Past Forward:
Articles from the
Journal of American History

Volume 2: From the Civil War to the Present

Past Forward:
Articles from the
Journal of American
History

Volume 2: From the Civil War to the Present

EDITED BY JAMES SABATHNE AND JASON STACY

New York
OXFORD UNIVERSITY PRESS
in collaboration with *The Journal of American History*

Oxford University Press is a department of the University of Oxford. It furthers the University's objective of excellence in research, scholarship, and education by publishing worldwide.

Oxford New York
Auckland Cape Town Dar es Salaam Hong Kong Karachi
Kuala Lumpur Madrid Melbourne Mexico City Nairobi
New Delhi Shanghai Taipei Toronto

With offices in
Argentina Austria Brazil Chile Czech Republic France Greece
Guatemala Hungary Italy Japan Poland Portugal Singapore
South Korea Switzerland Thailand Turkey Ukraine Vietnam

For titles covered by Section 112 of the US Higher Education
Opportunity Act, please visit www.oup.com/us/he for the latest
information about pricing and alternate formats.

Published by Oxford University Press
198 Madison Avenue, New York, New York 10016
http://www.oup.com

Oxford is a registered trademark of Oxford University Press

Library of Congress Cataloging-in-Publication Data
Names: Sabathne, James, editor. | Stacy, Jason, 1970- editor.
Title: Past forward : articles from the Journal of American history / edited
   by James Sabathne and Jason Stacy.
Other titles: Journal of American history (Bloomington, Ind.)
Description: New York : Oxford University Press, 2017.
Identifiers: LCCN 2016017561 | ISBN 9780190299286 (v. 1) | ISBN 9780190299293 (v. 2)
Subjects: LCSH: United States--History.
Classification: LCC E173 .P275 2017 | DDC 973--dc23 LC record available at https://lccn.loc.
gov/2016017561

9 8 7 6 5 4 3 2 1

Printed in the United States of America
on acid-free paper

PAST FORWARD: ACKNOWLEDGMENTS

We appreciate the guidance from the good people at the Organization of American Historians, without whose help this project would not be possible. Ed Linenthal and Stephen Andrews provided important early encouragement, and Nancy Croker, throughout, proved to be an essential resource and advocate.

Many thanks to Brian Wheel, Brianna Provenzano, Tili Sokolov, Marissa Dadiw and the rest of the editorial staff at Oxford University Press for making such a beautiful book. Thanks also to Jeanine Alexander, Randall Briggs, Jeff Enright, Todd Hering, Stacey Jarvis, Rebecca Kelley, Stephen Klawiter, Betsy Newmark, Frank Shoemaker, and the 3 anonymous readers who reviewed the manuscript.

James Sabathne is glad for opportunity to publicly acknowledge those who guided and influenced him, especially his parents, Chris and Connie Sabathne, who offered boundless love and support and valuable life lessons from the outset. James also wishes to thank the community at the University of Cincinnati, especially Hope Earls, Roger and Judith Daniels, and Gene and Dottie Lewis, whose excellent companionship continue to feed his passion for scholarship and his belly. Likewise, James is thankful for his good friends Jason and Michelle Stacy, and his wife Tracy. Lastly, James thanks his many muses–those who inspired his ongoing search for interesting, meaningful, and thought-provoking history–the thousands of dynamic and engaging students in his classes at Jacobs, Auburn, and Hononegah high schools. Among these he found two very special favorites who taught him the most, Payton and Camden Sabathne.

Jason Stacy thanks his colleagues at Southern Illinois University Edwardsville for their support and good cheer and especially Michelle, Abigail and Margaret Stacy, whose love makes everything possible.

Most importantly, James and Jason wish to thank the authors who contributed their excellent historical scholarship to these volumes. We are excited to share their outstanding work with US history students.

CONTENTS

~⌒

A Guide for Students on Active Reading and Reading Historically

In this introduction, we encourage you to think like a historian. The methods suggested here assume you are a student engaged in a formal study of US history, likely at the college survey level. Successful history students read actively, engage in deep analytical thinking, and create memorable records of their thoughts for later reference. This introduction in particular, along with this book in general, will help you be a successful student of history.

ACTIVE READING

Reading academic history presents a complicated challenge. What is called simply "reading" actually includes interpretation, recognition of important parts, and remembering what you read for later reference. Due to the difficulty of combining reading, interpreting, thinking, and remembering, students often honestly report, "I read, but I don't remember what I have read." You can overcome this common experience by reading actively. Active reading allows you to complete a series of tasks that separate the processes of reading, interpreting, and remembering before recombining them in the form of notes. Active reading calls for concentrated reading of a short section of text, an interpretation of the short section, the translation of ideas into your own words, and, if you judge them important, a brief recording of those ideas. We favor active reading in the form of annotations on the pages of the text. Most students, given a bit of practice, find annotations written in the margins the fastest and most efficient form of active reading. Try these steps to help you annotate something you read:

1. Select a manageable section to read (usually a paragraph).
2. Focus on reading and interpreting that section quickly.
3. Decide whether any aspects of the section merit remembering. Usually paragraphs present an argument; what the author is trying to prove. The author's argument is most often what you will want to remember.
4. Convert what you want to remember into a brief version expressed in your own words.
5. Write your brief annotation in the margins (next to text source if possible).

Annotating in our recommended fashion suits the way most people read and learn. Rare individuals read and absorb a complicated and lengthy text in a single uninterrupted sitting. Most people, however, consume texts in a piecemeal fashion one section at a time. If you annotate, you can approach a long text one manageable part at a time and create an easily understood personal record in your own words. The process of translating the author's text into your own words will increase your ability to recall those ideas later. If you find yourself easily distracted, try the annotation methods mentioned earlier to help you later remember the challenging history you read. With a moment of focus, you can quickly interpret and record in the margins arguments and evidence of a single paragraph. Annotating will allow you to read in whatever time you have—ten minutes while riding a bus, fifteen minutes at your doctor's office, or twenty minutes while waiting in line at the department of motor vehicles. The annotations you create will be an easily accessible personal record of your reading. You will also find that your annotations are easier to study later and review quickly since the ideas in your annotations reflect your thinking and trigger your memory of a section.

We think there are many good reasons that you should look up unfamiliar vocabulary as a part of the process of interpreting the text and translating it into meaningful annotations. Using a dictionary will help you develop key skills related to interpreting and thinking. Your ability to understand and employ specific and nuanced vocabulary defines your capacity to think, learn, and express ideas. Difficult vocabulary you encounter often represents a particular expression of a concept. Historians use specific and nuanced words to express complicated ideas. Look up unfamiliar words to ensure you capture the author's meaning, to advance your ability to interpret sophisticated texts, and to aid your own thinking. Building your vocabulary in this way also heightens your ability to express complicated thoughts. If you do not have access to a dictionary, use context clues to make sense of unfamiliar words. Given widespread access to the internet and dictionary applications, these times should be few and far between.

Although we recommend in-text annotations, some people prefer to record their notes in other locations. You might use post-it notes to record your annotations and stick them over the origin paragraph, or record your notes on separate paper, or even make your notes digitally on a tablet or laptop. Whatever method you use to annotate a text, remember that the process of taking small sections and translating them into your own words aids both understanding and memory.

PAYING ATTENTION TO THE PARAMETERS
OF HISTORICAL ESSAYS

To practice good historical thinking, you should know the parameters of what you read. Here is a handy list of the common parameters of a piece of historical writing:

1. Author
2. Title

3. Topic and Subtopics (What)
4. Chronological Scope (When)
5. Geographic Setting (Where)

Although we recommend you note these five basic essay parameters, perhaps at the end of the essay itself, the annotations that you make while you read will often capture most of them. If it helps, apply a simple marking that calls your attention to the author and title. If the author includes the chronological scope in the title or subtitle (by including the dates "1840–1855," for example), connect the label "when" to the date range. Find room in the margins to write other essay parameters: "topic," "subtopics," "where," and, if the author did not provide the chronological scope as a part of the title, "when."

Historians often convey important information in the titles of their essays, which is one reason they are worth your attention. Sometimes they hint at their central argument in the beginning and sometimes they offer up the biggest topics. It is important to remember both the author and the title of an essay so that when you refer to an essay in a discussion, a dinner conversation, or in writing a response to an examination question, you can identify the author and title for your reader or listener.

Also remember that all writing by historians has a main topic, and often subtopics. The main topic is what you would describe as the single biggest unifying subject of the essay. If the author divides the essay into smaller component parts, note these as subtopics. A good place to organize your annotations of the main topic and subtopics of an essay is in the space at the beginning or the end of the essay itself.

Once you read and annotate an essay in this volume, you will have noted its basic parameters (author, title, main topic and subtopics, when, and where) and the author's important ideas. These annotations can appear in the margins of the essay itself, though annotations of more general ideas and topics may be more usefully placed at the beginning or the end of the essay. No matter where you annotate, doing so will help you understand the essay and remember its important points and facts.

THINKING AS A BRIDGE FROM INTERPRETING TO REMEMBERING

We want you to think in a variety of ways to deepen your understanding of an author's ideas, hone critical historical thinking skills, and establish your thoughts in response to the essay. In the process, you will generate useful memories of what you read. Next are a few strategies to help you understand and remember a historical essay.

A great first step is to locate and label the author's thesis. Searching for, thinking about, committing to, and labeling an author's thesis requires you to process what the author wrote and understand the author's argument. Can you locate a statement, or statements, expressing the overriding argument of the author? Consider the entirety of the essay, and, if possible, locate the author's statement, or statements, that make up the thesis. When locating a potential thesis, consider carefully whether it suits the entirety of the essay. Most of the time, thesis statements encapsulate all of an author's arguments, so a thesis statement can be quite long, even multiple sentences or a whole paragraph.

Author's occasionally write historical essays in which they do not include a clearly stated thesis. You may find an essay with no stated thesis frustrating, and ought to consider raising that issue during a discussion of the piece, as well as noting the lack of a thesis in your annotations. Traditionally, authors state their thesis near the beginning of an essay. Some authors, however, structure their writing differently by elaborating on a number of introductory arguments (often summarizing what other historians have argued) before stating their thesis. Some historians only reveal the clear statement of their thesis in the very last pages or even sentences. If you locate a potential thesis near the end of an essay, you might double-check the beginning of the essay to see if you missed an earlier statement that amounts to the author's thesis. Sometimes a thesis can only be understood holistically, or after reading and understanding the entire essay. An essay whose thesis requires a holistic reading often contains certain themes that give some hint of the overall thesis. For example, if an author discusses women during the American Revolution, a holistic understanding of the entire essay may make the author's arguments about women during the American Revolution apparent.

Another strategy to help you understand and remember historical essays is to identify the supporting arguments the author uses to support the thesis. Reread your annotations and mark each one that represents a major argument or idea. You can circle each annotation that interprets one of the author's main ideas, or place an asterisk next to them, or highlight them with a marker. Use whatever symbol works for you.

Once you have identified the author's thesis and supporting arguments, consider how an essay supports, refutes, changes, or adds to what you know about a topic and to your knowledge in general. Can you connect what you read to current events? Perhaps the essay shows stark differences from the course of current events. Another important way to think about the essay is to consider the ways in which the author's arguments and subjects connect to other history you read or know. Does this essay remind you of the work of any other historians? Or, does the content of the essay remind you of other historical events you studied in class? When you answer these questions, you will likely come up with examples since historical subjects connect both to events that came before and after. These connections allow you to engage in comparative thinking. What was similar about the events, both past and present? And what were significant differences between them? Another useful line of reasoning considers whether the current reading connects to your knowledge of other academic disciplines such as literature, philosophy, rhetoric, science, or art. Think about how the essay you read might influence your understanding of broad historical patterns. Did this essay show a continuation of the historical trends of prior eras? Did the essay bring to light some new developments and reveal important historical changes?

Historians also think historiographically. *Historiography* is the study of the study of history. When historians think historiographically, they read historical essays not only for content but also for consideration of how other historians have used sources and the ways in which historical context shaped a particular historical analysis. Getting to know an author and his or her work will help you start to identify the ways in which history is a kind of discussion among historians. Academic history emerges from ongoing conversations and arguments of scholars. Historians build upon the research of their colleagues and give credit to the work of other historians in their essays and citations. Scholars researching the same topics arrive at varying conclusions, and sometimes note whose work they argue against in their writing. In making their arguments, using or supporting the work of earlier historians, and trying to disprove other researchers' ideas, scholars often refer to other authors. So, when you think historiographically, you will see that this book is a collection of discussions among historians with their own personalities and interests. Remembering which historians argued what about a particular topic will be your first step toward historiographical thinking.

Another aspect of historiographical thinking recognizes that the events and culture of a particular time and place exert an influence over a historian's work. You will notice in this book that there are short author biographies at the end of each essay. Many of the authors describe the ways in which historical events shaped their own historical writing. For example, one historian who lived during the civil rights movement of the 1960s noted that this historical event shaped his interest in the Civil War and the emancipation of enslaved blacks in the South. To understand a historical essay more fully, we advocate that you note the date of publication of any history you read. The questions historians ask and answer originate in their interests and concerns—as do the conclusions they reach.

Historiographical thinking also requires an analysis of the evidence a historian employs. For example, if a historian uses *The New York Times* to prove an argument about a coal strike in Pennsylvania, you might ask: Why not use some newspapers from Pittsburgh as well? Why did this historian depend on sources from New York City? When you analyze a historian's sources, you will find ways in which the evidence employed offers insight about the history, the historian, and the nature of the field of history. Think about the numbers, variety, and types of sources the author used. Historians analyze sources and question, or they assert their sources' relative merits, and/or limitations, but in all cases, historians make choices when utilizing sources. These choices reflect a historian's sense of audience and purpose. Even the best sources speak to limited topics. Part of thinking historically involves analyzing and weighing the usefulness of a historian's chosen sources.

Lastly, we advocate that you engage in thinking related to evaluation and criticism. Judge the essay. What was successful about the essay? In what ways did the author fail? Did you like it? Why or why not? Was it well written? Were the author's arguments sufficiently supported with historical evidence? Did the author express an analytical argument clearly? Did the author omit key information or topics? If you were the historian, how would you have improved the essay?

In sum, by engaging in meaningful thinking and reflection, you increase your creation of useful memories of history. Moreover, you practice analytical thinking, which will be useful in everything you do.

TECHNIQUES THAT AID REMEMBERING

The easiest approach to increase your recall is to reread your annotations. You will find rereading annotations is much more efficient than rereading the original essay. Reread and study your annotations and you will increase your chances of remembering the basic essay parameters, thesis, topics and subtopics, and main ideas. Adding the products of your thoughts to your annotated essay increases the usefulness of studying the annotated essay. If margin space allows, add new features to your annotated essay, but if space is short, you can staple an extra page or pages to the essay. Consider including the following:

1. A list of the main ideas or a mini-outline, including the author's thesis and the most important supporting arguments.
2. A list of your ideas for discussion. This has the added advantage of recording not only the author's ideas but also your personal analysis and thoughts about the essay.
3. A brief self-reflection at the end of your annotated essay. Your reflection might be as short as a sentence or two in which you capture your impressions of the essay's ideas and arguments.
4. A single analytical, idea-focused paragraph. Integrate a brief treatment of the author's thesis and supporting arguments, with your thoughts and evaluations. Your paragraph should avoid retelling the content and instead focus on important arguments and ideas of the author, and your thoughts about those ideas. One paragraph is an appropriate length comprising a more likely "memorable" comprehensive piece of thinking about the essay. Students that distill the author's arguments as well as their thoughts and evaluations into one paragraph create a product of a size, length, and importance that is more "memorable."

Your annotated essays with accompanying reflective writing make great study tools for final exams or preparation for class discussions or debates. An annotated essay makes it easy to refresh your memory of something you read ten weeks ago, or even two years in the past. And, of course, these annotations will serve as the beginning of your own essays about the past. Once you have gathered an author's arguments, weighed the evidence, and reflected on the merits and the shortcomings of an essay, you have entered the historical dialogue. You are thinking like a historian!

CHAPTER ONE

"A Rare Phenomenon of Philological Vegetation": The Word "Contraband" and the Meanings of Emancipation in the United States[1]

Kate Masur

In his 1888 history of black military service during the Civil War, the African American historian George Washington Williams reminded readers that early in the war, the U.S. general Benjamin F. Butler had made the "startling and revolutionary" decision to label slaves fleeing to army lines "contraband of war." . . . In late May 1861, just weeks after the war began, three enslaved men escaped to U.S-occupied Fortress Monroe, on the central coast of Virginia. Their owner, a Confederate colonel, had planned to send them south to labor for the Confederacy and soon ordered an aide to collect them. Butler, commander at the fort, was reluctant to return such valuable resources to the Rebels and recognized that the men's labor might serve the Union cause. But it was difficult to justify retaining the men against their owner's will. At this early stage in the war, the United States government was wary of confiscating Confederate property and opposed to emancipating slaves. Butler improvised. He declared the men "contraband of war," a move that provided a legal veneer for holding the men and avoided challenging their status as property. "There was considerable comment in the press, in the pulpit, and in political as well as military circles," Williams wrote. And yet, he concluded, Butler's policy of holding human beings as contraband—a policy that left unchallenged the "false idea" of human property—"died almost before the country was certain it ever had official countenance."[2]

The federal government never nationalized Butler's "contraband" policy; laws and executive orders quickly superseded his declaration. Yet as a name for

[1]Interested students are encouraged to read this essay in the original form. Kate Masur, "'A Rare Phenomenon of Philological Vegetation': The Word 'Contraband' and the Meanings of Emancipation in the United States," *Journal of American History* 93, no. 4 (March 2007), 1050–84.

[2]George Washington Williams, *A History of the Negro Troops in the War of the Rebellion, 1861–1865* (1888; New York, 1969), 70–72.

fleeing slaves, "contraband" had significance beyond Williams's estimate and beyond anything Butler could have predicted. Such slaves became critical to the U.S. war effort, weakening the Confederacy by their flight and offering the Union valuable information and labor power. On battlefields and navy ships and in all manner of correspondence, those fugitives became "contrabands" in the parlance of military officials. Even more intriguing, the term jumped immediately into popular culture. Refugees from slavery were portrayed as contrabands by minstrel performers, on collectible postcards, in cartoons, drawings, and oil paintings, and in publications ranging from the Democratic humor weekly *Vanity Fair* to the abolitionist *National Anti-Slavery Standard*. "Never was a word so speedily adopted by so many people in so short a time," wrote the New York lawyer and army officer Charles Cooper Nott in late 1862. The word "leaped instantaneously to its new place, jostling aside the circumlocution 'colored people,' the extrajudicial 'persons of African descent,' the scientific 'negro,' the slang 'nigger,' and the debasing 'slave.'" As Nott recognized, "contraband" was a new and noteworthy addition to the already extensive vocabulary of race and servitude in the United States. He predicted that "those who love to ponder over the changes of language and watch its new uses and unconscious growth, must find in it a rare phenomenon of philological vegetation."[3]

The "rare phenomenon" observed by Nott—the sudden explosion of "contraband" into popular culture—reflected Northern preoccupation with the meanings of emancipation and the future status of African Americans in the United States. As Nott and his contemporaries realized, people could choose among a range of words to refer to people of African descent, and different terms implied different views about black citizenship, dignity, and identity. The choice of the term "contraband" and the myriad ways people imagined the "contrabands" tell much about how Northerners, black and white, sought to make sense of the prospect of emancipation. Most fundamentally, the new usage of "contraband" signaled that the nation was at a crossroads. In the absence of other appropriate designations for fleeing slaves, the term was a placeholder whose appeal would fade once it became clear that the war would secure permanent emancipation. Because "contraband" had long been used to describe property, the term also implied the transitional status of the people to whom it referred. They were neither property with a clear owner (as in slavery) nor free people, but something in between. Some contemporaries debated and discussed the term itself: what it signified, whether and how to use it, and for how long. More often, however, people adopted it unselfconsciously and used it to express their own views on emancipation or on the character, needs, and desires of the nascent freedpeople.

Following both Nott and the cultural historian Raymond Williams, one might say that contraband is a "keyword" in the history of emancipation, race, and citizenship in the United States. Williams argued that the multiple meanings

---

[3][Charles Cooper Nott], *The Coming Contraband: A Reason against the Emancipation Proclamation, not given by Mr. Justice Curtis, to whom it is addressed, by an Officer in the Field* (New York, 1862), 2–3.

of a keyword are "inextricably bound up with the problems it [is] being used to discuss."[4] Similarly, the meanings and connotations ascribed to the term "contraband" were inseparable from the questions prospective emancipation forced Northerners to address, and they thus shed light on those questions. "Contraband" became a crucial term in the Northern debate over whether escapees from slavery were citizens in embryo or a threat to the Republic, whether they deserved respect, pity, or proscription. For Northern African Americans, the term also provided a new way of talking about difference, of defining their relationship to those just liberated from bondage.

Although Civil War-era Northerners used "contraband" in a novel way, both the word and the encounter between fleeing slaves and white Northerners were already encumbered with meanings. In international law, the term "contraband" carried connotations of property and wartime subterfuge. Applied to escaping slaves during the Civil War, it called up familiar tropes about enslavement and race, including conventions from minstrelsy and images of both aggressiveness and extreme dependency. Because all contrabands were fleeing slaves and all enslaved people were understood to be racially "negro," the term "contraband" implied racial blackness. As a term for fleeing slaves, it also tended to connote poverty, dependence, and desperation. Indeed, even those Northerners with the most expansive visions of freedom and human equality—white abolitionists and African Americans—used the term with a degree of condescension or at least an emphasis on the distinctiveness of former slaves.

Yet the contrabands of Northern popular music, literature, and illustration were also endowed with new ideas born of the ferment of war, including the notion that former slaves could be soldiers and citizens as well as speculation on the possibilities and implications of their dispersal into the North. While overt racism figured in some representations of contrabands, in many—as in the rhetoric of abolitionists or black Northerners—race was less at issue than the degradation to which people had been subjected as slaves. The contrabands of Northerners' imagination also congealed ideas about gender, citizenship, and the legacies of subjugation. Thus, Northern references to contrabands were not a simple rhetorical reenslavement. Nor did African Americans reject the term outright.[5] To the contrary, widespread adoption of the term, the debates over it, and its limitations together illuminate the critical Civil War-era debate about the future of African Americans and of democracy in the United States. . . .

The dramatic possibility raised by the escapees at Fortress Monroe—that the war would lead to the emancipation of some 4 million enslaved people— seemed to invite the adoption of a new term. . . . [T]he term "contraband," while . . . signifying transitional status, reflected the ad hoc machinations of an army at

---

[4]Ibid., 2; Raymond Williams, *Keywords: A Vocabulary of Culture and Society* (London, 1976), 13. On the importance of cultural forms in the history of race and racism, see Thomas C. Holt, "Marking: Race, Race-Making, and the Writing of History," *American Historical Review* 100 (Feb. 1995), 1–20.

[5]Alice Fahs, *The Imagined Civil War: Popular Literature of the North and South, 1861–1865* (Chapel Hill, 2001), 152; Ella Forbes, *African American Women during the Civil War* (New York, 1998), 9–10.

war, not a full-fledged government policy . . . even in the absence of much government encouragement, Northerners rushed to adopt the new term. From the moment Butler's decision was publicized, Northerners joined their own battle to infuse "contraband" with meaning.

Benjamin Butler originally applied the term "contraband of war" to fleeing slaves to provide a rationale for retaining them without challenging the concept of human chattel. In March 1861, in his inaugural address, Abraham Lincoln had promised that he had "no purpose, directly or indirectly, to interfere with the institution of slavery in the States where it exists." That May, when the three fugitives arrived at Fortress Monroe, the federal government was still pledged to Lincoln's promise. Yet Butler recognized that the three male field hands would be "very serviceable" in the U.S. war effort, and he was loath to see their labor benefit the Confederacy. Thus, when confronted by their owners' deputy, Butler argued that he was entitled to hold the men as property destined for use in the enemy's war effort. The aide departed without his boss's slaves, and Secretary of War Simon Cameron soon approved Butler's decisions to hold the fugitives and to employ them as laborers in his quartermaster's department.[6]

Butler's designation of the fleeing slaves as contraband of war was clever but legally untenable. In international law, the principle of contraband of war was part of a doctrine concerning the rights of neutral parties in wartime. Neutrals could trade with belligerent nations without fear of interception unless they were carrying goods that a belligerent would use to make war. Such goods were deemed contraband of war and subject to confiscation. A centuries-old tradition held that arms and ammunition were obvious contraband. Most nineteenth-century Anglo-American commentators also agreed that when intended for use in war, goods with peacetime uses—timber, horses, raw materials, and food, for example—could be confiscated.[7] As "property" destined for military use, fugitive slaves escaping labor for the Confederacy could qualify as contraband under such a definition.

Yet the principle of contraband of war was not applicable at Fortress Monroe, and Butler, a lawyer, knew it. The doctrine concerned the shipment of property by neutral parties, and there were no neutral parties in the Fortress Monroe confrontation. Butler could theoretically have invoked a different tradition in international law to retain the fugitives. Legal theorists generally approved the outright confiscation of enemy property in wartime, particularly of articles used in war.

---

[6]Abraham Lincoln, "First Inaugural Address," in *Abraham Lincoln, Slavery, and the Civil War: Selected Writings and Speeches,* ed. Michael P. Johnson (New York, 2001), 109; Benjamin F. Butler to Lt. Gen. Winfield Scott, May 24, 1861, in *The Civil War cd-rom: The War of the Rebellion; A Compilation of the Official Records of the Union and Confederate Armies,* dev. Philip Oliver (1 cd-rom, version 1.5, Guild Press of Indiana, Carmel, 1997), ser. 1, vol. II, 649–52; Butler to Scott, May 27, 1861, with reply by the Secretary of War, May 30, 1861, ibid., ser. 2, vol. I, 754–55; Edward L. Pierce, "The Contrabands at Fortress Monroe," *Atlantic Monthly* 8 (Nov. 1861), 626–30.

[7]See, for example, Joseph Moseley, *What Is Contraband of War and What Is Not: Comprising All the American and English Authorities on the Subject* (London, 1861), 8–9; James Kent, *Commentaries on American Law,* vol. I (Boston, 1860), 143–50; and Emer de Vattel, *The Law of Nations; or, Principles of the Law of Nature, Applied to the Conduct and Affairs of Nations and Sovereigns* (Philadelphia, 1852). Those works are available online in *The Making of Modern Law* (Thomson Gale, 2004–).

But if Butler had confiscated the fugitives as enemy property, he would most likely have faced censure for advancing a policy well beyond that of the Lincoln administration. In May 1861 the U.S. government had neither forged a policy toward Confederate property of any kind nor fully acknowledged the Confederacy as a belligerent nation. And, as Lincoln's inauguration promise not to interfere with slavery implied, emancipation was by no means a government policy. Butler's invocation of contraband of war thus avoided the pitfalls of both confiscation and emancipation. "The truth is," Butler reflected in his 1892 memoir, "as a lawyer I was never very proud of it, but as an executive officer I was very much comforted with it as a means of doing my duty."[8]

Butler's contraband policy was legally weak but culturally powerful. . . . As Lincoln's secretaries later wrote in their biography of the president, "Within a few days, a new phrase was on every one's lips, and the newspapers were full of editorials chuckling over the happy conception of treating fugitive slaves of rebel masters as contraband of war." It was not long, the biographers recalled, before the term was shortened and "every negro in and about the army became familiarly known and designated as a 'contraband.'"[9]

Northerners avidly followed the emergence of contrabands as principals in the drama of war and wondered what would happen to slavery and enslaved people in a protracted conflict. To abolitionists, events at Fortress Monroe signaled what they hoped would be the beginning of the end of slavery, although many—especially African American activists—also criticized the government's reluctance to declare the slaves free. One white abolitionist in Washington wrote to a friend, "I hope those hundred slaves at Monroe may be declared 'contraband'— twill be the signal for such a stampede!" Northern moderates and conservatives could be content that Butler's dictum cleverly divested Confederates of property while in theory leaving slavery intact. The *New York Herald* praised Butler as a "strict constructionist" and lauded the contraband policy as one that would please "those who regard slaves as absolute property" as well as radicals, who would be "content to abide by [Butler's] conclusions," if not by his principles. . . . Not surprisingly, Confederates were less happy. The *Charleston Mercury,* for example, condemned Butler's decree as evidence of the Union's hypocrisy. "Now, Cuffee and Sambo are slaves, or they are not," the paper insisted. "If slaves, they should be delivered to their owners. If not slaves, by what right is their labor coerced?" According to the *Mercury,* the logically inconsistent policy was evidence that the United States would go to any lengths to crush the Confederacy, a signal

---

[8]Benjamin F. Butler, *Autobiography and Personal Reminiscences of Major-General Benj. F. Butler* (Boston, 1892), 259. Pierce, "Contrabands at Fortress Monroe," 627. The New York lawyer Charles Cooper Nott called the moniker "a good professional joke." [Nott], *Coming Contraband,* 2. Mark Grimsley, *The Hard Hand of War: Union Military Policy toward Southern Civilians, 1861–1865* (New York, 1995), 11–17, 123; Guelzo, *Lincoln's Emancipation Proclamation,* 31–33, 41–43; and Silvana R. Siddali, *From Property to Person: Slavery and the Confiscation Acts, 1861–1862* (Baton Rouge, 2005).

[9]John G. Nicolay and John Hay, *Abraham Lincoln: A History* (10 vols., New York, 1890), IV, 388–89.

that the Confederacy must in response "smite unsparingly, with sweeping vengeance, and not merely conquer but destroy!"[10]

Fugitives from slavery made themselves indispensable to the Union war effort by walking away from those who claimed to own them and by offering direct aid to the Union. . . . By late July 1861, some nine hundred former slaves, men, women, and children, had escaped to Fortress Monroe. Early fugitives at the fort were surprised to hear themselves called "contraband." Edward L. Pierce, designated by Butler to supervise them, reported that when they asked about the strange moniker, "we did not attempt an explanation."[11] Many U.S. commanders followed Butler's lead in setting fugitives to work on fortifications and employing them around camps as servants, cooks, and teamsters. Not all military leaders agreed with the course Butler had established, however. Reflecting the broader Northern ambivalence about the status of fugitive slaves, in fall 1861 army commanders in Maryland, Kentucky, and Missouri ordered their subordinates to keep fugitives out of the federal lines. But slaves' determination to press forward, combined with white soldiers' growing reluctance to remand slaves to their owners, soon made such a policy untenable. Commanders quickly realized that fugitives offered not only their laboring bodies but also useful knowledge about local terrain, civilians' morale, and Confederate positions and strategy. As military officials grappled with the largely unanticipated influx, U.S. forces advanced further into the Confederacy and fugitives escaped to army camps by the thousand. Those fugitives— as well as the enslaved men, women, and children whose homes came within Union lines as armies advanced—were often called contrabands. . . .[12]

Abolitionists' and missionaries' early missives helped establish enduring representational conventions that reflected ambivalence about the contrabands and what they could become. These ostensibly sympathetic writers emphasized

---

[10]Gulielma Breed to Emily Howland, May 28, 1861 (addendum dated May 29), Emily Howland Papers (Division of Rare and Manuscript Collections, Cornell University Library, Ithaca, N.Y.); "Gen. Butler on Contraband Goods," *The New York Herald,* May 29, 1861; "Negro Slaves Contraband of War," *Charleston Mercury,* July 26, 1861. (I consulted *The New York Herald* and some issues of *The Christian Recorder* online at Accessible Archives.) Pierce, "Contrabands at Fortress Monroe," 626–27.

[11]Pierce, "Contrabands at Fortress Monroe," 627. *Private and Official Correspondence of Gen. Benjamin F. Butler during the Civil War Period* (5 vols., Norwood, Mass., 1917), I, 186. Sylvia R. Frey, *Water from the Rock: Black Resistance in a Revolutionary Age* (Princeton, 1991); Ira Berlin, *Many Thousands Gone: The First Two Centuries of Slavery in North America* (Cambridge, Mass., 1998), 220, 228–357; Adam Rothman, *Slave Country: American Expansion and the Origins of the Deep South* (Cambridge, Mass., 2005), 156–58; and Laurent Dubois, *A Colony of Citizens: Revolution and Slave Emancipation in the French Caribbean, 1787–1804* (Chapel Hill, 2004), 85–168.

[12]Berlin et al., eds., *Freedom,* ser. 1, vol. I, 18, 26–27, 417; Ira Berlin, "Who Freed the Slaves," in *Union and Emancipation: Essays on Politics and Race in the Civil War Era,* ed. David W. Blight and Brooks D. Simpson (Kent, 1997), 105–21; and William W. Freehling, *The South vs. the South: How Anti-Confederate Southerners Shaped the Course of the Civil War* (New York, 2002), esp. 96–104. Oliver, dev., *Civil War cd-rom: War of the Rebellion,* ser. 1, vol. III, 143–44, ser. 1, vol. VI, 175, ser. 1, vol. IV, 337, ser. 1, vol. III, 255. The navy used the term even more promiscuously than the army, in part because naval secretary Gideon Welles codified its use in an order of September 25, 1861, outlining a separate pay grade for "contrabands" in naval service. See Joseph P. Reidy, "Black Men in Navy Blue during the Civil War," *Prologue* 33 (Fall 2001), 155–67.

Figure 1.1
"Stampede Among the Negroes in Virginia—Their Arrival at Fortress
Monroe," Central panel in a multipanel wood engraving, *Frank Leslie's
Illustrated Weekly,* June 8, 1861, pp. 56–57. Courtesy Library of Congress,
Prints and Photographs Division, LC-USZ62-31165.

the chaos and comedy that ensued when contrabands arrived at federal encamp-
ments. They described contrabands as victims of a war they could not understand, as illiterate, unworldly, and disorderly in their appearance and personal
relationships. Artists' sketches printed as engravings in magazines and weekly
newspapers depicted groups of contrabands as heterogeneous and pathetic. Artists portrayed motley crowds featuring people of all ages, all shades, and both
sexes, wearing all manner of clothing and carrying disheveled collections of belongings. (See figures 1.1 and 1.2.) White soldiers were shown overseeing the
groups, often on horseback, suggesting the contrabands' need for white men's
supervision.[13] Such conventions were patronizing in their portrayal of the contrabands as undignified and dependent, but they did accommodate abolitionists'
conviction that contrabands, although damaged by enslavement, were susceptible

[13]1861 coverage in *National Anti-Slavery Standard;* Moncure D. Conway, *Testimonies Concerning
Slavery* (1864; New York, 1969), 107; Circular, April 1862, *The Christian Recorder,* May 24, 1862; letter
of J. G. McKee, *Colored Citizen,* Nov. 7, 1863, in *The Negro's Civil War: How American Negroes Felt and
Acted during the War for the Union,* ed. James M. McPherson (New York, 1965), 140–41; Cousin Sarah
to Howland, Jan. 26, 1863, Howland Papers; Anna M. Powell to "Dear Friends," Jan. 11, 1866, ibid.;
"The Contrabands at Port Royal," *Liberator,* Dec. 12, 1862, p. 198; James B. Rogers, *War Pictures: Experiences and Observations of a Chaplain in the U.S. Army, in the War of the Southern Rebellion* (Chicago,
1863), 110–13, 121–38; Pierce, "Contrabands at Fortress Monroe," 635–36; and "The Lounger," *Harper's
Weekly,* Jan. 11, 1862, p. 18. "Morning Muster of the 'Contrabands' at Fortress Monroe, on Their Way
to Their Day's Work Under the Pay and Direction of the U.S.," ibid., Nov. 2, 1861, p. 373; and "Contrabands Coming into Our Lines Under the Proclamation," *Harper's Weekly,* May 9, 1863, p. 293.

Figure 1.2
"Contrabands Coming into Camp in Consequence of the
Proclamation." Wood engraving based on a sketch by Alfred R.
Waud, *Harper's Weekly,* Jan. 31, 1863, p. 68. Courtesy Library of Congress,
Prints and Photographs Division, LC-USZ62-88812.

to the civilizing institutions of Christianity, family, and waged labor. The descriptions therefore reinforced efforts to aid the contrabands materially and to reform them spiritually. But the representations could also suggest that incipient emancipation presented a crisis, that the liberation of millions of slaves would lead to chaos and upheaval for which the nation was ill prepared.

The wartime rupture in slavery and the question of what would become of escaping slaves also preoccupied Northern African Americans. For decades, black activists had trained their attention on enslaved people in the South, fighting for abolition and aiding fugitives who made their way to free territory. Now that slavery seemed to be crumbling and the possibility of abolition within reach, they watched closely and—in church-based organizations, benevolent societies, and newspapers—discussed what action to take. Like white abolitionists, Northern African Americans freighted their representations of contrabands with ideas about slaves' abjection and their need for uplift. One black resident of Xenia, Ohio, reminded the Northern black readers of the *Christian Recorder,* the official organ of the African Methodist Episcopal Church, that the neediest "contrabands" were "now no longer brutes and chattels, but women and children; and if we do not stretch forth our arms to their relief, the curse is upon our head. . . ." If Northern African Americans did not act quickly, the writer hinted, the moment might be lost and the contrabands consigned to barbarism. His rhetoric and his call to action suggested both the distance many Northern black people felt from slaves and their sense of special responsibility to reach out. . . .[14]

---

[14]J. C. Maxwell, "Contrabands," *Christian Recorder,* Dec. 6, 1862; William C. Burke to Ralph R. Gurley, Sept. 29, 1863, in *Slaves No More: Letters from Liberia, 1833–1869,* ed. Bell I. Wiley (Lexington, Ky., 1980), 214.

Stirred by communiqués from colleagues in the South that described contrabands arriving destitute and ignorant in U.S. army camps, white and black activists recruited people into the largely segregated aid societies that burgeoned early in the war. Such organizations held benefit concerts, raised money, and sent food, clothing, and blankets to the fugitives. In the aid movement, the term "contraband" invoked the liminal and needy status of fugitives, innocents caught between bondage and freedom. Northern activists' use of the term thus both generated meaningful relief and highlighted the fugitives' powerlessness and destitution. . . . [T]he aid movement emphasized the helplessness of contrabands to insist that the fugitives deserved sympathy and support.[15]

Many reports on contrabands came to the North via mainstream newspapers. Escaping slaves were newsworthy because their existence made the question of emancipation unavoidable; because they provided labor power to the Union; because the government had to develop policies to pay, house, and feed them; and because they had unparalleled access to information about the Confederacy. One figure, the "intelligent contraband," became a critical part of the Northern iconography of race and war. It is not clear whether the press or the military invented the terms "intelligent contraband" and "reliable contraband," but the terms arose because fugitives from slavery provided critical information for the Union. By spring 1862, military officials routinely referred to information gleaned from "intelligent" or "reliable" contrabands. In their correspondence, military men assessed the supposed "intelligence" of contrabands in deciding whether their reports were credible. The frequency with which military people employed the term "intelligent" to modify "contraband" is striking, whether directly or in variations such as a reference to "seven Contrabands who . . . are bright and intelligent and can give us a great deal of information."[16] Army personnel used the modifiers "intelligent" and "reliable" to confer intellectual authority on people who otherwise had virtually none, as if the adjectives restored what the term "contraband" had eclipsed: a possibility that fugitive slaves could be worldly, knowledgeable, and an asset to the Union effort. Indeed, by distinguishing certain escapees as trustworthy, the phrase "intelligent contraband" subtly reinforced the commonplace assumption among Northern whites that *most* slaves were not worth taking seriously. . . .[17]

Northerners' attitudes toward the information offered by contrabands reflected varying hopes and concerns about the role of black people in the future of

---

[15]"Musical Intelligence," *Dwight's Journal of Music*, March 29, 1862, p. 414; "Concert at National Hall," *The Christian Recorder*, Nov. 22, 1862; H.M.T. to Editor, ibid., Jan. 10, 1863; and "The Hutchinson Family," ibid., March 7, 1863. Elizabeth B. Clark, "'The Sacred Rights of the Weak': Pain, Sympathy, and the Culture of Individual Rights in Antebellum America," *Journal of American History* 82 (Sept. 1995), 463–93.

[16]Berlin et al., eds., *Freedom*, ser. 1, vol. I, 302. Oliver, dev., *Civil War cd-rom: War of the Rebellion*, ser. 1, vol. VI, 266–67, ser. 1, vol. LI, no. 1, 675–76, ser. 1, vol. XXIV, 223–24, ser. 1, vol. XXX, no. 3, 778, ser. 1, vol. XLI, no. 2, 382, ser. 1, vol. XXXIX, no. 2, 122–23. Quarles, *Negro in the Civil War*, 78–92.

[17]G. E. Bryant to A. A. G. Rawlins, May 24, 1863, in *Freedom*, ser. 1, vol. I, ed. Berlin et al., 307. For conflicts about publishing sensitive information, see J. G. Randall, "The Newspaper Problem in Its Bearing upon Military Secrecy during the Civil War," *American Historical Review* 23 (Jan. 1918), 303–23; Louis M. Starr, *Bohemian Brigade: Civil War Newsmen in Action* (1954; Madison, 1987).

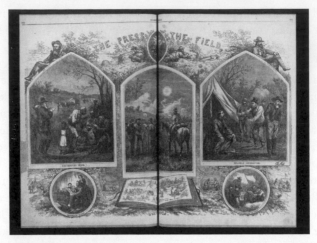

Figure 1.3
"Contraband News," part of "The Press, the Field, the
Sketchbook." Wood engraving based on a sketch by Thomas
Nast, *Harper's Weekly*, April 30, 1864, p. 280. Courtesy Library of
Congress, Prints and Photographs Division, LC-USZ62-123476.

the nation. . . . In representing escapees as active allies, Republican publications
helped refute the popular image of slaves as passive, ignorant, and a burden on
the armed forces. Reflecting the prevailing idea that active citizenship was gendered male, scenes portraying the exchange of information represented the
"contraband" as a man. For instance, a *Harper's Weekly* illustration showed an
individual black man talking with a reporter while several women and children
looked on. (See figures 1.3 and 1.4.) A stark contrast with depictions of large

Figure 1.4
The Reliable Contraband." Copper-plate etching in Life Studies
of the Great Army, by Edwin Forbes (New York, 1876), plate 23.
Courtesy Library of Congress, Prints and Photographs Division, LC-USZ62-
15833.

groups of contrabands that emphasized disorder and chaos, such por-
trayals of individual fugitive slave
men conveying information to the
Union at great peril to themselves
implied that such men might have the
independence of thought and
action—the "manhood"—to sustain
themselves in freedom.[18]

Conversely, the many white
Northerners who believed black
people to be naturally capricious or
stupid saw the "intelligent contraband" as a contradiction in terms. To
them, reports that U.S. forces relied
on slaves for information were evidence that the war was being poorly
prosecuted and, perhaps worse, that
the government was elevating fugitive
slaves to the status of men.... A *New
York Times* reporter traveling with the
army in Mississippi ridiculed an
African American guide who failed to
lead U.S. soldiers to a bridge as "one of

THE HIGHLY INTELLIGENT CONTRABAND,

Figure 1.5
"The Highly Intelligent Contraband." Wood
engraving by Bobbett and Hooper, *Vanity Fair,*
April 26, 1862, p. 203. Courtesy Library of
Congress, Rare Books Room.

those 'intelligent contrabands' developed during the present war ... who have
been of such singular service in all cases to the National Government." The Democratic press consistently challenged the army's trust in information provided by
fleeing slaves, believing slaves were not only ignorant, but deceitful. A *Vanity Fair*
cartoon mockingly titled "The Highly Intelligent Contraband" depicted a black
man with simian features signaling innate racial inferiority and lack of intelligence
(see figure 1.5)....[19]

---

[18]"The Slavery Question," *Harper's Weekly,* Dec. 7, 1861, p. 770; "Domestic Intelligence," ibid.,
Jan. 18, 1862, p. 35; "Our Special Correspondence with the Land Forces," *New York Herald,* July 19,
1863; Frank Moore, *Anecdotes, Poetry and Incidents of the War: North and South, 1860–1865* (New
York, 1867), 263–64, 268, 298–99, 374; and Allan Pinkerton, *The Spy of the Rebellion* (New York,
1883), 194, 245, 343–93. François Furstenberg, "Beyond Freedom and Slavery: Autonomy, Virtue,
and Resistance in Early American Political Discourse," *Journal of American History* 89 (March
2003), 1295–1330. Cooper, Holt, and Scott, *Beyond Slavery,* 17–18.

[19]"The War in Mississippi," *The New York Times,* Dec. 18, 1862; "The Highly Intelligent Con-
traband," *Vanity Fair,* April 26, 1862, p. 203. "Advance of the Army," *The New York Times,* June 1,
1862; "An Original but Doubtful View," ibid., Oct. 14, 1862; "The Condition of the South," ibid.,
Dec. 25, 1862; "More Delusive Prophesies," ibid., March 30, 1863; "Negro News," ibid., June 12, 1863;
"A Main Cause of the Defeat at Charleston," *The New York Herald,* April 17, 1863; "A Disorder and a
Com plaint," *Vanity Fair,* April 19, 1862, p. 188; and "Humors of the War," ibid., Aug. 16, 1862,
p. 138. "Light on a Dark Subject," ibid., June 14, 1862, p. 286; "Greeley's Vision," ibid., Aug. 30, 1862,
p. 102; and "Broadway Menagerie," *The New York Times,* Jan. 13, 1863, p. 7.

In fact, few freedpeople migrated North during the war, and with foreign im-migration diminished and many white men in the military, slaves posed little danger to the livelihoods of Northern white working people. Nevertheless, activat-ing Northerners' long-standing fears that slave emancipation would harm Northern free labor proved politically effective for the wartime Democrats, who insisted that ex-slaves, often referred to contemptuously as "contrabands," were on the verge of flooding the North. The sense of mobility and indeterminate status inherent in the term "contraband" was especially suited to arguments about the potential negative influence of black migrants on northern society. In January 1863 a white Ohioan informed his brother of the arrest of four men "of the class known now-a-days as contrabands." "They are the advance guard of that great army which is advancing northward to take possession of our jails and penitentiaries," he predicted. "Ere long we will be compelled to build new ones for their accommodation."[20]

By fall 1862—facing a growing population of slaves within the army's lines and a political imperative to persuade Northern whites that fugitive slaves would remain in the South—the U.S. government finally formulated a policy toward slaves in occupied areas of the Confederacy. The army would create "contraband camps" in the Confederacy and on its periphery, both to assuage white Northerners' fears of an exodus of African Americans to the North and to allow military officials to centralize relief efforts. The name given the camps reflected the intention that they be temporary holding areas for displaced people and serve a population—the contrabands—whose status remained am-biguous. Contraband camps became hubs for the distribution of rations and clothing and laboratories for a great experiment in remaking Southern society on a foundation of free labor. In practice, the camps also became social and political centers for freedpeople, who organized churches, schools, and civic

---

[20]Quoted in Frank L. Klement, *The Copperheads in the Middle West* (Chicago, 1960), 46. For the argument over contrabands' migration north, see "The Cry of Nig., Nig., Nigger," *Springfield Illinois Daily State Journal,* Oct. 16, 1862; "Mr. Swett on Immigration," ibid., Oct. 22, 1862; "Contra-band Labor in Illinois," *The Chicago Tribune,* Oct. 8, 1862; "The Contraband Hegira," ibid., Nov. 1, 1862; "Negro Immigration," *Liberator,* Oct. 31, 1862 (quoting *Indianapolis Indiana State Sentinel*); "Contrabands and What They Cost!," *Albany Atlas and Argus,* Jan. 29, 1863; and Charles Ward, *Contrabands: Suggesting an Apprenticeship, Under the Auspices of Government, to Build the Pacific Rail Road, January 8, 1863* (Salem, Mass., 1866). Arthur C. Cole, *The Era of the Civil War, 1848–1870* (Springfield, Ill., 1919), 334–35; Oliver, dev., *Civil War cd-rom: War of the Rebellion,* ser. 2, vol. V, 521–22; "The Song of the Contraband," *Vanity Fair,* May 10, 1862, p. 229; "Liberty. A Romance," ibid., 7 (Feb. 1863), 22; Klement, *Copperheads in the Middle West,* 16; and Iver Bernstein, *The New York City Draft Riots: Their Significance for American Society and Politics in the Age of the Civil War* (New York, 1990), 111–13. Forrest G. Wood, *Black Scare: The Racist Response to Emancipation and Reconstruction* (Berkeley, 1968); V. Jacque Voegeli, *Free but Not Equal: The Midwest and the Negro during the Civil War* (Chicago, 1967); V. Jacque Voegeli, "A Rejected Alternative: Union Policy and the Relocation of Southern 'Contrabands' at the Dawn of Emancipation," *Journal of Southern History* 69 (Nov. 2003), 765–90; Jean H. Baker, *Affairs of Party: The Political Culture of Northern Democrats in the Mid-Nineteenth Century* (Ithaca, 1983), 212–58; and Leslie A. Schwalm, "'Overrun with Free Negroes': Emancipation and Wartime Migration in the Upper Midwest," *Civil War History,* 50 (June 2004), 145–74. Michael P. Johnson, "Out of Egypt: The Migration of Former Slaves to the Midwest during the 1860s in Comparative Perspective," in *Crossing Boundaries: Comparative History of Black People in Diaspora,* ed. Darlene Clark Hine and Jacqueline McLeod (Bloomington, 1999), 223–45.

associations as they began to build lives outside the authority of slave owners. Life in the camps could be brutal, however. Conditions were often abysmal, and residents frequently suffered from disease, exposure, malnutrition, and swindling and abuse by soldiers. . . .[21]

As the government took steps to keep escapees in the South, artists and writers who favored emancipation worked to counter negative images of contraband migrants by portraying them as docile laborers and even as fonts of morality and Christianity. They publicized the industriousness of contrabands in army camps and speculated that freed slaves would help ameliorate labor shortages in the North. A short story entitled "Our Contraband," published in *Harper's New Monthly Magazine* in August 1863, addressed Northerners' concerns about integrating former slaves into the Northern, urban economy. In the story a New York society matron takes Aggie, a black teenager newly arrived from Virginia, into her home as a servant, sensing that, although the girl has been unmanageable in the homes of other white people, she can be reformed. The project is a disaster. The matron's husband and Irish servants oppose the plan, and the girl proves inconsistent in her housekeeping and care of the children. Moreover, Aggie seems culturally unassimilable, singing strange songs at inappropriate moments and manifesting mysterious religious beliefs. Finally, Aggie flees the home but finds Christianity and proper morality by living with, and working for, a Quaker woman. The story's logic did not permit the freed girl to be anything other than a domestic servant to white people, but it suggested that in the right milieu, "our contraband" would prove a good laborer and a good Christian.[22]

Since contrabands were so often portrayed as pathetic, threatening, or exotic, many African American writers were uncomfortable with the term. Some called for wholesale rejection of it, while many others used it with caveats. African Americans' first objection was to a policy based, in the words of the historian George Washington Williams, on "false idea" that people could own other people. In January 1862 Frederick Douglass condemned the term as "a name that will apply better to a pistol, than to a person." A pseudonymous correspondent for the *Christian Recorder* argued that despite the term's "popularity and general use" in reference to fleeing slaves, "this word is objectionable, because it is properly applicable to *things*, and not to *persons*." Moreover, "when used in reference to *persons*, it is disparaging to them, if not degrading." The writer advised, "Such use

---

[21]On life inside the camps, see n. 5 above and Steven Hahn, *A Nation under Our Feet: Black Political Struggles in the Rural South from Slavery to the Great Migration* (Cambridge, Mass., 2003), 72–79, 82; Leon F. Litwack, *Been in the Storm So Long: The Aftermath of Slavery* (New York, 1979), 3–166; Cam Walker, "Corinth: The Story of a Contraband Camp," *Civil War History* 20 (March 1974), 5–22; and Martha Mitchell Bigelow, "Freedmen of the Mississippi Valley, 1862–1865," ibid., 8 (March 1962), 38–47. On the evolution of U.S. policy toward fugitive slaves in army camps, see Voegeli, *Free but Not Equal*, 95–117; and Berlin et al., eds., *Freedom*, ser. 1, vol. II, 30–32, 41–43, 62–63.

[22]Mary E. Dodge, "Our Contraband," *Harper's New Monthly Magazine* 27 (Aug. 1863), 395–403. *Facts Concerning the Freedmen;* E. L. Pierce, "The Freedmen at Port Royal," *Atlantic Monthly* 12 (Sept. 1863), 308–10; and "'Work's Over'—Scenes among the Beaufort Contrabands," *Harper's Weekly*, Dec. 21, 1861, cover, 803. David Sears to Henry Wilson, July 23, 1861, in *Contrabands and Vagrants*, by David Sears (n.d., n.p.). Schwalm, "'Overrun with Free Negroes.'"

ought, therefore, to be discontinued, especially by colored speakers and writers," recommending instead the word "refugee," which meant "a PERSON seeking shelter or protection from oppression or wrong."[23]

African Americans did not discontinue use of the term, which was already in widespread use in the aid movement and the military. But many African American writers and some white ones attempted to strike a balance by drawing attention to its artificial or provisional nature when they used the term. Some referred to "so-called contrabands," emphasizing that "contraband" was not their term, but someone else's. Others placed quotation marks around the term. From South Carolina, the activist and former slave Harriet Tubman reported to allies in Boston on the Rebels' "most valuable livestock, known up in your region as 'contrabands.'"[24] The phrasing highlighted the multiple ways people viewed African Americans in occupied South Carolina. If Rebels viewed them as "livestock" and Yankees saw them as "contrabands," Tubman no doubt saw them as human beings. But even African Americans who recognized and objected to the term's negative connotations may have embraced its newness and flexibility; perhaps no other term seemed to capture the fugitives' spontaneous exodus from slavery or their ambiguous status once they had fled. Perhaps "contraband" seemed more neutral than other designations commonly used by whites.

Like African Americans, white people understood that the words they chose to refer to black people said much about their broader perspectives on race, citizenship, and inequality. During the war, newspapers and journals were flush with words for people of African descent and with commentaries on the proliferation of terms. One conservative periodical joked that Lincoln had preferred "negroes" in 1859, "colored men" in 1860, "intelligent contrabands" in 1861, and "free Americans of African descent" in 1862. In an ostensibly humorous account of a Northerner's travels in the South, the narrator referred to a black man as "The Sable Brother—alias the Son of Ham—alias the Image of God carved in Ebony—alias the Oppressed Type—alias the Contraband—alias the Irrepressible Nigger—alias the Chattel—alias the Darky—alias the Collud Pusson—alias the Great Cause—alias the Goose."[25] Such litanies emphasized the unstable status of people in the nation and way that each term could imply an entire worldview. "The sable brother," for example, denoted interracial fraternity and was associated with the abolitionist movement, whereas "the irrepressible nigger" alluded to the Democratic party's

[23]"The Great Speech. Frederick Douglass on the War," *The Christian Recorder*, Jan. 18, 1862; Senex, "Contraband," ibid., Aug. 9, 1862.

[24]Harriet Tubman, letter, June 30, 1863, in *Black Abolitionist Papers*, ed. Ripley et al., V, 221. Oct. 28, 1862, in *The Journals of Charlotte Forten Grimke*, ed. Brenda Stevenson (New York, 1988), 388; and James F. Jones, letter, May 8, 1864, in *A Grand Army of Black Men: Letters from African-American Soldiers in the Union Army, 1861–1865*, ed. Edwin S. Redkey (New York, 1992), 142. For use of "so-called" with "contrabands," see George A. Rue to Editor, *The Christian Recorder*, Aug. 9, 1862; H.M.T. to Editor, ibid., Oct. 18, 1862; Mr. Edward Young and Rev. Henry Davis to Editor, ibid., Nov. 15, 1862; and J.H.H. to Editor, ibid., March 21, 1863.

[25]*The Old Guard* 1 (June 1863), 144; "Through the Cotton States," *Knickerbocker; or, New York Monthly Magazine* 58 (Oct. 1861), 316. "Greeley's Vision"; Elizabeth Hyde Botume, *First Days Amongst the Contrabands* (1893; New York, 1968), 18; and "Contraband of War," *Harper's Weekly*, June 29, 1861, p. 416.

frustration with the dominance of slavery in national politics. Indeed, the derogatory term "nigger" was widely used in the Democratic press, among white soldiers, and elsewhere, while Republicans self-consciously eschewed it, at least in print. In the 1863 short story, "Our Contraband," the author signals that the family's Irish servants are racist by having them use such terms as "big black nigger" and, in dialect, "nagers." When the narrator refers to the ex-slave servant, Aggie, as a "contraband," the term is often placed in quotes, highlighting the provisional nature of both Aggie's status and the term itself. At the end of the story, when the narrator discovers that Aggie has found live-in work in a Quaker's home, she refers to Aggie as a "colored girl," as if her departure from the narrator's household—one that had never fully accepted her—had rendered her more human and freer than the term "contraband" could acknowledge.[26]

In minstrelsy, the most popular form of entertainment in the antebellum United States, white performers blacked their faces with burnt cork and caricatured African American songs, dances, and speech before largely working-class audiences. Many ostensibly humorous representations of contrabands harked back to minstrel performance. Consistent with minstrel traditions of selling representations of black people and performance, publishers printed decorative envelopes showing caricatured contrabands and a collectible card photograph featuring an "intelligent contraband. . . ."[27] Minstrel-style contraband humor was ubiquitous in Republican, Democratic, and even white abolitionist publications and—in the latter—reflected the limitations of racially egalitarian thinking in the period. Drawing on racist stereotypes elaborated in minstrelsy, the abolitionist *National Anti-Slavery Standard* portrayed African Americans as either simple and naïve or pretentious. Scores of anecdotes portrayed "intelligent

[26]Dodge, "Our Contraband," 396–97, 402. For examples of Republicans attributing the derogatory word "nigger" to others (especially Democrats) and studiously avoiding it themselves, see Mary Logan, *Reminiscences of the Civil War and Reconstruction*, ed. George Worthington Adams (Carbondale, 1970), 80, 84, 86; "The Vallandighamers and the 'Niggers,'" *Springfield Illinois Daily State Journal*, Oct. 15, 1862; "The Cry of Nig., Nig., Nigger," ibid., Oct. 16, 1862; and Root, *Contraband Christmas*, 17. Randall C. Jimerson, *The Private Civil War: Popular Thought during the Sectional Conflict* (Baton Rouge, 1988), 86–123; and Bell Irvin Wiley, *The Life of Billy Yank: The Common Soldier of the Union* (New York, 1951). Patrick Rael, *Black Identity and Black Protest in the Antebellum North* (Chapel Hill, 2002), 82–117. See also Randall Kennedy, *Nigger: The Strange Career of a Troublesome Word* (New York, 2002).

[27]"Stephen C. Foster and Negro Minstrelsy," *Atlantic Monthly* 20 (Nov. 1867), 609. William R. Weiss Jr., *The Catalog of Union Civil War Patriotic Covers* (Bethlehem, Penn., 1995), 285. *Vanity Fair*, June 15, 1861, p. 280. *Arthur's Home Magazine*, 28 (Dec. 1866), back matter. For additional "contraband" envelopes, see Eva V. Carline, "When Cotton Was King," *Overland Monthly* 36 (July 1900), 21. Sarah Emma Edmonds, *Memoirs of a Soldier, Nurse and Spy. A Woman's Adventures in the Union Army*, ed. Elizabeth D. Leonard (1865; DeKalb, 1999), 57; Dodge, "Our Contraband," 401; and Charles King, "A Contraband Christmas," *Harper's Weekly*, Dec. 19, 1896, pp. 1246–50. Lott, *Love and Theft: Blackface Minstrelsy and the American Working Class* (New York, 1993); Robert C. Toll, *Blacking Up: The Minstrel Show in Nineteenth-Century America* (New York, 1974); W. T. Lhamon, *Raising Cain: Blackface Performance from Jim Crow to Hip Hop* (Cambridge, Mass., 1998); Annemarie Bean, James V. Hatch, and Brooks McNamara, eds., *Inside the Minstrel Mask: Readings in Nineteenth-Century Blackface Minstrelsy* (Hanover, 1996); and David R. Roediger, *The Wages of Whiteness: Race and the Making of the American Working Class* (New York, 1991), 115–31.

contrabands" who proved ignorant of their surroundings or of the vicissitudes of the war.

Contrabands pervaded popular music, which became a key area for Northern representation of contrabands and, by extension, for speculation on the meanings of emancipation. As slave emancipation unfolded amid military occupation in parts of the Confederacy, activists reported on and transcribed examples of contraband singing, abolitionists wrote versions of what they *imagined* the contrabands would sing, and songwriters penned minstrel songs with contraband narrators. In keeping with whites' long-standing interest in African American dance, illustrators depicted contrabands dancing, and someone invented and marketed a "dancing contraband" doll.[28] The spread of songs about (and ostensibly by) contrabands, especially in 1861 and 1862, illuminates Northerners' keen interest in representing and defining the soon to be freed. The characteristics Northerners attributed to contrabands, in music as elsewhere, revealed their own divergent predictions about emancipation's consequences.

The proliferation of contraband music began with the encounter between fugitive slaves and white antislavery activists. Early white visitors to Fortress Monroe described being entranced by the singing of the fugitive slaves, and Lewis Lockwood, a minister and the first representative of the American Missionary Association to travel south to work with slaves, reported on "a prime deliverance melody" whose refrain was "Let my people go." At the behest of Lockwood and others, that song was titled *Go Down, Moses; or, The Song of the Contrabands,* widely printed in the Republican and antislavery press, and published as a parlor music arrangement in December 1861. Although the music historian Dena J. Epstein criticized the arrangement as unfaithful to the actual tones and cadences of the song as it was sung at Fortress Monroe, its publication as parlor music, however domesticated, gave Northerners a chance to bring "the song of the contrabands" into their homes. The song's impact is suggested by appropriations and parodies of its chorus, "Let my people go," in both antislavery songs and Democratic ones that twisted the refrain for antiemancipation, antiblack purposes.[29]

---

[28]"American Art and Artists," *Christian Examiner* 77 (Sept. 1864), 183. Winslow Homer, "A Bivouac Fire on the Potomac," *Harper's Weekly,* Dec. 21, 1861, pp. 808–9; Robert Knox Sneden, *The Eye of the Storm: A Civil War Odyssey* (New York, 2000), 134; and "The Banks Expedition—Extempore Musical and Terpsichorean Entertainment at the U.S. Arsenal, Baton Rouge," *Frank Leslie's Illustrated Newspaper,* Jan. 31, 1863, p. 292. Ronald Radano, "Denoting Difference: The Writing of the Slave Spirituals," *Critical Inquiry* 22 (Spring 1996), 509; and Sherrill V. Martin, "Music of Black Americans during the War Years," in *Feel the Spirit: Studies in Nineteenth-Century Afro-American Music,* ed. George R. Keck and Sherrill V. Martin (New York, 1988), 1–16. Lott, *Love and Theft;* Karen M. Adams, "The Black Image in the Paintings of William Sidney Mount," *American Art Journal* 7 (Nov. 1975), 42–59; Dena J. Epstein, *Sinful Tunes and Spirituals: Black Folk Music to the Civil War* (Urbana, 1977); and Ronald Radano, *Lying Up a Nation: Race and Black Music* (Chicago, 2003).

[29]"Mission to the Contrabands," *National Anti-Slavery Standard,* Oct. 12, 1861. "Contraband Singing," ibid., Sept. 7, 1861. For twenty verses of the song, plus the chorus, see "The Contrabands' Freedom Hymn," ibid., Dec. 21, 1861. Thomas Baker, arr., *The Song of the Contrabands. "O Let My People Go"* (New York, 1861); and *Harp of Freedom (Part I)* (New York, 1862), 2–3. A twelve-verse

Activists quickly put *Go Down, Moses* and other music by and about virtuous contrabands to service in their movement to aid the fugitives. To them, the song's message of liberation ("tell King Pharaoh, to let my people go!") constituted evidence of slaves' desire for freedom and refuted widespread suspicions that the enslaved were happy as they were. The song's biblical theme also announced the fleeing slaves' Christian faith and thus their susceptibility to moral uplift. One movement songbook printed *Go Down, Moses* alongside a song titled *Oh, Help the Contraband,* whose eight verses describe contra-bands coming north, willing to work and happy to taste freedom. The song concludes

> No more the stinging lash; No more the awful brand But knowledge, freedom, home, and Cash, For every "contraband." We come, we come, we come with joy to meet you, We come, we come our liberty to gain.[30]

By ascribing to the contrabands the ideals expected of the Northern middle class, the song encouraged its Northern singers to see escaping slaves as citizens in the making, potentially productive members of society. Whether attributed to slaves or authored by Northern activists, "contraband songs" of the antislavery movement sought to generate sympathy and to spur activism. They brought Southern slaves figuratively closer to Northerners by suggesting that their music and their values could be assimilated into Northern culture. . . .

The flight of enslaved people to Union lines and renditions of their music also inspired white songwriters to compose minstrel-style contraband songs designed for an audience outside the antislavery movement. Songs featuring "contraband" in the title and published as sheet music included *Ole Shady; or, The Song of the Contraband, Intelligent Contraband,* and *The Old Contraband.* (See figures 1.6 and 1.7.) As in most antebellum minstrel songs, a black man speaking in dialect narrated the minstrel-style contraband songs of the Civil War. Northern contraband songs mingled jokes about slave ignorance or pretension with sentimental renderings of the narrator's yearning to reunite with lost family members, to see his former owner taken down a peg, and—ultimately—to be free. In mixing ridicule with respect, the songs were consistent with a minstrel tradition that, as Eric Lott has persuasively argued for the antebellum period, was a complex cultural form that expressed not just white racism but also strands of desire and

---

"parody," using the same verse structure, urged the government to speed emancipation. Its refrain was, "Then go down, freemen, Away down to Dixie's land, And tell Uncle Sam To let my people go." Ibid. "Let the Bondmen Go!," *National Anti-Slavery Standard,* Jan. 18, 1862. For a Democratic parody "Dedicated to those who are partial to Contraband Melodies," see "O. Let Those People Go," *Vanity Fair,* Feb. 8, 1862, p. 68. Music historians regard the song as the first spiritual to be transcribed for a Northern audience. Other contemporary songs that incorporated variations of the chorus "let my people go" include G. F. Wurzel [pseud.], *De Day ob Liberty's Comin'* (Chicago, 1862); and Manuel Fenollosa, *Emancipation Hymn: Quartette & Chorus* (Boston, 1863). On Lockwood at Fortress Monroe, see Richardson, *Christian Reconstruction,* 4–14; and "Oh! Let My People Go. The Song of the Contrabands," *Continental Monthly* 2 (July 1862), 112–13. Epstein, *Sinful Tunes and Spirituals,* 247–49.

[30]*Harp of Freedom,* 27. "The Harp of Freedom," advertisement, *National Anti-Slavery Standard,* April 5, 1862; and "The Harp of Freedom," advertisement, *The New York Times,* March 22, 1862.

Figure 1.6
"Contraband" of Port Royal, poetry by John G. Whittier, music by Ferdinand Mayer (Boston, 1862). Courtesy Duke University, Rare Book, Manuscript, and Special Collections Library.

Figure 1.7
The Old Contraband. Song and Chorus, words by John L. Zieber, music by Rudolph Wittig (Philadelphia, 1865). Courtesy Brown University, John Hay Library, Sheet Music Collection.

identification.[31] The wartime flight of slaves to Union lines and the flexible term "contraband" added new grist for the genre. By definition, fugitives from slavery challenged antebellum minstrelsy's vision of slaves as content with simple lives in the pastoral South. Minstrel contraband songs reinforced ideas about inherent racial difference by emphasizing the slaves' supposed dialect and, in illustrated song sheets, supposed phenotypic differences from whites. Yet contraband narrators who, like real escapees, took dramatic risks to become free, exalted in liberation, and professed loyalty to the Union cause encouraged Northern audiences to reconsider their preconception that slaves were fundamentally different from the ostensibly freedom-loving Northern white working class. In the changed context—in which black men could aspire to military service and citizenship—male minstrel characters who longed to see their wives and children, enlisted in the army, or sought work in the North raised the possibility that black men desired, and could achieve, mainstream ideals of political and social manhood.

Most minstrel contraband songs commented on current events but then faded from popular memory. A few, however, had more staying power. The song *Kingdom Coming* exemplifies the geographical mobility and complex meanings that wartime contraband songs could accrue. The song, composed by the white midwestern songwriter Henry C. Work, was introduced in the spring of 1862 by the renowned Christy's Minstrels, a troupe of white men who performed in blackface. Its narrator describes (in supposed Southern black dialect) a plantation

---

[31]Lott, *Love and Theft*, 18–20.

owner's panicked flight from home as the Yankees invade. The lyrics portray the cowardice of a sun-darkened slave owner:

> He drill so much dey call him Cap'an,
> An he get so dreffel tann'd,
> I spec he try an' fool dem Yankees
> For to tink he's contraband.

The image of a plantation owner trying to pass as contraband is consistent with the sense of racialized subversion so often implicit in the term "contraband." The war has turned the planter into a desperate fugitive and the slaves into masters of the plantation. In subsequent verses, the liberated slaves move into the owner's house, raid his kitchen, and lock the overseer in the cellar as they revel in their freedom.[32]

Kingdom Coming enjoyed enormous popularity, selling more than 20,000 copies in its first seven months. White people who sang the song gave voice to the feelings of liberation and celebration that Work had put in the narrator's mouth. Indeed, considering its popularity, *Kingdom Coming* may have done more than the abolitionist contraband songs to introduce white people to the excitement and upheaval accompanying the advent of freedom to the South. The chorus ran

> De massa run? ha, ha!
> De darkey stay? ho, ho!
> It mus' be now de kingdom comin',
> An' de year ob Jubilo!

U.S. soldiers, both black and white, carried *Kingdom Coming* to the South, and Southern African Americans adopted it, sang it, changed the words, and sometimes took credit for its creation. Well into the twentieth century, African Americans in the South sang *Kingdom Coming*, a testament to the complex ways minstrel music could be appropriated and transformed. The song, sometimes subtitled *The Contraband's Song*, also continued to be published as a minstrel tune.[33]

---

[32]Henry C. Work, *Kingdom Coming* (Chicago, 1862).

[33]Dena J. Epstein, *Music Publishing in Chicago before 1871: The Firm of Root & Cady* (Detroit, 1969), 45–46. Kenneth A. Bernard, *Lincoln and the Music of the Civil War* (Caldwell, 1966), 99–100, 294, 295, 296, 299; J.R.M. to Editor, *Song Messenger of the North-West*, 1 (Aug. 1863), 78; J.R.M. to Editor, ibid. (Nov. 1863), 126–27. Richard Harwell, *Confederate Music* (Chapel Hill, 1950), 89–90, 125. For contemporary reports of slaves singing *Kingdom Coming*, see "How the Slaves Receive Our Troops," *Song Messenger of the North-West* 1 (July 1863), 57; "The Contraband's Kingdom," ibid. (Aug. 1863), 66–67. *Old Southern Songs of the Period of the Confederacy: The Dixie Trophy Collection;* compiled by Kate E. Staton, Tarboro, N.C. (New York, 1926), 101–2; and William E. Barton, *Old Plantation Hymns* (Boston, 1899), 25. Henry M. Belden and Arthur Palmer Hudson, eds., *The Frank C. Brown Collection of North Carolina Folklore* (7 vols., Durham, 1952–1964), II, 541–43; George P. Rawick, ed., *The American Slave: A Composite Autobiography* (19 vols., Westport, 1972), II, part 2, p. 197, IV, part 2, pp. 28–29, XVIII, 232; and Newman I. White, *American Negro Folk-Songs* (Cambridge, Mass., 1928), 170–71. On continuing publication of *Kingdom Coming* as a minstrel song, see *Minstrel Songs, Old and New* (Boston, 1882), 180–81; Albert E. Wier, ed., *Songs of the Sunny South* (New York, 1929), 27; and T. T. Burleigh, ed., *Negro Minstrel Melodies* (New York, 1910), 50–51. In meticulous research, Dena J. Epstein found no evidence that *Kingdom Coming* had existed as a slave song before its publication in Chicago in 1862. Epstein, *Music Publishing in Chicago*, 45–46.

Popular music thus proposed a variety of contraband protagonists, from the exotic yet Christian singer of *Go Down, Moses* to the ideal free laborer of *Oh, Help the Contraband* to the caricatured figures of many minstrel songs. At any moment, the dynamics of performance and reception shaped the songs' meanings. *Kingdom Coming,* for example, had different valences when sung by white minstrels in blackface for white Northern audiences, by former slaves for one another, or by former slaves for a white Northern audience—all of which happened. In all genres of contraband songs that circulated in the North—nascent spirituals, abolitionist songs, or minstrel songs—the contraband figure served as a proxy for people's fantasies about who slaves were and what they would do with their freedom.

As the federal government shifted from a policy of upholding slavery to one of emancipating slaves and enlisting black men as soldiers, new narrative possibilities opened for imagined contrabands. Throughout 1862 Americans debated whether black men should be allowed to serve in the U.S. army in combat roles, knowing that if they did, their path to eventual citizenship would be shortened. The military's employment of African American women and men contrabands as laborers had engendered little public debate. For more than a century, warring powers in the United States and throughout the Western Hemisphere had employed enslaved laborers in supporting roles. Arming black men was far more controversial. In the United States, the prospect of black enlistment in the Union cause challenged prevailing ideas about African Americans' roles in both war and peace. Most Northern white people believed (despite contrary evidence from earlier conflicts) that black men, especially those who had been enslaved, could not accommodate themselves to military discipline and lacked the courage required for soldiering. In addition, because republican governments had historically linked military service with citizenship rights, Northerners knew that arming black men would increase the likelihood that, once the war was over, black men could claim the political and civil rights of citizens. As the historian Laurent Dubois has written, when military conflicts in the Western Hemisphere raised the possibility of arming large numbers of slaves, "many whites feared, with good reason, that the presence of men of African descent in the military undermined and threatened racial hierarchy."[34]

Black leaders were especially vocal in urging the Lincoln administration to accept black men as soldiers, a move that would strengthen their claims to citizenship after the war. As a source of military manpower, black laborers within army lines loomed large in their campaign. Yet the emphasis on the passivity and naïveté of contrabands conflicted with the vision of such men as soldiers. In a January 1862 address, Frederick Douglass chastised the Lincoln administration for seeing fleeing slaves as contrabands, not soldiers. "The Washington Government wants men for its army, but thus far, it has not had the boldness to recognize the manhood of the race

---

[34]Dubois, *Colony of Citizens,* 225. For a comparative discussion, see Christopher Leslie Brown and Philip D. Morgan, *Arming Slaves: From Classical Times to the Modern Age* (New Haven, 2006). For slave labor in other Western Hemisphere wars, see Frey, *Water from the Rock,* esp. 121–22; Berlin, *Many Thousands Gone,* 230, 261, 296–97; Rothman, *Slave Country,* 148–50; Roger N. Buckley, *Slaves in Red Coats: The British West India Regiments, 1795–1815* (New Haven, 1979), 5; and Peter M. Voelz, *Slave and Soldier: The Military Impact of Blacks in the Colonial Americas* (New York, 1993), 59–65.

to which I belong. It only sees in the slave an article of commerce—a contraband." Douglass contrasted the government's use of "contraband"—which, he believed, implied that slaves were passive or inert—with his own vision of ex-slave soldiers as avatars of racial manhood. The poet James Madison Bell envisioned the transformation of contrabands into "men" in an 1862 poem titled, "What Shall We Do with the Contrabands?" "I would not have the wrath of the rebels to cease," Bell wrote,

> Till the Contrabands join in securing a peace, Whose glory shall vanish the last galling chain, And win for their race an undying respect.

The poem urged the conversion of passive contrabands into active soldiers striking a blow for their own freedom. Rather than suggest what "we" should do with the contrabands, Bell insisted that they must do for themselves. The contrabands must fight to "purge from their race . . . The stigma and scorn now attending the slave." Given the opportunity, advocates of black enlistment argued, men contrabands would show their real mettle; as they helped secure a victory for the United States, they would lay the groundwork for incorporation into the nation as citizens. Women too could be citizens, but ex-slave men's military service, which represented sacrifice for the nation and independent action, gave them a special platform from which to claim new (and gendered) rights.[35]

Black recruitment to the U.S. army began during 1862 and was legitimated by the Emancipation Proclamation, which took effect on January 1, 1863. Those developments changed the context for popular use of the term "contraband." Republicans seeking to emphasize the more permanent basis of emancipation began self-consciously replacing "contraband" with "freedman" and occasionally with "freedpeople." Colloquially, however, in military circles, in minstrelsy and other forms of popular culture, and in everyday language, "contraband" persisted well beyond January 1863. The government continued to issue "contraband rations"; the army continued to operate "contraband camps." The 1864 edition of Webster's dictionary institutionalized the new definition of contraband ("a negro slave") and explained that Gen. Benjamin Butler had invented the definition in 1861. As the dictionary suggested, the new definition of "contraband" had transcended the vicissitudes of policy and continued, in the popular lexicon, to evoke ideas about slavery, emancipation, race, and dependence.[36]

---

[35]"The Great Speech, Frederick Douglass on the War"; James Madison Bell, "What Shall We Do with the Contrabands?," in *Black Abolitionist Papers*, ed. Ripley et al., V, 138–39. Junius to Editor, *The Christian Recorder,* May 23, 1863; and Williams, *History of the Negro Troops in the War of the Rebellion.* Cooper, Holt, and Scott, *Beyond Slavery,* 17–18. Dubois, *Colony of Citizens,* 224–27, 150, 160–62, 192–94; and Ada Ferrer, *Insurgent Cuba: Race, Nation, and Revolution, 1868–1898* (Chapel Hill, 1999), 37–42, 125–26.

[36]Noah Webster, *A Dictionary of the English Language* (Springfield, Mass., 1864), 285. A current definition for "contraband" is "a slave who during the American Civil War escaped to or was brought within the Union lines," according to *Merriam-Webster's Online Dictionary,* http://m-w.com/dictionary/contraband. For "contraband rations," see Col. John Eaton to Gen. O. O. Howard, June 22, 1865, Letters Sent, vol. 1, DC Asst. Comr., Records of the Bureau of Freedmen, Refugees, and Abandoned Lands, rg 105 (National Archives, Washington, D.C.); and *Second Annual Report of the Western Freedmen's Aid Commission, Cincinnati, Ohio* (Cincinnati, 1865), 10.

Figure 1.8
Thomas Waterman Wood, *The Contraband*. Oil on canvas, 1866. The Metropolitan Museum of Art, Gift of Charles Stewart Smith, 1884 (84.12b). Image © The Metropolitan Museum of Art.

Figure 1.9
Thomas Waterman Wood, *The Recruit*. Oil on canvas, 1866. The Metropolitan Museum of Art, Gift of Charles Stewart Smith, 1884 (84.12b). Image © The Metropolitan Museum of Art.

After the Emancipation Proclamation, many white writers and artists followed the lead of the black activists Douglass and Bell in adopting a contraband-to-soldier narrative. White writers and artists, however, often suggested that white people made the contraband's transformation possible. In Louisa May Alcott's short story "My Contraband," a white woman nurse meets "her" contraband, Robert, in an army hospital and tries to reform him. She gives him a Bible and sends him to Boston, well known as the headquarters of abolitionism. The nurse's pedagogical efforts pay off, as Robert enrolls in the Fifty-fourth Massachusetts Volunteer Infantry Regiment, prepared to make the ultimate sacrifice for the nation. The story represents Robert as transformed from contraband into man by his embrace of Christian morality and military enlistment. All that remains is for him to prove himself on the battlefield, which he does at Fort Wagner, South Carolina.[37]

A series of paintings by Thomas Waterman Wood also dramatized the imagined transition from contraband to soldier and potential citizen. Wood, well known in his era as a painter of portraits and narrative scenes from everyday life,

---

[37]The story was first published as "The Brothers," a title chosen by the editor of the *Atlantic Monthly*. In personal correspondence Louisa May Alcott referred to the story as "the 'Contraband'"; it was republished as "My Contraband"; in *Hospital Sketches; And Camp and Fireside Stories*, by Louisa May Alcott (Boston, 1869). Louisa May Alcott, "The Brothers," *Atlantic Monthly* 12 (Nov. 1863), 584–95; Elizabeth Young, *Disarming the Nation: Women's Writing and the American Civil War* (Chicago, 1999), 329n64.

Figure 1.10

Thomas Waterman Wood, *The Veteran*. Oil on canvas, 1866. The Metropolitan Museum of Art, Gift of Charles Stewart Smith, 1884 (84.12c). Image © The Metropolitan Museum of Art.

spent much of the Civil War in Louisville, Kentucky, where he painted a series now known as *A Bit of War History*. (See figures 1.8, 1.9, and 1.10.) The three paintings, completed in 1866, were exhibited by the prestigious National Academy of Design in New York and reproduced as woodcuts in *Harper's Weekly*. The first painting, titled *The Contraband*, shows a man arriving in a provost marshal's office carrying a walking stick and a small bag of belongings. He raises his hat in a deferential greeting. A rifle and other soldier's accoutrements rest against a chair. The second, *The Recruit*, finds the man in soldier's uniform, with the rifle over his shoulder. With his left leg bent, he takes a more aggressive stance than the contraband in the first painting. In the last, *The Veteran*, the man—now on crutches with one leg missing—salutes with his hand, a sign of allegiance to the nation he has sacrificed to defend.[38]

The paintings suggest that military service endows the contraband with manhood and that as a veteran the man is due respect. Indeed, the veteran's missing limb symbolizes the compact of citizenship: men who make sacrifices for the nation are rewarded with rights of the transformation from contraband to citizen. The veteran, disabled or even emasculated, cannot be the autonomous individual so important to contemporary visions of masculine citizenship. The slave, transmuted through soldier to veteran, remains literally and figuratively dependent on a "crutch" to move forward. Only the middle figure, the soldier, represents the self-sufficient ideal citizen. Nor did Alcott find a way to envision postwar citizenship for her contraband character. Robert dies a heroic death in South Carolina, thus freeing Alcott from any need to propose a role for emancipated people in the nation's future.

While black enlistment created new opportunities to imagine contrabands as soldiers and future citizens, it also placed Northern African American men in a new and often difficult relationship to Southern contrabands. Many Northern black soldiers had no firsthand knowledge of the South and considered slavery both unfamiliar and horrific. Military service brought thousands of them into direct contact with slaves, pushing the Northerners to reconsider how they were

---

[38]Thomas Waterman Wood, "The Contraband, Recruit, and Veteran," *Harper's Weekly*, May 4, 1867, p. 284; Natalie Spassky et al., *American Paintings in the Metropolitan Museum of Art* (3 vols., New York, 1985), II, 196–99.

both connected to and different from those just emerging from bondage. James Henry Gooding—a black noncommissioned officer in the Massachusetts Fifty-fourth who had lived in New Bedford, Massachusetts, before the war—wrote from Beaufort, South Carolina, to a New Bedford newspaper, "The contrabands did not believe we were coming; one of them said, 'I nebber bleeve black Yankee comee here help culer men.' They think now the kingdom is coming sure enough." Like many African American soldiers, Gooding wrote admiringly of newly emancipated people. "So far as I have seen, they appear to understand the *causes* of the war better than a great many Northern editors," he commented, even as his rendering of the contrabands' dialect emphasized their difference from him. . . .[39]

The soldiers were immersed in a military culture in which the term "contraband" served to distinguish black men who worked as civilian laborers from those who worked as soldiers. And African American soldiers had a complicated relationship to the contraband laborers who built fortifications, dug trenches, and managed supply trains alongside them. White officers, loath to recognize the distinction between black soldiers and black civilian laborers, often assigned black soldiers to manual labor never required of white soldiers. Moreover, contrabands were commonly understood as the most interchangeable and degraded of laborers. For black soldiers, then, emphasizing the distance between themselves and civilian laborers became a way of demanding respect for their service. The practical importance of such a distinction became especially clear when, in June 1863, the secretary of war announced that black soldiers would be paid $10 per month, less $3 worth of clothing, a salary significantly less than the $13 per month paid to white soldiers. In September 1863, Gooding addressed President Lincoln about the issue. "Now the main question is, Are we Soldiers, or are we Labourers?" he asked rhetorically. "We of this Regt. were not enlisted under any 'contraband' act," he insisted, referring to the July 1862 Militia Act, which had established the rate of pay for African American military employees at $10 monthly.[40]

Yet Gooding demonstrated respect for the work of contraband laborers. "We do not wish to be understood, as rating our Service, of more Value to the

---

[39]James Henry Gooding to Editors, June 8, 1863, in *On the Altar of Freedom: A Black Soldier's Civil War Letters from the Front*, ed. Virginia M. Adams (New York, 1992), 26–27. G.E.S., letter, Nov. 20, 1862, in *Grand Army of Black Men*, ed. Redkey, 22–23; William Waring, letter, Feb. 15, 1865, ibid., 75; A. J. Bedfold, letter, Nov. 7, 1864, ibid., 150. See also G.E.S., letter, *Christian Recorder*, April 9, 1864; John H. W. N. Collins to Editor, ibid., May 20, 1865; and Wm. T. Fountain to Brother Weaver, ibid., May 28, 1864.

[40]Ira Berlin et al., eds., *Freedom: A Documentary History of Emancipation*, ser. 2, vol. III: *The Black Military Experience* (New York, 1982), 385–86. For contrabands as degraded laborers, see Berlin et al., eds., *Freedom*, ser. 1, vol. II, 251–53, 256, 266–68, 293, 298–99, 305–6. For the assignment of black soldiers to manual labor, see Williams, *History of the Negro Troops in the War of the Rebellion*, 162–66; Joseph T. Glatthaar, *Forged in Battle: The Civil War Alliance of Black Soldiers and White Officers* (1990; Baton Rouge, 2000), 182–85; and Oliver, dev., *Civil War cd-rom: War of the Rebellion*, ser. 1, vol. XLI, no. 2, p. 566, ser. 1, vol. XXVIII, no. 2, p. 95. Berlin et al., eds., *Freedom*, ser. 2, vol. III, 363, 388–89, 362–68; Herman Belz, "Law, Politics, and Race in the Struggle for Equal Pay during the Civil War," *Civil War History* 22 (Sept. 1976), 197–213; and Glatthaar, *Forged in Battle*, 169–76.

Government, than the service of the exslave," he wrote. "Their Service is un-doubtedly worth much to the Nation, but Congress made express, provision touching their case, as slaves freed by military necessity." "Not so with us," Good-ing insisted. "Freemen from birth, and consequently, having the advantage of *thinking*, and acting for ourselves, so far as the Laws would allow us. We do not consider ourselves fit subjects for the Contraband act."[41] In his protest Gooding drew a tentative line between those who had been free before the war and former slaves who, he suggested, had lacked opportunities to make decisions as indepen-dent actors and therefore did not merit the same pay as "freemen." His argument for equal pay excluded the great many black soldiers who had been enslaved at the beginning of the war, including those of four South Carolina regiments stationed not far from the Massachusetts Fifty-fourth.

Gooding's effort to honor the labor of the contrabands even as he insisted that "freemen from birth" deserved more pay suggested both the difficulty and utility of the term "contraband" for African Americans who had been free at the war's outset. During the war and at least into the Reconstruction period, African Americans used the term to distinguish newcomers from old residents, to allude to poverty and need, and sometimes to draw distinctions in religious and cultural traditions. For example, in 1866 the Northern black teacher Re-becca Primus reported from Maryland's Eastern Shore that local whites refused to pay "colored men & women . . . sufficient wages & if the people will not accept their terms they send off and get 'contrabands,' as they are here denomi-nated." For Primus, as for many black observers, "contraband" marked an im-portant distinction between local black people and recently emancipated migrants. If white people used the proximity of unemployed contrabands to justify paying longtime black residents poorly, the black residents themselves saw the contrabands as a threat to their economic livelihood. Much later, W. E. B. Du Bois, who was born in 1868, recalled that the "'contrabands'" who had mi-grated to his hometown in Massachusetts, "on the whole were well received" by the small and long-standing local black population. Yet he remembered that "the older group" of black residents "held some of its social distinctions and the newcomers astonished us by forming a little Negro Methodist Zion Church, which we sometimes attended. . . ."[42]

African Americans thus adopted the term "contraband" as a medium in which to express the meanings of differences between the newly freed and those

---

[41]Berlin et al., eds., *Freedom*, ser. 2, vol. III, 386.

[42]Rebecca Primus to "Parents & Sister," April 7, 1866, in *Beloved Sisters and Loving Friends,* ed. Griffin, 118; W. E. Burghardt DuBois, *Dusk of Dawn: An Essay toward an Autobiography of a Race Concept* (1940; New Brunswick, 1984), 15. In this passage Du Bois placed "contraband" in quotation marks. For objections by formerly free blacks to being treated like "contrabands" by military forces, see Berlin et al., eds., *Freedom,* ser. 1, vol. II, 273–75, 296–97, 307, 313–14; and Ira Berlin et al., eds., *Freedom: A Documentary History of Emancipation,* ser. 1, vol. III: *The Wartime Genesis of Free Labor: The Lower South* (New York, 1990), 570. "Contrabands," *The Christian Recorder,* April 5, 1862; W. J. Davis to Bro. Weaver, ibid., Nov. 15, 1862; "Letter from Keokuk, Iowa," ibid., April 18, 1863; and S. M. Giles to Editor, ibid., Nov. 21, 1863.

who had been free before the war. As Northern African Americans in the aid movement recognized, the racism of the broader society tended to force black people together, encouraging them to see distinctions as far less important than the collectivity. Nonetheless, differences of religion, regional origin, status, and experience with slavery *were* important, particularly as emancipation obliterated one of the starkest differences among African Americans, that between slave and free. When Northern African Americans used "contraband" to set themselves apart, descriptions of difference often shaded into suggestions of their own superiority, not of race, but of education and experience. Writers such as Bell and Bruce were likewise interested in the contrabands' distinctiveness, but they portrayed contrabands, not as objects of philanthropy, but as heroic agents of racial destiny. Possessed of preternatural bravery and integrity, Bell's and Bruce's contrabands would light the path to citizenship and vindicate the manhood of the entire race. The myriad connotations African Americans gave to "contraband" (and their choices of when and how to use the term) thus reflected a struggle to give linguistic expression to tensions between group identity and difference newly delineated at the moment of emancipation. Class differences among African Americans would later become more visible and the language of class more straightforward. For the time being, "contraband" was a shorthand that could suggest a variety of differences without naming them explicitly.[43]

Among politically active Republicans, use of the term "contraband" declined following the promulgation of the Emancipation Proclamation. Although the proclamation exempted enslaved people in loyal states and in parts of the Confederacy, and although it was not enforceable in Confederate-held areas, it marked a watershed in Union policy, for it forecast permanent emancipation and a new, more secure status for escapees from slavery. White and black Republicans now strove to replace the indeterminacy of "contraband" with the permanence of "freedman." Particularly conscious of the significance of that linguistic shift was the Boston-based white abolitionist Edward L. Pierce, who supervised contrabands at Fortress Monroe in 1861 and later at Port Royal, South Carolina. In a September 1863 article, Pierce reported, "These people were first called contrabands at Fortress Monroe; but at Port Royal . . . they were generally referred to as freedmen. These terms are milestones in our progress," he wrote, "and they are yet to be lost in the better and more comprehensive designation of citizens, or, when discrimination is convenient, citizens of African descent."[44]

---

[43]Emma Jones Lapsansky, "Friends, Wives, and Strivings: Networks and Community Values among Nineteenth-Century Philadelphia Afroamerican Elites," *Pennsylvania Magazine of History and Biography* 108 (Jan. 1984), 3–24; and Elsa Barkley Brown, "Negotiating and Transforming the Public Sphere: African American Political Life in the Transition from Slavery to Freedom," *Public Culture* 7 (Winter 1994), 107–46.

[44]Pierce, "Freedmen at Port Royal," 292. See also *Second Annual Report of the Western Freedmen's Aid Commission,* 6; H. Clay Trumbull, *War Memories of an Army Chaplain* (New York, 1898), 402; and Levi Coffin, *Reminiscences of Levi Coffin, the Reputed President of the Underground Railroad* (1876; New York, 1968), 620. Dubois, *Colony of Citizens,* 143–44, 150–51, 252–57; and Hebe Maria Mattos de Castro, "El color inexistente Relaciones raciales y trabajo rural en Rio de Janeiro tras la abolición de la

"Freedmen" took hold, leaving unfulfilled Pierce's prediction of a term that did not imply race or distinguish between the recently emancipated and those who had always been free. The War Department ratified the term in March 1863, when it commissioned the American Freedmen's Inquiry Commission. Congress later placed its imprimatur on the term in founding the Bureau of Freedmen, Refugees, and Abandoned Lands (popularly known as the Freedmen's Bureau) in spring 1865. The term "refugees" in the bureau's name referred to displaced white Unionists in the South whose sympathies made them essentially stateless when the Confederacy came into existence. The U.S. government offered such people limited support, through the military during the war and through the new bureau afterward. "Refugee" never caught on as a word for displaced (and implicitly Unionist) African Americans, notwithstanding the *Christian Recorder* correspondent's call for the term's use in place of "contraband." Indeed, the use of "freedmen" and "refugee" side by side in the name of the new federal bureau reflected a segregated world view in which white people were linked to their prior status as citizens, black people to their prior status as slaves, a people without a country to lose.[45]

Despite the persistence of segregating language, the government took steps between 1865 and 1869 to secure citizenship for African Americans via new constitutional amendments that abolished slavery, defined everyone born in the United States as a citizen, and prohibited racial discrimination in voting rights. In practice, the amendments did little to guarantee the rights of African Americans, but formally they settled the question of the place of former slaves in the national body politic. As the pseudonymous humorist Petroleum G. Nasby wrote to his pseudonymous friend Mark Twain in 1869, "The Reliable Contraband is contraband no more, but a citizen of the United States."[46]

As time-bound terms such as "contraband" and "freedman" receded into history, the egalitarianism of "citizen" would be modified by adjectives such as "colored" or supplanted entirely by nouns such as "negro." Yet the word "contraband" had become so integral to Northerners' experiences of the Civil War that contrabands appeared frequently in the memoirs, reminiscences, histories, and fictions of the Civil War published toward the end of the nineteenth century. Reflecting the reactionary tenor of the times, in white people's writing the complexities of the wartime use of "contraband"—especially the visions of contrabands as invaluable

---

esclavitud" (The nonexistent color: Race relations and rural work in Rio de Janeiro after the abolition of slavery), *Historia Social* (Valencia, Spain), 22 (1995), 83–100.

[45]On federal aid to Unionists of the South, see Stephen V. Ash, "Poor Whites in the Occupied South, 1861–1865," *Journal of Southern History* 57 (Feb. 1991), 39–62. On how the bureau came to serve white refugees as well as freedmen, see Herman Belz, "The Freedmen's Bureau Act of 1865 and the Principle of No Discrimination According to Color," *Civil War History* 21 (Fall 1975), 197–217. The term "refugee" had come into widespread use in late seventeenth-century England to designate Huguenot exiles from France. Until well into the twentieth century, it was used interchangeably with others such as "exile" and "émigré" to describe people who had been ejected or displaced, usually as a result of state policies. Nevzat Soguk, *States and Strangers: Refugees and Displacements of Statecraft* (Minneapolis, 1999), 58–61, 81–83.

[46]Albert Bigelow Paine, *Mark Twain* (4 vols., New York, 1912), I, 386.

to the U.S. government during the war, as objects of empathy, or as nascent citizens—fell away in favor of the minstrel-style, comic characterizations also found in wartime art and writing.[47] Contraband characters in late nineteenth-century writing the Civil War often provided a humorous element. White writers represented contrabands as passive, impoverished, picturesque, often dishonest, and—where relevant—unassimilable into Northern life. Such writers used "contraband" for escaping slaves in the Civil War period but not typically for African Americans in the present. One exception was the invocation of "intelligent contraband" and "reliable contraband" to refer to present-day sources of suspect information. A racialized symbol of haplessness and dishonesty, the "intelligent contraband" became part of the scaffolding of an increasingly racist society.[48]

Military officials and civilian relief workers who wrote memoirs of their wartime experiences often recounted the origin of the new meaning of "contraband" at Fortress Monroe, and they frequently alluded to the term's popularity during the war. Protective of his legacy, Benjamin Butler took space in his 1892 autobiography to refute a charge that he had not invented the moniker, publishing a letter from a former Confederate officer who said he had heard Butler declare the fugitives at Fortress Monroe "contraband of war."[49] Subsequent historians have given Butler's encounter with the three fugitives a place in history, training their attention on the unfolding events at Fortress Monroe; on wartime questions about slavery and property rights; and on the trajectory of U.S. policy from upholding slavery to destroying it. While those are worthy subjects, they do not account for the vast and enthusiastic popular appropriation of the

---

[47]See Rosella Rice, "Mother Bickerdyke," *Arthur's Home Magazine* 50 (Dec. 1882), 738–41; S. L. Gracey, "The Flight of the Contrabands," *Outing, an Illustrated Monthly Magazine of Recreation* 7 (Feb. 1886), 546; John T. Doyle, "An Episode of the Civil War," *Overland Monthly* 9 (May 1887), 539–41; Sara D. Halsted, "Little Jethro," ibid., 5 (May 1885), 484–87; John Habberton, "My Friend Moses," *Scribner's Monthly* 13 (Jan. 1877), 399–404; Mary E. C. Wyeth, "Moses an' Aaron," ibid., 14 (Aug. 1877), 542–46; King, "Contraband Christmas"; and Charles McIlvaine, "A Little Contraband," in *The St. Nicholas Anthology*, ed. Henry Steele Commager (1947; New York, 1983), 153–60. Rare exceptions include Pinkerton, *Spy of the Rebellion*, 194, 245, 343–93; and Edwin Forbes, *Thirty Years After: An Artist's Story of the Great War* (20 vols., New York, 1890–1891), XV, 233.

[48]George W. Hosmer, "The Hidden River," *Harper's Weekly*, Nov. 2, 1889, p. 881; "Promoting Immigration," *The New York Times*, Oct. 24, 1879; untitled, ibid., Feb. 13, 1885; Editorial, ibid., July 22, 1885; "A Reminder," *The Washington Post*, Nov. 19, 1899; Editorial, ibid., Feb. 25, 1878; "Current Comment," ibid., Aug. 19, 1882; and Thomas W. Higginson, "The Next Step in Journalism," *Current Literature* 8 (Dec. 1891), 486.

[49]See Butler, *Autobiography and Personal Reminiscences*, 256–64. For nonfiction that sought to secure the Civil War meaning of "contraband" for the future, see Nicolay and Hay, *Abraham Lincoln*, IV, 387–89; Forbes, *Thirty Years After*, 233; Albert Bushnell Hart, ed., *The Romance of the Civil War* (New York, 1903); John Eaton, *Grant, Lincoln, and the Freedmen: Reminiscences of the Civil War* (New York, 1907), esp. 1–14, 46–61; Elizabeth Nicholson, "A Contraband Camp," *Indiana History Bulletin* 1 (Sept. 1924), 134–40; Trumbull, *War Memories of an Army Chaplain*, 374, 386, 394–89; and Williams, *History of the Negro Troops in the War of the Rebellion*, 70–72.

term "contraband," a phenomenon contemporaries acknowledged but rarely analyzed.

Circulation of the term "contraband" exposed the constraints on Northerners' visions for former slaves. The brutal racism exemplified by *Vanity Fair*'s illustration of "The Highly Intelligent Contraband" stood at one end of the spectrum of possibilities, but the other end was not necessarily defined by acceptance of the recently emancipated as full citizens. Indeed, it was almost impossible to divorce the term from its connotations of difference and inferiority. Even white egalitarians, such as Thomas Waterman Wood, who envisioned dignity and citizenship for former slaves also tended to see them as helpless or incomplete. And although African Americans who had been free at the war's beginning, such as Henry Gooding, expressed no doubts about the fundamental humanity of former slaves, their invocation of "contraband" usually marked the differences they perceived—economic, cultural, or religious—between themselves and the newly emancipated.

The inability of most Northern whites to imagine former slaves as full citizens, unmodified by race or previous condition, had tragic consequences. But the racist repression with which the Civil War period ended should not erase the rich Northern debate about the meanings of slave emancipation. As enslaved people pressed for their own freedom throughout the South, Northerners imagined them as contrabands. In drawing them, joking and singing about them, and telling stories about them, Northerners sought to fill with meaning a term that was, by definition, transitional and unstable. The word's multiple valences and novelty provided creative latitude for wordsmiths and illustrators who used it to explore the implications of social upheaval, military conflict, the demise of slavery, and supposed racial difference. In the wartime context, imagined contrabands could be menacing migrants, the butt of jokes, citizen-soldiers in the making, ideal free laborers, objects of pity and reform, or avatars of racial uplift. The individual contraband could be a vessel for speculation on black manhood, while groups of contrabands could represent questions about the impact of enslavement or the nature of race. For Northern African Americans the term helped name distinctions of status at a moment when emancipation required a rethinking of their relationship to those who had long been held in bondage.

Looking forward from 1861, no one knew who would win the war or whether it would bring an end to slavery. In that period of deep uncertainty, Northerners used the term "contraband" to face questions common to all societies experiencing abolition during the long nineteenth century, questions about the meanings of race, former slaves' willingness to work for wages, the relationship between formerly free blacks and those who had been enslaved, and the terms under which freedpeople would become part of the body politic. Contemporaries who self-consciously reflected on the usage of "contraband" registered their understanding that naming the people then emerging from bondage was a critical step in cementing their future. Those critics rightly recognized the importance of language in creating a foundation for inclusion in, or exclusion from, the nation. The proliferation of contrabands in popular culture did not constitute a rethinking of scientific ideas about race but a debate over the boundaries of the body politic, the meanings of citizenship and dependency, and the legacies of slavery. For their own part, freedpeople drew on a rich palate of experience and ideology to make sense of their own lives. Yet the imagined contrabands of art, literature, and propaganda reveal much about a nation in the midst of a revolutionary transformation.

Kate Masur

As a historian, I focus on the problem of slavery and its legacies in American history. I trace some of my interest in history to my AP US History class at Oak Park River Forest High School and my teacher, Michael Averbach. That class was hard! Mr. Averbach threw us into the scholarly debates among the men considered to be the greatest historians of the post–World War II era, and he demanded that we understand history not just as facts but as a struggle over interpretation. In college I gravitated to cultural studies and media studies, a background that made me alert to the cartoons, jokes, songs, and other popular culture forms I examined in my article on "contrabands" in this collection. Most of my other work explores the intersection of law, politics, and the lives of everyday people. My first book looked at the abolition of slavery and the era of Reconstruction in Washington, D.C. I am now writing about liberty, policing, and the rights of free African Americans from the early nineteenth century through the Civil War. I teach in the History Department at Northwestern University, where I aspire to help students see that American history is fun, interesting, and relevant to our lives in the present.

QUESTIONS FOR CONSIDERATION

1. How did the context of the Civil War make the term "contraband" popular?
2. Popular opinion in the North was ambivalent about the status of formerly enslaved African Americans. How did the term "contraband" help Northerners redefine the status of former slaves? Was this redefinition ultimately beneficial or detrimental to recently freed African Americans?
3. How did Northern Republicans use escaped African Americans in their cause to convince Americans to end slavery? Conversely, how did Northerners who rejected emancipation use the idea of "intelligent contrabands" as a way to criticize the war effort?
4. Describe three other ways in which "contrabands" were portrayed in popular media. What does each of these tell you about their creator's perspectives and motivations?
5. How did "contraband music" help shape Northern opinion of these escaped African Americans?
6. Describe how the Emancipation Proclamation and the recruitment of formerly enslaved African Americans into the US Army further transformed the image of the "contraband." How did the paintings of Thomas Waterman Wood "dramatize" this transformation?
7. Characterize the ways in which African American writers in the North negotiated the term "contraband"?

CHAPTER TWO

֍

Rights and the Constitution in Black Life during the Civil War and Reconstruction[1]

Eric Foner

Early in 1873 a northern correspondent in Mississippi commented on the remarkable changes the previous decade had wrought in the behavior and self-image of southern blacks. "One hardly realizes the fact," he wrote, "that the many negroes one sees here . . . have been slaves a few short years ago, at least as far as their demeanor goes as individuals newly invested with all the rights and privileges of an American citizen. They appreciate their new condition thoroughly, and flaunt their independence." As the writer intimated, the conception of themselves as equal citizens of the American republic galvanized blacks' political and social activity during Reconstruction. Recent studies have made clear how the persistent agitation of Radical Republicans and abolitionists, and the political crisis created by the impasse between Andrew Johnson and Congress over Reconstruction policy, produced the Civil Rights Act of 1866 and the Fourteenth and Fifteenth amendments—measures that embodied a new national commitment to the principle of equality before the law.[2] But the conception of citizens' rights enshrined in national law and the federal Constitution during Reconstruction also came, as it were, from below. In seeking to invest emancipation with a broad definition of equal rights, blacks challenged the nation to live up to the full implications of its democratic creed and helped set in motion events that fundamentally altered the definition of citizenship for all Americans.

The transformation of blacks' role within American society began during the Civil War. For the nearly four million slaves, for the tiny, despised black population of the free states, and for the free blacks of the South, the war held out the

---

[1] Interested students are encouraged to read this essay in the original form. Eric Foner, "Rights and the Constitution in Black Life during the Civil War and Reconstruction" *The Journal of American History* 74, no. 3, "The Constitution and American Life: A Special Issue" (Dec. 1987).

[2] *Jewish Times* (New York), Feb. 7, 1873; Robert J. Kaczorowski, "To Begin the Nation Anew: Congress, Citizenship, and Civil Rights after the Civil War," *American Historical Review* 92 (Feb. 1987), 45–68.

hope of a radical change in American race relations. Each of those groups took actions that helped propel a reluctant white America down the road not simply to abolition but also to a constitutional recognition of the principle of civil and political equality regardless of race—a concept utterly unprecedented in the preceding two and a half centuries of American history.

It is now widely accepted that the actions of thousands of slaves who in the first years of the war abandoned their masters and headed for the Union lines helped undermine the South's peculiar institution and accelerated the Lincoln administration's progress toward emancipation. More directly pertinent to the question of the former slaves' rights as free men and women, however, was the massive enrollment of blacks in military service, which began in earnest in 1863. By the war's end some 180,000 blacks had served in the Union army—over one-fifth of the adult male black population of the United States below the age of forty-five. The "logical result" of black military service, one senator observed in 1864, was that "the black man is henceforth to assume a new status among us." Although treated with anything but equality in access to promotion and, initially, in pay, black soldiers played a crucial role not simply in winning the Civil War but also in defining the war's consequences. Their service helped transform both the nation's treatment of blacks and blacks' conception of themselves. . . .[3]

From Oliver Cromwell's New Model Army to the militias raised during the American Revolution to guerrilla armies of our own day, military service has often been a politicizing and radicalizing experience. For black troops, especially the vast majority who had known bondage, the army's impact was particularly profound. "No negro who has ever been a soldier," wrote one northern official in 1865, "can again be imposed upon; they have learnt what it is to be free and they will infuse their feelings into others." Black troops flaunted their contempt for symbols of slavery and relished the opportunity to exert authority over southern whites. One soldier celebrated his ability to walk "fearlessly and boldly through the streets [of New Orleans] . . . without being

Photo 2.1

Company E, Fourth U.S. Colored Troops, at Fort Lincoln, Washington, D.C. Courtesy Prints and Photos Division, Library of Congress.

---

[3]Ira Berlin, Joseph P. Reidy, and Leslie S. Rowland, eds., *Freedom: A Documentary History of Emancipation, 1861–1867*, Series 2: *The Black Military Experience* (New York, 1982), passim; Mary Berry, *Military Necessity and Civil Rights Policy: Black Citizenship and the Constitution, 1861–1868* (Port Washington, N.Y., 1977), 41–57, 62–74; Herman Belz, *A New Birth of Freedom: The Republican Party and Freedmen's Rights, 1861–1866* (Westport, 1976).

required to take off his cap at every step." For men of talent and ambition, the army flung open a door to position and respectability. From the army would come many of the black political leaders of Radical Reconstruction, including at least forty-one delegates to state constitutional conventions, sixty legislators, and four congressmen.[4]

Why

In time, the black contribution to the Union war effort would fade from the nation's collective memory. But it remained a vital part of the black community's sense of its own history. "They say," an Alabama planter reported in 1867, "the Yankees never could have whipped the South without the aid of the negroes." Here lay a crucial justification for blacks' self-confident claim to equal citizenship during Reconstruction, a claim anticipated in the soldiers' long battle for equal pay during the war. At the Arkansas Constitutional Convention of 1868, former slave William Murphey held his silence for weeks in deference to more accomplished white delegates (who, he pointed out, had "obtained the means of education by the black man's sweat"). But when some of those delegates questioned blacks' right to the suffrage, Murphey felt compelled to protest: "Has not the man who conquers upon the field of battle, gained any rights? Have we gained none by the sacrifice of our brethren?"[5]

Among northern blacks as well, the war inspired hopes for a broad expansion of their rights within American society. The small northern black political leadership of ministers, professionals, fugitive slaves, and members of abolitionist societies had long searched for a means of improving the condition of blacks in the free states and of striking a blow against the peculiar institution. In the antebellum decades, a majority had embraced what Vincent Harding calls the "Great Tradition," an affirmation of Americanism that insisted that blacks formed an integral part of the nation and were entitled to the same rights and opportunities white citizens enjoyed. In the 1850s, however, many northern blacks had despaired of ever finding a secure and equal place in American life, and a growing number of black leaders had come to espouse emigration to the Caribbean or Africa, reflecting both an incipient racial nationalism and a pessimism about black prospects in the United States. . . .[6]

The Civil War produced an abrupt shift from the pessimism of the 1850s to a renewed spirit of patriotism, restoring northern blacks' faith in the larger society. Even before the Emancipation Proclamation, a California black foresaw the dawning of a new day for his people:

---

[4]George D. Reynolds to Stuart Eldridge, Oct. 5, 1865, Registered Letters Received, ser. 2052, Mississippi Assistant Commissioner, Records of the Bureau of Refugees, Freedmen, and Abandoned Lands, RG 105 (National Archives); Leon F. Litwack, *Been in the Storm So Long: The Aftermath of Slavery* (New York, 1979), 96–102.

[5]John H. Parrish to Henry Watson, Jr., June 20, 1867, Henry Watson, Jr., Papers (Perkins Library, Duke University, Durham, N.C.); *Debates and Proceedings of the Convention Which Assembled at Little Rock, January 7, 1868* . . . (Little Rock, 1868), 629.

[6]Vincent Harding, *There Is a River: The Black Struggle for Freedom in America* (New York, 1981), 117–39, 172–94.

Everything among us indicates a change in our condition, and [we must] prepare to act in a different sphere from that in which we have heretofore acted. . . . Our relation to this government is changing daily. . . . Old things are passing away, and eventually old prejudices must follow. The revolution has begun, and time alone must decide where it is to end.

Emancipation further transformed the black response to American nationality. Symbolic, perhaps, was the fact that Martin R. Delany, the "father of black nationalism" and during the 1850s an advocate of emigration, now recruited blacks for the Union army and then joined himself. "I am proud to be an American citizen," declared black abolitionist Robert Purvis in 1863, recalling how, when the federal government was "a slaveholding oligarchy," he had denounced the country as "the basest despotism" on earth. Frederick Douglass, throughout his life the most insistent advocate of the now-reinvigorated Great Tradition, emerged as black America's premier spokesman, welcomed at the White House, his speeches widely reprinted in the northern press, his own life, he believed, exemplifying how America might move beyond racism to a society founded on universal human rights. Throughout the war Douglass insisted that the logical and essential corollaries of emancipation were the end of all color discrimination, complete equality before the law, and the enfranchisement of black men—the "full and complete adoption" of blacks "into the great national family of America."[7]

Meeting at Syracuse, New York, in October 1864, a national black convention reflected the optimism rekindled by the Civil War. The convention's spirit was very much that of the Great Tradition. . . . The convention galvanized a black assault on the northern color line that in the war's final months won some modest but significant victories. In February 1865 the first black lawyer, John S. Rock of Boston, was admitted to the bar of the Supreme Court. . . . Slowly, the North's racial barriers began to fall. In 1863 California first permitted blacks to testify in criminal cases; in 1865 Illinois repealed its law barring blacks from entering the state, . . . and Massachusetts passed the first comprehensive public accommodations law in American history. During the war, New York City, San Francisco, Cincinnati, and Cleveland desegregated their streetcars.[8]

Under pressure of emancipation, black military service, and the activity of northern blacks and their white allies, racial prejudice bent but did not break. No

---

[7]Harding, *There Is a River*, 233–35; James M. McPherson, ed., *The Negro's Civil War* (New York, 1967), 251–52; Philip S. Foner, ed., *The Voice of Black America* (2 vols., New York, 1975), I, 293–94, 318; Philip S. Foner, ed., *The Life and Writings of Frederick Douglass* (4 vols., New York, 1950–1955), III, 292, 348–52, 396.

[8]*Proceedings of the National Convention of Colored Men Held in the City of Syracuse, N.Y.* (Boston, 1864), 4–6, 19, 53–56; George A. Levesque, "Boston's Black Brahmin: Dr. John S. Rock," *Civil War History*, 26 (Dec. 1980), 336; Robert J. Chandler, "Friends in Time of Need: Republicans and Black Civil Rights in California during the Civil War Era," *Arizona and the West* 11 (Winter 1982), 329; Roger D. Bridges, "Equality Deferred: Civil Rights for Illinois Blacks, 1865–1885," *Journal of the Illinois State Historical Society* 74 (Spring 1981), 82–87; *Christian Recorder*, Nov. 19, 1864; Milton R. Konvitz, *A Century of Civil Rights* (New York, 1961), 155–56.

northern state outside of New England allowed blacks to vote on equal terms
with whites. Yet by the war's end, the issue of black suffrage occupied center stage
in American politics. The sudden prominence of the black suffrage issue was a
direct result of the political mobilization of the free blacks of New Orleans, who
compelled Congress and the president to grapple with the question as reconstructed Louisiana sought readmission to the Union.

In New Orleans lived the largest free black community of the Deep South,
whose members' wealth, social standing, education, and unique history set
them apart not only from slaves but also from most other free persons of color.
Descendants of unions between French settlers and black women or of wealthy
mulatto emigrants from revolutionary Haiti, many of the city's free blacks spoke
only French and educated their children at private academies in New Orleans or
Paris. Although denied the suffrage, they possessed far more rights than their
counterparts in other states and owned some two million dollars' worth of
property on the eve of the war. That self-conscious community, with a strong
sense of its collective history and a network of privately supported schools,
orphanages, and benevolent societies, was well positioned to advance its own
interests once Union troops occupied the Crescent City. At first, free blacks
spoke only for themselves, for as one who came to know the community well
later recounted:

> They tended to separate their struggle from that of the Negroes; some believed
> that they would achieve their cause more quickly if they abandoned the black to
> his fate. In their eyes, they were nearer to the white man; they were more
> advanced than the slave in all respects.... A strange error in a society in which
> prejudice weighed equally against all those who had African blood in their
> veins, no matter how small the amount.[9]

By January 1864 Lincoln appears to have privately endorsed the enrollment
of freeborn blacks as voters in Louisiana. But Gen. Nathaniel P. Banks, to whom
he had entrusted Louisiana's wartime Reconstruction, viewed even a limited
black suffrage as a threat to his efforts to win white support for a constitutional
convention that would abolish slavery in the state. In March 1864 two representatives of the free black community, Arnold Bertonneau, a wealthy wine dealer, and
Jean Baptiste Roudanez, a plantation engineer, arrived in Washington, D.C., to
present a petition for the suffrage. The day after their meeting, Lincoln wrote
Gov. Michael Hahn of Louisiana concerning the coming convention: "I barely
suggest for your private consideration, whether some of the colored people not be
let in—as for instance, the very intelligent, and especially those who have fought

---

[9]Laura Foner, "The Free People of Color in Louisiana and St. Domingue," *Journal of Social
History* 3 (Summer 1970), 406–30; Ted Tunnell, "Free Negroes and the Freedmen: Black Politics in
New Orleans during the Civil War," *Southern Studies* 19 (Spring 1980), 6–7; Donald E. Everett,
"Demands of the New Orleans Free Colored Population for Political Equality, 1862–1865," *Louisiana
Historical Quarterly* 38 (April 1955), 43–49; Jean-Charles Houzeau, *My Passage at the New Orleans
"Tribune": A Memoir of the Civil War Era*, ed. David C. Rankin, trans. Gerald F. Denault (Baton
Rouge, 1984), 81.

gallantly in our ranks. . . . But this is only a suggestion, not to the public, but to you alone."[10]

Hardly a ringing endorsement of black suffrage, Lincoln's letter nonetheless represented his first quasi-official statement on black voting. Moreover, it proposed to expand the suffrage considerably beyond the freeborn population for whom Bertonneau and Roudanez spoke. The letter illustrated the flexibility and capacity to compromise that were the hallmarks of Lincoln's political leadership. Such qualities, however, were in short supply in wartime Louisiana, for when the constitutional convention met, it abolished slavery but made no gesture toward black voting rights. Indeed, reported one observer, "prejudice against the colored people is exhibited continually, prejudice bitter and vulgar." Some delegates demanded the expulsion of all blacks from the state—even though, as one member pointed out, black troops were at that very moment guarding the convention hall. The convention widened a preexisting division in Unionist ranks, and it propelled the free black community down the road to universal manhood suffrage.[11]

The voice of Louisiana's politically articulate free blacks was the *New Orleans Tribune*, a newspaper founded by Dr. Louis C. Roudanez, the wealthy son of a French merchant and a free woman of color, and edited by Jean-Charles Houzeau, a Belgian aristocrat who had been converted to the revolutionary ideas of 1848 and had emigrated to the United States in the 1850s. In Houzeau, the *Tribune*'s proprietors found a man whose political outlook, like their own, had been shaped by the heritage of the Enlightenment and the French Revolution. In Roudanez and the others associated with the newspaper, Houzeau recognized "the vanguard of the African population of the United States." In late 1864 the *Tribune* made the momentous decision to demand suffrage for the freedmen, the free blacks' "*dormant* partners." It went on to develop a coherent radical program embracing the vote, equality before the law, the desegregation of Louisiana's schools, the opening of New Orleans streetcars to blacks, and the division of plantation lands among the freedmen. For the moment, however, black suffrage remained the Louisiana movement's central demand. Within the state, it did not receive a hearing. But in Washington the movement's complaints against the Louisiana government found a sympathetic audience. Contact with the cultured, economically successful New Orleans group challenged the racist assumptions widespread even in Republican circles and doubtless influenced Lincoln's own evolution toward a more egalitarian approach to Reconstruction. Because of Louisiana, black suffrage became a live issue in the Congress that assembled in

---

[10]Fred H. Harrington, *Fighting Politician: Major General N. P Banks* (Philadelphia, 1948), 143–46; LaWanda Cox, *Lincoln and Black Freedom: A Study in Presidential Leadership* (Columbia, 1981), 79–95; Houzeau, *My Passage*, 25n34; Roy P. Basler, ed., *The Collected Works of Abraham Lincoln* (9 vols., New Brunswick, 1953), VII, 243.

[11]"Diary and Correspondence of Salmon P. Chase," *Annual Report of the American Historical Association*, 1902, p. 438; *Debates in the Convention for the Revision and Amendment of the Constitution of the State of Louisiana* (New Orleans, 1864), 155, 213–14, 394, 556; Cox, *Lincoln and Black Freedom*, 97–99.

December 1864, torpedoing efforts to forge an agreement between Lincoln and Congress on a plan of Reconstruction and preventing the seating of Louisiana's newly elected senators.[12]

Despite the Louisiana impasse, the second session of the Thirty-eighth Congress was indeed a historic occasion, for in January Congress gave final approval to the Thirteenth Amendment, abolishing slavery throughout the Union. "The one question of the age is *settled*," exulted Congressman Cornelius Cole of California. But the amendment closed one question only to open a host of others. Did emancipation imply any additional rights for the former slaves? "What is freedom?" James A. Garfield would soon ask. "Is it the bare privilege of not being chained? . . . If this is all, then freedom is a bitter mockery, a cruel delusion." Rather than being a predetermined category or static concept, however, "freedom" itself became a terrain of conflict in the aftermath of emancipation, its substance open to different and sometimes contradictory interpretations, its content changing for both blacks and whites in the years following the Civil War. And as the former slaves entered the nation's public life after the war, they sought to breathe life into the promise of freedom.[13]

"The Negroes are to be pitied," wrote a South Carolina educator and minister. "They do not understand the liberty which has been conferred upon them." In fact, blacks carried out of bondage an understanding of their new condition shaped both by their experience as slaves and by observation of the free society around them. What one planter called their "wild notions of right and freedom" encompassed first of all an end to the myriad injustices associated with slavery— separation of families, punishment by the lash, denial of access to education. . . . "If I cannot do like a white man I am not free," Henry Adams told his former master in 1865. "I see how the poor white people do. I ought to do so too, or else I am a slave."[14]

Underpinning blacks' individual aspirations lay a broader theme: their quest for independence from white control, for autonomy both as individuals and as members of a community itself being transformed as a result of emancipation. In countless ways, blacks in 1865 sought to "throw off the badge of servitude," to overturn the real and symbolic authority whites had exercised over every aspect of their lives. Some took new names that reflected the lofty hopes inspired by emancipation—Deliverance Belin, Hope Mitchell, Chance Great. Others relished

[12]Houzeau, *My Passage*, 2–5, 19–39, 75, 78–80, 96–97; *New Orleans Tribune*, Aug. 4, Aug. 11, Aug. 13, Sept. 10, Sept. 24, Dec. 29, 1864, Jan. 10–15, 1865; Cox, *Lincoln and Black Freedom*, 103–27; Michael Les Benedict, *A Compromise of Principle: Congressional Republicans and Reconstruction 1863–1869* (New York, 1974), 84–97.

[13]Cornelius Cole, *Memoirs of Cornelius Cole* (New York, 1908), 220; Burke A. Hinsdale, ed., *The Works of James Abram Garfield* (2 vols., Boston, 1882–1883), I, 86.

[14]John H. Moore, ed., *The Juhl Letters to the "Charleston Courier"* (Athens, 1974), 20; Will Martin to Benjamin G. Humphreys, Dec. 5, 1865, Mississippi Governor's Papers (Mississippi Department of Archives and History, Jackson); Nathaniel P. Banks, *Emancipated Labor in Louisiana* (n.p., 1864), 7; U.S. Congress, Senate, *Report and Testimony of the Select Committee of the United States Senate to Investigate the Causes of the Removal of the Negroes from the Southern States to the Northern States*, 46 Cong., 2 sess., Senate rept. 693, pt. 2, p. 191.

opportunities to flaunt their liberation from the infinite regulations, significant and trivial, associated with slavery. Freedmen held mass meetings unrestrained by white surveillance; they acquired dogs, guns, and liquor (all forbidden them under slavery); and they refused to yield the sidewalk to whites. Blacks dressed as they pleased and left plantations when they desired. They withdrew from churches controlled by whites and created autonomous churches, stabilized and strengthened the families they had brought out of slavery, and established a network of independent schools and benevolent societies.[15]

In no other realm of southern life did blacks' effort to define the terms of their own freedom or to identify the "rights" arising from emancipation with independence from white control have implications so explosive for the entire society as in the economy. Blacks brought out of slavery a conception of themselves as a "Working Class of People," in the words of a group of Georgia freedmen who had been unjustly deprived of the fruits of their labor . . . [For] Baptist minister Garrison Frazier . . . [slavery] meant one man's "receiving . . . the work of another man, and not by his consent." Freedom he defined as "placing us where we could reap the fruit of our own labor." Yet more than simply receiving wages, blacks demanded the right to control the conditions under which they worked, to free themselves from subordination to white authority, and to carve out the greatest possible measure of economic autonomy.[16]

The desire to escape from white supervision and to establish a modicum of economic independence profoundly shaped blacks' economic choices during Reconstruction. It led them to resist working in gangs under overseers and to prefer leasing land for a fixed rent to working for wages. Above all, it inspired their quest for land of their own. Without land, there could be no economic autonomy, blacks believed, for their labor would continue to be subject to exploitation by their former owners. "Gib us our own land and we take care ourselves," a Charleston black told northern correspondent Whitelaw Reid, "but widout land, de ole massas can hire or starve us, as dey please."[17]

Numerous freedmen emerged from slavery convinced they had a "right" to a portion of their former owners' land. In part, their belief stemmed from actions of the federal government—the Freedmen's Bureau Act of early 1865, which held out the prospect of the division of confiscated and abandoned land among blacks and white refugees, and General Sherman's Field Order 15, which set aside a portion of the South Carolina and Georgia Lowcountry for exclusive settlement by blacks. In addition, blacks insisted it was only fair that "the land ought to belong to the man who (alone) could work it," as one former slave told [a] rice planter. . . . Most

---

[15]Eliza F. Andrews, *The War-Time Journal of a Georgia Girl* (New York, 1908), 347; George C. Rogers, Jr., *The History of Georgetown County, South Carolina* (Columbia, 1970), 439–41; Litwack, *Been in the Storm So Long*, passim.

[16]Edward Magdol, *A Right to the Land: Essays on the Freedmen's Community* (Westport, 1977), 273; "Colloquy with Colored Ministers," *Journal of Negro History* 16 (Jan. 1931), 88–94.

[17]Charles Colcock Jones, Jr., to Eva Jones, Nov. 7, 1865, Charles Colcock Jones, Jr., Collection (University of Georgia Library, Athens); *Southern Cultivator*, March 1867, p. 69; Whitelaw Reid, *After the War: A Southern Tour* (Cincinnati, 1866), 59.

often, however, blacks insisted their past labor entitled them to a portion of their owners' estates. "They have an idea that they have a certain right to the property of their former masters, that they have earned it," reported a North Carolina Freedmen's Bureau official. In its most sophisticated form, the claim to land rested on an appreciation of the role of black labor in the evolution of the nation's economy. When the army evicted blacks it had earlier settled on land near Yorktown, Virginia, freedman Bayley Wyat gave an impromptu speech of protest:

> We has a right to the land where we are located. For why? I tell you. Our wives, our children, our husbands, has been sold over and over again to purchase the lands we now located upon; for that reason we have a divine right to the land. . . . And den didn't we cleare the land, and raise de crops ob corn, ob cotton, ob tobacco, ob rice, ob sugar, ob everything. And den didn't dem large cities in de North grow up on de cotton and de sugars and de rice dat we made? . . . I say dey has grown rich, and my people is poor.[18]

If the goal of autonomy inspired blacks to withdraw from religious and other institutions controlled by whites and to attempt to work out their own economic destinies, in the polity freedom implied inclusion rather than separation. Indeed, the attempt to win recognition of their equal rights as citizens quickly emerged as the animating impulse of black politics during Reconstruction. Achieving a measure of political power seemed indispensable to attaining the other goals of the black community, including access to the South's economic resources, equal treatment in the courts, and protection against violence. But apart from its specific uses, in the United States the ballot was itself an emblem of citizenship. In a professedly democratic political culture, the ballot did more than identify who could vote—it defined a collective public life, as woman suffrage advocates so tirelessly pointed out. . . . Democrats were repelled by the very idea of including blacks in the common public life defined by the suffrage. . . . The United States, Frederick Douglass reminded the nation, differed profoundly from societies accustomed to fixed social classes and historically defined gradations of civil and political rights:

> If I were in a monarchial government, . . . where the few bore rule and the many were subject, there would be no special stigma resting upon me, because I did not exercise the elective franchise. . . . But here, where universal suffrage is the fundamental idea of the Government, to rule us out is to make us an exception, to brand us with the stigma of inferiority.[19]

The statewide conventions held throughout the South during 1865 and early 1866 offered evidence of the early spread of political mobilization among the South's freedmen. Several hundred delegates attended the gatherings, some

---

[18]Reid, *After the War*, 335; U.S. Congress, Senate, *Reports of Assistant Commissioners of the Freedmen's Bureau, 1865–66*, 39 Cong., 1 sess., Senate exec. doc. 27, p. 84; Edward B. Heyward to Katherine Heyward, May 5, 1867, Heyward Family Papers (South Caroliniana Library, University of South Carolina, Columbia); *A Freedman's Speech* (Philadelphia, 1867).

[19]*Congressional Globe*, 39 Cong., 1 sess., Feb. 16, 1866, p. 880; Foner, ed., *Life and Writings of Frederick Douglass*, IV, 159.

selected by local meetings specially convened for the purpose, others by
churches, fraternal societies, and black
army units, still others simply self-
appointed. Although the delegates
"ranged all colors and apparently all conditions," urban free mulattoes took the
most prominent roles, whereas former
slaves, although in attendance, were
almost entirely absent from positions of
leadership. Numerous black soldiers,
ministers, and artisans also took part, as
well as a significant number of recent
black arrivals from the North.[20]

The conventions' major preoccupa-
tions proved to be the suffrage and
equality before the law. In justifying the
demand for the vote, the delegates
invoked the nation's republican traditions, especially the Declaration of Independence, "the broadest, the deepest, the
most comprehensive and truthful definition of human freedom that was ever

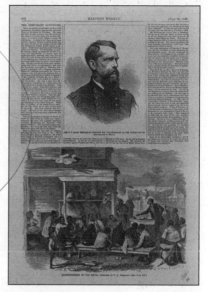

Photo 2.2

"Electioneering at the South." Political
meetings often involved the entire
community. Reproduced from *Harper's
Weekly*, July 25, 1868. Courtesy Prints and
Photos Division, Library of Congress.

given to the world," as black Freedmen's Bureau official John M. Langston put
it. . . . Eleven Alabama blacks complaining in 1865 of contract frauds, injustice
before the courts, and other abuses concluded their petition with a revealing
masterpiece of understatement: "this is not the persuit of happiness."[21]

There was more to the invocation of the Declaration of Independence than
merely familiar wording. Like northern blacks steeped in the Great Tradition of
prewar protest, the freedmen and southern free blacks saw emancipation as
enabling the nation to live up to the full implications of its republican creed—a
goal that could only be achieved by leaving behind the legacy of racial proscription and by absorbing blacks fully into the civil and political order. Isham Sweat,
a slave-born barber who wrote the address issued by North Carolina's convention
and went on to sit in the state legislature, told northern journalist John R. Dennett
that Congress should "declare that no state had a republican form of government
if every free man in it was not equal before the law." Another 1865 speaker destined

[20]John R. Dennett, *The South As It Is: 1865–1866*, ed. Henry M. Christman (New York, 1965),
148–50; Reid, *After the War*, 81; *Nashville Colored Tennessean*, Aug. 12, 1865; J. W. Blackwell to
Andrew Johnson, Nov. 24, 1865, Andrew Johnson Papers (Manuscripts Division, Library of
Congress); Peter Kolchin, *First Freedom: The Responses of Alabama's Blacks to Emancipation and
Reconstruction* (Westport, 1972), 152–53.

[21]John M. Langston, *Freedom and Citizenship* (Washington, D.C., 1883), 99–100, 110; Prince
Murrell and ten others to Gen. Wager Swayne, Dec. 17, 1865, Unregistered Letters Received, ser. 9, Alabama Assistant Commissioner, Records of the Bureau of Refugees, Freedmen, and Abandoned Lands.

for Reconstruction prominence, Louisiana's Oscar J. Dunn, described the absence of "discrimination among men," of "privileges founded upon birth-right," and of "hereditary distinctions" as the essence of America's political heritage. . . .[22]

Like their northern counterparts during the Civil War, southern blacks now proclaimed their identification with the nation's history, destiny, and political system. The very abundance of letters and petitions addressed by black gatherings and ordinary freedmen to officials of the army, to the Freedmen's Bureau, and to state and federal authorities, revealed a belief that the political order was at least partially open to black influence. "We are Americans," declared an address from a Norfolk black meeting, "we know no other country, we love the land of our birth." It went on to remind white Virginians that in 1619 "our fathers as well as yours were toiling in the plantations on James River" and that a black man, Crispus Attucks, shed "the first blood" in the American Revolution. And, of course, blacks fought and died to save the Union. America, resolved another Virginia meeting, was "now *our* country—made emphatically so by the blood of our brethren" in the Union army.[23]

Despite the insistent language of individual speeches, the conventions' resolutions and public addresses generally adopted a moderate tone, revealing both a realistic assessment of the political situation during Presidential Reconstruction and the fact that political mobilization had proceeded more quickly in southern cities than in the Black Belt where most freedmen lived. . . . The ferment rippling through the southern countryside found little echo at the state conventions of 1865 and 1866, a reflection of the paucity of Black Belt representation. Far different was the situation in 1867 when, in the aftermath of the Reconstruction Act, a wave of political mobilization swept the rural South.[24]

Like emancipation, the advent of black suffrage inspired freedmen with a millennial sense of living at the dawn of a new era. Former slaves now stood on an equal footing with whites, a black speaker told a Savannah mass meeting, and before them lay "a field, too vast for contemplation." As in 1865, blacks found countless ways of pursuing aspirations for autonomy and equality and of seizing the opportunity to press for further change. Strikes broke out during the spring of 1867 among black longshoremen in the South's major port cities and quickly spread to other workers, including Richmond, Virginia, coopers and Selma, Alabama, restaurant workers. . . . Three blacks refused to leave a whites-only Richmond

---

[22]Peter D. Klingman, *Josiah Walls* (Gainesville, 1976), 72–73; Dennett, *South As It Is*, 176; Sidney Andrews, *The South Since the War* (Boston, 1866), 125; *Proceedings of the Republican Party of Louisiana* (New Orleans, 1865), 4–5.

[23]*Equal Suffrage: Address from the Colored Citizens of Norfolk, Va., to the People of the United States* (New Bedford, 1865), 1, 8; Joseph R. Johnson to O. O. Howard, Aug. 4, 1865, Unregistered Letters Received, ser. 457, District of Columbia Assistant Commissioner, Records of the Bureau of Refugees, Freedmen, and Abandoned Lands.

[24]Roberta Sue Alexander, *North Carolina Faces the Freedmen: Race Relations during Presidential Reconstruction, 1865–67* (Durham, 1985), 28; Philip S. Foner and George E. Walker, eds., *Proceedings of the Black National and State Conventions, 1865–1900* (Philadelphia, 1986-), I, 189–94; *Proceedings of the Freedmen's Convention of Georgia* (Augusta, 1866), 20, 30.

streetcar, and crowds flocked to the scene shouting, "Let's have our rights." In New Orleans, groups commandeered segregated horse-drawn streetcars and drove them around the city in triumph. By midsummer, integrated transportation had come to these and other cities.[25]

But in 1867 politics emerged as the principal focus of black aspirations. Itinerant lecturers, black and white, brought the message of equality to the heart of the rural South. In Monroe County, Alabama, where no black political meeting had occurred before, freedmen crowded around the speaker shouting, "God bless you, bless God for this." Richmond's tobacco factories were forced to close on August 1 because so many black laborers quit work to attend the Republican state convention. Black churches, schools, and, indeed, every other institution of the black community became highly politicized. Every African Methodist Episcopal minister in Georgia was said to be engaged in Republican organizing, and political materials were read aloud at "churches, societies, leagues, clubs, balls, picnics, and all other gatherings." One plantation manager summed up the situation: "You never saw a people more excited on the subject of politics than are the negroes of the South. They are perfectly wild."[26]

Photo 2.3

"The First Vote." The three men voting exemplify key elements of black political leadership: the artisan (with tools in his pocket), the urbanite, and the soldier. Reproduced from *Harper's Weekly*, November 16, 1867. Courtesy Prints and Photos Division, Library of Congress.

In Union Leagues, Republican gatherings, and impromptu local meetings, ordinary blacks in 1867 and 1868 staked their claim to equal citizenship in the American republic. A black organizer in Georgia voiced the prevailing sentiment: "He was no nigger now. He was a citizen and was going to have all the rights of the white man, and would take no less."[27]

At their most utopian, blacks now envisioned a society purged of all racial distinctions. That does not mean they lacked a sense of racial identity, for blacks

---

[25]*Savannah Daily News and Herald*, March 19, 1867; Philip S. Foner and Ronald L. Lewis, eds., *The Black Worker: A Documentary History from Colonial Times to the Present* (8 vols., Philadelphia, 1978–1984), I, 3 52–53; Peter J. Rachleff, *Black Labor in the South: Richmond, Virginia, 1865–1890* (Philadelphia, 1984), 42–43; *Mobile Daily Advertiser and Register*, April 2, 1867; Roger A. Fischer, "A Pioneer Protest: The New Orleans Street-Car Controversy of 1867," *Journal of Negro History* 53 (July 1968), 219–33.

[26]Samuel S. Gardner to O. D. Kinsman, July 23, 1867, Wager Swayne Papers (Alabama State Department of Archives and History, Montgomery); Magdol, *Right to the Land*, 42; Henry M. Turner to Thomas L. Tullock, July 23, 1867, copies, Robert C. Schenck Papers (Rutherford B. Hayes Library, Fremont, Ohio); Parrish to Watson Aug. 6, 1867, Watson Papers.

[27]Joseph P. Reidy, "Masters and Slaves, Planters and Freedmen: The Transition from Slavery to Freedom in Central Georgia, 1820–1880" (Ph.D. diss., Northern Illinois University, 1982), 253.

remained proud of the accomplishments of black soldiers and preferred black teachers for their children and black churches in which to worship. But in the polity, those who had so long been proscribed because of color defined equality as color-blind. "I heard a white man say," black teacher Robert G. Fitzgerald recorded in his diary, "today is the black man's day; tommorrow will be the white man's. I thought, poor man, those days of distinction between colors is about over, in this (now) free country." . . .[28]

Nor did blacks evince much interest in emigration during Radical Reconstruction. Over twelve hundred emigrants from Georgia and South Carolina had sailed for Liberia under American Colonization Society auspices during 1866 and 1867, "tired of the unprovoked scorn and prejudice we daily and hourly suffer." But the optimism kindled in 1867 brought the emigration movement to an abrupt halt. "You could not get one of them to think of going to Liberia now," wrote a white colonizationist. . . . Throughout Reconstruction, blacks took pride in parading on July 4, "the day," a Charleston, South Carolina, diarist observed, "the Niggers now celebrate, and the whites stay home." As late as 1876, a speaker at a black convention aroused "positive signs of disapproval" by mentioning emigration. "Damn Africa," one delegate declared. "If Smith wants to go, let him; we'll stay in America."[29]

Blacks' secular claim to equality was, in part, underpinned by a religious messianism deeply rooted in the black experience. As slaves, blacks had come to think of themselves as analogous to the Jews in Egypt, an oppressed people whom God, in the fullness of time, would deliver from bondage. And they endowed the Civil War and emancipation with spiritual import, comprehending those events through the language of Christian faith. A Tennessee newspaper commented in 1869 that freedmen habitually referred to slavery as "Paul's Time" and to Reconstruction as "Isaiah's Time," referring perhaps to Paul's message of obedience and humility and to Isaiah's prophecy of cataclysmic change, a "new heaven and a new earth" brought about by violence. Black religion reinforced black republicanism, for as Rev. J. M. P. Williams, a Mississippi legislator, put it in 1871, "of one blood God did make all men to dwell upon the face of the earth . . . hence their common origin, destiny and equal rights."[30]

---

[28]Robert G. Fitzgerald Diary, April 22, 1868, Robert G. Fitzgerald Papers (Schomburg Center for Research in Black Culture, New York); *New National Era*, Aug. 31, 1871.

[29]Francis B. Simkins, "The Problems of South Carolina Agriculture after the Civil War, *North Carolina Historical Review*, 7 (Jan. 1930), 54–55; Wyatt Moore to William Coppinger, July 5, 1866, American Colonization Society Papers (Manuscripts Division, Library of Congress); E. M. Pendleton to Coppinger, March 18, 1867, ibid.; P. Sterling Stuckey, "The Spell of Africa: The Development of Black Nationalist Theory, 1829–1945" (Ph.D. diss., Northwestern University, 1973), 91–92; Proceedings of the Southern States Convention of Colored Men, Held in Columbia, South Carolina (Columbia, 1871), 99–100; Jacob Schirmer Diary, July 4, 1867, July 4, 1872 (South Carolina Historical Society, Charleston); *Cincinnati Commercial*, April 10, 1876.

[30]Clarence G. Walker, *A Rock in a Weary Land: The African Methodist Episcopal Church during the Civil War and Reconstruction* (Baton Rouge, 1982), 125; Stephen V. Ash, *A House Dividing: War, Emancipation, and Society in Middle Tennessee, 1860–1870* (Baton Rouge, 1987), ch. 9; Address to the Citizens of Adams County, by Rev. J. M. P Williams, broadside, March 1871, Ames Family Papers (Sophia Smith Collection, Smith College, Northampton, Mass.).

Politics in 1867, unlike two years earlier, also assimilated the freedmen's economic longings. Many northern and southern freeborn leaders, it is true, clung to free labor nostrums that portrayed hard work and individual accumulation as the only legitimate route to the acquisition of property. It was, however, an inopportune moment to preach self-help to Black Belt freedmen, for successive crop failures had left those on share contracts with little or no income and had produced a precipitous decline in cash wages. "We have tried [plantation labor] three years," wrote an Alabama black, "and are worse off than when we started. . . . We cannot accumulate enough to get a home." Drawing on widespread dissatisfaction with a contract system that appeared to consign them permanently to poverty, rural blacks raised, once again, the demand for land.[31]

The land issue animated grass-roots black politics in 1867. The Reconstruction Act rekindled the belief that the federal government intended to provide freedmen with homesteads. In Alabama, freedmen delivered "inflammatory" speeches asserting that "all the wealth of the white man has been made by negro labor, and that the negroes were entitled to their fair share of all these accumulations." "Didn't you clear the white folks' land," asked one orator. "Yes," voices answered from the crowd, "and we have a right to it!" . . .[32]

By mid-1867, planter William Henry Trescot observed, blacks had become convinced that membership in the Union League "will in some way, they do not exactly know how, secure them the possession of the land." Yet that was only one among the multiplicity of purposes blacks sought to achieve through Reconstruction politics. In a society marked by vast economic disparities and by a growing racial separation in social and religious life, the polity became the only area where black and white encountered each other on a basis of equality—sitting alongside one another on juries, in legislatures, and at political conventions; voting together on election day. For individuals, politics offered a rare opportunity for respectable, financially rewarding employment. And although elective office and the vote remained male preserves, black women shared in the political mobilization. They took part in rallies, parades, and mass meetings, voted on resolutions (to the consternation of some male participants), and formed their own auxiliaries to aid in electioneering. During the 1868 campaign, Yazoo, Mississippi, whites found their homes invaded by buttons depicting Gen. Ulysses S. Grant that were defiantly worn by black maids and cooks.[33]

---

[31]*Christian Recorder*, Jan. 7, Aug. 5, Sept. 9, Sept. 16, 1865; *Mobile Nationalist*, Oct. 24, 1867.

[32]Manuel Gottlieb, "The Land Question in Georgia during Reconstruction," *Science and Society* 3 (Summer 1939), 373–77; U.S. Congress, House of Representatives, *Testimony Taken by the Joint Committee to Enquire into the Condition of Affairs in the Late Insurrectionary States*, 42 Cong., 2 sess., House rept. 22, Alabama, 976; James S. Allen, *Reconstruction: The Battle for Democracy* (New York, 1937), 124.

[33]"Letter of William Henry Trescot on Reconstruction in South Carolina, 1867," *American Historical Review* 15 (April 1910), 575–76; *Richmond Dispatch*, Aug. 2, 1867; A. T. Morgan, *Yazoo: Or, on the Picket Line of Freedom in the South* (Washington, D.C., 1884), 231–33, 293; *Testimony Taken by the Joint Committee to Enquire into the Condition of Affairs in the Late Insurrectionary States*, Alabama, 684; ibid., Georgia, 1184.

Throughout Reconstruction, blacks remained "irrepressible democrats." "Negroes all crazy on politics again," noted a Mississippi plantation manager in the fall of 1873. "Every tenth negro a candidate for office." And the Republican party—the party of emancipation and black suffrage—became as central an institution of the black community as the church and the school. When not deterred by violence, blacks eagerly attended political gatherings and voted in extraordinary numbers; their turnout in many elections exceeded 90 percent. Despite the failure of land distribution, the end of Reconstruction would come not because property-less blacks succumbed to economic coercion but because a politically tenacious black community fell victim to violence, fraud, and national abandonment. Long after they had been stripped of the franchise, blacks would recall the act of voting as a defiance of inherited norms of white superiority and would regard "the loss of suffrage as being the loss of freedom."[34]

. . . Blacks saw in political authority a countervailing power. "They look to legislation," commented an Alabama newspaper, "because in the very nature of things, they can look nowhere else." . . . Black legislators successfully advocated . . . measures advantageous to plantation laborers. Their success marked a remarkable departure from the days of slavery and Presidential Reconstruction, when public authority was geared to upholding the interests of the planter class. On the local and state levels, black officials . . . pressed for the expansion of such public institutions as schools, hospitals, and asylums. They insisted, moreover, that the newly expanded state must be color-blind, demanding and often achieving laws prohibiting racial discrimination in public transportation and accommodations and, although generally amenable to separate schools for black and white, insisting that such segregation be a matter of choice, rather than being required by law. . . .[35]

Ultimately, however, blacks viewed the national government as the guarantor of their rights. Before 1860 blacks and their white allies had generally feared federal power, since the government at Washington seemed under the control of the "Slave Power," and after 1850 they looked to state authorities to nullify the federal Fugitive Slave Act. But blacks who had come to freedom through an unprecedented exercise of national power . . . became increasingly hostile to ideas of states' rights and local autonomy. Until Americans abandoned the idea of "the right of each State to control its own affairs. . . ," wrote Frederick Douglass, "no general assertion of human rights can be of any practical value." Black political leaders did not share fears of "centralism" common even in Republican

---

[34][Belton O'Neall Townsend], "The Political Condition of South Carolina," *Atlantic Monthly* 39 (Feb. 1877), 192; A. D. Grambling to Stephen Duncan, Aug. 10, 1873, Stephen Duncan Papers, Natchez Trace Collection (Eugene C. Barker Texas History Center, University of Texas, Austin); Paul D. Escott, *Slavery Remembered* (Chapel Hill, 1979), 153–54; U.S. Congress, House of Representatives, *Election of 1868*, 41 Cong., 2 sess., House misc. doc. 154, pp. 181–82.

[35]Foner and Lewis, eds., *Black Worker*, II, 149; Eric Foner, *Nothing but Freedom: Emancipation and Its Legacy* (Baton Rouge, 1983), 39–73; Howard N. Rabinowitz, ed., *Southern Black Leaders of the Reconstruction Era* (Urbana, 1982), 211, 257–58; Charles Vincent, *Black Legislators in Louisiana during Reconstruction* (Baton Rouge 1976), 180, 199; Edmund L. Drago, *Black Politicians and Reconstruction in Georgia* (Baton Rouge, 1983), 89.

circles, and throughout Reconstruction they supported proposals for such vast
expansions of federal authority as Alabama black congressman James T. Rapier's
plan for a national educational system complete with federally mandated
textbooks.[36]

As Reconstruction progressed, the national Constitution took its place
alongside the Declaration of Independence as a central reference point in black
political discourse. A petition of Louisiana blacks calling for the removal of hostile local officials began with these familiar words: "We the people of Louisiana
in order to establish justice, insure domestic tranquility, promote the general
welfare . . . do ordain and establish this Constitution." Like many Radical Republicans, black political leaders found in the Constitution's clause guaranteeing to
each state a "republican form of government" a reservoir of federal power over
the states. . . . But blacks particularly identified the postwar amendments as definitions of a new national citizenship and as guarantees of federal authority to
protect the rights of individual citizens. The political crisis of 1866—which black
complaints against the injustices of Presidential Reconstruction had helped
create—had produced the Fourteenth Amendment, defining for the first time a
national citizenship with rights no state could abridge, embracing blacks and
whites equally. As a result, Martin R. Delany reported from South Carolina,
blacks believed "the Constitution had been purged of color by a Radical Congress." Indeed, blacks called for even more far-reaching constitutional changes
than northern Republicans were willing to accept. Black spokesmen, for instance,
supported a Fifteenth Amendment that explicitly guaranteed all male citizens
above the age of twenty-one the right to vote—wording far more sweeping than
the language actually adopted, which allowed states to restrict the suffrage for
any reason except that of race. . . .[37]

But more than any other issue, racial violence led blacks to identify the federal government as the ultimate guarantor of their rights. Increasingly, it became
clear that local and state authorities, even those elected by blacks, were either
unwilling or unable to put down the Ku Klux Klan and kindred organizations.
"We are more slave today in the hand of the wicked than we were before," read a
desperate plea from Alabama freedmen. "We need protection . . . only a standing
army in this place can give us our right and life." "Dear sir," read a letter written
during Mississippi's violent Redemption campaign of 1875, "did not the 14th
Article . . . say that no person shall be deprived of life nor property without due
process of law? It said all persons have equal protection of the laws but I say we
colored men don't get it at all. . . . Is that right, or is it not? No, sir, it is wrong."
Blacks enthusiastically supported the Enforcement Acts of 1870 and 1871, which

---

[36]Foner, ed., *Life and Writings of Frederick Douglass*, IV, 199; Foner and Lewis, eds., Black
Worker, I, 136.

[37]A. R. Henderson to Richard H. Cain, April 13, 1875, William P. Kellogg Papers (Louisiana
State University, Baton Rouge); *New National Era*, Aug. 31, 1871; William D. Forten to Charles
Sumner, Feb. 1, 1869, Charles Sumner Papers (Houghton Library, Harvard University, Cambridge,
Mass.).

effectively put an end to the Klan, and the Reconstruction era expansion of the powers of the federal judiciary. One black convention went so far as to insist that virtually all civil and criminal cases involving blacks be removable from state to federal courts, a mind-boggling enhancement of federal judicial authority.[38]

Throughout Reconstruction, blacks insisted that "those who freed them shall protect that freedom." Increasingly, however, blacks' expansive definition of federal authority put them at odds with mainstream white Republicans, who by the 1870s were retreating from the war-inspired vision of a powerful national state. Indeed, even among abolitionists, the persistent demands of blacks for federal action on their behalf raised fears that the freedmen were somehow not acting as autonomous citizens capable of defending their own interests. Frederick Douglass himself had concluded in 1865 that the persistent question "What shall we do with the Negro?" had only one answer: "Do nothing. . . . Give him a chance to stand on his own legs! Let him alone!" Douglass realized that the other face of benevolence is often paternalism and that in a society resting, if only rhetorically, on the principle of equality, "special efforts" on the freedmen's behalf might "serve to keep up the very prejudices, which it is so desirable to banish." It was precisely that image to which President Johnson had appealed in justifying his vetoes of the Freedmen's Bureau and Civil Rights bills in 1866. Douglass, of course, and most Republicans, believed equal civil rights and the vote were essential to enabling blacks to protect themselves. But by the 1870s, with those rights granted, blacks' demands for protection struck many whites, including reformers, as reflecting a desire to become privileged "wards of the nation."[39]

The fate of Charles Sumner's federal Civil Rights Bill, prohibiting racial discrimination in public accommodations, transportation, schools, churches, and cemeteries, illustrated how much black and white Republicans differed regarding what obligations the federal government had incurred by emancipating the slaves. Before galleries crowded with black spectators, black congressmen invoked both the personal experience of having been evicted from inns, hotels, and railroads and the black political ideology that had matured during Reconstruction. To James T. Rapier, discrimination was "anti-republican," recalling the class and religious inequalities of other lands—in Europe "they have princes, dukes, lords"; . . . in the United States "our distinction is color." Richard H. Cain reminded the House that "the black man's labor" had enriched the country; Robert B. Elliott recalled the sacrifices of black soldiers. But white Republicans considered the bill an embarrassment to the party. Not until 1875 did a watered-down version pass Congress. It contained only weak provisions for enforcement

---

[38]James Martin and five others to William H. Smith, May 25, 1869, Alabama Governor's Papers (Alabama State Department of Archives and History); William Crely to Adelbert Ames, Oct. 9, 1875, Mississippi Governor's Papers; *Report and Testimony of the Select Committee of the United States Senate to Investigate the Causes of the Removal of the Negroes from the Southern States to the Northern States*, pt. 2, p. 395.

[39]*Christian Recorder*, May 26, 1866; Foner, ed., *Life and Writings of Frederick Douglass*, III, 189; James D. Richardson, ed., *A Compilation of the Messages and Papers of the Presidents 1789–1897* (10 vols., Washington, D.C., 1896–1899), VI, 399–413; *National Anti-Slavery Standard*, Feb. 5, 1870.

and remained largely a dead letter until the Supreme Court ruled it unconstitutional in 1883.[40]

In the end, the broad conception of "rights" with which blacks attempted to imbue the social revolution of emancipation proved tragically insecure. Although some of the autonomy blacks had wrested for themselves in the early days of freedom was irreversible (control of their religious life, for example), the dream of economic independence had been dashed. . . . By the end of the century, the Fourteenth and Fifteenth amendments had been effectively nullified in the South. As Supreme Court Justice John Marshall Harlan put in 1883, the United States entered on "an era of constitutional law when the rights of freedom and American citizenship cannot receive from the nation that efficient protection which heretofore was unhesitatingly accorded to slavery and the rights of the master." During Reconstruction, political involvement, economic self-help, and family and institution building had all formed parts of a coherent ideology of black community advancement. After the South's "Redemption," that ideology separated into its component parts, and blacks' conception of their "rights" turned inward. Assuming a defensive posture, blacks concentrated on strengthening their community and surviving in the face of a patently unjust political and social order, rather than directly challenging the new status quo.

A disaster for blacks, the collapse of Reconstruction was also a tragedy that deeply affected the future development of the nation as a whole. If racism contributed to the undoing of Reconstruction, by the same token Reconstruction's demise and the emergence of blacks as a disfranchised class of dependent laborers greatly facilitated racism's further spread, so that by the early twentieth century it had become more deeply embedded in the nation's culture and politics than at any time since the beginning of the antislavery crusade. Meanwhile, the activist state's association with the aspirations of blacks discredited it in the eyes of many white Americans. And the removal of a significant portion of the laboring population from public life shifted the center of gravity of American politics to the right, complicating the tasks of reformers for generations to come. Long into the twentieth century, the South remained a one-party region under the control of a reactionary ruling elite whose national power weakened the prospects not simply of change in racial matters but of progressive legislation in many other realms.[41]

In this year of the United States Constitution's bicentennial, it is sobering to reflect how frail the constitutional recognition of blacks' citizenship rights proved as a guarantee of racial equality among American citizens. Well might blacks bitterly echo the words of Reconstruction congressman Joseph Rainey: "tell me nothing of a constitution which fails to shelter beneath its rightful power the people of a country."[42]

---

[40]Alfred H. Kelly, "The Congressional Controversy over School Segregation, 1867–1875, *American Historical Review* 64 (April 1959), 552; *Congressional Record*, 43 Cong., 1 sess., Dec. 19, 1873, p. 344; ibid., Jan. 5, 1874, p. 382; ibid., Jan. 6, 1874, pp. 407–9; ibid., Jan. 10, 1874, p. 565; ibid., Jan. 24, 1874, pp. 901–2; ibid., June 9, 1874, pp. 4782, 4785; ibid., 2 sess., Feb. 3, 1875, p. 945; Bertram Wyatt-Brown, "The Civil Rights Act of 1875," *Western Political Quarterly* 18 (Dec. 1965), 763–65; John Hope Franklin, "The Enforcement of the Civil Rights Act of 1875," *Prologue* 6 (Winter 1974), 225–35.

[41]Konvitz, *Century of Civil Rights*, 118.

[42]*Congressional Globe*, 42 Cong., 1 sess., March 27, 1871, pp. 294–95.

Eric Foner

I grew up in a historically oriented family (my father and uncle were historians). But when I entered college many years ago, I hoped to be an astronomer. It was an inspiring teacher, Professor James P. Shenton, whose course on the Civil War era was my first history class in college, who persuaded me to change my focus. Moreover, the 1960s were a time of great social upheaval in the United States. The civil rights revolution led me, and many of my contemporaries, to seek in history an explanation for the events transforming the world around us. I became interested in the subjects that have shaped most of my teaching and writing—the struggle against slavery, the effort during Reconstruction to create a more equal society, the contested meaning of freedom in a society shaped in considerable degree by the legacy of slavery and segregation. Another great teacher, Richard Hofstadter, who supervised my doctoral dissertation, taught me another lesson—that historians should write in a style accessible to readers outside the academic world, and that we have an obligation to bring good, up-to-date history to the broadest possible audience. Over the years, I have written for newspapers and magazines, have curated two museum exhibitions, and have worked on various television historical documentaries.

QUESTIONS FOR CONSIDERATION

1. According to Foner, what have "recent studies" shown regarding the progress free blacks made since Emancipation? What does he claim those studies have overlooked?
2. How did military service allow formerly enslaved blacks to claim civil rights? In what ways does this support Foner's contention that civil rights for blacks also came "from below"?
3. According to Foner, in what ways did the Emancipation represent a "turning point" for blacks regarding their faith in the possibilities of civil rights? What civil rights might blacks have hoped for in this new period?
4. Find three examples of formerly enslaved blacks claiming economic and political rights "from below." What actions by the federal government seemed to support these claims?
5. Describe an example of formerly enslaved blacks using religious arguments for civil rights. How did the context of nineteenth-century America make these arguments possible?
6. Foner claims that whites and formerly enslaved blacks disagreed on the role the federal government played in civil rights. Briefly describe the differences. What might explain the different ideas about the role of the federal government?
7. In what ways did the political, social, and economic status of blacks change after Emancipation? In what ways did it remain the same as before the Civil War?

CHAPTER THREE

Producing Poverty: Local Government and the Economic Development in a New South County, 1874–1884[1]

Wayne K. Durrill

Throughout the postwar South, planters and merchants actively sought to develop the region's economy, substituting capitalist agriculture for the trade in surplus goods that had been produced earlier by slaves and subsistence farmers. To facilitate that change, they built railroads, organized new networks of credit and exchange, and promoted scientific farming methods. Those constructive efforts were heralded by promoters at the time and have been chronicled by historians since. Recently, however, scholars of the New South have focused on a less attractive side of postwar economic development. The Conservatives' accession to power after 1870 ensured passage and enforcement of lien, mortgage, and vagrancy laws that channeled control of land and labor into landlords' and employers' hands. In addition, fence and game laws closed off many persons' access to natural resources that sustained life apart from ties to planters and merchants. How these and other measures transformed the southern economy, however, remains the subject of intense debate.[2]

In the nineteenth century, Union County's landscape consisted of low hills and broad valleys south of the unnavigable Rocky River. Its soils included rich

---

[1]Interested students are encouraged to read this essay in the original form. Wayne K. Durrill, "Producing Poverty: Local Government and Economic Development in a New South County, 1874–1884," *The Journal of American History* 71, no. 4 (March 1985), 764–81.

[2]C. Vann Woodward, *Origins of the New South, 1877–1913* (Baton Rouge, 1951), 107–41; David L. Carlton, *Mill and Town in South Carolina, 1880–1920* (Baton Rouge, 1982), 1–39; Roger L. Ransom and Richard Sutch, *One Kind of Freedom: The Economic Consequences of Emancipation* (New York, 1977), 88–199; Harold D. Woodman, *King Cotton and His Retainers: Financing and Marketing the Cotton Crop of the South, 1880–1925* (Lexington, Ky., 1968), 43–359; Steven Hahn, "Hunting, Fishing and Foraging: Common Rights and Class Relations in the Postbellum South, " *Radical History Review* 26 (1982), 37–64; Steven Hahn, *The Roots of Southern Populism: Yeoman Farmers and the Transformation of the Georgia Upcountry, 1850–1890* (New York, 1983); J. Crawford King, Jr., "The Closing of the Southern Range: An Exploratory Study, " *Journal of Southern History* 48 (Feb. 1982), 53–70; Lacy K. Ford, "Rednecks and Merchants: Economic Development and Social Tensions in the South Carolina Upcountry, 1865–1900," *Journal of American History* 71 (Sept. 1984), 294–318.

brown loams with some patches of clay and stone outcroppings. In the north, close to the Rocky River, the soil was thinner and supported mainly stands of hardwood timber. Subsistence farmers hunted wild game and herded hogs and sheep in those hills. In the south, near the South Carolina border, planters found the darker, richer soil suitable for extensive corn and cotton cultivation. By 1870 the county boasted of one sizable town, Monroe, the county seat. It straddled two main wagon roads that connected the county to external markets. Monroe, however, saw little trade because the cost of transport remained high without a railroad. The town served mainly to house the small county government and a handful of lawyers.[3]

Before 1870 small farmers dominated the northern townships' economy and politics. They planted corn and wheat in small clearings amounting to 66,572 of the county's more than 300,000 acres in 1860. From that acreage Union County farmers as a whole harvested 301,175 bushels of corn, 76,321 bushels of wheat, and smaller amounts of sweet potatoes, peas, beans, and wool. The remaining 236,900 acres of woodlands supported 6,544 cattle, 11,641 sheep, and 20,074 hogs. Most local farmers derived their livelihoods chiefly from "great droves [of hogs] in the woods [that lay] in beds of 75 to 100." Hogs and corn provided not only a subsistence to small farmers but also a basis for political power. Stock dealers organized subsistence farmers as Democrats before the war and as Republicans afterward. In the southern townships planters dominated local economic and political activity. They operated small plantations ranging from 100 to 500 acres, and in 1860 produced 3,045 400-pound bales of cotton. However, they also raised a subsistence first, cultivating cotton mainly for cash to purchase items that could not be produced at home. One Union County planter's son recalled in later years that "Grand-father's and father's . . . chief cultivation was corn, but cotton was the money crop." Cotton provided the wealth that enabled planters to develop an elaborate web of debts among their friends, neighbors, and relatives. Out of those personal dependencies, planters fashioned evangelical churches and political parties, in which they acted as elders and magistrates to dominate neighborhood affairs.[4]

Union County's residents differed in many particulars, but all adopted a self-sufficient way of life. They based their economy on an assumption of abundance that made possible the direct production of most goods. They had many natural

[3]C. B. Williams, W. E. Hem, J. K. Plummer, and W. F. Pate, "County Soil Report No. 3, Report on Union County Soils and Agriculture," *Bulletin of the North Carolina Department of Agriculture* 38 (July 1917), 5–43; H. Nelson Walden, *History of Union County* (Monroe, N.C., 1964), 49–53; A. M. I. Stack and R. F. I. Beasley, *Sketches of Monroe and Union County* (Charlotte, N.C., 1902), 6–10.

[4]U. S. Department of the Interior, Census Office, *Agriculture of the United States in 1860 Compiled from the Original Results of the Eighth Census* (Washington, D.C., 1864), 108–11; J. Raymond Shute interview by Wayne K. Durrill, June 25, 1982, transcript, p. 8, Southern Oral History Program (Southern Historical Collection, University of North Carolina, Chapel Hill); George T. Winchester, *A Story of Union County and the History of Pleasant Grove Camp Ground* (Mineral Springs, N.C., 1937), 87–89; John Brevard Alexander, *Reminiscences of the Past Sixty Years* (Charlotte, N.C., 1908), 115, 168; Robert E. Gallman, "Self-Sufficiency in the Cotton Economy of the Antebellum South," *Agricultural History* 44 (Jan. 1970), 5–23.

resources—land, water, forests, game—and they possessed a large labor force, although county northerners and southerners differed on how to organize that labor. Subsistence farmers relied on kinsmen and friends, while planters used slaves. But both divisions of labor derived from personal dependencies—women on men, blacks on whites, and in the southern townships, the poor on the wealthy. An assumption of abundance also implied direct exchange. If a certain item could not be produced at home, someone in the county could grow it or make it. Union County residents, therefore, formed what they called a "market" among themselves—for example, rotating from house to house the responsibility for killing livestock to supply an entire neighborhood. That practice extended as well to the work of skilled craftsmen and to large projects such as barn raisings. Through direct production and exchange, farmers and planters assured themselves of a modest livelihood that rendered the economic world outside Union County largely irrelevant.[5]

After 1870 the county's economy underwent changes that permanently subordinated direct production and exchange to an indirect economy based on cash. "The greatest yield with the smallest outlay of capital and labor is what we aim at," according to one local writer. The goal now was profit, an ever-increasing ratio of input to output, in which a farmer's control over supplies and his family's labor was mediated through local merchants. A simple subsistence no longer sufficed to satisfy those who would develop Union County's economy.[6]

In practice, profitable agriculture required a complete alteration of farming methods as well as goals. In place of raising edible, usable crops, farmers sought to raise grains and tubers, which could be sold for cash or fed to improved breeds of livestock. The new crop mix would produce an intensive agriculture, as contrasted to subsistence farmers' extensive herding and slash-and-burn planting. Intensive cultivation would rely on investment in fertilizers, better seeds, and improved livestock to replace the use of common lands. Intensive agriculture, however, did not mean one-crop planting. Developers argued publicly that the price of cotton simply could not repay a farmer's investment no matter how efficient the operation. . . . Diversified commodities production would profit Union County's residents most.[7]

Union County developers, mainly town merchants and a few commercial planters, came to power in 1870 as Republican influence began to wane in the state and the nation. Many had arrived only recently from the South Carolina upcountry, being the sons of merchants and commercial planters on the periphery of Charleston's antebellum trading territory. These young men formed a cohesive and active group. After 1870 they opened wholesale trading houses, organized a local Masonic lodge, founded the Bank of Monroe, established the

[5]Byron W. Lathan, *The Lathan-Belk Families and In-Laws, 1710–1979* (Monroe, N.C., 1979), 87–89, 113–14, 375; Alexander, *Reminiscences*, 151, 198. For the cattle trade in Monroe, see *Monroe Enquirer*, June 29, 1875, p. 1.

[6]*Monroe Enquirer*, Feb. 5, 1877, p. 4.

[7]Ibid., April 30, 1877, p. 2.

town's first Methodist church, and persuaded old Whigs and some Democrats to join the newly organized local Conservative party. In the election of 1870, they dominated the county board of commissioners for the first time and thereafter made the board the political engine by which to push local development forward. In 1871 the board hired an agent to persuade the Wilmington, Charlotte, and Rutherford Railroad to locate in the county. Later that same year the board funded $60,000 in bonds to finance the railroad's construction. The board also raised tax rates to pay for the bonds by 1877. Once the railroad neared completion in 1874, the commissioners began to build and to improve the roads that fed the county's rapidly developing railroad towns. They approved dozens of petitions from landowners in 1874 that transformed private, country roads into publicly maintained thoroughfares.[8]

After 1874 taxation became the core of local development policy. From that year forward, the board of commissioners raised tax rates annually from 53 cents on $100 assessed valuation in 1873 to 94 cents in 1879. The board also raised poll taxes from 70 cents in 1873 to $1.68 in 1879. At the same time, the board took the power to assign valuations on personal property out of taxpayers' hands. Before the Civil War local residents themselves customarily listed their possessions with a local assessor, usually a neighboring planter. They based their returns on an estimate of what their real and personal property would bring at a forced sale, obviously a very low value. In 1874 the commissioners published a standard scale of valuations for most personal property found on farms—horses, mules, cattle, hogs, cotton, wagons, sheep, goats, corn, flour, bacon, cotton gins, and buggies. The new standard scale quickly raised valuations on all personal property.[9]

Union County's tax policies did not fall on all residents with the same force. For example, while total county tax revenues rose from $10,436 in 1870 to $34,825 in 1873 and ended the decade at $21,790, the average valuation of farmland declined from $2.99 in 1870 to $2.98 in 1880. Large landowners who had already listed their land therefore likely paid little more in taxes per acre than they had before 1870. Tax revenue from other sources, however, rose. The number of acres listed for taxation increased from 289,689 in 1870 to a high of 378,403 in 1873, finally ending the decade at 371,168. These figures suggest that many smaller farmers found themselves obliged to make a return and to pay taxes on their land for the first time. Some of the increase, however, may represent land recently purchased by large landholders, hence just entered on the tax rolls. Moreover, many county residents found themselves paying personal property taxes for the first time. That was so because North Carolina decreased its tax exemption on

[8]Union County Board of Commissioners' Minutes, vol. 1, Oct. 2, 1871, p. 146 (North Carolina Division of Archives and History); ibid., Nov. 6, 1871, p. 150; Shute interview, 1, 2, 6, 7, 17; LeGette Blythe, *William Henry Belk, Merchant of the South* (Chapel Hill, 1958), 29–57.

[9]Union County Board of Commissioners' Minutes, vol. 1, June 2, 1873, p. 243; ibid., March 3, 1874, p. 287; ibid., April 18, 1874, pp. 282–83; ibid., May [n.d.], 1875, p. 348; ibid., April 12, 1876, p. 412; ibid., June 6, 1876, p. 423; ibid., Aug. 6, 1877, p. 523; ibid., vol. 2, Aug. 4, 1879, p. 65; *Executive and Legislative Documents Laid before the General Assembly of North Carolina, Session 1870–'71* (Raleigh, 1871), doc. no. 3, p. 231.

personal property from $200 in 1868 to only $25 in 1879. As a result, valuations on one form of personal property, farm equipment, rose from $11,075 in 1870 to $303,827 just five years later. Finally, the number of polls returned rose dramatically from 1,089 in 1870 to 2,434 in 1879. The figures taken together suggest a wholesale addition to the tax rolls of small farmers' property.[10]

By the mid-1870s new cash taxes posed a serious dilemma for Union County's subsistence farmers and herders. They could grow cash crops to pay the levies, or they could continue to produce a subsistence and find themselves charged with failure to pay assessed taxes. Many simply neglected to list their taxable property. In 1876 the chairman of the board of commissioners warned *Monroe Enquirer* readers that "such delinquencies [have] been each year increasing" and that failure to list property for taxation constituted "a misdemeanor and could result in a fine and imprisonment." At the very least, the county assessed delinquent farmers double taxes for the years in which they did not list their property. When residents refused altogether to pay taxes, they found their land attached and advertised for sale. In 1875 the county sheriff posted final tax lists for 1873–1874 and warned that "all property upon which the tax has not been paid will be advertised for sale at once." Between 1875 and 1879 the sheriff advertised for sale 347 pieces of land amounting to 47,977 acres. In fact, most land offered for sale never passed from its owner's possession. The threat of sale usually induced local residents to pay overdue taxes only hours before the sheriff's auction.[11]

Union County residents who refused to pay taxes were sometimes seized and imprisoned in the county jail under the state's insolvency laws. That practice violated the state's constitutional prohibition on imprisoning debtors. The county commissioners found, however, that a tax burden could be considered a legal debt to the state and county. Then, under state insolvency laws, debtors had two choices: They could sign insolvency oaths and allow the government to take a lien on all existing and future property held or produced by the debtor. Alternatively, debtors could wait in jail for friends or kinsmen to pay their taxes and jail fees, thereby retaining their present and future property. Many local tax dodgers chose the latter course. By 1877 the county's jail overflowed, and, therefore, the commissioners began hiring out prisoners to local merchants. Many of the prisoners served terms of forty to sixty days, and sometimes longer. Union County

---

[10]*Executive and Legislative Documents Laid before the General Assembly of North Carolina*, Sessions including: 1871–'72, 1872–'73, 1873–'74, 1874–'75, 1876–77; *Public Documents of the General Assembly of North Carolina*, Session 1879; *North Carolina Executive and Legislative Documents*, Session 1881; *Executive and Legislative Documents of the State of North Carolina*, Session 1883; "An Act to Provide for the Collection of Taxes by the State, "Public Laws of the State of North Carolina Passed by the General Assembly at Its Session 1868–'69 (Raleigh, 1869), 165–66; "An Act to Provide for the Levying and Collection of Taxes, " Laws and Resolutions of the State of North Carolina Passed by the General Assembly at Its Session 1879 (Raleigh, 1879), 109–110; Union County Board of Commissioners' Minutes, vol. 3, April 2, 1888, p. 46.

[11]William H. Battle, *Battle's Revisal of the Public Statutes of North* Carolina (Raleigh, 1873), 764; *Monroe Enquirer*, July 20, 1875, p. 3; ibid., Nov. 23, 1875, p. 3; ibid., Dec. 7, 1875, p. 3; ibid., April 3, 1876, p. 3.

residents thus found themselves compelled to work for an employer, although without benefit of wages.[12]

Those who further evaded assessors appear to have been arrested on charges of insanity or vagrancy. On one notable day in 1878, the sheriff arrested five people in Monroe Township on charges of insanity. A hastily assembled jury convicted all the defendants and sent them to the poorhouse. By 1879 the board of commissioners began to pay bounties for the arrest of vagrants. In April one man received one dollar "for apprehending and bringing William Fincher a pauper to [the] Poorhouse." The poorhouse to which those people found themselves remanded was in reality a fortified cotton plantation. Located two miles south of Monroe, it consisted of two houses, one for paupers and one for the insane, a barn and outbuildings, and several hundred acres planted in cotton by the inmates. The commissioners expected the poorhouse to train inmates so that they might "get out and earn [their] own support" in the new commercial economy.[13]

Persons who persisted in foraging and herding attracted the attention of local landowners acting as magistrates. The landowners hoped to force herders and hunters off common lands by enforcing existing trespass laws. In July 1875 five planters published a notice in the *Monroe Enquirer* that forbade hunting and fishing on their lands by "all persons . . . either with or without dogs, or in anyway trespassing on our lands." They warned that the "law will be strictly enforced against any person found so doing." Six months later twelve other planters extended trespass regulations to include all manner of foraging. They prohibited "fishing or hunting, either in the day or night time, with or without dogs or guns, and cutting or hauling timber, wood, or pine, on the land of the undersigned." So that readers would not mistake the warning's target, the landowners noted: "Gentlemen will easily respect this notice—rascals will be required to do so."[14]

In 1878 Union County magistrates expanded their efforts to enforce property rights. One group forbade the "making of roads, or traveling with horses or wagons or on foot," whether on existing private roads or elsewhere on their land, "on pain of being prosecuted by us according to law." Other landowners argued

---

[12]William T. Dortch, John Manning, and John S. Henderson, eds., *The Code of North Carolina, Enacted March 2, 1883* (2 vols., New York, 1883), II, 683; "An Act Concerning the Estates of Insolvent and Imprisoned Debtors," *Public Laws of the State of North Carolina, 1868–'69*, 388–400; *Moore vs. Green*, 73 N.C. 330 (1875) at 394; Union County Board of Commissioners' Minutes, vol. 1, July 1, 1872, pp. 179–81; ibid., Nov. 23, 1872, pp. 207–8; ibid., May 26, 1877, p. 513; ibid., June 4, 1877, p. 519; ibid., Nov. 5, 1877, p. 546; ibid., April 1, 1878, pp. 583–86; ibid., May 6, 1878, pp. 590, 595; ibid., Feb. 3, 1879, p. 48; ibid., vol. 2, Aug. 5, 1879, pp. 70–73; "An Act to Provide for the Levying and Collection of Taxes," *Laws and Resolutions of the State of North Carolina*, 1879, 103–33. Thomas M. Cooley, *Treatise on the Law of Taxation, Including the Law of Local Assessment* (Chicago, 1876), 14; *Report of the Tax Commission of the State of North Carolina* (Raleigh, 1886), 6. For the first recorded case in Union County of an imprisoned debtor's taking the insolvency oath, see Union County Board of Commissioners' Minutes, vol. 1, Sept. 4, 1871, p. 143.

[13]Dortch, Manning, and Henderson, eds., *Code of North Carolina*, 29–32, 481–82; Union County Board of Commissioners' Minutes, vol. 1, May 6, 1878, pp. 592, 594; ibid., vol. 2, Dec. 6, 1881, pp. 237, 239; ibid., Feb. 11, 1882, pp. 248–49.

[14]*Monroe Enquirer*, July 13, 1875, p. 4; ibid., Dec. 7, 1875, p. 3.

that it was not the trespass of men but of their dogs that constituted the greatest breach of property rights. Some believed that dogs attacked sheep and therefore ought to be prevented from roaming freely. They proposed a statewide tax on dogs. Others argued that the mere possession of dogs did not create the difficulty. Rather, as one Union County man noted, an owner's failure to prevent his dogs from crossing property lines did: "It is the running at large of dogs which does the harm. Every dog which leaves his master['s] premises and intrudes on another ought to be shot."[15] By those means, property owners asserted their exclusive possession of land and of other resources that subsistence producers had exploited with impunity for decades.

In large measure, local developers achieved the economic expansion they sought. Cotton production jumped from 1,196 bales in 1870 to 8,336 in 1880. Trade boomed in the county's railroad towns. Moreover, such expansion did not alter the county's basic self-sufficiency. Corn production rose from 203,032 bushels in 1870 to 338,520 in 1880, while the number of cattle, sheep, and hogs also increased. Developers' efforts, however, produced other consequences that later transformed the local economy into something less than robust. Taxation left small farmers little choice but to exchange their physical labor for cash, not for the expectation of a future exchange. And trespass laws left county residents no alternative but to cease all labor that produced food and fuel without recourse to money. Those policies thus substituted an indirect mechanism, cash, in either wages or profits, in place of direct production and exchange. Merchants and commercial planters, by interposing themselves between producers and their labor's product, had created local markets for both commodities and labor.[16]

Union County's developers did not hesitate to take advantage of those changes. In August 1875 Monroe's leading merchants opened the Peoples Bank of Monroe, the county's first full-time lending institution. The bank took deposits and paid interest on them for the first time in the county's history. It also lent money in exchange for mortgages on real estate and on cotton in storage. Two months later Monroe's largest wholesale houses ceased to sell goods on credit, except in cases involving very large contracts. Because the bank lent money only to property owners and because merchants demanded cash for their goods, landless farmers and herders lacked access to capital that would enable them to enter the cash economy as independent commercial farmers. They could participate only as sharecroppers, renters, or wage laborers. A year later local landowners further strengthened their hand by enforcing the new Landlord and Tenant Act. The law replaced the mechanic's lien with legislation requiring that, in any rental or cropping agreement, landlords retain possession of all crops until their

---

[15]Ibid., April 1, 1878, p. 3; ibid., Nov. 19, 1877, p. 3.

[16]U.S. Department of the Interior, Census Office, *Ninth Census*, vol. III: *The Statistics of the Wealth and Industry of the United States* (Washington, D.C., 1872), 218–19; U.S. Department of the Interior, Census Office, Tenth Census, vol. III: *Report on the Productions of Agriculture* (Washington, D.C., 1883), 78–79; "Report on the Cotton Production of the State of North Carolina," ibid., vol. VI: *Report on Cotton Production in the United States*, June 1, 1880 (Washington, D.C., 1884), pt. 2, p. 5.

tenants had paid due rents in full and carried out "all other stipulations." In those ways Union County developers dominated local commodities and labor markets by restricting access to the means by which poor people might produce a living. For poor men and women, their economy of abundance suddenly became an economy of scarcity.[17]

By 1880 hundreds of Union County farmers had entered local cash markets. Some made the transition on their own farms by producing cotton as well as a subsistence for themselves. Most, however, participated in the cash economy as either renters or sharecroppers. In 1879 tenants operated almost two-thirds of the farms that encompassed less than 100 acres—that is, 413 out of 670 farms. Many of those tenants probably came from very small farms that had been swallowed up in land sales to merchants and commercial planters. The number of farms comprising less than 10 acres, for example, declined from 111 in 1870 to 23 in 1880; those from 20 to 49 acres fell from 816 to 430. At the same time, many former subsistence farmers and herders evidently became wage laborers on the larger farms in the county. How many made that transition cannot be determined exactly. We know only that in 1880 Union County's farm laborers were paid $51,492 in wages, which at the going rate of $100 for a year's labor, indicates that perhaps 515 persons labored in the fields for wages.[18]

Those who now labored for wages or farmed for rent or shares soon saw themselves as having interests that differed from their employers' or creditors'. Robberies and assaults increased, particularly in the springs of 1878 and 1879 when cotton prices bottomed out at levels so low that the newspaper ceased to publish local quotations. . . . Finally, the number of fires increased dramatically. In 1878 and 1879 fifteen substantial buildings, several connected with local merchants, went up in flames, eleven of which fires the newspaper reported as the work of incendiaries. Arson cases included a ginhouse, a smokehouse, a rural whiskey shop owned by a Monroe merchant, two large gristmills, a school, and three Methodist churches. Other fires included four houses and a large wholesale store. The newspaper had reported no fires in the three years previous to 1878.[19]

Violence reached a peak during the harvest of 1879. Attacks against property owners that once had been attempted anonymously now became public and very personal events. J. M. Bowers, for example, had worked for years as a tenant on Joseph McNeely's farm in Sandy Ridge Township, a cotton-producing area in southwestern Union County. The two had quarreled all summer over the management of

[17]*Monroe Enquirer,* Feb. 28, 1876, p. 2; ibid., Feb. 12, 1877, p. 3; ibid., Aug. 24, 1878, p. 4; ibid., Oct. 5, 1878, p. 3.

[18]Census Office, *Ninth Census,* III, 218–19; Census Office, *Tenth Census,* III, 78–79; *Third Annual Report of the Bureau of Labor Statistics of the State of North Carolina for the Year 1889* (Raleigh, 1890), 127–28.

[19]*Monroe Enquirer,* Dec. 17, 1877, p. 3; ibid., Feb. 25, 1878, p. 3; ibid., March 18, 1878, p. 3; ibid., April 6, 1878, p. 3; ibid., April 13, 1878, p. 3; ibid., May 11, 1878, p. 3; ibid., May 25, 1878, p. 3; ibid., Aug. 17, 1878, p. 3; ibid., Aug. 24, 1878, p. 3; ibid., Dec. 7, 1878, p. 3; ibid., Jan. 18, 1879, p. 3; ibid., March 15, 1879, p. 3; ibid., Nov. 1, 1879, p. 3; ibid., Jan. 24, 1880, p. 3.

Bowers' crop, and in October they finally came to blows. "A difficulty sprang up in regard to the division of some corn they were then engaged in hauling." McNeely went to his house close by to get his gun, leaving his son to guard the corn while Bowers and his wife, already armed, continued to dispute the division. A melee ensued from which McNeely's son emerged with several gashes and a shotgun wound. Both sides then called on neighborhood magistrates and had warrants sworn out for the others' arrest. At a subsequent trial the McNeelys consented to buy the Bowers' interest in the crop, and Bowers and his wife agreed to leave the county. Elsewhere in Union County that week, two men fought with pistols at a corn shucking, and another young man was shot and killed at a ginhouse near Monroe. A local newspaper editor noted "a growing tendency to the use of the pistol in our own immediate locality."[20]

Union County's violence ought to have warned developers that something was amiss. Local arsonists . . . and murderers did not commit their depredations randomly. They attacked the property and the persons of those who had dedicated themselves to commercial expansion. This suggests that such unorganized terrorism not only expressed displeasure with individuals but also constituted a disjointed opposition to the new commercial economy itself. . . .[21]

. . . The economic crisis that had provoked . . . open conflict eased in the last two weeks of November 1879. Cotton prices climbed steadily from a low of 6 1/2 to 9 7/8 cents per pound in February 1878 to just over 12 cents per pound in February 1880. That did not signal an end to the county's troubles, however. Indeed, local cotton dealers warned that the increase in prices resulted from efforts by New York brokers to corner the world cotton market. Prices paid to tenants for cotton surely would drop again, and with that change would come renewed conflict.[22]

In January 1879 Union County developers ignored signs of distress among local farmers and pressed on with a campaign for further economic growth. They and their capitalist brethren from around the state met in Raleigh at a session of the North Carolina General Assembly. All sought to conserve and to concentrate their funds for investment. Merchants demanded abolition of the purchase tax levied on items they bought with their liquid capital. Landowners agitated for lower tax rates on real estate. These changes in state fiscal policy would reduce government revenues, hence, they hoped, their own expenses. But other developers, headed by Gov. Thomas J. Jarvis, objected to lower state expenditures. They proposed to increase state spending for development purposes, primarily for railroads and for the state agriculture department, but without raising tax rates.[23]

[20]Ibid., Nov. 1, 1879, p. 3.

[21]Ibid.

[22]Ibid., Dec. 6, 1879, p. 2; ibid., Dec. 13, 1879, p. 2.

[23]*Raleigh News*, Jan. 17, 1879, p. 1; ibid., Jan. 28, 1879, p. 2; ibid., Jan. 31, 1879, p. 2; Elgiva D. Watson, "'The Election Campaign of Governor Jarvis, 1880: A Study of the Issues," *North Carolina Historical Review* 48 (Summer 1971), 276–300.

The solution to those conflicting demands lay in "equalization" as embodied in the Machinery Act of 1879. Equalization meant creating new assessment procedures designed to locate property that previously had escaped taxation. Such procedures, the governor hoped, would "in a few years double the taxable value of [the state's] property." Equal taxation, however, did not necessarily imply equitable taxation. The governor, in fact, went on to assure capitalists that the new assessing procedures would result in no increase in tax rates and that taxes on capital actually would decline. The tax burden then would shift to those who had paid few taxes in the past, primarily the poor who would become the unwitting financiers of further economic expansion.[24]

At the same assembly meeting, Union County's representative, D. A. Covington, agitated for a local-option stock law. Such a law, local developers believed, would enable farmers to protect their intensively cultivated fields from marauding cattle and hogs. Farmers then could reclaim "old fields" left idle in the past and begin intensive cultivation using fertilizers, machinery, and improved seeds. They could also justify the expense of purchasing and husbanding purebred cattle, sheep, and hogs. In addition, the developers argued, such a law would save the cost of fencing crops, would reduce litigation over trespassing, and would facilitate the division of plantations now considered "unwieldy and unprofitable to their owners" into tenant farms.[25]

At the heart of the new agriculture and its stock laws lay the further enforcement of property rights. A resident of adjacent Mecklenburg County informed *Monroe Enquirer* readers that adoption of the stock law in his neighborhood "learned men to regard the lives and property of their fellow men, and thereby advanced the cause of civilization"—and presumably capitalist agriculture. As trespass laws had enforced commercial farmers' rights to their lawfully owned resources, stock laws would extend that protection to the proceeds of their investments. That argument, however, appealed mainly to landowners. Union County's surviving subsistence farmers lamented that there would be no place for their roving stock under the new system of intensive cultivation. One planter warned developers: "I never knew anything more unpopular when first mentioned."[26]

Union County's commissioners renewed their campaign for commercial development in May 1879. . . . They called an unprecedented meeting in Monroe of all the county's assessors to explain the Machinery Act's purpose and provisions. The law required assessors, not taxpayers, to make entirely new estimates of the value of local real and personal property. The valuations would reflect the "*true value* of an item, and not what it would *likely bring if put to a forced sale*." To enforce the novel procedures, assessors also acquired expanded judicial

---

[24]Hugh Talmage Lefler and Albert Ray Newsome, *The History of a Southern State: North Carolina* (Chapel Hill, 1973), 542–45; Watson, "Election Campaign of Governor Jarvis," 276–300; Jerry Lee Cross, "Political Metamorphosis: An Historical Profile of the Democratic Party in North Carolina, 1800–1892" (Ph.D. diss., State University of New York, Binghamton, 1976), 207–209; *Raleigh News*, Jan. 10, 1879, p. 1; ibid., Jan. 12, 1879, p. 3; ibid., Jan. 16, 1879, p. 2; ibid., Feb. 1, 1879, p. 2.

[25]*Monroe Enquirer*, Sept. 1, 1877, p. 1.

[26]Ibid.

powers, including the right to "send for persons and papers, and to examine witnesses." The law further required the appointment of two "assessors-at-large" to correct and to revise tax lists, to hear complaints, and to ensure that township assessors indeed valued property at its "ad valorem" worth. Whatever the outcome of the new procedures, the Machinery Act prohibited assessors from lowering a township's aggregate assessment.[27]

The *Monroe Enquirer* editor explained the anticipated effect: "The tax on each hundred dollars' worth will be less, but the aggregate valuation will be greater." That prediction proved accurate. Land valuations in Union County rose dramatically from $2.93 per acre in 1880 to $4.49 in 1889. Similarly, the valuation of cattle, the primary item of cash exchange for subsistence farmers, jumped from $5.68 in 1880 to $12.87 in 1889. Hence, in 1880 the county's revenues promised such a rapid increase as a result of broadening the tax base that the board of commissioners cut county tax rates drastically. Between 1879 and 1881 the local tax rate declined from $.92 per $100 valuation to $.09½. Poll-tax rates also dropped, from $1.68 to $.28½.[28]

In order to collect revenue from new taxpayers, Union County's sheriff arrested more men for nonpayment of taxes, while the board of commissioners farmed out more offenders to local merchants. In 1884 the board also sold the old poorhouse, bought a larger farm, and built brick houses, stables, and a new barn for the inmates. As a result of those efforts, poor men and women began to flee the county, many to cotton mills in neighboring Charlotte, leaving their unpaid tax bills behind. In May 1888 the board for the first time sent local tax lists to neighboring counties to which Union County tax dodgers had escaped.[29]

While it sought out new taxpayers, Union County's board granted large reductions in tax valuations to landlords and merchants who petitioned for the favor. One Monroe merchant, for example, requested and received a reduction in valuation from $150 to $50 on a lot in Monroe for 1879 and complete "relief" on that lot's valuation for 1875. The board granted reductions also to whole townships that supported the board's development program. In 1883, after hearing petitions and complaints from several landowners, the commissioners authorized

[27]"Act to Provide for the Levying and Collection of Taxes," 103–33. Cf. "An Act to Provide for the Collection of Taxes by the State, Known as the Machinery Act," *Laws and Resolutions of the State of North Carolina Passed by the General Assembly at Its Session 1876–77* (Raleigh, 1877), 255–82; and Union County Board of Commissioners' Minutes, vol. 2, May 5, 1879, p. 54.

[28]*Monroe Enquirer*, April 11, 1879, p. 3; Executive and Legislative Documents of the State of North Carolina, Session 1883 & Session 1885; Executive and Legislative Documents Laid before the General Assembly of North Carolina, Session 1887 (Raleigh, 1887), doc. no. 5, pp. 261–68, and statement I; ibid., doc. no. 5, pp. 259, 279–86, and statement I [two different documents no. 5 were printed in 1887]; Public Documents of the State of North Carolina, Session 1889 (Raleigh, 1889), doc. no. 5, p. 293, and statement I; ibid., doc. no. 6, pp. 270, 277, and statement I; Public Documents of the State of North Carolina, Session 1891 (Raleigh, 1891), doc. no. 5, p. 267, and statement L; ibid., doc. no. 6, p. 228, and statement K; Union County Board of Commissioners' Minutes, vol. 2, Aug. 1, 1881, p. 209.

[29]Union County Board of Commissioners' Minutes, vol. 2, Nov. 6, 1882, p. 316; ibid., May 7, 1883, p. 356; ibid., April 8, 1884, pp. 420–22; ibid., vol. 3, May 7, 1888, p. 49.

across-the-board reductions in valuations ranging from 20 to 50 percent for every township in the county except one, New Salem. Subsistence farmers there had defeated stock laws and prohibition regulations in 1881 and 1882. In 1891 the board lowered all assessments in Vance Township, a newly organized area with a vigorous merchant community, while it raised New Salem's valuations yet again by 8 percent.[30]

In the 1880s Union County's tax policies did not generate increased tax revenues as they had in the mid-1870s. Total county revenue, in fact, dropped from $21,790 in 1879 to a low of $3,023 in 1881, rose again later to a high of $16,679, and ended the decade at $11,848 in 1890. State tax revenues from Union County, meanwhile, rose only gradually from $5,835 in 1880 to a high of $8,916 in 1883 and ended the decade at $7,179. Tax revenues produced by different forms of wealth meanwhile changed dramatically. Tax revenue produced by land rose from $1,310 in 1880 to $4,432 in 1885, whereas revenue from merchants' inventories declined from $493 in 1881 to a low of $312 in 1885 and ended the decade at $335. Similarly, valuations on different forms of capital varied substantially. Local valuations on lands rose from $1,082,593 in 1880 to a high of $1,675,449 in 1886 and declined to $1,359,119 in 1890, while the valuation of merchants' goods fell from $19,940 in 1881 to a low of $5,207 in 1885. Most impressive perhaps, valuations on personal property rose from $606,453 in 1880 to a high of $1,208,017 in 1884 and receded to $1,045,184 in 1890. These figures suggest that Union County's assessing procedures located new land, personal property, and polls for inclusion on the tax lists, while the board's exemptions to merchants and planters kept local capitalists' funds out of the tax collector's hands.[31]

With capital in hand, local developers turned to the task of protecting new investments, chiefly in cotton-producing tenant farms. The 1879 local-option stock law permitted township residents to vote for the first time on whether to enforce such regulations within a township's boundaries. The law allowed for the fencing of whole townships, for a special tax to finance the building and maintenance of fences, and for stiff penalties for violation. Persons who willfully injured or destroyed a public fence or who allowed their livestock to run at large within a fenced township faced fines of up to fifty dollars and jail sentences amounting to thirty days. Livestock found illegally at large could be impounded. If not redeemed, the animals could be sold after ten days' public notice was given, proceeds going to the errant beast's captor.[32]

[30]Ibid., vol. 2, Feb. 3, 1879, p. 32; ibid., Aug. 13, 1883, p. 374; ibid., vol. 3, April 2, 1888, p. 46; ibid., Aug. 3, 1891, p. 187.

[31]Ibid., vol. 3, April 2, 1888, p. 46; *Executive and Legislative Documents,* [from] 1870–'71, 1872–'73, 1873–'74, 1874–'75, 1876–77, 1883; *Public Documents of the General Assembly of North Carolina, Session 1879,* doc. no. 4, pp. 344, 359–67, doc. no. 5, pp. 263, 277–92; *North Carolina Executive and Legislative Documents, Session 1881,* doc. no. 3, pp. 178, 192–206, doc. no. 4, pp. 182, 197–211; "Act to Provide for the Collection of Taxes," 165–66 and 109–110.

[32]"An Act to Prevent Live Stock from Running at Large within Rowan, Davie, Cabarrus, and Other Counties," *Laws and Resolutions of the State of North Carolina, 1879,* 252–64.

Union County's commercial farmers had begun enclosing their lands in 1877. Some landowners formed private associations among themselves, joining their fences together and enforcing existing trespass laws on their property. Others approached the board of commissioners for permission to erect gates across public roads that passed through their lands. But effective fencing was delayed until 1882. Between 1879 and 1882 local developers organized a series of township elections that failed to approve the local-option stock law as a result of stiff local resistance. In October 1879 the first local stock-law election took place in Sandy Ridge Township, south of Monroe in the heart of Union County's cotton belt. Developers carried on a vigorous campaign there and predicted a "close race." In the November election, however, the measure failed by a vote of 175 to 97, with most favorable votes cast by commercial farmers. One writer noted that "the land owners at both precincts were, as a majority, in favor of 'Stock Law' and so voted."[33]

By 1882 Union County's board of commissioners felt that there existed sufficient support for the stock law to justify a countywide election. In February the board held elections in every township. Two townships, Goose Creek and Sandy Ridge, approved the measure and were ordered fenced. The results appeared so promising that the board ordered a second countywide election in March. Goose Creek and Sandy Ridge confirmed their votes, and Monroe Township also approved the law. The remaining townships, however, defeated the fence law by a combined vote of 826 to 194. The commissioners then deferred further elections on the stock-law question for the moment, appointed fence keepers for Monroe Township, and ordered that a fence be built around the township to connect with existing fences encircling Sandy Ridge and Goose Creek.[34]

The commissioners did not, however, abandon efforts to secure countywide adoption of the stock law. They simply changed tactics, now holding elections in each township one at a time, beginning in September 1882 with Jackson Township, where the closest defeats had occurred earlier. The board then held elections in one precinct of Lane Creek Township, where the vote had been relatively close. The outcomes of those elections do not appear in the board's records, but by January 1884 the commissioners had secured adoption of the 1879 stock law in every township. They declared the law in force throughout the county and ordered that all public fences be taken down, the rails sold, and all gates across public roads removed. Only private fences remained in the county, but to pen farmers' animals rather than to enclose crops. Commercial farmers now could protect their investments in crops and livestock at a minimal expense.[35]

[33] *Monroe Enquirer,* June 15, 1875, p. 4; ibid., Sept. 1, 1877, p. 1; ibid., Nov. 22, 1879, p. 3; Union County Board of Commissioners' Minutes, vol. 1, Feb. 4, 1878, p. 542; ibid., March 4, 1878, p. 567; ibid., vol. 2, Feb. 3, 1879, p. 32; ibid., March 3, 1879, p. 37; ibid., Oct. 6, 1879, pp. 82–83; ibid., Jan. 3, 1881, p. 167; ibid., Sept. 5, 1881, p. 213.

[34] Union County Board of Commissioners' Minutes, vol. 2, Jan. 2, 1882, p. 241; ibid., March 18, 1882, pp. 262–63; ibid., March 22, 1882, p. 264; ibid., April 12, 1882, pp. 273–74; ibid., May 1, 1882, pp. 275–76.

[35] Ibid., Sept. 4, 1882, p. 305; ibid., July 2, 1883, p. 367; ibid., Jan. 7, 1884, p. 399; ibid., Feb. 4, 1884, p. 409; ibid., Oct. 6, 1884, p. 497.

The equalization and stock-law campaigns together produced a profound change in Union County agriculture between 1880 and 1890. The total acreage under cultivation increased from 86,428 to 120,790. Old fields, which had decreased from 62,255 acres in 1870 to 40,587 in 1880, disappeared altogether by 1890. The agricultural expansion, however, produced only a modest increase in the output of cotton and did so at the expense of local food production. The number of 400-pound bales of cotton produced in the county rose from 8,336 in 1880 to 8,889 in 1890. Corn production, however, declined modestly from 338,520 bushels in 1880 to 327,731 in 1890. But from 1879 to 1888 the number of cattle produced in Union County declined from 11,668 to 5,054. The number of sheep decreased from 19,993 in 1880 to 5,885 in 1887. And the number of hogs dropped from 21,805 in 1878 to 6,597 in 1887. The slump in food production occurred unfortunately at a time when cotton prices declined steadily and food prices increased. As a result, the total value of Union County's agricultural production actually declined from $795,589 in 1880 to $724,270 in 1890, despite an expansion of cultivated land, a rise in overall production (including cotton), and a substantial increase in the value of the county's livestock production from $316,793 in 1880 to $384,350 in 1889. Land now produced cotton and corn and supported fewer, but more valuable, animals—all for external cash trade.[36]

Equalization and stock laws also produced important changes in land tenure. Although most small landowners continued to own and farm their land, two new kinds of farms appeared in Union County. First, small cotton plantations were eclipsed by large commercial operations, probably employing black wage laborers. The number of farms comprising 500 to 999 acres increased from 62 to 71, and the number of those exceeding 1,000 acres went from 7 to 21. Second, there was a large increase in the number of small tenant farms, probably operated by whites. The number of renters who farmed 20 to 49 acres, for example, increased from 3 in 1880 to 69 in 1890, and the number of sharecroppers who farmed plots ranging from 20 to 49 acres rose from 148 in 1880 to 449 in 1890.[37]

In sum, Union County's tax policies and stock laws promoted economic expansion, but they did not produce prosperity for most persons. Nearly 500 families for the first time grew cotton that constantly dropped in price. Moreover, they purchased foods at prices that rose in part because they produced less corn and livestock. Even many families that continued to own their land faced the prospect of losing everything to creditors. In 1890, 252 of Union County's farm-owning families owed money on land or a house that amounted to 45.5 percent of their property's total value. In addition, there were those who

[36]Census Office, *Tenth Census*, III, 129, 201, 237; U.S. Department of the Interior, Census Office, *Eleventh Census*, vol. VI: *Report on the Statistics of Agriculture of the United States* (Washington, D.C., 1895), 222, 379, 396; *Executive and Legislative Documents*, Session 1881 and 1883; *Public Documents of the State of North Carolina, Session 1889* [and] *1891*.

[37]Census Office, *Eleventh Census*, VI, 170–71.

labored for wages on the larger plantations. Men received between $6 and $13 per month; planters paid women about 20 percent less. In 1888 one Union County planter noted that "the laborers in my neighborhood are negroes and they are very much demoralized." Another planter observed that "the condition of the wage-hand and tenant [renter] is very bad in this county," although he thought that sharecroppers had fared even worse. Finally, even persons who escaped the countryside to seek work in Union County's railroad towns found little New South prosperity for themselves. In 1888 laborers in Monroe reported "a large surplus of labor here" and "a great want of steady employment." According to a "mechanic" in Monroe, "We have to work at a very low price, and then cannot get work much over half the time, the consequence is, we are obliged to run in debt to live." As a result, another Monroe laborer reported, "many working people are leaving here and seeking employment where they can get better wages."[38]

Economic decline among Union County farmers led to violence once again, but now committed by the developers. In what the *Monroe Express* called a "homicidal mania," disputes between employers and employees escalated to armed conflict, ending in uncounted (and doubtless many unreported) attacks, including at least nine deaths in a five-year period. McKee Secrest, who ran a saw mill three miles west of Monroe, for example, shot and killed his employee, Washington Helms, in August 1881. Secrest had employed Helms for several years and had authorized his employee to "take up a certain amount of credit at a store in Monroe." On the day of the murder, both parties appeared in Monroe, where Secrest claimed that Helms had overspent his credit limit and owed him some additional money besides. Later a quarrel ensued, and Secrest shot and killed his employee. Secrest was arrested and later indicted by a grand jury for murder. . . .[39]

The essential conflict between a developing capitalist economy and political and social power based on dependencies endured in Union County, as it did throughout the New South. . . . Development continued apace, and cotton tenantry spread to every part of the county. Poverty became and remained through 1940 the chief product of economic development in Union County. Perhaps some local residents recalled their forebears' belief, now demonstrated, that New South economic development was "taking the peoples Libertyes away by law power."[40]

---

[38] *First Annual Report of the Bureau of Labor Statistics of the State of North Carolina for the Year 1887* (Raleigh, 1887), 110; *Second Annual Report of the Bureau of Labor Statistics of the State of North Carolina for the Year 1888* (Raleigh, 1888), 135–203; *Fifth Annual Report of the Bureau of Labor Statistics of the State of North Carolina for the Year 1891* (Raleigh, 1892), 102–4.

[39] *Anson Times*, Sept. 1, 1881, p. 3.

[40] "To the Hon Legislature of North Carolina," June 7, 1852, petitions, box 8, Legislative Papers, sess. 1852 (North Carolina Division of Archives and History, Raleigh).

Wayne K. Durrill

William K. Durrill's research interests are primarily in nineteenth-century US history, especially the American South. He has written on topics as diverse as flag ceremonies in the Confederacy, the South during Reconstruction, and black communities before the Civil War. His book, *War of Another Kind: A Southern Community in the Great Rebellion* (1990) explores the disintegration of Southern social structures during the Civil War. In 1984, he received the Louis Pelzer Memorial Award from the Organization of American Historians for "Producing Poverty: Local Government and Economic Development in a New South County, 1874–1884," which appears in edited form in this volume. He is a professor of history at the University of Cincinnati.

QUESTIONS FOR CONSIDERATION

1. According to Durrill, in what ways did farming change in the South after 1870? In what ways did it remain the same?
2. How did the rise of "Conservative" politicians after 1870 help bring about these changes? What laws were passed to further these economic changes?
3. In what did ways merchants and commercial planters help foster economic changes?
4. Describe three ways in which small farmers reacted to economic changes.
5. Durrill makes the following claim at the end of his article: "Poverty became and remained through 1940 the chief product of economic development in Union County." Which factor, in your opinion, was the primary cause of this poverty in the midst of economic development? What was a secondary factor that was nonetheless important?
6. In what ways did these changes in the Southern economy after 1870 happen within the context of national industrialization in the last quarter of the nineteenth century?
7. What are some similarities and some differences between the situation of small white farmers in Durrill's article and black farmers after Emancipation as described in Foner's article located in this volume?

CHAPTER FOUR

Feminist Politics in the 1920s:
The National Woman's Party[1]

Nancy F. Cott

The National Woman's Party (NWP) is not well known. . . . Insofar as it is known, the party has a paradoxical image. In histories of the suffrage movement in the 1910s, it appears as the militant, "left" wing; in histories of women's reform movements of the 1920s, it appears as a clique of prosperous business and professional women, repellent to the Left. The one organization of women that openly declared itself feminist, it has attracted most of historians' blame for the "demise" of feminism after woman suffrage was obtained. . . .[2]

The NWP grew from the Congressional Union, the suffrage organization that Alice Paul and Lucy Burns founded when they broke with the leadership of the National American Woman Suffrage Association (NAWSA) early in 1913. Paul and Burns distinguished their approach from the mainstream, . . . as their Congressional Union evolved into the Woman's Party (1916) and the NWP (1917). A group of, by, and for women, it concentrated on the federal (rather than state) government, aiming to amend the United States Constitution to gain woman's rights. It used flamboyant publicity tactics, including street marches, . . . and . . . picketing of the White House and the Capitol. It also followed a "political" (rather than simply educative) strategy, trying to marshal women's votes in the states

---

[1]Interested students are encouraged to read this essay in the original form. Nancy F. Cott, "Feminist Politics in the 1920s: The National Woman's Party," *The Journal of American History* 71, no. 1 (June 1984), 43–68.

[2]See Ida Husted Harper, ed., *The History of Woman Suffrage*, vols. 5 and 6, 1900–1920 (New York, 1922); Eleanor Flexner, *Century of Struggle: The Woman 's Rights Movement in the United States* (Cambridge, Mass., 1959); Aileen S. Kraditor, *The Ideas of the Woman Suffrage Movement, 1890–1920* (New York, 1965); William P. O'Neill, *Everyone Was Brave: The Rise and Fall of Feminism in America* (Chicago, 1969); William Henry Chafe, *The American Woman: Her Changing Social, Economic, and Political Roles, 1920–1970* (New York, 1972); J. Stanley Lemons, *The Woman Citizen: Social Feminism in the 1920s* (Urbana, 1973); Susan D. Becker, *The Origins of the Equal Rights Amendment: American Feminism between the Wars* (Westport, Conn., 1981). The National Woman's Party Papers, deposited at the Library of Congress, are available in two microfilm sets, "National Woman's Party Papers: The Suffrage Years, 1913–1920" [hereafter NWP-P, 1913–1920] (Microfilming Corporation of America, 1982); and "National Woman's Party Papers, 1913–1974" [hereafter NWP-P, 1913–1974] (Microfilming Corporation of America, 1979).

where women were enfranchised to force "the party in power" (the Democratic party) to pass a woman suffrage amendment. Between 1914 and 1919, the group took risks; . . . and did not fail to rankle the stalwarts of the mainstream NAWSA. The party appealed to working-class women and . . . to left-wing women because of its militant tactics and its opposition to the government during wartime. It side-stepped gentility, at the same time that it appealed to wealthy socialites because of its newsworthiness and its strategy of lobbying national legislators, besides exhorting the man on the street. In 1914 Alva Belmont (widow to Vanderbilt and Belmont millions) became the party's financial angel and an important voice.[3]

. . . The NWP made waves beyond its size because of the variety, devotion, and vigor of its organizers and members.[4] The organization charted a course . . . toward a constitutional amendment for woman suffrage; and its heterogeneous member-ship worked toward that goal under control from above. "There is no difference of opinion in regard to Alice Paul in the Woman's Party," wrote Inez Haynes Irwin, the group's historian. "With one accord, they say 'She is the Party.' They regard her with an admiration which verges on awe." Paul seems never to have imagined any other than a tightly knit, ideologically pure, vanguard party. Though V. I. Lenin was probably far from her ken or sympathy, Paul's leadership style might be called "Leninist". . . . By virtually all accounts of the 1910s, Paul was charismatic . . . [Doris] Stevens declared, "I have seen her very presence in headquarters change in the twinkling of an eye the mood of fifty people. It is not through their affections that she moves them, but through a naked force, a vital force which is indefinable but of which one simply cannot be unaware."[5] Paul hewed to a narrow course with superb determination, letting other considerations fall aside. "The point is first, who is our enemy," she enunciated in August 1914, initiating the policy of "holding the party in power responsible," "and then, how shall that enemy be attacked?" "To count in an election you do not have to be the biggest Party; you have to be simply

---

[3]See Loretta Ellen Zimmerman, "Alice Paul and the National Woman's Party, 1912–1920," (Ph.D. diss., Tulane University, 1964); Sidney Roderick Bland, "Techniques of Persuasion: The National Woman's Party and Woman Suffrage, 1913–1919" (Ph.D. diss., George Washington University, 1972); and Christine A. Lunardini, "From Equal Suffrage to Equal Rights: The National Woman's Party, 1913–1923" (Ph.D. diss., Princeton University, 1981); Doris Stevens, *Jailed for Freedom* (New York, 1920); Inez Haynes Irwin, *The Story of the Woman's Party* (New York, 1921); and Caroline Katzenstein, *Lifting the Curtain: The State and National Woman Suffrage Campaigns in Pennsylvania as I Saw Them* (Philadelphia, 1955).

[4]Mabel Vernon interview by Amelia R. Fry, 1976, "Mabel Vernon: Speaker for Suffrage and Petitioner for Peace," 190–91, Suffragists Oral History Project (Bancroft Library, University of California, Berkeley); Alice Paul interview by Amelia R. Fry, 1976, "Conversations with Alice Paul: Woman Suffrage and the Equal Rights Amendment," 327, Suffragists Oral History Project; Loretta Ellen Zimmerman, "Alice Paul and the National Woman's Party,"243; Elsie Hill to Mrs. Dorothy C. Rice, March 30, 1921, NWP-P, 1913–1974; Inez Haynes Irwin, *Angels and Amazons: A Hundred Years of American Women* (Garden City, N.Y., 1933), 392.

[5]Irwin, *Story of the Woman's Party*, 15; Stevens, *Jailed for Freedom*, 17, 10–11; Marjory Nelson, "Ladies in the Streets: A Sociological Analysis of the National Woman's Party, 1910–1930" (Ph.D. diss., State University of New York at Buffalo, 1976), 315, 320–21; Bland, "Techniques of Persuasion," 78–79, 178. See also Lunardini, "From Equal Suffrage to Equal Rights," 118; Lavinia Dock referred tongue-in-cheek to "our Comrade Alice Paul Lenin." Lavinia Dock to Emma Wold, Jan. 1921, NWP-P, 1913–1974.

an independent Party that will stand for one object and that cannot be diverted from that object," she clarified two years later.[6] So long as Paul's object commanded as much fervor as the constitutional route to woman suffrage did, she was highly effective in inspiring and leading a vanguard party.

The NWP's 1917 strategy of picketing the White House (to persuade President Woodrow Wilson to lead the Congress to pass woman suffrage) and carrying the "strike" to jail when pickets were arrested was its most daring media ploy, but its decision in 1917 to decline any organizational declaration regarding the United States entry into the World War was equally indicative of its course. While the NAWSA pledged women's patriotism to the war effort, the NWP . . . refused commitment. In consequence . . . the NWP became a haven for socialist and pacifist suffragists and a de facto proponent of civil liberties during the war and postwar years 1917–1919. Although the NWP's direct action remained nonviolent, defensible as a form of free speech, some NAWSA loyalists decried the NWP as "the I.W.W. of the suffrage movement"; the police who held back NWP demonstrators at Wilson's 1919 embarkation for Europe called them "cannibals" and "Bolsheviks." Despite the NAWSA leadership's conviction that NWP actions were traitorous and counterproductive, and despite NWP scorn for the NAWSA's distrust, the different approaches of the two organizations seem to have complemented one another. The NWP endowed woman suffrage with high drama, and the NAWSA insistently pursued its legislative plan to increase through state victories the number of states whose senators and congressmen would support a constitutional amendment for woman suffrage. . . .[7]

The year 1920 was a crucial one for every woman suffrage organization, not only because the principal goal was attained, but also because that attainment was conditioned by world-historical events—the World War, the Russian Revolution, labor unrest on an unprecedented scale, the Red Scare, economic recession that made contemporaries sense that one era had ended and another had begun. . . .

By July 1920, a month before the final ratification of the Nineteenth Amendment, Belmont was stressing the need for the NWP to continue as an organization to "obtain for women full equality with men in all phases of life and make them a power in the life of the state," and Paul had enunciated as a worthy goal some form of "blanket" legislation that would remove all legal discriminations against women.[8] From September 1920 through February 1921, the party's inner circle, the National Executive Committee, met monthly to hash out resolutions to

[6]Irwin, *Story of the Woman's Party*, 75, 151.

[7]*New York Times*, Feb. 10, 1919, p. 4; Stevens, *Jailed for Freedom*, 332; Mari Jo Buhle, *Women and American Socialism, 1870–1920* (Urbana, 1981), 237–38; Carole A. Nichols, "A New Force in Politics: The Suffragists' Experience in Connecticut" (M.A. essay, Sarah Lawrence College, May 1979), esp. 39–43; Stevens, *Jailed for Freedom*, 250–51; Bland, "Techniques of Persuasion," 134–38; Flexner, *Century of Struggle*, 290–92; David Morgan, *Suffragists and Democrats: The Politics of Woman Suffrage in* America (East Lansing, 1972), 121–23; and Anne F. Scott and Andrew M. Scott, *One Half the People: The Fight for Woman Suffrage* (Philadelphia, 1975), 40–42.

[8]National Executive Committee, NWP, minutes, July 9, 1920, reel 114, part A, series 2, "National Woman's Party Papers, 1913–1974"; *New York Times*, July 18, 1920, sec. 6, p. 6; Peter Geidel, "The National Woman's Party and the Origins of the Equal Rights Amendment, 1920–23," *Historian*, 42 (Aug. 1980), 562.

present at the grand convention in February . . . [T]he leadership moved undeviatingly toward the majority resolution offered at the convention: that the NWP disband but immediately regroup under the same name, with its "immediate work" being "the removal of the legal disabilities of women."[9]

Hundreds of women arrived at the February convention expecting to vent their opinions on the future of the organization. . . . Crystal Eastman, a feminist-pacifist-socialist lawyer and cultural radical who had been among the inner circle since CU days, presented her program: to remove legal and customary barriers to women's self-realization, to remake marriage laws and public opinion to eliminate the homemaker-childrearer's economic dependence, to end laws prohibiting birth control, and to renovate the laws of inheritance, divorce, child custody, and sexual morality on the basis of sexual equality. Eastman predicted that "nobody that has a thread of modern feminism will care a rap" for the NWP if it adopted the "old-fashioned" aim to remove legal disabilities. Her proposals were voted down, nonetheless, almost two to one.[10]

The votes in support of the majority resolution—to disband, to regroup immediately under the same name, and to adopt the program of ending women's legal disabilities—were strong enough to suggest that the convention willingly supported Paul. . . . Eastman, in the *Liberator*, and Freda Kirchwey, in the *Nation*, wrote acerbic articles characterizing the NWP leadership as a "steamroller" and a "machine." Party members who identified themselves with the political Left, as Eastman and Kirchwey did, were generally disappointed with the convention's outcome. . . . Agnes Leach of New York objected that legal disabilities were "felt chiefly by women of property," who could take care of themselves. . . .[11]

Once a new initiation fee of ten dollars and annual dues of ten dollars were set, more were alienated. Beulah Amidon of South Dakota refused to recruit members at so high a fee, which she felt made the party "at once a conservative, property-holding, upper-crust group" with whom she was "out of sympathy." . . . The temporary chairman of the new party, Elsie Hill of Connecticut, who had joined as an organizer in 1913, remonstrated that both the Socialist party and the Industrial Workers of the World (IWW) asked for one dollar per month, or twelve dollars per year, from their members, that the nominal membership fee required by the NWP during the suffrage campaign had made Paul and others into "beggars" of rich women, and that the organization now had to be self-supporting. "The work must be supported by those who feel the need, and direction of it must be in the hands of those who really care."[12]

---

[9]National Executive Committee, NWP, minutes, Sept. 10, Oct. 8, Nov. 16, Dec. 10, 1920, Jan. 22, Feb. 14, 1921, NWP-P, 1913–1974.

[10]Charles DeBenedetti, *Origins of the Modem American Peace Movement, 1915–1929* (Millwood, N.Y., 1978), 86–97; Charles Chatfield, *For Peace and Justice: Pacifism in America, 1914–1941* (Knoxville, 1971), 147–50; NWP Convention, transcript, Feb. 15–18, 1921, pp. 129–34.

[11]Crystal Eastman, "Alice Paul's Convention," *Liberator* 4 (April 1921), 9–10; Freda Kirchwey, "Alice Paul Pulls the Strings," *Nation*, March 2, 1921, pp. 332–33. Rebecca Hourwich to Hill, May 6, 1921, NWP-P, 1913–1974; Agnes B. Leach to Paul, March 25, 1921, ibid.; Leach to Mrs. [Elizabeth] Rogers, Feb. 25, 1921, ibid.; Sylvie Thygeson to Hill, March 30, 1921, ibid.

[12]Beulah Amidon to National Woman's Party, n.d. [April 1921], NWP-P, 1913–1974"; to Emma C. Bancroft, March 26, 1921, ibid.

Hill's response to a convention delegate displeased with the dismissal of disarmament shed additional light on the party's stance at that transitional moment. . . . In Hill's view the "natural thing" for women was "always to be drawn hither and thither and give their feeble undominating support to many very appealing issues," . . . [and] "that women have got to be more powerful in society before they can aid conclusively the real issues which affect them vitally." . . . Hill felt strongly that "the greatest work" for the NWP was "to stick to the fight to increase the power of women, and their daring to use what power they have in securing immediate results, instead of merely announcing many beliefs." . . .[13]

The machinations surrounding the convention made it clear that the NWP's single-issue politics and top-down control were intentional preferences of its leadership. . . . In 1916 the party had determined to align women voters against Wilson purely because of the suffrage question. . . . In 1917 the party had refused to take an organizational stand on the World War, to avoid committing its membership to anything but woman suffrage. In 1920–1921 the goal of woman suffrage having been won, the party's leadership moved to define a new single issue. To "remove all remaining forms of the subjection of women" became the party's new rallying cry; but since, in Paul's view, people needed "a simple, concrete object" to be mobilized, the removal of legal disabilities was to be the immediate work. Women who stayed with the party in the 1920s accepted the conditions that Paul's leadership imposed. . . .[14]

The NWP's new priorities, and Paul's ruthlessness in paring away "diversions," were clarified in a little-known controversy over black women voters at the convention. Despite early links between the woman's rights and the antislavery movements, the suffrage movement after 1890 failed to take a stand against the oppression of blacks, knuckling under to the racism of the surrounding society, sacrificing principle and the interests or pride of black people, if that seemed advantageous to white women's obtaining the vote. . . . During its "militant" years the NWP sought and gained the support of some black women, including two outstanding leaders, Ida B. Wells-Barnett and Mary Church Terrell. . . .[15]

When the February 1921 convention was announced, Mary White Ovington, a white socialist, feminist, and founding member of the NAACP, wrote to all

---

[13]Hill to Willystine Goodsell, April 1, 1921, ibid.

[14]National Executive Committee, NWP, minutes, Jan. 22, 1921, ibid; Nichols, "New Force in Politics," 37–43.

[15]Kraditor, *Ideas of the Woman Suffrage Movement*, 163–218; Rosalyn Terborg-Penn, "Discrimination against Afro-American Women in the Woman's Movement, 1830–1920," in *The Afro-American Woman: Struggles and Images*, ed. Sharon Harley and Rosalyn Terborg-Penn (Port Washington, N.Y., 1978), 17–27; Angela Y. Davis, *Women, Race, and Class* (New York, 1981), 118; Bland, "Techniques of Persuasion," 53–55; Ida B. Wells-Barnett to Paul, March 21, 1921, NWP-P, 1913–1974; and Paul to Wells-Barnett, March 24, 1921, ibid; Ida B. Wells-Barnett, *Crusade for Justice: The Autobiography of Ida B. Wells*, ed. Alfreda M. Duster (Chicago, 1970); Mary Church Terrell, *A Colored Woman in a White World* (Washington, D.C., 1940), 316–17; NWP headquarters to Mary Church Terrell, April 24, 1919, item 631, container 5, Mary Church Terrell Papers (Library of Congress); NWP headquarters to Terrell [Jan. 1921], item 214, container 6, ibid.; and Walter White to Terrell, March 14, 1919, item 615, container 4, ibid.

members of the NWP National Advisory Council whom she knew personally, urging them to arrange for a black woman to address the group. Describing how prospective black voters in the South were being terrorized, Ovington stressed that black women would never vote unless their rights were upheld by all other women. She urged that the convention appoint a committee to investigate and take action on this issue. . . . The response from the NWP headquarters was negative. Headquarters secretary Emma Wold, writing for Paul, explained that the convention could give the podium only to groups with legislative programs for women or with feminist aims. The point was to ensure that the NWP, in choosing its goals, did not duplicate another group's work. Since Mary C. Talbert of the National Association of Colored Women's Clubs, the speaker whom Ovington recommended, represented a group with a "racial," not "feminist," intent, she could not be featured. Wold emphasized that it was the definition of the convention program rather than lack of concern about blacks that caused this refusal. She encouraged the appointment of black women as delegates who could speak from the floor. Headquarters did make efforts to facilitate the inclusion of blacks in state delegations. . . .[16]

Black women's formal presentation of their concerns at the convention was more significant, however, and here there was no satisfaction. . . . When Florence Kelley, leader of the National Consumers' League and a member of the NWP National Executive Committee, intervened on behalf of Ovington's plea, Paul gave her a more complicated explanation. Next on the NWP's agenda, Paul said, and "by far the most important item of their immediate program" was to push for legislation "enforcing" woman suffrage by means of federal penal sanctions against any state registration or election official who discriminated against women. The proposed legislation was presumably aimed at southern states that disfranchised black women. Paul gave Kelley the impression that she feared Talbert's "inflaming" the southerners at the convention, once the enforcement bill became known. Kelley concluded that "Miss Paul, as a Quaker woman is of course entirely in sympathy with Mrs. Talbert and her work" but "as a tactician" denied the request for Talbert to speak from the podium. The NWP did in fact have an enforcement bill introduced to Congress, on December 30, 1920, by Wesley Jones, Republican senator from Washington.[17]

A group of black women subsequently took up the second part of Ovington's request, for an investigation of voting rights violations. Early in February a large

---

[16]Mary White Ovington to Harriot Stanton Blatch, Dec. 3, 1920, "National Woman's Party 1920–21" folder, container 384, series C, NAACP Papers (Library of Congress); Ovington to NWP Advisory Council members, Dec. 6, Dec. 23, 1920, ibid.;Wold to Blatch, Dec. 29, 1920, ibid.; Ovington to Lucy Burns, Dec. 17, 1920, with appended handwritten note by Burns to NWP headquarters, NWP-P, 1913–1974; Wold to Burns, Jan. 14, 1921, ibid.

[17]Florence Kelley to Ovington, Dec. 22, 1920, "National Woman's Party 1920–21" folder, container 384, series C, NAACP Papers; *Congressional Record*, 66 Cong., 3 sess., Dec. 30, 1920, p. 808; Mary Winsor to Ovington, Dec. 31, 1920, "National Woman's Party 1920–21" folder, container 384, series C, NAACP Papers; clipping sent by Mary Talbert to Ovington, ibid.; Anna A. Clemons to Secretary of the NWP, Oct. 10, 1920, NWP-P, 1913–1974; Headquarters Secretary [Wold] to Miss Clemons, Oct. 20, 1920, ibid.; Clemons to Wold, Oct. 24, 1920, ibid.; Wold to Clemons, Oct. 28, 1920, ibid.; and Wold to Clemons, Nov. 2, 1920, ibid.

delegation claiming to represent five million black women in fourteen states called on Paul to point out violations of black voting rights in 1920 and to ask for the opportunity to call the NWP's attention to that travesty of the Nineteenth Amendment. Paul gave them only the same opportunity other individuals had—to speak as delegates from the convention floor. At the convention Ella Rush Murray, a white delegate from New York and member of the National Advisory Council, managed to present a minority resolution directing the NWP to form a committee to pressure Congress to investigate violations of the Nineteenth Amendment.... The resolution was voted down. In the *Nation* Kirchwey asserted that "Miss Paul was indifferent to" the appeal of the black women and "resented the presence of the delegation." Kirchwey reported that black delegates were denied use of the elevator at the convention; moreover, she voiced a rumor that the NWP had agreed not to raise the race issue as a price for the ratification of woman suffrage in the South.[18]

Paul's view of the matter differed entirely. In a lengthy letter to the *Nation* (never printed and perhaps not even sent) and in letters to her intimates, Paul denied all of Kirchwey's damaging allegations. The elevator story was a mistake: black women had been asked by the elevator boy to use the stairs but so had all the white women, until someone complained, whereupon everyone was allowed to use the elevator. Paul asserted, more significantly, that the NWP had never made a "deal" to ignore the racial question in the South but always as a general policy ignored all issues outside the woman suffrage amendment. She maintained that she had made sure, after receiving the black delegation, that they had the same opportunity everyone else did to present their views from the convention floor, although she anticipated southern white delegates' hostility. Indeed, the entire white delegation from North Carolina at first refused to register, in protest against the black women's presence, and only with difficulty were persuaded to attend at all; they stayed away from the ceremonial dinner, where they would have had to eat with black women....[19] In Paul's view no discrimination and no "machine" had operated. The convention had passed over black voting rights, as it had passed over disarmament and birth control, because its consensus genuinely formed around another goal, that of eliminating women's legal disabilities....[20]

---

[18]Inez Richardson to Paul, Feb. 2, 1921, NWP-P, 1913–1974; Paul to Mrs. Lawrence [Dora] Lewis, March 23, 1921, ibid.; Paul to Mrs. John Rogers, March 24, 1921, ibid.; Ella Rush Murray, "The Woman's Party and the Violation of the 19th Amendment," *Crisis* 21 (April 1921), 259–61; NWP Convention, transcript, Feb. 15–18, 1921, p. 61; Kirchwey, "Alice Paul Pulls the Strings," 333; Kelley to Mrs. [Dora] Lewis, Feb. 28, March 7, 1921, NWP-P, 1913–1974; Ella Rush Murray to editor, *Nation*, March 23, 1921, p. 434.

[19]Paul to Mrs. Lawrence [Dora] Lewis, March 23, 1921, NWP-P, 1913–74; Paul to Mrs. John Rogers, March 24, 1921, ibid.; Dora Lewis to Mrs. Brannon, March 9, 1921, ibid.; National Chairman [Elsie Hill] to Olympia Brown, March 8, 1921, ibid.; Dora Lewis to "Dearest Paulie" [Paul], April 11, 1921, ibid.

[20]Kirchwey, "Alice Paul Pulls the Strings," 332, 333; Juliet Barrett Roublee to Paul, Feb. 5, 1921, NWP-P, 1913–1974; NWP headquarters secretary to Roublee, Feb. 8, 1921, ibid.; Mary Ware Dennett, to Paul, Jan. 21, Feb. 3, 1921, ibid.; Mrs. Lawrence Lewis to Dennett, Feb. 4, 1921, ibid.; Marion May to Paul, Feb. 9, [1921], ibid.; Wold to Ethel McC. Adamson, Feb. 12, 1921, ibid.; Wold to Dennett, telegram, Feb. 14, 1921, ibid.

It was a great credit to Paul and her immediate lieutenants that they asserted the ongoing need for an association dedicated to women's power, not to social service or to good government, but to "the removal of all remaining forms of subjection" of the female sex. The treatment of black women's concerns at the convention forewarned, however, that the party's interpretation of equal rights would narrow, rather than expand, its purview and its constituency. Paul presumed that equality of legal rights was, like woman suffrage, a "purely feminist" program on which women could unite regardless of their disagreements on other issues. Instead of encompassing the issue of black women's voting rights in the circle of women's legal equality, Paul regarded it as a diversion, and she regarded it as a diversion because black women were suffering an injustice imposed, not by sex, but by race—black men were similarly disfranchised. . . . That Paul's outlook was at least as much due to her conception of the viability of single-issue politics as it was to racism is strongly suggested by her similar attitude at the convention toward birth control as a "diversion" from the principal route. The party's refusal to declare on any issue besides the woman suffrage amendment had been consistent with heterogeneity among its membership during the suffrage campaign, and Paul envisioned no difference in procedure for the future. But in the case of black women's voting rights, Paul's newly defined "simple, concrete object" excluded a group of women. The black women's question at the convention was the first clear indication that in claiming to make equal rights—intrinsically so much thornier to define and to pursue than suffrage was—stand for and speak to all women, the NWP would stand for and speak to fewer and fewer women.[21]

Besides those who did not join the reorganized NWP because their principal goal, suffrage, had been achieved, many women more strongly committed to black rights, pacifism, birth control, or social revolution departed. "I do not feel the interest in the new Woman's Party which seems to fill the hearts of some of the old group," wrote Jessie Hardy MacKaye, deserting to pacifism. . . . Two months after the convention, the new NWP had 151 paid members—as compared with a membership total between 35,000 and 60,000 at its height in 1919–1920. By dunning people for earlier pledges as small as $1, by selling whatever was salable from the old headquarters, by enlisting new "founders" at $1,000 apiece, and charging $10 for new members to join, the NWP paid off its $12,000 debt from the suffrage years in fairly short order, nonetheless. Small and large donations—the latter mainly from Belmont—kept the group solvent.[22] And membership grew, though it never exceeded—and probably fell far below—the party's claim of 10,000 during the 1920s. Recognizing the motivation toward feminism among women at work, especially in professional and semiprofessional fields, the NWP

---

[21]Nelson, "Ladies in the Streets," 201–6; Caroline Spencer to Paul, Oct. 10, 1920, NWP-P, 1913–1974.

[22]Jessie Hardy MacKaye to Hill, March 21, 1921, NWP-P, 1913–1974; Pollitzer to Mrs. [Dora] Lewis, April 13, 1921, ibid.; Hill to Rice, March 30, 1921, ibid.; Irwin, *Angels and Amazons*, 392–93; Dora Lewis to Mrs. Alva Belmont, March 9, 1921, NWP-P, 1913–1974; Becker, *Origins of the Equal Rights Amendment*, 38–41.

recruited members by structuring occupational councils: the Government Workers, Industrial Workers, Physicians, Homemakers councils, and so on, headed whenever possible by famous women such as Ruth Hale (journalists), Zona Gale (Authors), Lavinia Dock (Nurses), and Ethel Barrymore (Actresses).[23]

To translate "the removal of legal disabilities" into legislation was the prime task. Paul had been experimenting with forms for a constitutional amendment to end sex discrimination in law even before the convention gave its mandate. As a sequel to their strategy in the suffrage campaign, NWP leaders clearly preferred the "clean sweep" approach of amending the Constitution.... Party leaders began surveying state legal codes for sex discriminations, conferring with lawyers, drumming up attendance for a delegation to President Warren G. Harding, and drafting numerous versions of equal rights legislation and amendments for the state as well as the federal level.[24]

When the issue of laws that protected women's hours, wages, and conditions of work came up, as it immediately did, NWP leaders at first made exceptions to their blanket legislation plans. For example, in March 1921 Paul advised the chairman of the Massachusetts NWP to

> be very certain that none of the legislation which you introduce in any way disturbs any protective legislation that may have been passed in your state for the welfare of women. I do not think we want to interfere in any way with the so called welfare legislation that has been passed at the instance of the Consumers League and other organizations for the purpose of protecting women from night work and from too long hours of labor, even though this legislation may not be equal for men and women. That is, it seems to me when there is an inequality in which the position of women is better than that of men, we do not want to bring the standard for women down to that of men, but want, on the contrary, to bring that of men up to the standard existing for women.

... Members of women's groups who had led in creating sex-based protective legislation were becoming nervous and distrustful, suspecting that the NWP was less interested in preserving labor laws than in attaining "equal rights" and fearing that any blanket legislation, even with safeguarding clauses, would endanger welfare provisions for women and would throw the question of industrial protection into the reactionary courts.[25]

[23]*New York Times*, May 29, 1922, p. 10; Ethel Smith to Belle Sherwin, May 10, 1926, folder 42, National Women's Trade Union League Papers (Schlesinger Library); Mary Anderson to Mary Mundt, Sept. 24, 1926, folder 11, Mary Anderson Papers (Schlesinger Library); National Council, NWP, minutes, Dec. 5, 1927, NWP-P, 1913–1974; E. A. Crosby to Alma Lutz, May 23, 1936, folder 68, Lutz Collection; "Report of Organization Chairman," draft, folder 23, Lutz Collection.

[24]Katherine Fisher to Paul, Nov. 8, 1920, NWP-P, 1913–1974; Paul to Hill, telegram, Jan. 4, 1921, ibid.; Eva Epstein Shaw to Paul, Jan. 4, 1921, ibid.; Boeckel to Mr. Brigham, Jan. 28, 1921, ibid.

[25]Paul to Katherine Morey, March 20, 1921, NWP-P, 1913–1974." Similar sentiments are in Hill to Kelley [early 1921], ibid.; Hill to Mrs. Florence Kennedy [Kelley], March 21, 1921, ibid.; Temporary Secretary to Shippen Lewis, April 1, 1921, ibid.; Hill to Shippen Lewis, April 7, 1921, ibid.; rough draft of Paul to Florence Sanville, April 2, 1921, ibid; Peter Geidel, "The National Woman's Party and the Origins of the Equal Rights Amendment" (M.A. thesis, Columbia University, 1977), chapter 3.

Meanwhile, differences of opinion within the NWP were surfacing. A few members had for some time seen sex-based protective legislation as only another form of sex discrimination and opposed it. . . . Paul seems to have favored [protective] legislation early on. Before the suffrage campaign she (like many other suffragists) had worked in settlement houses and with wage-earning women. Her letters of 1920–1921 affirming her desire to preserve labor legislation for women sound sincere. During 1921, however, Gail Laughlin . . . who . . . opposed labor legislation restricted to women, seems to have exerted greater influence on Paul. . . . By late November the handwriting appeared on the wall as Paul explained . . ., "Personally, I do not believe in special protective labor legislation for women. It seems to me that protective labor legislation should be enacted for women and men alike in a trade or in a geographical district and not along sex lines. I think that enacting labor laws along sex lines is erecting another handicap for women in the economic struggle." The NWP was still trying to draft an amendment that would preserve special labor legislation, nonetheless, and continued to introduce state equal rights bills with safeguards through the following spring.[26]

At Kelley's behest, Paul and three other NWP members met in December 1921 with leaders of the League of Women Voters, the National Women's Trade Union League, the Woman's Christian Temperance Union, and the General Federation of Women's Clubs to discuss the amendment now proposed by the NWP: "No political, civil or legal disabilities or inequalities on account of sex, or on account of marriage unless applying alike to both sexes, shall exist within the United States or any place subject to their jurisdiction." Kelley asked Paul to hold the amendment back until the safety of the labor laws could be assured; she proposed that "civil" and "legal" be removed from the wording. . . . Kelley disapproved of blanket equal rights measures, regardless of safeguards, thinking they were "as dangerous as anything can possibly be" in the hands of the courts. At the meeting Paul was her one-issue self, asserting that pursuit of equal legal rights, not concern for other legislation, was her organization's mandate. . . . Two other NWP members present, however—Dora Lewis and Maud Younger— said they strongly supported the eight-hour day and minimum wage for women. . . . Paul refused Kelley's suggestion about wording because, she said, it would render the amendment worthless, but she welcomed others. Ethel Smith of the Women's Trade Union League and Maud Wood Park of the League of Women Voters left the meeting very worried about "a cleavage among women . . . which would be most deplorable and harmful to women's interests" though not at all willing themselves to temper their opposition to an equal rights amendment. Kelley was deeply distressed about the threat to welfare legislation. All felt that compromise was unlikely. By mid-1922 Kelley's, Ethel Smith's, and Park's organizations, and the American Federation of Labor (AFL) and the

26Paul to Jane Norman Smith, Nov. 29, 1921, folder 110, Jane Norman Smith Collection (Schlesinger Library).

American Home Economics Association besides, had gone on record opposing blanket equal rights legislation.[27]

Already, each side on the question of an equal rights amendment thought the other intransigent, although debate within the NWP went on. At the February meeting of the National Advisory Council, Caroline Spencer of Colorado introduced an amendment worded, "Equality of the sexes shall not be denied or abridged on account of sex or marriage. " She argued that the NWP should not be concerned with the fate of special labor legislation. . . . In April, Laughlin communicated her views, which became definitive. She mollified those who still favored sex-based labor legislation by reasoning, lawyer-like, that the equal rights amendment declared women's freedom of contract no more strongly than did the Fifth and Fourteenth amendments, already on the books and more than once overridden in the name of the state's police power. Laughlin herself strongly opposed sex-based legislation. "If women can be segregated as a class for special legislation along any line," she asserted, "the same classification can be used for special restrictions along any other line which may, at any time, appeal to the caprice or prejudice of our legislatures." If sex-based laws were not abolished and prohibited, "the advancement of women in business and industry will be stopped and women relegated to the lowest, worst paid labor."[28]

. . . At a grand conference staged in Seneca Falls, New York, in November 1923 to commemorate the seventy-fifth anniversary of Stanton's Declaration of Sentiments, the NWP introduced an equal rights amendment stating, "Men and women shall have equal rights throughout the United States and every place subject to its jurisdiction. " The amendment was introduced into Congress on December 10, 1923.[29]

Forging ahead, the NWP cut its links with most women connected to the labor movement, who remained convinced of the need for sex-specific protection. The few NWP members with strong labor attachments, such as [Harriet Stanton] Blatch, insisted that trade union organizing, not special legislation, should protect women workers' interests. The NWP presented its opposition to sex-based legislation as a positive program of industrial equality, but only a handful of working-class activists agreed. Representatives of the AFL and of several

---

[27]"Conference on So-called 'Equal Rights' Amendment Proposed by the National Woman's Party [Dec. 4, 1921]," typescript, reel 2, National Women's Trade Union League Papers (Library of Congress); "Conference Held December 4, 1921," NWP-P,1913–1974; Kelley to Hill, March 23, 1921, ibid; Ethel Smith to Members and Friends, Dec. 12, 1921, folder 378, Consumers League of Massachusetts Collection (Schlesinger Library); Pollitzer to Jane Norman Smith, Jan. 5, 1922, folder 110, Jane Norman Smith Collection.

[28]National Council, NWP, minutes, Feb. 14, 1921, NWP-P, 1913–1974; See also National Council, NWP, minutes, Dec. 17, 1921, ibid; Gail Laughlin to Fellow Members of National Council, April 7, 1921, National Council, NWP, minutes, April 11, 1921, NWP-P, 1913–1974; Geidel, "National Woman's Party and the Origin of the Equal Rights Amendment" [Historian], 576–77; Paul to Jane Norman Smith, Feb. 20, 1923, folder 111, Jane Norman Smith Collection.

[29]National Council, NWP, minutes, June 19, 1923, NWP-P, 1913–1974.

international unions as well as a lengthy list of women's groups voiced opposition at the first Senate subcommittee hearings on the equal rights amendment. . . .[30]

The arguments against the equal rights amendment offered by the various groups overlapped. They assumed that an amendment would invalidate sex-based labor laws or, at least, throw them (and welfare laws designed for mothers and widows) into the courts for protracted argument, during which time women would lose needed benefits. They argued that sex discriminations would be more efficiently and accurately removed from legal codes by attacking each case. Opponents of the amendment asserted that women workers, wary of employers' freedom to exploit them, valued sex-based labor legislation and that maximum-hour laws for women had benefited men, too, in factories where male workers could not continue operations once female employees had left for the day. . . . They declared that only the elite who did not have to work at all or professional women whose conditions of work were entirely different could possibly denigrate the benefits of protective laws. They regularly accused the NWP of being the unwitting tool (at best) or the paid servant of rapacious business interests, although no proof was ever brought forward.[31]

In the NWP's view the equal rights amendment was the logical sequel to woman suffrage, the fulfillment of Susan B. Anthony's vision. The many differences in state codes and practices in sex discriminations made a constitutional amendment the most direct route to equal rights. Protective laws that classed women with children as "the industrial and political wards of the state" only manifested women's long history of economic dependence and served to preserve the most lucrative and interesting jobs for men. . . . By eliminating "anachronism" in the law, the amendment would encourage women to become self-respecting citizens, to slough off their history of subservience and their embedded

---

[30]*Equal Rights*, Dec. 22, 1923, p. 358; Mary Anderson, *Woman at Work: The Autobiography of Mary Anderson as Told to Mary N. Winslow* (Minneapolis, 1951), 159–72; Becker, *Origins of the Equal Rights Amendment*, 198–234; Judith Anne Sealander, "The Woman's Bureau, 1920–1950: Federal Reaction to Female Wage Earning" (Ph.D. diss., Duke University, 1977), 196–220; Blatch to Hill, March 22, NWP-P, 1913–1974; Blatch to Headquarters, April 8, 1921, ibid.

[31]Florence Kelley, "Shall Women Be Equal before the Law? No," *Nation*, April 12, 1922, p. 421; Florence Kelley, "The Equal Rights Amendment: Why Other Women Groups Oppose It," *Good Housekeeping* 78 (March 1924), 19, 162–65; Kelley to Mrs. [Dora] Lewis, March 7, 1921, NWP-P, 1913–1974; Kelley to Freda Kirchwey, Jan. 16, 1922, "Equal Rights Amendment Correspondence" folder, box C4, National Consumers' League Papers (Library of Congress); Silas Bent, "The Women's War," *New York Times*, Jan. 14, 1923; Ethel M. Smith, "Working Women's Case against 'Equal Rights,'" *New York Times*, Jan. 20, 1924; Ethel M. Smith, "What Is Sex Equality and What Are the Feminists Trying to Accomplish," *Century Magazine* 118 (May 1929), 96–106; Mary Van Kleeck, "Women and Machines," *Atlantic Monthly* 127 (Feb. 1921), 250–60; Alice Hamilton, draft of letter to Mrs. [Edith Houghton] Hooker, Jan. 16, 1922, folder 19, Alice Hamilton Collection (Schlesinger Library); Alice Hamilton, "The Blanket Amendment—A Debate: II—Protection for Women Workers," *Forum* 72 (Aug. 1924), 152–60; Elizabeth Glendower Evans, "The Woman's Party—Right or Wrong? I. The Woman's Party Is Wrong," *New Republic*, Sept. 26, 1923, p. 123; Mary Anderson, "Should There Be Labor Laws for Women? Yes," *Good Housekeeping* 81 (Sept. 1925), 53, 166, 169–70, 173–74, 176, 179–80; Clara Mortenson Beyer, "Do Women Want Protection? What Is Equality?" *Nation*, Jan. 31, 1923, p. 116.

psychology of the unpaid worker. Women workers' real interests lay in obtaining equal access to job opportunities and to trade union organization, the NWP maintained. . . . At the same time, the NWP expressed no opposition to protective labor legislation as such or to protection of motherhood, so long as neither legally treated women "as a class."[32]

This is not the place to analyze the controversy over the equal rights amendment in its full complexity, except to say that the opponents' attempts to portray the amendment as "class" legislation were simplistic, just as the proponents' attempts to portray it as legislation affecting only sex equality understated the case. Neither side acknowledged the real ambiguities and complications of the workings of sex-based protective legislation at the time. While the antiamendment side was right, in that protective laws had improved conditions for the great majority of women in industry, the proamendment side was also right, in that the laws had limited women's opportunities in the labor market and had helped to sustain the notion that women were dependent and secondary wage earners.[33] Supporters of protective legislation did not see that their expectations of women, rooted in biological and customary notions of women's place and purpose, helped to confirm women's second-class position in the economy. Nor did advocates of the equal rights amendment recognize the need protective legislation addressed or acknowledge that their program of equal rights would not in itself free women's economic opportunity from the stranglehold of the domestic stereotype.

When the Supreme Court in 1923 used reasoning consonant with the NWP's to invalidate the minimum-wage law covering women in the District of Columbia, the party's new newspaper, *Equal Rights*, applauded but deferred: "It is not within the province of the Woman's Party, as a purely feminist organization, to discuss the constitutional question involved or to discuss the merits of minimum wage legislation as a method of bettering labor conditions. On these points we

---

[32]Elsie Hill, "Shall Women Be Equal before the Law? Yes!" *Nation*, April 12, 1922, pp. 419–20; Doris Stevens, "The Blanket Amendment—A Debate: I—Suffrage Does Not Give Equality," *Forum* 72 (Aug. 1924), 145–52; Harriot Stanton Blatch, "Do Women Want Protection? Wrapping Women in Cotton-Wool," *Nation*, Jan. 31, 1923, pp. 115–16; Lemons, *Woman Citizen*, 184–99; Chafe, *American Woman*, 112–32; O'Neill, *Everyone Was Brave*, 274–94; Becker, *Origins of the Equal Rights Amendment*, 121–51; Geidel, "The National Woman's Party and the Origins of the Equal Rights Amendment" [M.A. thesis]; Sheila M. Rothman, *Woman's Proper Place: A History of Changing Ideals and Practices, 1870 to the Present* (New York, 1978), 153–65; Alice Kessler-Harris, *Out to Work: A History of Wage-Earning Women in the United States* (New York, 1982), 194–95, 205–12; Josephine Goldmark, *Impatient Crusader* (Urbana, 1953), 180–88.

[33]Kessler-Harris, *Out to Work*, 200–205, 212–14; James Weinstein, *The Corporate Ideal in the Liberal State, 1900–1918* (Boston, 1968), 43–45; Elizabeth Faulkner Baker, "At the Crossroads in the Legal Protection of Women in Industry," *Annals of the American Academy of Political and Social Science*, 143 (May 1929), esp. 277; Rothman, *Woman's Proper Place*, 162–64; Nancy Schrom Dye, *As Equals and as Sisters: Feminism, the Labor Movement, and the Women's Trade Union League of New York* (Columbia, Mo., 1980), 159–60; Olive Banks, *Faces of Feminism: A Study of Feminism as a Social Movement* (New York, 1981), 115; and Judith A. Baer, *The Chains of Protection: The Judicial Response to Women's Labor Legislation* (Westport, Conn., 1978).

express no opinion."[34] Just as black voting rights had been judged outside the "purely feminist;" so was the betterment of labor conditions. That single-mindedness made the NWP virtually anathema to labor and the Left. In the 1920s context of Republican domination, with business in the saddle and with labor interests losing out in both trade union organization and state protection, to express no policy but equal rights for women was to affirm the status quo in every other respect. . . .

The NWP followed its exclusion-in-effect of blacks and of labor interests—though in the case of the latter the process was certainly not one-sided—with a decision in 1928 that alienated its adherents and potential adherents among Democrats. Standing on its head the earlier policy of "holding the party in power responsible" for failure to pass the desired amendment, the NWP formally endorsed the Republican ticket. Herbert Hoover's vice-presidential running mate, Charles Curtis, had been responsible for introducing the equal rights amendment in the Senate. The NWP had sent speakers to exhort equal rights planks to both the Republican and the Democratic conventions in the summer of 1928, with mixed results. The Democratic party adopted a straddling plank that linked women's welfare with children's; the Republican party endorsed the notion of women's equality but not the amendment. At a special conference at headquarters early in September, the NWP under the chairmanship of Jane Norman Smith decided to endorse Hoover and Curtis.

The rationale was that the Republican ticket, with Curtis on it, offered the best likelihood of success for the equal rights amendment. Alfred E. Smith, the Democratic candidate, had made clear his support for sex-based protective legislation. The Socialist candidate, Norman Thomas, had stated his opposition to the amendment. The Prohibitionist candidate endorsed the amendment, but he was not on the ballot in every state. NWP publicity emphasized that solely the parties' positions relative to the amendment dictated its endorsement; its intent was to make the amendment an election issue. Formally and informally the NWP reminded all that it was following its characteristic mode of pressure on whatever party needed pressing: in 1916 it had thrown its weight against the Democrats; in 1920 it had picketed the Republican convention to speed ratification of the woman suffrage amendment by recalcitrant Republican-controlled state legislatures; in 1924 it had supported independent and third-party female candidates for Congress (all running against Republicans). The 1928 position was another instance of "remaining independent to use our votes in the way that we decide will be of greatest help to Equal Rights."[35]

---

[34]*Equal Rights*, April 21, 1923, p. 76.

[35]*Equal Rights*, June 23, 1928, p. 155; ibid., July 7, 1928, p. 171; ibid., July 14, 1928, pp. 181–82;ibid., Sept. 22, 1928, pp. 258–61; ibid., Sept 29, 1928, p. 269; ibid., Nov. 3, 1928, p. 306; National Council, NWP, minutes, Sept. 11, 1928, NWP-P, 1913–1974; Jane Norman Smith to Member of the Woman's Party, Oct. 8, 1928, ibid.; Vernon to Mrs. Rilla Nelson, Sept. 17, 1928, box 1, Lucia Voorhes Grimes Collection, Michigan Historical Collections (Bentley Historical Library, University of Michigan, Ann Arbor).

That decision aroused immediate—and in some cases fatal—remonstrance from some leading members, both old and new. Lavinia Dock, one of the party's remaining socialists, most picturesquely objected, "I could no more cast a vote for the Republican Party than I could swallow a large, smooth, green caterpillar"; Sue Shelton White, a Tennessee Democrat, disavowed the party's choice and never came back to the fold; Emma C. Johnson, a founder six or seven years earlier, saw the decision as "a fair piece of 'railroading,'" judged that the organization had "grossly betrayed women," and tendered her resignation. Most objectors made the point that Curtis would not be president and that Hoover—who had appointed Margaret Dreier Robins, a National Women's Trade Union League leader and clear opponent of the equal rights amendment, head of his campaign among industrial working women—promised no brighter prospects for the amendment than did Alfred E. Smith. The basis for the endorsement seemed even flimsier when on October 26, 1928, Hoover made a statement opposing any change in protective labor laws applying to women. . . .[36]

Paul was not present during official moves toward the endorsement, but the action had her hallmarks: the decision was made at the top, the focus on the equal rights amendment was single-minded, and much more sympathy for the Republican than for the Democratic party was manifest. Although Paul usually avoided high office in the NWP during the 1920s, there is little question that her wishes determined major policy decisions. In 1928 Paul saw the opportunity to repeat the strategy of 1916, regardless that true parallels were lacking. . . .[37]

The authoritarian character of the NWP leadership became obvious to any who really participated in its work. As several women who were invited to serve on the National Advisory Council in 1921 commented, even that second-tier group had never been "advisory" nor been asked for "council."[38] In 1928 not only the endorsement of Hoover but also the NWP's turn toward international work for equal rights gave evidence that the ruling coterie ruled, regardless of whether any mass base supported their aims. . . . Paul, studying international law in the 1920s, framed her aims more and more abstractly and legalistically; her interest in international organization was spurred by Belmont's grandiose visions of an "International Parliament of Women." Belmont lived in France from 1920 until her death in 1933, and Paul constantly curried her favor to keep financial support flowing. Although the extent of Belmont's

---

[36]Sue Shelton White to Member of the Woman's Party, Nov. 20, 1928, box 1, Grimes Collection; Sue S[helton] White to Miss Lucia V. Grimes, Dec. 28, 1929, ibid.; Sue Shelton White to Jane Norman Smith, Sept. 15, 1928, folder 35, Sue Shelton White Collection (Schlesinger Library); Dock to Party, Oct. 2, [1928], NWP-P, 1913–1974; Emma C. Johnson to NWP, Oct. 18, 1928, ibid.

[37]NWP correspondence through the 1920s makes Paul's leadership clear. Susan Ware, *Beyond Suffrage: Women in the New Deal* (Cambridge, Mass., 1981), 33–38; and Clarke A. Chambers, *Seedtime of Reform: American Social Service and Social Action, 1918–1933* (Minneapolis, 1963), 260–61; Flyer [c. 1920], "Republican Party Record on Woman Suffrage," folder 12, Margaret S. Roberts Collection (Schlesinger Library); and Stevens, Jailed for Freedom, 250.

[38]Adamson to Hill, March 18, 1921, NWP-P, 1913–1974; MacKaye to Hill, March 21, [1921], ibid.

power over NWP decisions is not clear . . . she held the office of president for years and unquestionably had her greatest influence in fostering the party's international efforts. . . .[39]

Hooker's dispute with Jane Norman Smith in 1933–1934 and an intraparty schism that shortly resulted manifested a crisis that had been building since 1928 because of such factors as action at the top, disregard for inviting or involving membership participation, and more distant and more legalistic application of the concept of equal rights. Those practices dimmed the beacon of the NWP's feminist ideas, beset anyway by the depression economy. Hooker noted early in 1934 that the treasury for the previous year showed five or six hundred paid members. But Hooker's attempts at that point to build up the state organizations and to collaborate with other women's groups on aims they shared were flattened by "the most spectacular exhibition of autocracy," Hooker herself said. "The steam roller plied back and forth." Another member who saw galvanizing more women as a priority also had "practically no hope that it will be given any serious thought by any considerable group of the leaders; for these leaders are too largely made up of pioneers who are gripped by conservatism. They will not face facts. . . . One's having been 'jailed for the CAUSE' seems to make one an oracle." In forming a vanguard party, Paul seems to have been oblivious to Lenin's warning, "Be it remembered that in order to become the vanguard, we must attract other classes." Or, as Hooker editorialized in not-so-veiled language in the throes of the 1934 crisis, "the leaders are powerless unless they have massed behind them ever-growing and evermore insistent followers. . . . If the rank and file of women do not realize their subjection, how can they be expected to struggle to free themselves?"[40]

Although it was not so obvious before 1928, the NWP neglected what had been, historically, a crucial element in building the woman movement: the *process* of grass-roots participation. That neglect was not fatal during the suffrage movement, since the party entered rather late and, as Carrie Chapman Catt later bitterly said, "played the cuckoo, and laid its eggs in nests that had cost much to build."[41] In the 1920s the NWP continued its reputation for working at the top, lobbying presidents and members of Congress; it staged brilliant events attended by notable people and carried out daring exploits for publicity; it attracted some

[39]Becker, *Origins of the Equal Rights Amendment*, 161–86; National Council, NWP, minutes, Oct. 9, 1928, Jan. 15, 1929, NWP-P, 1913–1974.

[40]Hooker to Lutz, Jan. 5, 1934, folder 66, Lutz Collection; Mary Wilhelmine Williams to Lutz, April 22, 1934, folder 76, ibid.; Hooker to Stevens, Nov. 19, 1934, folder H, box IV, Stevens unprocessed adenda no. 76–246 (Schlesinger Library); James Weinstein, *Ambiguous Legacy: The Left in American Politics* (New York, 1975), 31; *Equal Rights*, June 23, 1934, p. 162. See also Hooker to Lutz, March 13, 1935, folder 67, Lutz Collection; Jane Norman Smith to Lutz, Feb. 6, 1932, folder 58, ibid.; Jane Norman Smith to Lutz and Marguerite Smith, Dec. 9, 1933, folder 98, ibid.

[41]Carrie Chapman Catt to Margaret Corbett Ashby, Oct. 20, 1925, "International Woman's Suffrage Alliance, 1925" folder, series 2, box 52, League of Women Voters Papers (Library of Congress).

individuals of artistic and professional renown, such as poet Edna St. Vincent Millay, artist Georgia O'Keeffe, and aviator Amelia Earhart. The ideas, researches, and perceptions of its small number of proponents were outstandingly acute: *Equal Rights* tracked instances of sex discrimination and of women's accomplishments around the world, editorialized about sex-role conditioning and the hypocrisies of gender hierarchy, published historical, autobiographical, and speculative essays on women's condition, and recorded the legislative progress of equal rights. Yet party leaders, who called themselves "Feminists," never recognized that cumulative grass-roots movement, as historian Ellen DuBois points out, was essential to the woman's rights legacy they saw themselves heir to.[42]

The significance of the suffrage movement, DuBois emphasizes, is that it was a *movement*, in which "increasing numbers of women would be transformed through the process of acting deliberately and collectively to achieve the equality and independence that enfranchisement seemed to promise." Sara Evans's history of the beginnings of the women's liberation movement in the late 1960s likewise emphasizes the importance of deliberative and collective *process* in the transformation of consciousness on an effective scale. DuBois's argument for the mid-nineteenth century applies to the much more recent period as well: that "it was women's involvement in the movement" itself that "created the basis for new social relations between men and women." The NWP, however, left out process entirely and focused single-mindedly on its *goal* of equal rights, conceived ever more abstractly. The equal rights amendment, supposed to be the first step in an agenda to end women's subjection, became itself the panacea. Stevens recognized this when in an acid critique of 1946 she wrote, "To my way of thinking the NWP in its direction since 1923 has lost more [and] more of that great feminist tradition handed on to our care from the 18th century. We are bogged down in legal formalism." The "dead hand" of Paul prevented anyone from "revitalizing the feminist climate": "the sad, bleak truth is that AP [Alice Paul] dislikes people . . . can't be bothered with members. . . . No sooner does a struggling state org[anization] show signs of life than, I am told, AP picks off their best workers for money and 'lobbying' . . . men on whom they have no claim. . . . One of our pioneers said lately, 'if AP had died 25 years ago, we'd now have the amendment.'"[43]

The failure to ratify the equal rights amendment in the 1980s indicates how obstacle-ridden the path of the amendment has been and thus how wrong, in one respect, that commentator on Paul was; yet Stevens's lament had a firm basis. Certainly a mix of historical factors in the 1920s conditioned the NWP's

---

[42]Ellen Carol DuBois, *Feminism and Suffrage: The Emergence of an Independent Women's Movement in America, 1848–1869* (Ithaca, 1978), 18, 24.

[43]*Ibid.*, 201; Sara Evans, *Personal Politics: The Roots of Women's Liberation in the Civil Rights Movement and the New Left* (New York, 1979); Doris [Stevens] to Betty [Gram Swing], Jan. 8, 1946, box IV, Stevens unprocessed adenda no. 76-246.

fate: the impasse over sex-based protective legislation was one; the defensive antisocialist trend of American politics was another; the panache of self-seeking in the younger generation was a third—not to speak of the deep-rootedness of gender hierarchy in the culture at large. But the NWP just as certainly had its dynamic, forged in the suffrage struggle and applied and misapplied obsessively after that. Though a full and fair treatment of the NWP would require richer detailing of its members, leaders, and activities, that dynamic is clear. It is not to dismiss the NWP's efforts—its carrying the banner of equal rights at state, federal, and international levels, its sustenance of a community of interest among its members, its serving as a resource for women seeking feminist affiliation to acknowledge that after 1928 its once-envisioned vanguard role was no more. . . .

Initiated in a vision of inclusiveness, a stand for all women, the NWP campaign for equal rights devolved into a practice of exclusiveness and a defense of the status quo with regard to everything but the gender question. That devolution owed in great part to Paul's assumption that equal rights (like suffrage, in her view), a demand relevant to all women, was separable from all other issues. Paul posed women's political options in either-or, rather than both-and, terms: "work for women" (which meant equal rights) or something else. Within that framework NWP loyalists chose equal rights. Women who had any other priority were "followers of men, worms of the dust," in the vitriolic words of Caroline Spencer, "who cannot see that the tyranny of half the race over the other half is the first wrong to be righted, and its overthrow, the greatest revolution conceivable."[44]

As a result of its construction of the gender imperative, the NWP made equal rights an abstract goal, because placing it in the context of social reality would have required stands on social and political issues that affected women but that were not strictly gender questions. (The suffrage battle might have provided a different lesson, regarding the separability of women's rights from politics in general, but perhaps only long retrospect allows us to see that feminist movements flourish best in the midst of other reforming politics and in alliance with other reforming aims.) With some justice Mary Anderson accused the NWP of putting the "woman question" first and of demanding that "the solution of all others should be determined solely by what is done with women's problems."[45] A tremendous irony lies here. The NWP set out to erase legislation that treated women "as a class" but predicated its feminism on construing women as a class, that "other half" of the human race. Its dilemma was the dilemma of twentieth-century feminism, that it required gender consciousness for its basis while it aimed for the dissolution of prescribed gender roles.

---

[44]Spencer to Pollitzer, April 30, 1921, NWP-P, 1913–1974.
[45]Anderson, "Should There Be Labor Laws for Women?" 53.

Nancy F. Cott

I am the Jonathan Trumbull Professor of American History at Harvard University, focusing on issues of gender, sexuality, feminism, and marriage. Before 2002, I taught at Yale University for twenty-six years and led in founding its Women's Studies Program in the late 1970s. I became a historian because of the women's movement circa 1970. Feminism reeducated me, making it possible to see women as subjects in history (and agents of change) as never before. My commitment to graduate school was waning when I got the opportunity to teach a couple of courses at a women's college—and was allowed to teach a course in women's history, something not on the books at the time. Teaching that fledgling course in US women's history (assigning only primary-source documents) got me hooked on the field's importance. I then wrote a dissertation that centrally concerned women's consciousness—something that the women's movement cued me to examine. It became my first book, *The Bonds of Womanhood: 'Woman's Sphere' in New England, 1780–1835* (1977). My article in this anthology stemmed from research on *The Grounding of Modern Feminism* (1987). I began that inquiry in the late 1970s when media claimed the women's movement was dead—though I knew it was not. I then wondered whether the 1910s feminist movement had really disappeared after suffrage—as 1920s media claimed. More recently, my book *Public Vows: A History of Marriage and the Nation* (2000) was sparked partly by the way that same-sex couples' demands to marry put a spotlight on the state's role in marriage.

QUESTIONS FOR CONSIDERATION

1. According to Cott, what have been the three main views of historians of the NWP?
2. In what ways did the Alice Paul and the NWP's tactics differ from other women's rights organizations? How was the NWP characterized by more moderate women's rights organizations because of these tactics?
3. After the passage of the Nineteenth Amendment, Paul and the NWP concentrated on social and legal reforms for women. Describe two of these reforms. How were these social reforms connected to the goal of women's suffrage?
4. At the height of its influence in 1921, the NWP suffered a split between its membership and leadership. What were the primary issues that caused the split? In what ways did this split reflect broader debates about class and race?
5. How did arguments over an equal rights amendment ideologically and tactically divide the NWP? In what ways did Paul's tactics exacerbate this division?
6. Describe four historical factors that ultimately caused the NWP's failure to pass an Equal Rights Amendment. Make sure that two of these causes are long term and two are short term.

≺◦≻

CHAPTER FIVE

The Architecture of Race in American Immigration Law: A Reexamination of the Immigration Act of 1924[1]

Mae M. Ngai

On February 4, 1929, Dr. Joseph A. Hill presented a plan for immigration quotas based on national origin to the United States Senate immigration committee. Hill was the chief statistician of the Census Bureau and chairman of the Quota Board. . . . Congress had mandated the board to allocate the quotas under the Immigration Act of 1924. That law restricted immigration into the United States to 150,000 a year based on quotas, which were to be allotted to countries in the same proportion that the American people traced their origins to those countries, through immigration or the immigration of their forebears. . . . [2]

In early 1929 it was still not at all certain that the system mandated in 1924 would come into being. Congress had already postponed implementation of the quotas twice. . . . The issue hung in political suspension throughout the presidential election campaign of 1928. Herbert Hoover . . . kicked off his presidential campaign in August with a speech that described national origins quotas as impossible to determine "accurately and without hardship," an apparent appeal to German and Scandinavian voters in the Midwest. Observers noted that Hoover's Democratic rival, Al Smith, opposed the quotas in the North while favoring them before southern audiences.[3]

During the winter, the nativist lobby stepped up its own efforts, mobilizing mass petitions to Congress from the American Legion, the Grange, and the

---

[1]Interested students are encouraged to read this essay in the original form. Mae M. Ngai, "The Architecture of Race in American Immigration Law: A Reexamination of the Immigration Act of 1924," *The Journal of American History* 86, no. 1 (June 1999), 67–92.

[2]U.S. Congress, Senate, Committee on Immigration, *National Origins Provision of the Immigration Law*, 71 Cong., 2 sess., Feb. 4, 1929, p. 16. The Immigration Act of 1924 stipulated that permanent immigration quotas were to go into effect on July 1, 1927. In the meantime, immigration was governed by temporary quotas, which were allocated to each European country at 2% of the number of foreign-born of each nationality in the 1890 census. The temporary formula gave 85% of the quotas to northern and western European nations. Act of May 26, 1924, chap. 190, 43 Stat. 153.

[3]U.S. Congress, Senate, *National Origin Provision of the Immigration Act of 1924*, 69 Cong., 2 sess., Dec. 16, 1926; U.S. Congress, Senate, *Immigration Quotas on the Basis of National Origins*, 70 Cong., 1 sess., Feb. 25, 1928; Robert Divine, *American Immigration Policy, 1924–1952* (New Haven, 1957), 40.

Daughters of the American Revolution. The patriotic societies took out a series of advertisements in the *Washington Post*, defending the "national origins basis . . . [as] the only one which does not discriminate for or against any" nation and exhorting members of Congress to stand firm against the efforts of "hyphenates" who would "play politics with the nation's blood stream." . . .[4] Congress had accepted the principle of national origins as fair and nondiscriminatory, but the claim to fairness would evaporate if the quotas could not be accurately determined. . . .[5] Nevertheless, as one of his first acts as president, Herbert Hoover proclaimed the quotas on March 22, 1929.[6]

Both academic and popular discourse have long criticized differential immigration quotas based on national origin as discriminatory. Yet the concept of "national origin" as a constitutive element of the American nation remains inadequately problematized. In part that is because most scholarship on the Immigration Act of 1924 has focused on the legislative process leading to the passage of the law. The central theme of that process was a race-based nativism, which favored the "Nordics" of northern and western Europe over the "undesirable races" of eastern and southern Europe. . . . The narrative of the politics of eugenics and restriction, however, emphasizes the passage of the Reed-Johnson Act as the end of the story, the triumph of Progressive Era nativism and the historical terminus of open immigration from Europe. That focus does not adequately explain and may, in fact, obscure from view other ideas about race, citizenship, and the nation that the new law both encoded and generated.[7]

More generally, the lack of critical analysis of "national origin" may also result from a presumption that nations and nationality are normative categories in the ordering of the world. . . . Recent scholarship has emphasized the need to historicize the nation-state and the cultures, identities, and relationships that it generates. Like race, [the] legal definitions and cultural meanings [of nation and nationality] can only be understood in the context of history.[8]

---

[4]Petitions in support of national origins quotas, from Daughters of the American Revolution, American Legion, Grange, file Sen. 70A-J17, box 179, Senate Records; *Washington Post* [Feb. 18, 1929];ibid., Feb. 25, 1929, p. 4; ibid., March 2, 1929, p. 4.

[5]Edward Hutchinson, *Legislative History of American Immigration Policy, 1790–1965* (Philadelphia, 1981), 205; John Higham, *Strangers in the Land: Patterns of American Nativism, 1865–1924* (1955; New Brunswick, 1985), 319–21; and Divine, *American Immigration Policy*, 1–51.

[6]*Proclamation by the President of the United States of America*, no. 1872, March 22, 1929, 46 Stat. 2984.

[7]Higham, *Strangers in the Land*; Divine, *American Immigration Policy*; Philip Gleason, "American Identity and Americanization," in *Harvard Encyclopedia of American Ethnic Groups*, ed. Stephen Thernstrom (Cambridge, Mass., 1980); John Higham, *Send These to Me* (Baltimore, 1981); Carl Degler, *In Search of Human Nature: The Decline and Revival of Darwinism in American Social Thought* (New York, 1991); Stephen Jay Gould, *The Mismeasure of Man* (New York, 1981); Nancy Stepan, *The Idea of Race in Science* (London, 1982); and Elazar Barkan, *The Retreat of Scientific Racism: Changing Concepts of Race in Britain and the United States between the World Wars* (Cambridge, Eng., 1992).

[8]Eric Hobsbawm, *Nations and Nationalism Since 1780: Programme, Myth, Reality* (Cambridge, Eng., 1992), 192; Benedict Anderson, *Imagined Communities: Reflections on the Origins and Spread of Nationalism* (London, 1991); Gopal Balakrishnan, ed., *Mapping the Nation* (London, 1996); and Paul Gilroy, *The Black Atlantic: Modernity and Double Consciousness* (Cambridge, Mass., 1992).

This article argues that the Immigration Act of 1924 comprised a constellation of reconstructed racial categories, in which race and nationality—concepts that had been loosely conflated since the nineteenth century—disaggregated and realigned in new and uneven ways. At one level, the new immigration law differentiated Europeans according to nationality and ranked them in a hierarchy of desirability. At another level, the law constructed a white American race, in which persons of European descent shared a common whiteness that made them distinct from those deemed to be not white. Euro-Americans acquired both ethnicities—that is, nationality-based identities that were presumed to be transformable—and a racial identity based on whiteness that was presumed to be unchangeable. This distinction gave all Euro-Americans a stake in what Matthew Jacobson has called a "consanguine white race" and facilitated their Americanization. But, while Euro-Americans' ethnic and racial identities became uncoupled, non-European immigrants—among them Japanese, Chinese, Mexicans, and Filipinos—acquired ethnic and racial identities that were one and the same. The racialization of the latter groups' national origins rendered them unalterably foreign and unassimilable to the nation. The Immigration Act of 1924 thus established legal foundations for social processes that would unfold over the next several decades, processes that historians have called, for European immigrants, "becoming American" (or, more precisely, white Americans), while casting Mexicans as illegal aliens and foredooming Asians to permanent foreignness.[9]

Drawing upon Michael Omi and Howard Winant's concept of racial formation, which they define "as the sociohistorical process by which racial categories are created, inhabited, transformed, and destroyed," this article seeks to understand the role of immigration law and policy in the production of official knowledges of race and nationality.[10] The article examines three major aspects of the

---

[9]Matthew Jacobson, *Whiteness of a Different Color: European Immigrants and the Alchemy of Race* (Cambridge, Mass., 1998); James Barrett and David Roediger, "Inbetween Peoples: Race, Nationality, and the 'New Immigrant' Working Class," *Journal of American Ethnic History* 16 (Spring 1997), 3–44; Thomas Archdeacon, *Becoming American* (New York, 1988); Gleason, "American Identity and Americanization"; David Roediger, *Towards the Abolition of Whiteness* (London, 1994), 181–98; Kathleen Neils Conzen et al., "The Invention of Ethnicity: A Perspective from the USA," *Journal of American Ethnic History* 12 (Fall 1992), 3–41; and Russell Kazal, "Revisiting Assimilation: The Rise, Fall, and Reappraisal of a Concept in American Ethnic History," *American Historical Review* 100 (April 1995), 437–71; Lizabeth Cohen, *Making a New Deal: Industrial Workers in Chicago, 1919–1939* (Cambridge, Eng., 1990); Gary Gerstle, *Working Class Americanism: The Politics of Labor in a Textile City* (Cambridge, Eng., 1989); James Barrett, "Americanization from the Bottom Up: Immigration and the Remaking of the Working Class in the United States, 1880–1930," *Journal of American History* 79 (Dec. 1992), 997–1020; George Sanchez, *Becoming Mexican American: Ethnicity, Culture, and Identity in Chicano Los Angeles, 1900–1945* (New York, 1993), 209–26; David Gutierrez, *Walls and Mirrors: Mexican Americans, Mexican Immigrants, and the Politics of Ethnicity* (Berkeley, 1995), 69–116; Neil Foley, *The White Scourge: Mexicans, Blacks, and Poor Whites in Texas Cotton Culture* (Berkeley, 1997), 40–63; David Montejano, *Anglos and Mexicans in the Making of Texas* (Austin, 1987), 181–96; Lisa Lowe, *Immigrant Acts: On Asian American Cultural Politics* (Durham, 1996), 1–36; Ian Haney Lopez, *White by Law: The Legal Construction of Race* (New York, 1995); and Bill Ong Hing, *Making and Remaking Asian America through Immigration Policy* (Stanford, 1990).

[10]Michael Omi and Howard Winant, *Racial Formation in the United States from the 1960s to the 1990s* (New York, 1994), 55.

Immigration Act of 1924. First, it analyzes the invention of "national origins," which applied mostly to Europeans while distinguishing Europeans from non-Europeans, and the attendant process by which immigration quotas were determined as practical policy. The article then examines the evolution of the concept of "ineligibility to citizenship," a condition that applied to all Asians, justifying and perfecting their exclusion from immigration, and that completed "Asiatic" as a peculiarly American racial category. Finally, the article turns to the role that immigration law played in the racial formation of Mexican immigrants and Mexican Americans. While not subject to numerical quotas or restrictions on naturalization, Mexicans were profoundly affected by restrictive measures enacted in the 1920s, among them deportation policy, the creation of the Border Patrol, and the criminalization of unlawful entry.

This analysis of the Immigration Act of 1924 suggests that immigration law and policy were deeply implicated in a broader racial and ethnic remapping of the nation during the 1920s, a remapping that took place in mutually constituting realms of demography, economics, and law. . . .[11]

THE INVENTION OF NATIONAL ORIGINS

. . . Census and immigration records, upon which the Quota Board relied in making its calculations, were woefully incomplete. The census of 1790, the nation's first, did not include information about national origin or ancestry. The census did not differentiate the foreign-born until 1850 and did not identify the places of birth of parents of the native-born until 1890. Immigration was unrecorded before 1820 and not classified according to origin until 1899, when it was arranged, not by politically defined nation-states, but according to a taxonomy called "races and peoples." Emigration was not recorded until 1907. . . .[12]

To calculate the quotas, the Quota Board first had to conceptualize the categories that constituted the system. "National origin," "native stock," "nationality," and other categories in the system were not natural units of classification; they were constructed according to certain social values and political judgments. Race, never explicitly mentioned in the statute, nevertheless entered the calculus and subverted the conceptual foundations of the system in myriad ways. For example, the board defined "native stock," not as persons born in the United States, but as persons who descended from the white

[11]Gilbert Osofsky, *Harlem, the Making of a Ghetto: Negro New York, 1890–1930* (New York, 1968); Donald Massey and Nancy Denton, *American Apartheid: Segregation and the Making of the Underclass* (Cambridge, Mass., 1993).

[12]LaVerne Beales, "Distribution of White Population as Enumerated in 1920 According to Country of Origin," typescript, Oct. 16, 1924, file 16, box 2, Reports, Correspondence, and other Records relating to Immigration Quota Laws and National Origins Statistics, ca. 1920–1936, NN-374–63, Population Division, Records of the Census Bureau, RG 29 (National Archives); Minutes of Quota Board meeting, May 25, 1926, file 19, ibid.

population of the United States in 1790. It defined "foreign stock" as the descendants of all whites who immigrated to the United States after 1790.[13]

The law defined "nationality" according to country of birth. But that definition did not apply to the American nationality. The statute excluded non-European peoples residing in the United States from the population universe governing the quotas. The law stipulated that "'inhabitants in continental United States in 1920' does not include (1) immigrants from the [Western Hemisphere] or their descendants, (2) aliens ineligible to citizenship or their descendants, (3) the descendants of slave immigrants, or (4) the descendants of the American aborigines."[14]

The Quota Board used census race categories to make its calculations. It subtracted from the total United States population all blacks and mulattoes, eliding the difference between the "descendants of slave immigrants" and the descendants of free Negroes and voluntary immigrants from Africa. It also discounted all Chinese, Japanese, and South Asians as persons "ineligible to citizenship," including descendants of such people with American citizenship by native birth. Finally, it left out the populations of Hawaii, Puerto Rico, and Alaska, which American immigration law governed and whose native-born inhabitants were United States citizens.[15]

In other words, to the extent that the "inhabitants in continental United States in 1920" constituted a legal representation of the American nation, the law excised all nonwhite, non-European peoples from that vision, erasing them from the American nationality. The practical consequence of those erasures is clear enough. In 1920 African Americans accounted for approximately 9 percent of the total United States population. Had they been included in the base population governing the quotas, the African nations from which they originated would have received 9 percent of the total immigration quota, resulting in 13,000 fewer slots for the European nations.

Race altered the meaning of nationality in other ways as well. Formally, the quota system encompassed all countries in the world outside the Western Hemisphere. China, Japan, India, and Siam each received the minimum quota of 100, but the law excluded the native citizens of those countries from immigration because they were deemed to be racially ineligible to citizenship. Thus Congress created the oddity of immigration quotas for non-Chinese persons from China, non-Japanese persons from Japan, non-Indian persons from India, and so on. . . .

Thus while the national origins quota system was intended principally to restrict immigration from the nations of southern and eastern Europe and used the

[13]Joseph A. Hill, "The Problem of Determining the National Origin of the American People," paper delivered at the annual meeting of the Social Science Research Council, Hanover, N.H., Aug. 1926, p. 7, file 17, ibid.

[14]Act of May 26, 1924, sec. 12 (a), 43 Stat. 153; ibid., sec. 11 (d).

[15]S. W Boggs to W W Husband, Nov. 11, 1926, p. 3, file 30, box 3, Reports relating to Immigration Quota Laws, Census Records; Act of May 26, 1924, sec. 11 (d). Husband to Joseph Hill, May 6, 1922, file 30, box 3, Reports relating to Immigration Quota Laws, Census Records.

notion of national origins to justify discrimination against immigration from those nations, it did more than divide Europe. It also divided Europe from the non-European world. It defined the world formally by country and nationality but also by race, distinguishing between white persons from white countries and so-called colored races, whose members were imagined as having no countries of origin. . . .[16]

Like most of their contemporaries, members of Congress and the Quota Board treated race as evidence in itself of differences that they presumed were natural. Few, if any, doubted that the Census Bureau's categories of race were objective divisions of objective reality. Such confidence evinced the strength of race thinking generally as well as the progressivist faith in science, in this case, the sciences of demography and statistics. Indeed, few people doubted the census at all. The census carried the weight of official statistics; its power lay in the seeming objectivity of numbers and in its formalization of racial categories. Census data gave the quotas an imprimatur that was nearly unimpeachable. . . .

Demography, and the census itself, far from being the simple quantification of material reality, grew in the late nineteenth and early twentieth centuries as a language for interpreting the social world. As the historian Margo Anderson observes, census classifications that defined urban and rural populations, social and economic classes, and racial groups created a vocabulary for public discourse on the great social changes taking place in the United States—industrialization, urban growth, and, of course, immigration. In fact, the census was the favored form of scientific evidence cited by restrictionists and nativists during this period. That practice began with census officials. Francis A. Walker, the superintendent of the 1870 and 1880 censuses, was president of the Massachusetts Institute of Technology (MIT) and a brilliant scholar in the new field of statistics. He was also an ardent nativist and social Darwinist who believed immigrants from Italy, Hungary, Austria, and Russia were "vast masses of peasantry, degraded below our utmost conceptions . . . beaten men from beaten races, representing the worst failures in the struggle for existence."[17]

Analyzing census data, Walker developed the theory that by the 1880s immigration was retarding the natural birthrate of Americans, which he lauded . . . as evidence of the nation's greatness. Because immigrants crowded native-born Americans from unskilled jobs, Walker theorized, the latter adjusted to their limited job opportunities by having fewer children He considered immigration a "shock" to the principle of natural population increase.[18] His theory rested on the assumption that the nation possessed a natural character and teleology, to which immigration was external and unnatural. That assumption resonated with conventional views about America's providential mission and the general

[16]John Trevor, "An Analysis of the American Immigration Act of 1924," *International Conciliation* 202 (Sept. 1924), 58–59.

[17]Margo Anderson, *The American Census: A Social History* (New Haven, 1988), 133–34; Francis A. Walker, "Restriction of Immigration," *Atlantic Monthly* 77 (June 1896), 828.

[18]Higham, *Strangers in the Land*, 143; Francis A. Walker, "The Great Count of 1890," *Forum* 15 (June 1891), 406–18. See also Francis A. Walker, "Immigration and Degradation," ibid. (Aug. 1891), 634–44.

march of progress. Yet, it was rooted in a profoundly conservative viewpoint that the composition of the American nation should never change. . . .[19] Francis Walker's theory of the declining native birthrate and the census data upon which it was based became the foundation for the restrictionists' claim that immigration threatened to overwhelm the American nation. It anchored Madison Grant's thesis that the great Nordic race was in danger of extinction. . . .[20]

Like Francis Walker, Joseph Hill also came from an elite, old-line New England family. . . . He graduated from Phillips Exeter Academy and Harvard College (as had his father and grandfather). . . . Although Hill began his tenure at the Census Bureau in 1899, two years after Walker's death, he held many of the same views. In 1910, using previously unpublished and untabulated census data, Hill contributed to the Dillingham Commission's study of immigration two monographs that were of great importance to the restrictionist movement. . . . Not coincidentally, these studies provided additional empirical evidence for Francis Walker's theory of the retarded native birthrate.[21]

Since the mid-nineteenth century, scientific race theory had revolved around efforts to develop systems of racial classification and typology. In this vein, Hill strove for ever more precise categories of classification and comparisons of type. He added new questions to the census in 1910 and 1920 in the hope of elucidating differences in race and nationality in increasing detail. Hill restored the "mulatto" race category (which had been eliminated in the 1900 census) as well as questions to ascertain literacy, ability to speak English, mother tongue, number of children born and living, and length of time in the United States. He was particularly interested in creating indices to gauge assimilation. . . .[22]

In a sense, demographic data were to twentieth-century racists what craniometric data had been to race scientists during the nineteenth. Like the phrenologists who preceded them, the eugenicists worked backward from classifications they defined *a priori* and declared a causal relationship between the data and race. Instead of measuring skulls, they counted inmates in state institutions.

---

[19]Francis Walker, "Our Population in 1900," *Atlantic Monthly* 32 (Oct. 1873), 487–95; William Peterson, *The Politics of Population* (New York, 1964), 198–200.

[20]Madison Grant, *The Passing of the Great Race* (New York, 1916), 104; Edward Lewis, *Nation or Confusion? A Study of Our Immigration Problems* (New York, 1928), 79; Madison Grant and Charles Stewart Davison, eds., *The Alien in Our Midst*; or, "Selling Our Birthright for a Mess of Pottage" (New York, 1930), 15.

[21]*New York Herald Tribune*, Dec. 13, 1939, clipping, "Career and Funeral" file, box 3, Correspondence of Joseph Hill, Records of the Assistant Director of Statistical Standards, Records of the Chief Statistician, Administrative Records of the Census Bureau, RG 29 (National Archives); U.S. Congress, Senate, *Reports of the Immigration Commission*, "Occupations of the First and Second Generations of Immigrants in the US and Fecundity of Immigrant Women," 61 Cong., 2 sess., Jan. 12, 1910.

[22]Joseph Hill, "Some Results of the 1920 Population Census," *Journal of the American Statistical Association* 18 (Sept. 1922), 350–58; Joseph Hill, "Composition and Characteristics of Population," typescript, [1920], file C-22, box 146, Memoranda and Notes [of Joseph Hill], Records of the Assistant Director of Statistical Standards, Records of the Chief Statistician, Administrative Census Records; Joseph Hill, "Scope of the Fourteenth Census," typescript [1917–1919], "Papers written by Dr. Hill" file, box 4, Miscellaneous Records [of Joseph Hill], ibid.

If statistics showed that immigrants were less healthy, less educated, and poorer than native-born Americans, that was deemed evidence of the immigrants' inferior physical constitution, intelligence, and ambition.

Unlike Francis Walker, Joseph Hill did not aggressively campaign for restriction. He endorsed the national origins principle in a restrained way and otherwise scrupulously avoided taking political positions. Yet, like all scientists, he brought his own political views and values to his work—to the questions he asked, to the ways in which he classified data, and to the interpretations he drew from the data. In Hill's case, those politics had guided a proliferation of census data on the foreign-born that served the nativist movement.[23]

That is not to say that Hill's work was unscientific or unprofessional. To the contrary, he was a serious professional who worked according to the established methods and disciplinary requirements of his field. As Nancy Stepan has pointed out, scientific racism's power lay, in large part, in its adherence to scientific methodology and disciplinary standards. If race science were merely pseudoscience, it would have had far less currency.[24]

In fact, Hill agonized over the methodological problems in determining national origins. One of the most serious problems he confronted was the lack of reliable information about the national origins of the white native-stock population. . . . The census of 1790 did not record data on place of birth. A study conducted by the Census Bureau in 1909, *A Century of Population Growth*, classified the population of 1790 according to country of origin by analyzing the surnames of the heads of households recorded in the census. . . .[25] Hill decided to use *A Century of Population Growth* because no other data existed. But after protests mounted from groups of Irish, German, and Scandinavian Americans, he realized that the flawed report endangered the credibility of the entire exercise. With the help of a $10,000 grant from the American Council of Learned Societies, Hill enlisted Howard Barker, a genealogist, and Marcus Hansen, an immigration historian, to determine the national origins of the white population in 1790. Their conclusions, based on a more sophisticated method of analyzing surnames and reported to the Quota Board in 1928, adjusted the allocations of origins of the colonial stock considerably. Great Britain and Northern Ireland's share fell from 82 percent to 67 percent of the total, reducing its quota by 10,000.[26]

---

[23]Hill, "Problem of Determining the National Origin of the American People," 2–3.

[24]Stepan, *Idea of Race in Science*, xvi.

[25]Minutes of Quota Board meeting, June 23, 1926, file 19, box 1, Reports relating to Immigration Quota Laws, Census Records; Joseph Hill, "Memorandum for the Secretary," June 21, 1926, p. 3, file 15, box 1, Memoranda and Notes [of Joseph Hill], Administrative Census Records; William S. Rossiter, *A Century of Population Growth* (Washington, D.C., 1909); Joseph Hill, "Notes on Prof. Jameson's Paper on 'American Blood in 1775,'" typescript, [1924–1925], file 20, box 2, Reports relating to Immigration Quota Laws, Census Records.

[26]Hill, "Memorandum for the Secretary," 3; American Council of Learned Societies, "Report of Committee on Linguistic and National Stocks in the Population of the United States," *Annual Report of the American Historical Association* (3 vols., Washington, D.C., 1931), I, 124; Anderson, *American Census*, 148–49.

Assuming that Barker and Hansen discerned the national origins of the population in 1790 with fair accuracy, determining the national origins of the American population from that base, following their descendants forward in time from 1790 to 1920, was an entirely different matter. The methodology employed by the Quota Board analyzed the population in terms of numerical equivalents, not actual persons. Hill explained that the Quota Board could not "classify people into so many distinct groups of individual persons, each group representing the number of individual persons descending from a particular country." He continued,

> Even if we had complete genealogical records that would not be possible because there has been a great mixture of nationalities through inter-marriage since this country was first settled. So when the law speaks of the number of inhabitants having a particular national origin, the inhabitant must be looked upon as a unit of measure rather than a distinct person. That is to say, if we have, for example, four people each of whom had three English grandparents and one German grandparent, . . . we have the equivalent of three English inhabitants and one German inhabitant.[27]

Using numerical equivalents may have been the only available statistical method, but it revealed the fundamental problem of the whole project. The method treated national identities as immutable and transhistorical, passed down through generations without change. The Quota Board assumed that even if nationalities combined through intermarriage, they did not mix but remained in descendants as discrete, unalloyed parts that could be tallied as fractional equivalents. The board's view of national origin drew from the concept of race defined by bloodline and blood quantum, which was available in the established definition of Negro. Rather than apply the "one drop of blood" rule, however, the board conceived of intermarriage between European nationalities in Mendelian terms. But is a person with three English grandparents and one German grandparent really the numerical equivalent of her ancestors? Or does that person perhaps develop a different identity that is neither English nor German but syncretic, produced from cultural interchanges among families and communities and shaped by the contingencies of her own time and place? By reifying national origin, Congress and the Quota Board anticipated the term "ethnicity," inventing it, as Werner Sollors said, with the pretense of its being "eternal and essential" when, in fact, it is "pliable and unstable." Sollors's view of ethnicity as a "pseudo-historical" concept triggered by "the specificity of power relations at a given historical moment" fits well the notion of immigration quotas based on national origin.[28]

The Quota Board also ignored intermarriage between Euro-Americans and both African Americans and Native American Indians, never problematizing the effect of miscegenation on the "origins" of the white population. That was because no conceptual space for such consideration existed in the absolutism of American racial construction. Thus, even as the board proceeded from an assumption that

---

[27]Hill, "Problem of Determining the National Origin of the American People," 5–6.

[28]Werner Sollors, "Introduction: The Invention of Ethnicity," in *The Invention of Ethnicity*, ed. Werner Sollors (New York, 1989), xiv–xvi.

all bloodlines were inviolate, it conceptualized national origin and race in fundamentally different ways.[29]

Even when considered on its own terms, the task of calculating national origins was beset by methodological problems. The Quota Board had to make assumptions to fill the gaps in the data. Hill acknowledged that his computations involved "rather arbitrary assumptions," some of which did "violence to the facts." The most serious . . . was his decision to apply the same rate of natural increase to all national groups. Hill also weighted the population figures for each decade, giving each earlier decade greater numerical importance than the succeeding one, to allow for a larger proportion of descendants from earlier immigrants. The net result of these assumptions tilted the numbers toward the northern European nationalities.[30]

Hill himself expressed concern that the entire exercise rested on so many assumptions that the conclusions might not be viable. Ultimately, Hill rationalized, arguing that errors in the process would not significantly affect the outcome. . . . A more honest inquiry might have concluded that determining the national origins of the American people was theoretically suspect and methodologically impossible. But, once President Hoover promulgated the quotas in 1929, the "national origins" of the American people, and the racial hierarchies embedded in them, assumed the prestige of law and the mantle of fact.[31]

ELIGIBILITY TO CITIZENSHIP AND THE RULE OF RACIAL UNASSIMILABILITY

The system of quotas based on national origin was the first major pillar of the Immigration Act of 1924. The second was the exclusion of persons ineligible to citizenship. By one account, the provision barred half the world's population from entering the United States.[32]

---

[29]Gary Nash, "The Hidden History of Mestizo America," *Journal of American History* 82 (Dec. 1995), 941–64; Peggy Pascoe, "Miscegenation Law, Court Cases, and the Ideology of Race in Twentieth-Century America," ibid., 83 (June 1996), 44–69; and Joel Williamson, *New People: Miscegenation and Mulattos in the United States* (New York, 1984).

[30]Hill, "Memorandum for the Secretary," 2; Minutes of Quota Board meeting, May 25, 1926, p. 3, file 19, box 2, Reports relating to Immigration Quota Laws, Census Records; Hill to Secretary of State, Secretary of Commerce, Secretary of Labor, Feb. 15, 1928, in *Immigration Quotas on the Basis of National Origin*, 70 Cong., 1 sess., Feb. 28, 1929, S. Doc. 65, p. 9; LaVerne Beales, "Committee on Distribution of Population by National Origin," typescript, Dec. 1, 1924, file 16, box 2, Reports relating to Immigration Quota Laws, Census Records.

[31]Hill, "Memorandum for the Secretary," 2; Minutes of Quota Board meeting, May 25, 1926, p. 3, file 19, box 2, Reports relating to Immigration Quota Laws, Census Records; Hill, "Problem of Determining the National Origin of the American People," 21; Hill to Secretary of State, Secretary of Commerce, Secretary of Labor, Feb. 15, 1928, in *Immigration Quotas on the Basis of National Origin*, 7.

[32]Act of May 26, 1924, sec. 13 (c), 43 Stat. 152; Paul Scharrenberg, "America's Immigration Problem," Dec. 1926, p. 4, "Immigration Quotas" file, box 2, Paul Scharrenberg Papers.

Ineligibility to citizenship and exclusion applied to the peoples of all the nations of the Far East. Nearly all Asians had already been excluded, either by the Chinese exclusion laws or by the "barred Asiatic zone" that Congress created in 1917. The latter comprised the area from Afghanistan to the Pacific, save for Japan, which the State Department wished not to offend, and the Philippines, a United States territory. In 1907 the Japanese government had agreed to prevent laborers from emigrating to the United States, but nativists complained that the diplomatic agreement was ineffective. The exclusion of persons ineligible to citizenship by the Immigration Act of 1924 achieved statutory Japanese exclusion and completed Asiatic exclusion. Moreover, it codified the principle of racial exclusion, incorporating it into general immigration law, albeit through the euphemistic reference to "persons ineligible to citizenship," which remained in effect until 1952.[33]

Two major elements of twentieth-century American racial ideology evolved along with the racial requirement for citizenship: the legal definition of "white" and the rule of racial unassimilability. The origin of these concepts may be found in the Nationality Act of 1790, which granted the right to naturalized citizenship to "free white persons." After the Civil War and the passage of the Fourteenth Amendment, Congress amended the Nationality Act to extend the right to naturalize to "persons of African nativity or descent." The latter was a gratuitous gesture to the former slaves. No one seriously believed that "the [N]egroes of Africa [would] emigrate," a federal judge explained in 1880. . . .[34]

The Nationality Act of 1870 thus encoded racial prerequisites to citizenship according to the familiar classifications of black and white. European immigrants fit into that legal construct as white persons. . . . Although nativists commonly referred to southern and eastern Europeans as "undesirable races," their eligibility to citizenship as "white persons" was never challenged and the legality of naturalizing European immigrants was never an issue in public and political discourse. The Chinese Exclusion Act of 1882 declared Chinese ineligible to citizenship, but it remained unclear where Japanese, Asian Indians, Armenians, Syrians, Mexicans, and other peoples that immigrated into the United States in the late nineteenth and early twentieth century fit in the black-white construct of citizenship law. Although in 1906 the United States attorney general held Japanese and Asian Indians to be ineligible to citizenship, several hundred Japanese and Asian

---

[33]Act of May 6, 1882, 22 Stat. 58; Act of May 5, 1892, 27 Stat. 25; Act of April 29, 1902, 32 Stat. 176; Act of April 27, 1904, 33 Stat. 428; Act of Feb. 5, 1917, 39 Stat. 874; Act of June 27, 1952, 66 Stat. 163; Mary Coolidge, *Chinese Immigration* (New York, 1909); Alexander Saxton, *The Indispensable Enemy* (Berkeley, 1971); Sucheng Chan, ed., *Entry Denied: Exclusion and the Chinese Community in America, 1882–1943* (Philadelphia, 1990); and Lucy Salyer, *Laws Harsh as Tigers: Chinese Immigrants and the Shaping of Modern Immigration Law* (Chapel Hill, 1993); Yuji Ichioka, *The Issei: The World of First Generation Japanese Immigrants, 1880–1924* (New York, 1988); Roger Daniels, *The Politics of Prejudice: The Anti-Japanese Movement in California and the Struggle for Japanese Exclusion* (Berkeley, 1977); Joan Jensen, *Passage from India* (New Haven, 1988).

[34]Act of March 6, 1790, 1 Stat. 103; Act of July 14, 1870, 16 Stat. 25; Stanford Lyman, "The Race Question and Liberalism: Casuistries in American Constitutional Law," *International Journal of Politics, Culture, and Society* 5 (Winter 1991), 231.

Indians obtained naturalized citizenship during the first two decades of the century. Between 1887 and 1923 the federal courts heard twenty-five cases challenging the racial prerequisite to citizenship, culminating in two landmark rulings by the United States Supreme Court, *Ozawa v. United States* (1922) and *United States v. Thind* (1923). In each case, the court's decision turned on whether the petitioner could be considered a "white person" within the meaning of the statute.[35]

The judicial genealogy of the rules of racial eligibility to citizenship followed a racial logic different from that of the legislative discourse surrounding the quota laws. While the latter emphasized eugenics and the superiority of Nordics, scientific race theory proved inadequate to the classificatory challenge that eligibility to citizenship, and Asiatic exclusion generally, required of the law. As Ian Haney López has pointed out, the federal courts' rulings in naturalization cases increasingly rejected scientific explanations in favor of common understandings of race. No doubt this was because science was revealed to be an unreliable guide to racial exclusion. The few petitioners who successfully litigated their status as white persons did so with the aid of scientific race theories. In 1909 a federal court in Georgia ruled that George Najour, a Syrian, was eligible to citizenship. District Judge William Newman stated that "fair or dark complexion should not be allowed to control" determinations of race. He cited A. H. Keane's *The Worlds People* (1908), which divided the human race into four categories, noting that Keane "unhesitatingly place[d] the Syrians in the Caucasian or white division." Using similar logic, federal courts admitted Syrians, Armenians, and Asian Indians to citizenship as white persons in seven cases between 1909 and 1923.[36]

In *Ozawa* the Supreme Court struggled with the problem of racial classification. The Court acknowledged that color as an indicator of race was insufficient, given the "overlapping of races and a gradual merging of one into the other, without any practical line of separation." Yet, the Court resisted the logical conclusion that no scientific grounds for race existed. It sidestepped the problem of classification by simply asserting that white and Caucasian were one and the same, concluding, with circular reasoning, that Japanese cannot be Caucasian because they are not white.[37]

The Court resolved this problem in the *Thind* case, which it heard just a few months after *Ozawa*. Bhagat Singh Thind, a "high class Hindu," had argued his eligibility to citizenship as a white person based on his Aryan and Caucasian roots. Citing anthropological experts, Thind noted that the Aryans of India are a "tall, long-headed race with distinct European features, and their color on the average is not as dark as the Portuguese or Spanish." Because marrying outside of caste is strictly forbidden in India, Thind argued that he was a "pure Aryan."[38]

---

[35]Census Bureau, *Historical Statistics of the United States*, I, 114–15; Jensen, *Passage from India*, 247–48; Ichioka, Issei, 211; *Ozawa v. United States*, 260 U.S. 178 (1922); *United States v. Thind*, 261 U.S. 204 (1923); *People v. Hall*, 4 Cal. 399 (1854); Jensen, *Passage from India*, 12–14; Haney Lopez, *White by Law*, 51–52.

[36]Haney Lopez, *White by Law*, 65–77; In re Najour, 174 F. 735–36 (N.D. Ga. 1909).

[37]*Ozawa v. United States*, 197.

[38]Brief of Respondent at 10, 36, *United States v. Thind*.

The government rejected Thind's claim to whiteness as ridiculous. "In the popular conception," it stated, "he is an alien to the white race and part of the 'white man's burden'. . . . Whatever may be the white man's burden, the Hindu does not share it, rather he imposes it." The Court agreed, stating, "The word [Caucasian] by common usage has acquired a popular meaning, not clearly defined to be sure, but sufficiently so to enable us to say that its popular as distinguished from its scientific application is of appreciably narrower scope." In *Thind* the Court dismissed science altogether. The term "Caucasian," it said, "under scientific manipulation, has come to include far more than the unscientific mind suspects." Noting that Keane included Indians, Polynesians, and the Hamites of Africa in the Caucasian race, the Court commented dryly, "We venture to think that the average well-informed white American would *learn* with some degree of astonishment that the race to which he belongs is made up of such heterogeneous elements." The Court believed that the original framers of the law intended "to include only the type of man whom they knew as white . . . [those] from the British Isles and northwestern Europe . . . bone of their bone and flesh of their flesh." Furthermore, the meaning of white readily expanded to accommodate immigrants from "Eastern, Southern, and Mid Europe, among them Slavs and the dark-eyed, swarthy people of Alpine and Mediterranean stock." Those immigrants were "received [as] unquestionably akin to those already here and readily amalgamated with them."[39]

The Court's edict in *Thind*—"What we now hold is that the words 'free white persons' are words of common speech, to be interpreted with the understanding of the common man"—amounted to a concession to the socially constructed nature of race. Moreover, its acknowledgement of the assimilability of eastern and southern Europeans and its insistence on the unassimilability of Asians rendered a double meaning to assimilation. For Europeans, assimilation was a matter of socialization and citizenship its ultimate reward. Asians, no matter how committed to American ideals or practiced in American customs, remained racially unassimilable and unalterably foreign.[40]

Although *Ozawa* and *Thind* applied to Japanese and South Asians, respectively, the Court made a leap in racial logic to apply the rule of ineligibility to citizenship to Koreans, Thais, Vietnamese, Indonesians, and other peoples of Asian countries who represented discrete ethnic groups and, in contemporary anthropological terms, different racial groups. This involved a measure of casuistry, which used retroactive and circular reasoning. In the last paragraph of *Thind* the Court applied the rule of ineligibility to citizenship to the natives of all Asian countries, saying:

> It is not without significance in this connection that Congress, by the [Immigration] Act of 1917 . . . excluded from admission into this country all natives of Asia within designated limits of latitude and longitude, including the whole of

---

[39]Brief for the United States, 16, 19, ibid.; ibid., 209, 211.

[40]42 *US v. Thind* at 213; Jeff Lesser, "Always 'Outsiders': Asians, Naturalization, and the Supreme Court," *Amerasia Journal*, 12 (no. 1, 1985), 83–100.

India. This not only constitutes conclusive evidence of the congressional attitude of opposition to Asiatic immigration generally, but is persuasive of a
similar attitude towards Asiatic naturalization as well, since it is not likely that
Congress would be willing to accept as citizens a class of persons whom it
rejects as immigrants.[41]

In 1923, on the heels of *Ozawa* and *Thind*, the Court issued four rulings
upholding California and Washington state laws proscribing agricultural land
ownership by aliens ineligible to citizenship. Those laws had been passed in the
1910s to drive Japanese and other Asians out of farming. In *Terrace v. Thompson*, the Court held that the alien land laws fell within the states' police powers
to protect the public interest. Ironically, Japanese had taken up agriculture
during the first decade of the century in the belief that farming would facilitate
permanent settlement, civic responsibility, and assimilation. But if Japanese
embraced the Jeffersonian ideal, the nativists who dominated Progressive politics on the Pacific Coast concluded that Japan was conspiring to take California
away from white people. In a typical statement, United States senator James
Phelan, formerly the mayor of San Francisco and for thirty years a leading
California exclusionist, claimed in 1920 that Japanese land colonies in Merced
County "would have destroyed that section for white settlement ... and the
desirable element."[42]

... The Court contended that the alien land laws did not discriminate against
Japanese because the laws applied to all aliens ineligible to citizenship, eliding the
racial foundation of the concept.... The Court asserted, "One who is not a citizen
and cannot become one lacks an interest in, and the power to effectually work for
the welfare of the state, and so lacking, the state may rightfully deny him the right
to own or lease land estate within its boundaries. If one incapable of citizenship
may lease or own real estate, it is within the realm of possibility that every foot of
land within the state may pass to the ownership of non-citizens." ...[43]

Together, the naturalization and land cases solidified the concept "ineligible
to citizenship," providing the basis for Asiatic exclusion in the Immigration Act of
1924. There is no direct evidence that the Supreme Court intended to influence the
character of immigration legislation. But the timing of the decisions, coincident
with the congressional debates over immigration restriction, is striking, especially
since *Ozawa* and *Thind* had languished on the docket since World War I.[44]

The Supreme Court rulings on Asians in 1922–1923 and the Immigration
Act of 1924 thus completed the legal construction of "Asiatic" as a racial category.

---

[41]*United States v. Thind*, 215.

[42]*Terrace v. Thompson*, 263 U.S. 197 (1923) at 221; *Porterfield v. Webb*, 263 U.S. 225 (1923); *Frick
v. Webb*, 263 U.S. 225 (1923); and *Webb v. O'Brien*, 263 U.S. 313 (1923); James Phelan is quoted in U.S.
Congress, House, Committee on Immigration and Naturalization, *Japanese Immigration*, 66 Cong.,
2 sess., July 12–14, 1920, p. 20; Milton Konvitz, *The Alien and the Asiatic in American Law* (Ithaca,
1946), 161, 187–89; Ichioka, *Issei*, 146–56.

[43]*Truax v. Corrigan*, 257 U.S. 312, cited in *Terrace v. Thompson*, 263 U.S. at 218; *Terrace v.
Thompson*, 263 U.S. at 221.

[44]Ichioka, *Issei*, 223.

The "national origins" of Asians had become thoroughly racialized. This construct of race, based both on nationality and "common" or subjective understandings of race, differed from the language of eugenics that dominated the legislative discourse of immigration restriction, which was based on scientific race theory. Yet, the racialization of Asian nationalities was consistent with the overarching logic of the language in the Immigration Act of 1924, which, at the formal level, was based on categories of nationality and not of race. The act thus fit the modern tenor of classifying the world into nation-states and avoiding explicit racial language in the law. However, the underlying assumptions in the construction of those categories diverged in relationship to Europeans and Asiatics. The racial and national identities of the former became uncoupled while those of the latter became merged. The divergence pointed to a racial logic that determined which people could assimilate into the nation and which people could not. Thus, the shift in formal language from race to national origin did not mean that race ceased to operate, but rather that it became obfuscated.

FROM CONQUERED NATIVES TO ILLEGAL ALIENS

If Congress and the Court defined Asiatics as definitely not white, they found the problem of racially classifying Mexicans much more vexing. In the late 1920s the California Joint Immigration Committee and other nativist organizations sought to restrict immigration of Mexicans on grounds of their alleged racial ineligibility to citizenship. But not only did agricultural interests in the Southwest and diplomatic and business interests in Latin America impede restrictions on immigration from Mexico, Mexicans resisted easy racial classification because they fit no clear type.

The history of the Southwest as former Mexican territory, annexed by the United States as a result of the Mexican-American War, further complicated the meanings of race and citizenship. To be sure, Anglo-Americans never considered Mexicans their racial equals and, moreover, regarded them with the suspicion they had historically accorded genotypically mixed peoples. Yet, paradoxically, conquest mitigated the racialization of Mexicans in the United States. The Treaty of Guadalupe Hidalgo, which specified the terms of Mexico's defeat in 1848, gave Mexico's northern half to the United States and stipulated that all inhabitants in the ceded territory who did not either announce their intention to remain Mexican citizens or leave the territory in one year would automatically become citizens of the United States. American citizenship in this instance was not consistent with the liberal tradition of citizenship by consent. Rather, it indicated Mexicans' new status as a conquered population.[45]

---

[45]Gutierrez, *Walls and Mirrors*, 13–20; Reginald Horsman, *Race and Manifest Destiny: The Origins of American Anglo-Saxonism* (Cambridge, Mass., 1981), 210; Carey McWilliams, *North from Mexico: The Spanish-Speaking People of the United States* (New York, 1968), 51–52; Peter Schuck and Rogers Smith, *Citizenship without Consent: Illegal Aliens in the American Polity* (New Haven, 1985), 40; Tomas Amalguer, *Racial Fault Lines: The Historical Origins of White Supremacy in California* (Berkeley, 1993), 55–56.

In 1929 Secretary of Labor James Davis advised Albert Johnson of the House immigration committee (coauthor of the Immigration Act of 1924) that the precedent of mass naturalization made it impossible to apply the rule of racial ineligibility to Mexicans. The right to naturalize under the terms of the treaty had been upheld by a federal court in 1897, when Ricardo Rodriguez, a thirty-seven-year-old native of Mexico who had lived in San Antonio for ten years, petitioned to become a citizen. . . . The attorneys of the court contested his eligibility on grounds that "he is not a white person, nor an African, nor of African descent." In district court, Judge Thomas Maxey noted that "as to color, he may be classed with the copper-colored or red men. He has dark eyes, straight black hair, and high cheek bones." But, the judge concluded, because Rodriguez "knows nothing of the Aztecs or Toltecs, [h]e is not an Indian." . . .[46]

Judge Maxey conceded, "If the strict scientific classification of the anthropologist should be adopted, [Rodriguez] would probably not be classed as white." However, the constitution of the Texas Republic, the Treaty of Guadalupe Hidalgo, the Gadsden treaty, and other agreements between the United States and Mexico either "affirmatively confer[red] the rights of citizenship upon Mexicans, or tacitly recognize[d] in them the right of individual naturalization." Noting that such agreements covered "all Mexicans, without discrimination as to color," Judge Maxey concluded that Rodriguez was "embraced within the spirit and intent of our laws upon naturalization."[47]

In re Rodriguez foreshadowed *Thind* by acknowledging the subjectivity of racial identification. Despite the judge's perception that Rodriguez was probably Indian (or, at least, not white), the court bowed to Rodriguez's own claim that he was not Indian, Spanish, or African but, rather, "pure blooded Mexican." Secretary of Labor Davis also recognized that self-identification impeded race-based immigration policy. He said, "the Mexican people are of such a mixed stock and individuals have such a limited knowledge of their racial composition that it would be impossible for the most learned and experienced ethnologist or anthropologist to classify or determine their racial origin. Thus, making an effort to exclude them from admission or citizenship because of their racial status is practically impossible."[48]

Mexicans' legal status as white persons was unstable, however. By the late 1920s, a Mexican "race problem" had emerged in the Southwest, impelled by contradictions wrought by the burgeoning of commercial agriculture, an all-time high in Mexican immigration, and the formation of a migratory, landless agricultural proletariat and of segregated communities. Immigration policy was deeply implicated in the reorganization of the region's political economy. Although Congress was unwilling to impose quotas on Mexican immigration or to exclude Mexicans on racial grounds, it did seek to restrict Mexican immigration by

---

[46]James Davis to Albert Johnson, Feb. 14, 1929, HR71A-F 16.1, Records of the House of Representatives, RG 233 (National Archives); *In re Rodriguez*, 81 Fed. 337–338 (W.D. Texas, 1897).

[47]*In re Rodriguez*, 349, 354, 352, 354–55.

[48]Ibid. at 337; Davis to Johnson, Feb. 14, 1929, p. 5, file HR71A-F16.1, House Records.

administrative means. In 1929 the United States consuls in Mexico began more strictly to enforce existing provisions of the immigration law—the ban on contract labor, the literacy test, and the provision excluding any person "likely to become a public charge"—in order to refuse visas to all Mexican laborers save those with prior residence in the United States. The policy had an immediate effect. Immigration from Mexico, which had averaged 58,747 a year during the late 1920s, dropped to 12,703 in 1930 and 3,333 in 1931.[49]

That decrease, however, was only in legal immigration. Contemporaries estimated that illegal immigration ran as high as 100,000 a year throughout the 1920s. Unofficial entry was not new, as migration across the border had had an informal, unregulated character since the nineteenth century. But during the 1920s Congress made provisions for the enforcement of immigration laws that hardened the difference between legal and illegal immigration. It lifted the statute of limitations on deportation in 1924 and formed the Border Patrol in 1925. In 1929 Congress made unlawful entry a felony, a move that was intended to solve the problem of illegal immigration from Mexico. The number of Mexicans deported formally under warrant rose from 846 in 1920 to 8,438 in 1930. In addition, some 13,000 Mexicans a year were expelled as "voluntary departures" in the late 1920s and early 1930s.[50]

By the late 1920s the problem of illegal immigration became increasingly associated with Mexicans, as they came to constitute half of those deported formally under warrant and over 80 percent of all voluntary departures. Illegal European immigrants who were apprehended by the Immigration Service were also more likely to avoid deportation. Euro-American communities had achieved a measure of political representation and could count on religious and settlement organizations to advocate their interests. Euro-American communities also had greater access to legal assistance than did their Mexican counterparts. A contemporary study found that 20 percent of aliens in deportation hearings in New York City had legal counsel as compared to fewer than 2 percent in the Mexican border districts.[51]

---

[49]Divine, *American Immigration Policy*, 62–68; U.S. Department of State, "Latest Statistics on Immigration from Mexico," May 12, 1930, HR71-F16.4, House Records; Census Bureau, *Historical Statistics of the United States*, I, 107; Carey McWilliams, *Factories in the Field: The Story of Migratory Farm Labor in California* (Santa Barbara, 1971); Sanchez, *Becoming Mexican American*; Gutierrez, *Walls and Mirrors*; Montejano, *Anglos and Mexicans in the Making of Texas*; Lawrence Cardoso, *Mexican Emigration to the US* (Tucson, 1980); Mario Garcia, *Desert Immigrants* (New Haven, 1981); and Carlos Vélez-Ibáñez, *Border Visions: Mexican Cultures of the Southwest United States* (Tucson, 1996).

[50]Manuel García y Griego estimated the annual seasonal migration in the 1920s at 60,000 to 100,000. Manuel Garcia y Griego, "The Importation of Mexican Contract Laborers to the United States, 1942–1964: Antecedents, Operation, and Legacy," *Working Papers in US-Mexican Studies* (no. 11, 1981), 5; Robert McLean, "Tightening the Mexican Border," *Survey* 64 (April 1930), 29, 54; U.S. Department of Labor, Bureau of Immigration, *Annual Report of the Commissioner General of Immigration to the Secretary of Labor*, 1920–1931 (Washington, D.C.); Census Bureau, *Historical Statistics of the United States*, I, 115; Act of May 26, 1924, sec. 14, 43 Stat. 153; Act of Feb. 27, 1925, 43 Stat. 1949; Act of March 4, 1929, 45 Stat. 1551.

[51]Max Kohler, *Immigration and Aliens in the United States: Studies of American Immigration Laws and the Legal Status of Aliens in the US* (New York, 1936), 413.

"Illegal" became constitutive of "Mexican," referring, not to citizens of Mexico, but to a wholly negative racial category, which comprised both Mexican immigrants and Mexican Americans in the United States. The construction of Mexicans as an illegal and illegitimate foreign presence in their former homeland played a central role in the reorganization of the agricultural labor market in the 1920s. The development of commercial agriculture required the creation of a migratory work force and the destruction of all vestiges of the old *patrón-peón* relationships of mutual obligation that had characterized the late-nineteenth-century ranch economy. Casting Mexicans as foreign *distanced* them both from Anglo-Americans culturally and from the Southwest as a region: it stripped Mexicans of the claim of belonging they had had as natives, even as conquered natives. (The formation of segregated communities similarly served to detach Mexicans from their claims of belonging.) The distancing was a way by which the "other" was constructed, out of what Tzvetan Todorov called the failure (or refusal) to identify the self in the other. It differed from the colonial stance toward conquered native subjects, in which the other is a ward to be converted, civilized, and otherwise remolded in the colonialist's image; no such sense of responsibility inhered in commercial growers' relationship to migratory wage labor. Economic relations between absentee owners and migrant laborers were impersonal. As one grower told the economist Paul Taylor in 1929, "The relations between Mexican laborers and American employers . . . are regulated under economic, not personal pressure."[52]

In 1930 the Census Bureau enumerated Mexicans as a separate race, albeit with the imprecise definition of the Mexican race as persons born in Mexico or with parents born in Mexico and who "are not definitely white, Negro, Indian, Chinese, or Japanese." Distinguishing a separate race of illegitimate foreigners, official policy hardened the idea of Mexicans as a disposable labor force and facilitated the deportation and repatriation of over 400,000 Mexicans (half of them children with United States citizenship) during the Great Depression.[53]

The unassimilability of Mexicans to the American nation had long been argued by eugenicists and nativists, but the historical circumstances of conquest, the labor market, and foreign policy made it impossible to exclude Mexicans formally in the same manner as were Asians. Nevertheless, the fundamental nature

---

[52]Tzvetan Todorov, *The Conquest of America: The Question of the Other*, trans. Richard Howard (New York, 1984), 185; Paul Taylor, "Mexican Labor in the US: Dimmit County, Winter Garden District, South Texas," *University of California Publications in Economics* 6 (no. 5, 1930), 448.

[53]Joseph Hill, "Composition of the American Population by Race and Country of Origin," *Annals of the American Academy of Political and Social Science* 188 (Nov. 1936), 177–84; Paul Taylor, "Mexican Labor in the US: Migration Statistics IV," *University of California Publications in Economics* 12 (no. 3, 1933); Sanchez, *Becoming Mexican American;* Francisco Rodriguez Balderrama and Raymond Rodriguez Balderrama, *Decade of Betrayal: Mexican Repatriation in the 1930s* (Albuquerque, 1995); García y Griego, "Importation of Mexican Contract Laborers to the United States"; Camille Guerin-Gonzales, *Mexican Workers, American Dreams: Immigration, Repatriation, and California Farm Labor, 1900–1939* (New Brunswick, 1994); Abraham Hoffman, *Unwanted: Mexican Americans in the Great Depression: Repatriation Pressures, 1929–1939* (Tucson, 1974).

of restrictive policy created the problem of illegal immigration and placed it at the center of the modern Mexican race problem.

Lawmakers had invoked anthropology and scientific racism to create immigration restriction based on national origin, but it fell to civil servants in the executive branch to devise actual categories of identity for purposes of regulating immigration and immigrants. Indeed, the enumeration and classification of the American people enabled such regulation. As Vicente Rafael has suggested, the value of such population schedules to the modern state lay in their "render[ing] visible the entire field of [state] intervention." Thus the invention of national origins and unassimilable races was as much a project of state building as it was one of ideology. Indeed, if World War I marked the end of the "long nineteenth century," the United States emerged during the 1920s in full modern dress. Key to its modern persona was a comprehensive race policy that was unprecedented in scope and embedded in the law and in official practices at the federal level. Immigration policy and its specific constructions of race enabled the state to demarcate and police both the external boundaries and the internal spaces of the nation.[54]

Congress, the Quota Board, the Supreme Court, and the Immigration Service produced and reproduced categories of difference that turned on both nationality and race, reclassifying Americans as racialized subjects simultaneously along both axes. The Immigration Act of 1924 contributed to the racialization of immigrant groups around notions of whiteness, permanent foreignness, and illegality—categories of difference that have outlived the racial categories created by eugenics and post–World War I nativism. Those legacies remain with us to this day, as Lisa Lowe has described, in "racial formations that are the material trace of history."[55]

---

[54]Vicente Rafael, "White Love: Surveillance and Nationalist Resistance in the United States Colonization of the Philippines," in *Cultures of United States Imperialism*, ed. Amy Kaplan and Donald Pease (Durham, 1993), 188.

[55]Lowe, *Immigrant Acts*, 26.

Mae Ngai

I am a historian of American immigration, citizenship, national identity, and nationalism. I am interested in immigration in part because I am the daughter of immigrants; but more generally because immigration is one of the most controversial issues facing our time. My first book, *Impossible Subjects: Illegal Aliens and the Making of Modern America* (2004), explores the historical and legal emergence of "illegal aliens" in the twentieth century and investigates the means by which this concept shaped Americans' ideas about ethnicity, race, and citizenship. More recently I have been exploring the experiences of Chinese people in America. In 2010, I published *The Lucky Ones: One Family and the Extraordinary Invention of Chinese America*, a nineteenth-century biography about one of the first middle-class Chinese American families in the United States. I am currently at work on *Yellow and Gold: The Chinese Mining Diaspora, 1848–1908*, a study about Chinese gold miners and anti-Chinese racial politics in California, Australia, and South Africa. I continue to be interested in immigration matters and write commentaries on immigration history and policy for *The New York Times*, *The Washington Post*, *The Los Angeles Times*, and other publications. I am a professor of history at Columbia University.

QUESTIONS FOR CONSIDERATION

1. Ngai argues that "nation and nationality are socially constructed." What does this mean?
2. What, according to Ngai, was the effect of the Immigration Act on American conceptions of ethnicity?
3. The Immigration Act of 1924 was based on the percentages of "native stock" and "foreign stock" from the census of 1790. How were these categories determined? What categories of people were excluded from these definitions?
4. Ngai argues that eugenicists "worked backward from classifications they defined . . . and declared a causal relationship between data and race." What does she mean by this statement? And what can we infer from this statement about the role of historical context in the formation of social scientific theories?
5. Ngai, quoting another scholar, calls ethnicity "pseudo-historical" and "triggered" by "power relations in a given historical moment." How did ideas of different ethnicities reflect the historical context of the 1920s, especially in terms of the "power relations" of the period?
6. What problems arose in the attempt to define "races" scientifically? How did these problems manifest themselves in specific cases?
7. How did the Immigration Act of 1924 help redefine Asians and Mexicans as "ineligible" or "illegal" residents? What were the historical origins of this discrimination? How was the ethnicity of black Americans conceived in ways both similar and different to those of the immigrants described in Ngai's article? Consult Foner's article at the beginning of this volume for assistance.

CHAPTER SIX

Rethinking Paternalism: Power and Parochialism in a Southern Mill Village[1]

Mary Lethert Wingerd

In the restive summer of 1934, waves of worker insurgency shook the textile South. Years of unanswered industrial grievances culminated in a general strike unparalleled in the region, with over 170,000 southern mill hands ultimately joining ranks in protest. In Durham, North Carolina, the operatives of Mill 1, flagship of the Erwin Mills Company, immediately presented a united front of organized opposition. Picket lines also quickly sprang up around Erwin Mill 2, located eighty miles southeast of Durham in the town of Erwin. But such was not the case at Erwin Mill 3. In the village of Cooleemee, nestled in the western Piedmont of North Carolina far from any urban center, the mill whistle blew as usual and the full complement of hands reported for work. Despite pleading, persuasion, and even coercion from flying squadrons of organizers and operatives from other mills, the people of Cooleemee refused to go out. . . .[2] Nonetheless, it would be a mistake to conclude that workers in Cooleemee passively accepted management practices. Formal organization and militant opposition are not the only measures of resistance. Such a narrow definition fails to take into account the cultural and social contours that inform protest. . . .[3]

---

[1]Interested students are encouraged to read this essay in the original form. Mary Lethert Wingerd, "Rethinking Paternalism: Power and Parochialism in a Southern Mill Village," *The Journal of American History* 83, no. 3 (Dec. 1996), 872–902.

[2]"Flying squadrons" were caravans of striking workers who raced across the Piedmont in cars and trucks, spreading word of the strike and closing down as many mills as possible. On the strike and the events leading up to it, see Janet Irons, "Testing the New Deal: The General Strike of 1934" (Ph.D. diss., Duke University, 1988).

[3]Melton Alonza McLaurin, *Paternalism and Protest: Southern Cotton Mill Workers and Organized Labor, 1875–1905* (Westport, 1971), 16–40; Barbara S. Griffith, *The Crisis of American Labor: Operation Dixie and the Defeat of the CIO* (Philadelphia, 1988), 88–105; Bryant Simon, "Choosing between the Ham and the Union: Paternalism in the Cone Mills of Greensboro, 1925–1930," in *Hanging by a Thread: Social Change in Southern Textiles*, ed. Jeffrey Leiter, Michael D. Schulman, and Rhonda Zingraff (Ithaca, 1991), 81–89; Jacquelyn Dowd Hall et al., *Like a Family: The Making of a Southern Cotton Mill World* (New York, 1989); Douglas Flamming *Creating the Modern South: Millhands & Managers in Dalton, Georgia, 1884–1984* (Chapel Hill, 1992); Irons, "Testing the New Deal," 422, 425; and David L. Carlton, *Mill and Town in South Carolina, 1880–1920* (Baton Rouge, 1982), 162.

In 1937, just three years after the crushing defeat of the general strike, with the textile unions broken across the South, the operatives of the Cooleemee mill organized to form Local 251 of the Textile Workers Organizing Committee (TWOC), which was affiliated with the Committee for Industrial Organization (CIO). This action led to unionization of all Erwin's North Carolina mills—a feat of no small significance since Erwin was one of the "big four" in North Carolina textiles, employing over 5,500 workers in its three mill towns. Organized labor was facing virtual obliteration in the Piedmont when Erwin's workers organized, led by Cooleemee; they thereby *doubled* the union presence in North Carolina. The local continued to function in its members' behalf until the closing of the mill in 1969. Moreover, the union was described by the Textile Workers Union of America (TWUA) representative assigned to Cooleemee in 1941 as "the best local I've ever seen."[4]

The explanation for this shift from apparent passivity to activism lies in the community's interior dynamics, what political scientist James C. Scott has described as "infrapolitics": "the circumspect struggle waged daily by subordinate groups" in their confrontation with an unequal balance of power.[5] Thus, the underpinnings of the highly personalized world of southern industrial paternalism can be understood clearly only at the local level. Each community was fundamentally shaped by specific contingencies of personality and place, and identity of interests was determined by more than the sum of material circumstance. A close look at Cooleemee reveals a culture neither of resignation, of accommodation, nor of historically learned defeat.[6] Instead, below the surface of apparently placid labor relations, an elaborate culture of resistance operated within a locally circumscribed system of negotiation. In ways that were neither illogical nor peculiarly southern, workers used insularity to their advantage in complex negotiations of their rights. The strategies they employed were not exceptional. Rather, they corresponded to the modes of resistance practiced with differing success by a variety of rural people in their encounters with cultural and economic transition.[7] Drawing on ties of kinship and neighborhood and a precisely drawn definition of

---

[4]Donald McKee interview by Mary Wingerd, May 31, 1993, audiotape (in Mary Wingerd's possession), side 1; Paul David Richards, "The History of the Textile Workers Union of America, CIO, in the South, 1937–1945" (Ph.D. diss., University of Wisconsin, Madison, 1978), 164.

[5]James C. Scott, *Domination and the Arts of Resistance: Hidden Transcripts* (New Haven, 1990), 183–84; Robin D. G. Kelley, "'We Are Not What We Seem': Rethinking Black Working-Class Opposition in the Jim Crow South," *Journal of American History* 80 (June 1993), 111–12; Lawrence Goodwyn, *Breaking the Barrier: The Rise of Solidarity in Poland* (New York, 1991); and Lawrence Goodwyn, *Democratic Promise: The Populist Moment in* America (New York, 1976).

[6]John Gaventa, *Power and Powerlessness: Quiescence and Rebellion in an Appalachian Valley* (Urbana, 1982).

[7]McLaurin, *Paternalism and Protest*; Allen Tullos, *Habits of Industry: White Culture and the Transformation of the Carolina Piedmont* (Chapel Hill, 1989); and I. A. Newby, *Plain Folk in the New South: Social Change and Cultural Persistence, 1880–1915* (Baton Rouge, 1989). Jonathan Prude, *The Coming of Industrial Order: Town and Factory Life in Rural Massachusetts, 1810–1860* (Cambridge, Eng., 1983); and Thomas Dublin, *Women at Work: The Transformation of Work and Community in Lowell, Massachusetts, 1826–1860* (New York, 1979); Gerald Zahavi, *Workers, Managers, and Welfare Capitalism: The Shoeworkers and Tanners of Endicott Johnson, 1890–1950* (Urbana, 1988).

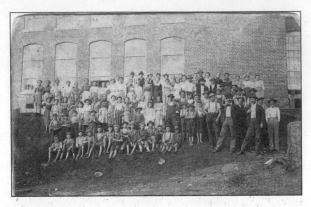

Photo 6.1
Spinning room work force, 1911, showing the assignment of jobs by sex and age. The job of spinner was categorized as women's work. "Doffer boys" removed the filled bobbins and quills from the spinning frames; as young as nine or ten years old, they were considered particularly adept because of their size and agility. The men were probably supervisors, machine fixers, and sweepers, the highest and the lowest occupations in the mill. Printed with permission of the Cooleemee Textile Heritage Center Archive.

community, the settled workers of Cooleemee labored to hold management accountable within a social contract, strategies that led directly to their unionization and deeply influenced the union they constructed.[8]

Coolemee conformed exactly to the well-known profile of a rural company town. The village was archetypal in its isolation and the degree of control the mill seemed to wield. At the turn of the century, when James and Benjamin Duke, the financial power behind Erwin Mills, began construction of their new state-of-the-art cotton mill community, they chose a site that would give new meaning to the term "isolated mill village." Drawing on the Dukes' extraordinary capital resources, Erwin Mills bought up approximately 5,000 acres of land surrounding the site of the new mill, effectively buttressing its workers from "outside influences." . . . In their early years, the mill and village were virtually inaccessible by road; materials moved to and from the mill by rail . . . , and passenger traffic was ferried in and out of the village mainly by boat. As late as 1924, the village could claim only two cars. Both belonged to management.[9]

---

[8]James C. Scott, *Weapons of the Weak: Everyday Forms of Peasant Resistance* (New Haven, 1985); David Thelen, *Paths of Resistance: Tradition and Dignity in Industrializing Missouri* (New York, 1986); and E. P. Thompson, *Customs in Common: Studies in Traditional Popular Culture* (New York, 1993).

[9]McLaurin, *Paternalism and Protest*, 155–57; Financial records, box 58, Cooleemee Series, Erwin Mills Papers (Special Collections Department, Duke University Library, Durham, N.C.); Jim Rumley, "Not Hemmed In," Cooleemee History Loom (Spring 1991), 1. T. M. Young, *The American Cotton Industry: A Study of Work and Workers, Contributed to the Manchester Guardian* (New York, 1903), 58–60; James W. Wall, *History of Davie County* (Spartanburg, 1985), 276–82; Margaret Skinner Parker, interview by W. Weldon Huske, March 7, 1976, transcript, pp. 1–6 (Southern Historical Collection, University of North Carolina, Chapel Hill).

Internally, the Dukes lavished funds on their version of a model company town, taking pains to provide amenities designed to keep workers in place and to determine who would do business within the village. Not only did they own the mill and all the land on which the village was situated; they owned every cottage, store-front, lamppost, and road in the unincorporated village, as well as thousands of acres of surrounding tenant farms. Erwin Mills embarked wholeheartedly on a sophisticated strategy of "benevolent paternalism" well in advance of most of the industry. From the outset, the company meticulously maintained the village, underwrote the building of churches and schools, stocked the company store with varied goods at competitive prices made accessible through generous terms of credit, and furnished recreational amenities for workers and their families.[10] The downside of all this seeming benevolence, however, was that Erwin Mills intended to control every aspect of workers' lives.

Nonetheless, despite management's efforts, the new industrial workers who migrated from the farms of the surrounding counties saw themselves neither as passive beneficiaries of the company's largess nor as helpless victims in the face of company control. On the contrary, they considered themselves active participants in constructing the meaning of community that would shape social and labor negotiations between workers and management in Cooleemee.

To understand these dynamics, it is important to keep in mind that in the village of Cooleemee community encompassed only a certain category of worker and its meaning had real geographical limits. Partly because of Cooleemee's isolation, partly in response to Erwin's management style, but to a great degree because of the way women and men chose to characterize themselves as workers, their identity was inseparable from the specific mill village they called home.

The Scotch-Irish, English, and German farm families who became the first generation of workers had embarked on industrial life with mixed feelings, strongly influenced by perspectives of age and gender. On one hand, the mill whistle promised opportunity and escape from the uncertainty and drudgery of the fields, and the bustling village seemed an energetic antidote to quiet country life. The younger people, particularly young women, experienced a heady new freedom from parental control. Describing her first impression of the village, spinner Lillie Bailey vividly exclaimed, "My first trip to Cooleemee, I thought I'd been to New York, it was so big. I'd been somewhere I'd been to Cooleemee." On the other hand, town life and wage work challenged traditional rural values, independence and status, especially for males. . . .[11]

Middle-class Southerners universally looked down on this new working class and the communities where they lived. Though Cooleemee's isolation

---

[10]Flamming, *Creating the Modern South*; Margaret Crawford, "Earle S. Draper and the Company Town in the American South," in *The Company Town*, ed. John S. Garner (New York, 1992), 139–72. The description of Cooleemee here relies primarily on oral histories, photographs, issues of the *Cooleemee Journal* and *Salisbury Post*, Young, *American Cotton Industry*, and Wall, *History of Davie County*.

[11]Lillie Bailey interview, in *Cooleemee: Memories Not Lost* (Cooleemee Historical Association, 1990) (videotape, 40 min.); G. A. Myers interview, ibid.; Lillian Spry interview by Wingerd, May 14, 1992, audiotape (in Wingerd's possession), side 1.

protected its residents from the daily slights that demeaned workers who lived on the edge of urban centers, they were well aware of the widespread contempt for their way of life—most intimately personified by the hauteur of middle-class Mocksville, just seven miles down the road and the only other town in Davie County. The antagonism between the two towns became legendary, and for generations Cooleemee people were typically accosted in Mocksville by taunts of "linthead" and "mill trash." . . .[12]

To protect themselves from the stings of Mocksville's disdain, mill people in Cooleemee used isolation as a fortress. Drawing on a culture of rural localism and kinship, they constructed a new identity, banding together behind a wall of community pride and solidarity. When spinner Sadie Hodges encountered a Mocksville man who advised her, "Now don't you tell nobody you're from Cooleemee. You know what Cooleemee is," Sadie staunchly replied, "I'm going to tell you something—I'm from Cooleemee and proud of it." Notably, working people in Cooleemee did not refute the reputation of mill hands in general. Instead, they closed ranks and described themselves as a "better class" of mill worker—better workers, more cultured, more educated, and, overall, "different." Rather than contesting the mill hand stereotype as universally unfair, they worked out a definition of themselves as exceptions to the rule.[13]

Thus, they identified themselves in opposition both to middle-class culture and to broader cultural characterizations of the working class. Their identity and loyalties were intrinsically tied to place, which linked workers, across class, with resident management in a shared, though contested, common culture as part of the "community" of Cooleemee.[14] Such pride in place was not unique to this village. Throughout the textile south, workers in isolated mill towns similarly defined themselves as "different" and "unique." The significance of this strategy lies in its capacity both to empower and to limit workers' struggles, making broad working-class solidarity difficult to achieve.

Place was a defining factor, but not the only factor. Of equal importance was participation in a value system that supported workers' established culture as well as Cooleemee's claims to exceptionalism. The solidarity that allowed workers to present a united face to the outside world was based on strict understandings of internal mutuality and morality, enforced by traditional ties of kinship, neighborhood, and church—as well as a prickly assertion of independence and

---

[12]Carlton, *Mill and Town in South Carolina*, 78–88, 129–70; Ray Jordan interview by Wingerd, March 25, 1992, notes, p. 3 (in Wingerd's possession). See also John Henry Nail interview by Lynn Rumley, March 13, 1990, videotape (Cooleemee Historical Association Archives, Cooleemee, N.C.); Sadie Hodges interview by Wingerd, May 28, 1992, audiotape (in Wingerd's possession), side 1.

[13]Hodges interview, May 28, 1992, side 1. Flamming, *Creating the Modern South*, 164; and Dale Newman, "Work and Community Life in a Southern Textile Town," *Labor History* 19 (Spring 1978), 207.

[14]Jordan interview, March 25, 1992, p. 4; Flamming, *Creating the Modern South*, 161; Werner Sollors, ed., *The Invention of Ethnicity* (New York, 1989); John Bodnar, *The Transplanted: A History of Immigrants in Urban America* (Bloomington, 1985); and Susan A. Glenn, *Daughters of the Shtetl: Life and Labor in the Immigrant Generation* (Ithaca, 1990), esp. 202–6.

pride. As extended families of the original workers poured into the village and those families inter-married, the web of obligation and support thickened and strengthened over generations, and residents' assertion that they were "just like a family" took on more than a metaphorical meaning.[15]

The shift from agriculturist to industrial worker was neither sharp nor immediately completed . . . For many years even those families who settled permanently in the village tended livestock, chickens, and gardens as well as power looms, accommodating rural rhythms of work to the demands of industrial time. Mabel Head rose every morning at five A.M. to slop the hogs before heading off to a day's work in the mill. . . .[16]

Some version of this rural / urban life-style existed in most of those southern mill villages located away from urban centers. But Cooleemee was exceptional in the scope of Erwin Mills' vast landholdings and the degree to which the company made them available for workers' use. Not only did the company provide common pasture for livestock, land for large-scale gardening, and common woodlots; it also gave workers free rein to hunt and fish its lands. Thus, though residents of Cooleemee had taken up wage work, their access to the countryside gave them breathing room and allowed them to retain a sense of self-sufficiency and independence. According to loom fixer Claudie Boger, "you could use their land just like it was yours."[17]

Just as workers adapted rural practices to town living, so they brought the values and social relations that had given order to their preindustrial lives, reshaping them to fit a social landscape fundamentally transformed by the looming presence of a cotton mill. Corn shuckings, hog killings, and, particularly, church activities formed the social nexus of village life, providing—even demanding—reinforcement of neighborly mutuality and community ties. Cooleemee became home to four mainstream denominations—Baptist, Methodist, Presbyterian, and Episcopalian—and members of each congregation participated enthusiastically in activities sponsored by the others. Bazaars, oyster stews, "wienie roasts," and an array of other social activities supplemented Bible study groups and church services to fill out Cooleemee's social calendar. . . .[18] The core families, those who lived within the village and who by their persistence defined the meaning of community, tended to remain in place throughout their working lives, creating stable and interlocking relationships that persisted over generations. . . . Daily personal interaction obligated managers as well as mill hands in a mutually binding, albeit unequal, social contract.[19]

---

[15]Boe Turner, "They Came from Wilkes," *Cooleemee History Loom* (Fall 1991), 3, 12.

[16]Mabel Head interview in *Cooleemee: Memories Not Lost*; Fred Pierce, Jessie and Fred Pierce interview by Wingerd, May 14, 1992, audiotape (in Wingerd's possession), side 1.

[17]Claudie Boger, Frances and Claudie Boger interview by Wingerd, May 27, 1992, audiotape (in Wingerd's possession), side 1, tape 2.

[18]Jessie and Fred Pierce interview, side 1; Ray Jordan interview, May 14, 1992, side 1; Spry interview, side 1.

[19]Jessie Pierce, Jessie and Fred Pierce interview, side 1; Ray Jordan interview, May 14, 1992, side 2; Nail interview; Sadie Jordan interview by Wingerd, May 14, 1992, audiotape (in Wingerd's possession), side 1.

. . . Without question company rules infringed on personal freedoms. However, management often turned a blind eye to the transgressions of valued workers, and regulations were enforced selectively to police the behavior of transient or less conventional operatives. . . . The expulsion of obstreperous elements from the village often supported the values of the settled cohort of workers, as evidenced by general acquiescence in the casting out of unfit church members. In addition, people expressed little disapproval of company policy that expelled unwed pregnant women from the village (though they considered it unduly harsh to force the entire family to leave town). . . .[20] It seems that community was defined narrowly by management and residents alike. Indeed, evidence of Ku Klux Klan activity in Cooleemee in the 1920s indicates that some workers occasionally played a very active role in enforcing a sanctioned code of conduct. According to one mill hand Klansman, the order was "just as Christian as any organization" and mobilized primarily to discipline white transgressors of community mores, "women and men not doing right, [such as] wife beating." In his words, "We had a right good secretary who'd write them letters—a warning. We wouldn't have to write a second one."[21]

The ominous march of the Klan through town also served as a chilling reminder to local African Americans that they were definitely not part of the community. Nor were they welcome as workers in the mill. Textile work throughout the Jim Crow South was almost exclusively the province of white labor. No African Americans resided in the village of Cooleemee proper, and black workers comprised only a minuscule proportion of the mill's work force, limited to janitorial roles and the dirtiest and most difficult tasks in the mill yard. Yet, though they were excluded from the self-described community, the small African American population nonetheless played a critical role in the construction of its identity. White workers enhanced their self-esteem and narrowed the gap between themselves and management through a common culture of white supremacy. . . . In addition, white mill workers regularly employed black women as domestics, an arrangement that enabled poorly paid whites to act out their own version of paternalism, with a distinctly racial cast. Thus, membership and status in the community of Cooleemee were determined by an intricate weighing of class, race, gender, and conduct.[22]

[20]27 Frances Boger, Frances and Claudie Boger interview, side 1, tape 1; Sadie Jordan interview, side 1; Hall et al., *Like a Family*, 164–67; Flamming, *Creating the Modern South*, 165; G. C. Waldrep III, "The Politics of Hope and Fear: The Struggle for Community in the Industrial South" (Ph.D. diss., Duke University, 1996), 240–72.

[21]Claudie Boger, Frances and Claudie Boger interview, side 1, tape 1; Russell Ridenhour interview by Rumley, Oct. 22, 1989, videotape (Cooleemee Historical Association Archives).

[22]Gary M. Fink, *The Fulton Bag and Cotton Mills Strike of 1914–1915: Espionage, Labor Conflict, and New South Industrial Relations* (Ithaca, 1993), 150; Hall et al., *Like a Family*, 66, 157; Jessie Pierce, Jessie and Fred Pierce interview, side 2; Hodges interview, May 14, 1992, side 1; and Harold Foster interview by Rumley, Feb. 15, 1990, videotape (Cooleemee Historical Association Archives); Foster interview; David Roediger, *The Wages of Whiteness: Race and the Making of the American Working Class* (New York, 1991).

The complicated web of social relations extended vertically through the mill hierarchy as well as laterally among the operatives. Management nurtured the concept of Cooleemee's exceptionalism to further its own ends. The qualities that workers ascribed to themselves neatly fit the profile of an ideal work force. And, in the minds of both company president William Erwin and J. W. Zachary, manager of the Cooleemee mill for over thirty years, the social landscape of "their" exceptional village also confirmed their vision of themselves as moral guardians and father figures to "their people." . . . Summing up his career as head of Erwin Mills, William Erwin wrote: "I would be glad for you to know that in dealing with several thousand operatives and families of same that I have striven unceasingly to uplift and make them better. In this work I have found pleasure and trust that in it I may be permitted to broaden my field of labor." . . .[23]

Herein was the hidden component of incipient worker power embedded in the social contract. If Cooleemee's workers were indeed exceptional, then they must be treated with the respect that their character demanded—both in the village and in the mill. Within the close confines of Cooleemee, neighbor worked next to neighbor at the looms and management lived right down the street. Workers and managers attended the same churches and sent their children to the same schools, and even managers' children usually worked for a time in the mill, all of which reinforced the respectability of mill work, in opposition to derogatory cultural stereotypes. By articulating a community identity that included managers, workers seized some power to hold them to its norms. As long as managers tied their own identities to the constructed conceptions of family and community, they were doubly bound. . . .[24]

This is not to say that Cooleemee's workers had achieved a cultural coup. The unwritten compact maintained by elaborate, customary social rituals was fragile. The cultural lure of paternalism for managers was always inextricably linked to economic self-interest. . . . Workers' negotiating leverage was effective only so long as management identified a stable, settled work force as a priority in its long-term profit projections. In the increasingly competitive international textile market, managers eventually discarded paternalistic practices for a more rationalized industrial capitalism. But in Cooleemee, for some thirty-four years, the compact remained largely intact. Throughout his tenure as manager, Zachary seemed committed to insuring the persistence of Cooleemee's core work force, and he carefully nurtured the illusion of democratic social relations and company largess. That illusion carried a price for management prerogative. According to village residents, supervisors who ignored the rituals of conduct that guided Cooleemee's labor or social relations seldom lasted long in the mill. Those who stayed quickly learned the acceptable code of etiquette or faced the consequences. . . .[25]

---

[23]Eugene D. Genovese, *Roll, Jordan, Roll: The World the Slaves Made* (New York, 1974), 70–87. For William Erwin's letter, see *Durham Morning Herald*, Feb. 29, 1932, p. 2.

[24]Pierce interview, side 1; Wall interview, p. 2. For evidence of the long-standing nature of this practice, see Manuscript Population Schedules, Davie County, North Carolina, Thirteenth Census of the United States, 1910 (microfilm: reel 1107), Records of the Bureau of the Census, RG 29 (National Archives, Washington, D.C.).

[25]Frances and Claudie Boger interview, side 2, tape 1; Parker interview, p. 8.

Within the limits of the self-described community of Cooleemee—and they were real limits—workers responded to breaches of the social contract with a solidarity that placed management decidedly outside the bonds of family. To mediate such tensions between management and labor and to undercut incipient class solidarity, Erwin filled its low-level management positions almost exclusively from the local work force.[26] The fact that the second hands and overseers—all male—were the fathers, sons, and neighbors of those they dealt with did smooth labor relations, but it also gave workers increased leverage in negotiating. . . . Work relations on the floor were inseparable from the dynamics that played out on the streets of the village—or even, in some instances, at the kitchen table. Members of a single family might find themselves on opposing sides of a labor dispute, further complicating loyalties and obligations.[27]

None of this is to suggest that Cooleemee's workers fundamentally changed the balance of power in the mill, nor did they delude themselves about their autonomy in this company town. Management's authority was a stifling presence at times. As one mill hand recalled: "He [the manager] was the king. You had to do what was his policy. He told my momma, 'Either get rid of the dog, keep him [tied] up or move out of Cooleemee.' That's the way the hammer was." . . .[28]

The folklore of the village attests to the critical importance workers imparted to assertions of independence and self-respect as they battled in this arena of unequal power relations. Three related themes dominate workers' reminiscences: talking back, walking out, and acting up in ways that were beyond the mill's control. . . .[29] When management transgressed customary work practices, workers stress, they responded with immediacy and solidarity in spontaneous walkouts. Though the details of these confrontations remain vivid in workers' memory, the results are seldom remembered. It seems the meaning of the story was in the act of assertion more than in its outcome. Self-evidently, such acts had limited effect on basic power relationships; however, they had far more than theatrical value. Workers used the rituals of social custom to articulate their sense of dignity and rights. In doing so, they reinforced their self-esteem and developed a collective confidence that, as events were to demonstrate, would serve them well in later years.[30]

The rhythms of life and work were inseparable, and the grievances that moved people to protest were conceived in broad, holistic terms. Workers recollect that wages were seldom an issue of contention, declaring, "we were poor but we didn't know it." Indeed, from at least 1920 through the mid-1940s, Erwin's

[26]Hall et al., *Like a Family*, 96–98.

[27]Ray Jordan interviews, May 28, 1992, side 1, and May 14, 1992, side 1; Sadie Jordan interview, side 1. See also Boger and Pierce interviews.

[28]Dave Hancock interview in *Cooleemee: Memories Not Lost*.

[29]Lawrence Miller interview in *Cooleemee: Memories Not Lost*.

[30]Goodwyn, *Breaking the Barrier*, 138–39; and Scott, *Domination and the Arts of Resistance*, 65–66.

wages, though never generous, outpaced the prevailing southern scale.[31] The wages were combined with noncash benefits provided by the company, and they were supplemented by family-raised livestock and produce. Thus in Cooleemee through 1934 the standard of living was less dependent on wages than in many other mill towns. When discontent periodically erupted, it was almost invariably over issues of respect, work practices, or traditional rights.[32]

By the time of the 1934 general strike, cutthroat competition in the industry and the resultant demands for increased productivity had created abysmal conditions in most southern textile communities, with workers subjected to ever-increasing work loads and deteriorating working conditions. The chief grievance was what mill hands called the stretch-out—the practice of assigning increasing numbers of machines to individual workers, reducing workers' control over both pace and method of production. Some manufacturers had begun implementing time-management practices as early as 1921, and by 1934 people were desperate for relief.[33]

But in Cooleemee, though mill management was tentatively experimenting with new combinations of piece rate and incentive schemes, time management and the attendant stretch-out had not yet invaded the mill in any systematic fashion. . . . Workers characterized working conditions in the mill as generally "pretty good" in 1934, in sharp contrast to conditions in other mills in the South. Perhaps workers saw this as further proof of their exceptionalism, or at least as a testament to the efficacy of community-based negotiating tactics.[34]

Thus it was that in 1934 Cooleemee's workers, with an ingrained suspicion of outsiders, saw little to induce them to cast their lot with mill hands in other textile communities. Nor were they receptive to the overtures of outside organizers. . . .[35] Holding themselves apart from broader working-class struggles, Cooleemee's workers chose instead to depend on one another and on a known quantity—their ability to negotiate personally with the management of their mill. According to Claudie Boger, a union leader in later years, "people in town felt like the company was part of them. They wasn't interested in fighting the company *at that particular time*."[36]

---

[31]"Report to the National War Labor Board, 1942," National War Labor Board Folder, box 49, Erwin Mills Papers.

[32]Irons, "Testing the New Deal," 2, 14, 267; Boger, Ray Jordan, Nail, and Sadie Jordan interviews.

[33]Daniel James Clark, "The TWUA in a Southern Mill Town: What Unionization Meant in Henderson, North Carolina" (Ph.D. diss., Duke University, 1989), 19–20; and Irons, "Testing the New Deal," 46–53.

[34]Wall interview, p. 3; and Claudie Boger, Frances and Claudie Boger interview, side 1, tape 1. Sadie Jordan interview, side 1; Frances and Claudie Boger interview, side 1, tape 1; and Spry interview, side 1.

[35]Griffith, *Crisis of American Labor*, 101–2, 167–69.

[36]Hodges interview, May 14, 1992, side 1; Claudie Boger, Frances and Claudie Boger interview, side 1, tape 1.

To reenlist any wavering loyalties, Kemp Lewis, William Erwin's successor, came to town at the onset of the strike, called a general meeting of the operatives, and promised, "you all stick with us and we'll stick with y'all later. If y'all will vote to work, we'll send the National Guard up here to protect you."[37] The workers did stick with the company, led by the older generation of workers who reassured themselves that the bonds of custom would provide immunity from the changes ripping apart the Piedmont. The younger people, who would later become the union's leaders, were held in check by the reins of parental authority. In 1934 young Draper Wood, who would play a key role in the organizing effort in 1937, decided to picket at the gates with the flying squadrons from other mills. But when his father heard that his son had stayed out, he put a hammer in his pocket "in case there was any trouble" and set out to "bring his boy in." Old Mr. Wood's motivations were complex; "he thought there was nobody like Erwin Mills," but at the same time he knew his son "would have been fired just like that." Other workers, skeptical of Erwin's good faith, may have been silenced by the intimidating evidence of the company's partnership with the state, manifested in the National Guard. Some people felt equally threatened by the strikers on one side and the National Guard on the other. Caught up in a war not of her making, Lillian Spry was afraid that the union people might force her to lose her job or convince her husband to join them. At the same time, she remembered hesitantly, "I never been scared so bad in all my life because they brought in the National Guards, and I just knowed they was going to come in to kill us all!" Power relations in Cooleemee were seldom so overtly displayed, and as townspeople anxiously awaited the arrival of the troops, they filled the churches in prayer services that besought the salvation of their community.[38]

Photo 6.2

The National Guard patrols in front of the Cooleemee mill during the 1934 general strike. The arrival of the National Guard, ostensibly deployed to "protect" workers, was an unmistakable reminder of the power relations that underlay claims of community in this **company town.** Printed with permission of the Cooleemee Textile Heritage Center Archive.

The decisive historical juncture for these workers occurred shortly after the defeat of the general strike. Despite Kemp Lewis's promise, time-management experts appeared in the Cooleemee mill. As John Henry Nail ironically observed, "In place of them sticking with us, they really stuck it to us. They brought a bunch of checkers in here and put more

---

[37]Nail interview.

[38]Claudie Boger, Frances and Claudie Boger interview, side 1, tape 1; Spry interview, side 1; Parker interview, p. 45.

work on us." . . .[39] By early 1935 the company had determined to bring the Cooleemee mill in line with its competitors' practices. In the face of the continuing depression, Erwin Mills abandoned any pretense that its workers were partners in the enterprise. With the bottom line at stake, profit took precedence over Erwin's vaunted paternalism and contracts of custom were unilaterally breached.

The intrusion of time-management experts not only increased work loads; it also affronted workers' dignity and skill. Claudie Boger was insulted to find his every move timed. "If you had to go to the bathroom, they'd follow you over to the bathroom door, stand there 'til you come out—note how much time you spent. . . . You was supposed to have six minutes of rest an hour and under the time system, every second that wasn't actually working was rest time. . . . Going to the bathroom, getting a drink of water, that was all rest time." Moreover, experienced mill hands were frustrated by the flaws in the evaluation system that would henceforth set the pace of their work. The "experts" seemed not to understand the intricacies of textile production: that coarse thread filled the spindles more quickly than fine, requiring more frequent tending of the spinning frames; that moving people from job to job upset important working relationships. As one worker explained, "You got used to a certain person doing your repair work, maybe doffing [removing filled bobbins from the spinning frames], but as you moved around, you changed the people that would do that for you. And that relationship that you'd worked up between you and your fixer and your doffer changed. That made a lot of difference—the people you worked with." Nor did the checkers take into account the way their watchful presence distorted normal work rhythms. "People would be nervous and they'd get shook up and scared they wasn't doing it right," or "some would work like a Trojan" at a pace that could not be realistically maintained. Frances Boger's work assignment went from sixteen looms to thirty-two. As she recalled:

> Before, folks had a job they could keep up, make a little rest on it, and talk to the next operator beside them, and everybody was just friendly-like and talking amongst themselves. But when they started the stretch-out, they didn't have nothing to do but just run, run, run on that job. And they resented it.

The new work patterns reduced workers' control over their labor; they also ended lunch breaks and informal social time in the mill and signaled a disrespect for the expertise in which Cooleemee mill hands took pride. When workers attempted to point out the problems in the system, they were frustrated to discover that their knowledge counted for little. Frances Boger ruefully remarked, "We had the experience and they had it on books."[40]

Initially, workers attempted to utilize traditional methods of resistance and self-assertion to stave off the hated changes, expressing their discontent in frequent, spontaneous walkouts, but old strategies no longer seemed effective. The

---

[39]Nail interview.

[40]Frances and Claudie Boger interview, side 2, tape 1; Sadie Jordan interview, side 2; Ray Jordan interview, May 14, 1992, side 2.

first time a checker appeared with his stopwatch in the weave room, outraged workers picked him up and threw him out the window.[41] Though this story has become one of Cooleemee's most cherished bits of folklore, the checkers stayed and the stretch-out continued. Ironically for Erwin Mills, however, the illusion of democratic social relations that managers had fostered to defuse worker protest had a power they had not anticipated. By acting out their independence and dignity in seemingly small and inconsequential ways over the years, workers had gradually developed the confidence and sense of entitlement to assert themselves when more was at stake. Drawing on a history of successful self-activity, rather than one of defeat, workers turned to unionization as a new means to enforce company accountability. . . .

When workers organized in 1937 their actions did not represent a sharp break with past practices, but an attempt to formalize and protect the negotiating parameters they had so carefully constructed. Just as their parents and grandparents had translated traditional social understandings to serve their interests as wageworkers in a company town, so the union generation would structure their union using the social strategies that had protected them in the past, in an ongoing dialectic of continuity and change.

In the years following 1934, traditional ways in the village were challenged as the hamlet became less of a cultural island. By 1937, door-to-door salesmen had discovered Cooleemee, hawking a variety of consumer goods on "easy credit" terms. Automobiles were no longer a rarity. The village square now boasted a movie theater, and strains of the *Saturday Night Barn Dance* could be heard from radios in nearly every home. Clearly, more than work loads were changing in this company town.[42]

Of course, the outside world was changing as well. New Deal reforms and victories for organized labor (outside the textile South) seemed to promise a new day for working people. Most southern textile workers, however, battered by the defeats of 1934, had neither the resources nor the optimism to take up the fight again. But in Cooleemee, where workers had been untouched by the consequences of the general strike, unions had a new appeal as a means to protect working-class interests. Some undecided mill hands were persuaded to sign union cards because they believed President Franklin D. Roosevelt had pledged his support and protection for labor's cause. Claudie Boger recalled that "FDR said in a speech that if he worked in a plant, the first thing he would do is join the union."[43] Even the considerable authority of Erwin Mills must have seemed no match for that of the president of the United States. Thus the drive to organize was fueled by a sense of expanded possibilities as well as by

---

[41]Claudie Boger, Frances and Claudie Boger interview, side 1, tape 1; Fred Pierce, Jessie and Fred Pierce interview, side 1.

[42]In 1942, among the 321 households in the village proper, there were 204 automobiles and 412 radios. Cooleemee Village Census, War Labor Board Folder, box 49, Erwin Mills Papers. See also Hodges interview, May 28, 1992, side 1; Hall et al., *Like a Family*, 137–62; Lizabeth Cohen, *Making a New Deal: Industrial Workers in Chicago, 1919–1939* (Cambridge, Eng., 1990), 99–158.

[43]Claudie Boger, Frances and Claudie Boger interview, side 1, tape 1.

new pressures in the workplace. Even so, the Cooleemee union would not be a classic oppositional union like the other CIO unions that formed in the same period, nor a company union. Instead it was a hybrid of the two, shaped by local experience and relationships. Perhaps it can most accurately be described as a community union. . . .

When workers in Cooleemee determined to organize, the thrust came initially from within the community, rather than from an outside organizing drive. Unionization represented a shift in leadership to the younger generation, but it did not entirely jettison the old social contract. All the leaders were children of the first generation of workers, less convinced of the company's reliability than their elders, but still known and trusted insiders, tied through kinship and friendship to nearly everyone in the village, and well versed in traditional Cooleemee modes of negotiating.[44]

Company management also had a stake in its long-standing style of labor relations. Most southern textile magnates stonewalled union efforts regardless of cost. . . . In contrast, Erwin Mills put up little overt resistance when faced with the prospect of unionization, surprising workers and organizers alike.[45] The reasons were complex. Still in the throes of the Depression, cutthroat competition, government regulation, and labor unrest all posed danger to the company's profitability. Company president, Kemp Lewis, feared that, with Franklin Roosevelt in the White House, anything might happen! In 1937 Lewis expressed his dismay to a fellow textile industrialist: "It would seem almost unbelievable unless we were witnessing it for a man of the ancestry and the family surrounding of Franklin Roosevelt to be sitting calmly by and watching the forces of disorder making rapid strides in dominating this country without opening his mouth." . . .[46]

. . . The undetermined role that the National Labor Relations Board (NLRB) would play in future labor negotiations also [distressed company officials]. Company counsel, William R. Perkins, regularly warned Lewis of possible NLRB actions "in these days of wild laws and decisions against employers." In addition, directives from New York repeatedly cautioned him to act with care:

> The Wagner Act is now the law of the land and must be obeyed. You are compelled, as I understand it, to negotiate with properly accredited representatives, but you are not obliged to comply with their demands. We can only hope that your discussions, whenever they take place, will lead to an amicable settlement.

In the spring of 1937 Lewis was under exceptional pressure as Erwin Mills' business began to rebound from depression lows. He reported over a half million

---

[44]Frances and Claudie Boger interview, side 1, tape 1; Ray Jordan interview, March 25, 1992, p. 5; Foster interview.

[45]McKee interview, side 2; Claudie Boger, Frances and Claudie Boger interview, side 1, tape 1. See also Richards, "History of the Textile Workers Union of America," 196–98.

[46]Kemp Lewis to B. B. Gossett, April 6, 1937, Correspondence File, box 46, Kemp Plummer Lewis Papers, Southern Historical Collection; Kemp Lewis to Louis Graves, July 23, 1937, ibid.; and Kemp Lewis to George Fooshe, May 11, 1937, ibid.

dollars gross profit in the first quarter, declaring, "If we are just let alone and have no labor trouble, we ought to have an unusually good year." But he feared labor trouble was on the horizon. . . .[47]

In consultation with Erwin Mills' major shareholders, Lewis apparently had determined that the wisest course was to eschew outright opposition, try to avoid NLRB sanctions, and keep the mills running. At the same time the company would focus its energies on crafting an institutionalized version of existing forms of negotiation, one that would bypass regional or national union representatives as much as possible in favor of personalized, local mediation. Lewis recognized that the success of this endeavor would depend on the quality of face-to-face interactions between workers and management, with or without a union. While he wasted no sympathy on the union itself, he attempted to draw a distinction between CIO organizers and local union activists in the work force:

> If trouble should come, we are not going to be a party to take any measures which will result in violence and personal injury, which will contribute toward antagonism, disrupting the morale of our mills. . . . the effect of which cannot be easily wiped out. If our employees should force this type of trouble on us, we would very much prefer to think of them from our standpoint as being mistaken and to refrain as far as we possibly can from having our minds dwell upon the individual cases. We must all recognize and keep it in our minds that these people are going to be promised a great many things by the organizers and the future will be painted in a very rosy hue to them if they join in this co-operative movement. . . . We are sincerely hopeful that we can get through it without any disruption of our relationship with our employees, and without appreciable lowering of the morale of our employees.[48]

Clearly, Lewis's response to "this co-operative movement" diverged from that of most of his fellow industrialists, in strategy if not intent. Thus, throughout the organizing campaign and the ensuing contract negotiations, neither workers nor management completely repudiated old bases of accountability, though the social fabric on which they relied wore increasingly thin. The TWUA may have treated the company as its implacable opponent, but at the ground level, at least in Cooleemee, the new order was not quite so apparent. Workers maneuvered to maintain customs that would protect community authority, and management strove to convince workers that problems could still be worked out in the company "family."

The result left labor relations in Cooleemee straddling old and new forms of negotiation. When the ballots were counted, the TWUA easily won representation rights as Cooleemee workers voted by more than three to one in favor of

---

[47]William R. Perkins to Kemp Lewis, April 11, 1940, William Perkins Folder, box 49, Erwin Mills Papers; J. C. Thorne to Kemp Lewis, May 14, 1937, Correspondence File, box 46, Lewis Papers; Kemp Lewis to Thorne, May 10, 1937, ibid.; Kemp Lewis to Fooshe, May 11, 1937, ibid.; Kemp Lewis to Thorne, March 15, 1937, ibid.; Thorne to Kemp Lewis, May 14, 1937, ibid.

[48]Kemp Lewis to R. H. Lewis, Dec. 4, 1937, Correspondence File, box 46, Lewis Papers; Kemp Lewis to P. B. Parks, Feb. 5, 1938, Correspondence Folder, box 48, Erwin Mills Papers; Kemp Lewis to E. M. Holt, April 2, 1937, ibid.

the union. But as contract negotiations (intended to cover all Erwin's North Carolina mills) stalled for over three years, grievances continued to be handled in much the old way—by individualized mediation between employees and management, with the added participation of local union representatives, and rituals of courtesy and respect protected valued bargaining chips on both sides of the table.[49]

During this period workers developed an enhanced collective confidence as members of a legally sanctioned bargaining group. At the same time, the company, hoping to minimize the union's demand for contractual constraints, practiced extreme caution both in implementing new work practices and in handling employee complaints. Lewis bombarded his managers with advice on "keeping discussions on a friendly basis, with no bitterness creeping in," and Edwin Holt, manager of the Cooleemee mill, in turn assured him, "we will do everything possible to keep these meetings harmonious and will see that every consideration is given for requests for hearing and what is said in the hearings." Working people in Cooleemee put increasing faith in the demonstrated ability of their representatives to negotiate successfully with management and drew the reasonable conclusion that they had succeeded in restabilizing labor relations to their advantage. In workers' minds the union had achieved precisely what they had intended. All that remained was to formalize the existing parameters of negotiation within a contract.[50]

The TWUA understandably put little faith in the informal constraints of community accountability and adamantly pressed for a binding arbitration clause in the contract. But, at the insistence of Cooleemee's rank and file, Local 251 overrode the objections of union negotiators, broke with workers in Erwin's other mills, and signed a contract *without* binding arbitration. Despite a superficial alliance with textile operatives in Erwin's other mills, the meaning of union remained parochially circumscribed by a definition of community exceptionalism that set them apart from other workers. In short, local issues moved workers to organize, and community dynamics, more than company policy, determined the particular meaning of union and the way locals would operate.[51]

In historical perspective the Cooleemee contract may seem to represent workers' short-sighted denial of the power relations in place, but from the workers' standpoint in 1941 their choice was not entirely illogical. Their union had experienced significant success in mediating grievances, and workers may well have believed that similar locally controlled negotiation would be the most effective strategy in battling future increases in work load. In fact, no version of the contracts that the TWUA

---

[49]See boxes 47–48, Labor Relations Series, Erwin Mills Papers.

[50]Holt to Kemp Lewis, March 5, 1941, Correspondence Folder, box 48, ibid.; Erwin Mills and TWUA contract negotiation meeting, minutes, March 26, 1941, TWUA Negotiations Folder, box 49, ibid.

[51]Minutes, March 21, 1941, ibid.; C. R. Harris memorandum re contract meeting, July 16, 1941, ibid.; Frances and Claudie Boger interview, tape 1, side 2; Foster interview; Ray Jordan interview, May 28, 1992.

presented Erwin Mills seriously contested management's right to control either the introduction of new technology or the pace of production. Thus, if the stretch-out were to be contained, it would not be by the union contract.[52]

To union members in Cooleemee, the CIO provided a useful institutionalized form, but it was only one weapon in the arsenal of opposition. Labor relations in Cooleemee remained largely community-driven and dependent on personal relationships. The local leadership proceeded to steer the union's affairs vigorously with little assistance from the national office. . . . Though the Cooleemee mill remained an open shop in accordance with North Carolina law, the union quickly achieved and maintained high participation, topping 93 percent in 1941. Its shop steward system was unusually inclusive, assuring broad participation by the rank and file in the decision-making process. . . .[53] Despite the national's preoccupation with issues of wages and hours, in Cooleemee throughout the 1940s, grievances continued to focus primarily on working conditions, seniority, and "the arrogance of overseers treating people differently."[54]

The union rapidly became not only the vehicle for labor relations but also the focal social institution of the village, involving the entire community in its many activities. The union took over the social role formerly played by mill management, sponsoring union picnics, beauty contests, fund-raising drives, and classes, as well as the village's annual Fourth of July and Christmas celebrations.[55] These events were not restricted to union members; they were open to all workers and their families, to Cooleemee's small merchant class, and to local management as well. Even as union activities began to demonstrate a more inclusive working-class consciousness, they maintained some of the old ties between workers and managers. Arbitration meetings were held in the union hall, but the hall itself was located above the company store on the village square.[56]

The local's bargaining tactics also retained striking elements of the old, informal, face-to-face negotiating style, as deeply embedded in community as in the workplace—with many of the old strengths and limitations. Cooleemee became widely known for its brand of vibrant unionism and for the union's ability to mediate individual grievances at the local level, so much so that workers from other mill communities looked to Cooleemee as an example and regularly sought the union's assistance in their organizing attempts. Cooleemee's workers, in turn, began to see their interests as tied to those of a larger working-class

[52]Reports to the National Labor Relations Board, Election Folder, box 48, Erwin Mills Papers; Contracts Folder, box 49, ibid.

[53]McKee interview, side 1; Claudie Boger, Frances and Claudie Boger interview, side 1, tape 1.

[54]Foster interview; McKee interview, side 1; Ray Jordan interview, May 14, 1992, side 1; and Claudie Boger, Frances and Claudie Boger interview, side 1, tape 1 and side 2, tape 2.

[55]*Textile Challenger*, 1951–1957.

[56]Richard C. Franck, "An Oral History of West Durham: A Report Submitted to the Durham Bicentennial," 1975, p. 9, Durham Bicentennial Commission Papers (Special Collections Department, Duke University Library).

Photo 6.3
The "roosting pole" in the village square, traditional gathering place for male mill hands, informally supplemented the union hall as the site for discussions of union and community business. Tellingly, this was a masculine preserve. Printed with permission of the Cooleemee Textile Heritage Center Archive.

community, including most immediately those employed in Erwin's other mills. In 1955 the membership made the significant decision to integrate the local, a step toward overcoming generations of inherited racism.[57]

Nonetheless, it will not do to romanticize the efficacy of community unionism. Despite an evolving union consciousness and considerable success in protecting certain worker rights, institutional abuses that derived from conditions outside the Cooleemee mill remained beyond the union's control. Primary among them was the stretch-out, which ultimately proceeded despite all efforts to restrain it.[58] In addition, the union's negotiating leverage was always limited by its tenuous presence in southern textiles.

After a failed organizing drive in the late 1940s, both the CIO and AFL abandoned the southern field. Yet, despite the weakness of organized labor in the region—or perhaps because of it—Erwin Mills came to terms with the union presence in its mills. Cooleemee's manager, Edwin Holt, looked forward to a signed contract in 1941, stating, "We do believe that a contract will do a lot towards straightening out questions that we are now having to answer with regard to work loads." In the opinion of workers and union representative Don McKee, the company regarded the union as a means to forestall costly, spontaneous walkouts and to regularize grievance mediation. McKee declared that he found "no antagonism coming from top management when they went in to negotiate

---

[57]Foster interview; Claudie Boger, Frances and Claudie Boger interview, side 2, tape 1; McKee interview.

[58]Spry interview, side 1.

contracts. They almost seemed to welcome collective bargaining." Thus, while workers used the union to preserve personal accountability, management viewed it as a move toward rationalized labor relations. Consequently, in Cooleemee the union occupied a middle ground between paternalism and contractualism that appeared to offer certain advantages to both sides.[59]

Workers had learned the skills to negotiate paternalism, and they continued to expand them, but the underlying structure of power was unchanged. The advantages accruing to them from community unionism persisted only so long as established relationships remained intact. These limitations were most vividly demonstrated when Burlington Industries purchased Erwin Mills in 1962. Following a corporate strategy unfettered by community constraints, Burlington swept unwritten and legally unprotected rights and obligations from the bargaining table. Workers became increasingly uneasy as one decision after another worked against their interests and against what they perceived as the long-term viability of the mill. Nonetheless, they were stunned by the magnitude of the consequences. In 1969 Burlington shut down the Cooleemee mill without discussion or even a day's notice, exposing the fragile base of community unionism and effectively destroying the community that had been built over generations. Frances Boger sadly recalled, "Not to brag, but we thought we had it made. It really knocked the breath out of you. At our age it was bad to have to get up and hunt for more work."[60]

The limitations of community unionism notwithstanding, the critical insight to be gained from the history of Cooleemee is that the union there did not spring from a newly discovered oppositional consciousness. It grew out of workers' years of experience in self-assertion and resistance—though not of the sort to elicit attention beyond the village boundaries. Neither fully oppositional nor deeply co-opted by management, their version of union reflected workers' understanding of how they could best protect themselves, and it was built on an accumulated, experiential logic of infrapolitical resistance. It mined the usable elements of the old system of rights and obligations, seeking to institutionalize them to counter a rapidly de-personalizing environment. The union's essential role was to keep the social fabric of Cooleemee intact. In the end, it was only a holding action, but in an industry that often seemed committed to crushing workers' rights, that in itself was an achievement. In the annals of southern labor history, even such a qualified achievement was rare. In many respects Cooleemee was an anomaly—as was Erwin Mills—and not representative of most southern mill towns. In fact, Cooleemee may present a best-case scenario of southern industrial paternalism at work. Therein lies its analytical value. The claims of

---

[59]Holt to Kemp Lewis, March 5, 1941, Correspondence Folder, box 48, Erwin Mills Papers; McKee interview, side 2; Claudie Boger, Frances and Claudie Boger interview, sides 1 and 2, tape 1; Ray Jordan interview, May 14, 1992, side 2; Fred Pierce interview, side 2; Claudie Boger, Frances and Claudie Boger interview, side 2, tape 1; Spry interview, side 1.

[60]Frances Boger, Frances and Claudie Boger interview, side 1, tape 1; Ray Jordan interview, May 28, 1992, side 2; Sadie Jordan interview, side 1; Fred Pierce, Jessie and Fred Pierce interview, side 2.

family and community that undergird paternalism were highly articulated in this village in ways that bound all its residents in varying degrees. The exceptional social space that prevailed in Cooleemee provides an opportunity to examine fully both the authority and the limits of community codes, an endeavor with applications well beyond the world of southern textiles.

The logic of resistance that operated in Cooleemee was framed as an intensely parochial "inside" struggle, as working people labored to exact some control over their lives and to reduce the forces aligned against them to a human dimension. In constructing a community that encompassed both management and the settled cohort of workers, the mill people of Cooleemee attempted to protect their interests by calling on a moral accountability based on shared identity, an identity partly constructed as strategy but also partly internalized. The qualified success they experienced precluded enduring alliances with a broader working-class movement for change.

Similar modes of resistance have been employed by a variety of subordinated people across time and space, and though such localistic strategies suffer from obvious inadequacies—the insular nature and tenuous enforceability of community obligation—they have been informed more often by an acute understanding of the realm of the possible than by a mystification of existing power relations. For people struggling in a world of limited options against powerful adversaries, the imperfect bonds of custom and culture could prove, at least for a time, the surest weapons at hand.

Mary Wingerd

I am an American historian who began my career focusing on issues of inequality in the twentieth century. But, as I searched for understanding of more recent events, I discovered that causes and conditions were often rooted deep in the past. I began my dissertation, which became my first book, trying to untangle the dynamics behind an important strike that occurred in 1934 and soon found myself looking for answers back in the mid-nineteenth century. My most recent book, *North Country: The Making of Minnesota*, took me on a journey to the seventeenth century. It traces the evolution of a multicultural society that Native people and Europeans created together and its subsequent destruction and replacement by the racial hierarchies that underlie so much of present-day inequality. The most important insight that I have gained over the course of my career is that we cannot chart a better future without a clear understanding of the past. Thus, the great importance of history. I fell in love with history as an undergraduate at Macalester College and had the great good fortune to earn my MA and PhD at Duke University under the guidance of Larry Goodwyn and William Chafe. My dissertation won the Urban History Prize and *North Country* also won two book awards. But nothing thrilled me more than to have my article, "Rethinking Paternalism," chosen to appear in the *Journal of American History* when I was a graduate student, and I am honored to have it chosen as part of this anthology. I live in my hometown of St. Paul, Minnesota, and teach American history and direct the graduate program in public history at St. Cloud State University.

QUESTIONS FOR CONSIDERATION

1. Describe at least two ways in which Erwin Mills sought to maintain social and economic control over the community of Cooleemee.
2. How did rivalry with nearby Mocksville help foster a sense of identity for the residents of Cooleemee? In what ways were citizens of Cooleemee proudly working class? In what ways did they seek to define themselves against other members of the working class?
3. Describe how the working-class residents of Cooleemee excluded or forcibly removed certain members of their community. In what ways did these actions reflect the broader context of the United States during this period?
4. How did new time management practices change worker–management relations? How did the election of Franklin Delano Roosevelt, the passage of the Wagner Act, and the creation of the National Labor Relations Board also help to foster a change in this relationship?
5. How did the older relationship between management and workers at Cooleemee continue to shape contract negotiations once the mill's workers unionized?
6. To what extent did the changes in the work environment at Cooleemee by the 1940s mirror that of the workers described in the articles by Foner and Durrill in this volume?

❦

In the Nation's Image: The Gendered Limits of Social Citizenship in the Depression Era[1]

Alice Kessler-Harris

When a workman suffers he suffers all the more comfortably . . . when he knows that behind him in his sorrow there is the nation to which he belongs. . . . England . . . has done nothing that is more worthy of her than that in the great hour of her need and in the midst of her innumerable anxieties, her first thought has been to sustain the manhood on which her fame so well reposes.[2]

. . . My experience in postwar Britain, and since then with other welfare states . . . illuminates a significant puzzle with respect to how the United States handled a similar transformative moment in the 1930s. Faced then with a crisis of major proportions, United States policy makers chose to expand social provision dramatically, but in ways so restrictive that they did not challenge the nation's sense of itself as a predominantly individualistic nation. Put another way, Americans chose to utilize an equivalent moment of transition—the Great Depression—not to reframe a particular national self-image, but to reaffirm it. In this essay, I want to use a transnational location to explore some of the latent meanings of this American experience. I propose that a transnational perspective can reveal some of the ways that particular ideas of "nation" function in the play of the imagination and memory to constrain policy and to construct meaning for what people do. The argument takes off from recent explorations of nationalism that emphasize the force of ideas in creating bonds among peoples not bound together by what Arjun Appadurai calls blood and kinship. Appadurai comments that

---

[1] Interested students are encouraged to read this essay in the original form. Alice Kessler-Harris, "In the Nation's Image: The Gendered Limits of Social Citizenship in the Depression Era," *The Journal of American History* 86, no. 3, The Nation and Beyond: Transnational Perspectives on United States History: A Special Issue (Dec. 1999),1251–79.

[2] Lord Snell, Baron of Plumstead, address to the Fifth National Conference of the American Association for Old Age Security in spring 1932, quoted in Abraham Epstein, *Insecurity: A Challenge to America* (New York, 1938), 31.

nations, "especially in multiethnic settings, are tenuous collective projects, not eternal natural facts."[3] Pushing this idea a step further, Liah Greenfeld describes a nation "as first and foremost an embodiment of an ideology," an idea that applies "more rigorously" to the United States because "at the outset, ideology, the firm convicton that the American society . . . was a *nation*, was the only thing that was certain." Its existence, as Homi Babha insists, is a "cultural construction," one that assumes historical specificity as it is written and narrated.[4]

In the depression 1930s, I suggest, Americans reflecting different social and economic interests imagined themselves preserving the manly independence of the Jeffersonian ideal. As they constructed policies to meet the crisis, influential policy makers and legislators drew on a deeply gendered, racialized, and sometimes nostalgic vision of the past that was ultimately rooted in Lockean perceptions of individual freedom and economic opportunity, untrammeled by government intervention. To legitimize their actions, they situated themselves in implicit and sometimes explicit comparison with their European counterparts, appealing to, and simultaneously building, a national identity from the ideas they chose as rationales for their positions. They protested their innocence of the "tyranny of Europe," which they imagined as the curse of the weak and dependent male; and they sought to ensure that the dignity of men would reside in their continuing capacity to support their homes. Their words . . . reveal how ideas and institutions adapted across time and space can sustain and affirm a sense of nation. Attention to these issues illuminates the boundaries of United States social policy initiatives in the 1930s and helps to explain something of their continuing direction.

. . . Americans of different social origins continue to live at best ambivalently and sometimes in abrasive discontent with even the most effective of government interventions. Two key . . . arenas illustrate the point. In the Old Age and Unemployment Insurance provisions of the 1935 Social Security Act . . . the United States created major new policy departures that appear to have had extensive public support.[5] Yet, unlike similar ideas that appeared elsewhere, they did not revise . . . the deeply rooted ideas about self-sufficiency that informed what it meant to be an American. Rather, their significance as new initiatives was cloaked

---

[3]Arjun Appadurai, *Modernity at Large: Cultural Dimensions of Globalization* (Minneapolis, 1992), 162; Appadurai notes that nations are sometimes constructed from ideas about blood and kinship and at others out of cultural connections. See Benedict Anderson, *Imagined Communities: Reflections on the Origin and Spread of Nationalism* (London, 1991); Eric Hobsbawm, "Mass-Producing Tradition," in *The Invention of Tradition*, ed. Eric Hobsbawm and Terence Ranger (Cambridge, Eng., 1992), 263–308; and Partha Chatterjee, *Nationalist Thought in the Colonial World: A Derivative Discourse* (Minneapolis, 1986).

[4]Liah Greenfeld, *Nationalism: Five Roads to Modernity* (Cambridge, Mass., 1992), 402–3. Homi K. Babha, "DissemiNation: Time, Narrative, and the Margins of the Modern Nation," in *Nation and Narration*, ed. Homi K. Babha (New York, 1990), 292.

[5]For access to the history of these programs, see Edward Berkowitz, *Americas Welfare State: From Roosevelt to Reagan* (Baltimore, 1991); Colin Gordon, *New Deals: Business, Labor, and Politics in America, 1920–1935* (Cambridge, Eng., 1994); and Stanley Vittoz, *New Deal Labor Policy and the American Industrial Economy* (Chapel Hill, 1987).

by a fog of rhetoric that clouded their purposes, limited their possibilities, and restrained their potentialities. Like the benefits offered by other countries, the initiatives of the 1930s have ameliorated some of the worst forms of poverty and economic insecurity, and, though perhaps less than most, they have modestly redistributed national income.[6] But these policies shared in a set of gendered economic assumptions and did not fundamentally challenge prevailing definitions of what the nation is and stands for. They have not transformed the central ideological beliefs that informed the American imagination. Nor were they intended to. . . .

Until the late 1970s, almost all prosperous Western industrial nations systematically siphoned off and effectively redistributed some of the profits of the market-place through strategies intended to sustain somewhat different forms of what each considered a "good society." Their efforts included public housing and transportation, child allowances, expanded family and maternity support systems, and near-universal health insurance, all of them affirming a larger sense of public responsibility. . . . Australia offers a case in point. In the first two-thirds of the twentieth century it curbed rampant individualism by locating government as the agency of collective conscience. Australians still generally think of their government as benignly intentioned and likely to be the instrument of positive change.[7]

By and large, the United States has taken a different path, limiting the scope and beneficiaries of social provision and shaping its national image . . . around individual entrepreneurial skills, much-vaunted opportunities to succeed, and the glories of making a contribution. . . . Voices eager to meld national interest with support for public well-being or collective responsibility to citizens have certainly been present in the United States, but they are harder to hear because so much of how most Americans imagine their relationship to their nation resonates with the language of nonintervention. To most Americans, the public good takes second place to the rhetoric of self-reliance, individual ambition, competition, and the fairness of the market. Clothed in the language of rights and freedoms, the pursuit of individual desire (often measured by the capacity to consume or accumulate goods) confirms a history that has rewarded individual self-interest and contested efforts to build a larger national community by rallying around collective responsibility. As a result, the United States has never had a welfare state or a vision of social justice comparable to most of those in other industrial nations where the elimination of poverty has been a primary goal. It has not developed universal health insurance or old-age pensions funded out of progressive tax revenue; it has meager unemployment protection and a

---

[6]Redistribution of income has been one of the acknowledged functions of the family-based income tax. See especially Edward J. McCaffery, *Taxing Women* (Chicago, 1997); and the classic Boris Bittker, "Federal Income Taxation and the Family," *Stanford Law Review* 27 (July 1975), 1389–1463.

[7]On the idea and limits of the "good society," see John Kenneth Galbraith, *The Affluent Society* (Boston, 1958); and more recently, Robert N. Bellah et al., *The Good Society* (New York, 1991), ch. 3. For Australian attitudes toward government, see Marian Sawer, "Reclaiming Social Liberalism: The Women's Movement and the State," in *Women and the State: Australian Perspectives*, ed. Renate Howe (Melbourne, 1993), 1–21.

mean-spirited provision for the poorest. Existing social provisions are continually eroded as illustrated by the steep decline in the real value of the minimum wage and of unemployment insurance, and aid to even the smallest dependent infants requires parental participation in wage work.

. . . Nations everywhere seem to utilize gender . . . as an important weapon in their nation-building arsenals. Whatever the particular differences among nations, gender participates in mediating the imagination, periodically refiguring the assumptions, constraints, imagery, and expectations that surround it. Examples are legion. Dorothy Ko's work on seventeenth-century China suggests that, among other uses, footbinding asserted the civilized quality of the Ming in the face of the conquering Qing. Nineteenth-century Czechoslovakian feminists claimed a national tradition of patriotism to justify demands for women's rights. . . . Early-twentieth-century Indians protested British rule and located their own nationalism in the spiritual domain of culture, where it remained resistant to Western pressures. Women, as the preservers and guardians of culture, became embodiments of that inner spirituality that rendered the British, perhaps predictably, more committed to wiping out such customs as child marriage and Sati that assigned women the special mission of preserving their national culture for perpetuity. More limited but equally powerful notions of male guardianship of family honor and community have participated in the development of many nations, including some in Islamic countries and in Latin America. . . .[8]

When we note how, under different historical circumstances, and with enormous frequency, the emancipation and repression of women are located in broad national agendas, we are pulled into asking how gender participated in the reframing that occurred in the 1930s in the United States. The evidence suggests . . . most powerfully that the social policies adopted in a decade of change utilized gender to reinforce traditional notions of liberty, individualism, and the effectiveness of the market and to undermine calls for collective action. By tying the benefits of social citizenship to racialized and gendered images of freedom and nation, the architects of American social policy turned crucial vehicles of economic security into markers of a powerful national ideology. A gendered view

---

[8]Dorothy Ko, *Teachers of the Inner Chambers: Women and Culture in Seventeenth-Century China* (Stanford, 1994), 148–51. Katherine David, "Czech Feminists and Nationalism in the Late Habsburg Monarchy: 'The First in Austria,'" *Journal of Women's History* 3 (Fall 1991), 26–45, esp. 27; Lata Mani, "Contentious Traditions: The Debate on Sati in Colonial India," in *Recasting Women: Essays in Indian Colonial History*, ed. Kumkum Sangari and Sudesh Vaid (New Brunswick, 1990), 88–126; Mrinalini Sinha, "Reading Mother India: Empire, Nation, and the Female Voice," *Journal of Women's History* 6 (Summer 1994), 6–44; see also Samita Sen, "Motherhood and Mothercraft: Gender and Nationalism in Bengal," *Gender and History* 5 (Summer 1993), 231–43; R. Radhakrishnan, "Nationalism, Gender, and the Narrative of Identity," in *Nationalisms and Sexualities*, ed. Andrew Parker et al. (New York, 1992), 77–95; Donna J. Guy, "'White Slavery,' Citizenship, and Nationality in Argentina," ibid., 201–17; Valentine M. Moghadam, "Revolution, Islam, and Women: Sexual Politics in Iran and Afghanistan," ibid., 424–46. The rape of women by soldiers in wartime is a classic example of the embodiment of male power over a victimized female/nation. On this, see especially Rhonda Copelon, "Gendered War Crimes: Reconceptualizing Rape in Time of War," in *Womens Rights, Human Rights: International Feminist Perspectives*, ed. Julie Peters and Andrea Wolper (New York, 1995), 197–217.

of the world subverted efforts to draw out solidaristic themes. It reconstructed and perpetuated notions of individualism by protecting male independence and autonomy in the labor market, reinforcing traditional notions that rights are defined by position in the family, and affirming women's status as dependent. Because traditional gender constraints, which are deeply imbricated with class and race, often seemed merely natural, they required little defense, allowing class and racial discriminations to piggyback on them.

Protective labor legislation, for example, has served as an arena within which national agendas are played out while gendered ritual and tradition are negotiated. Designed in the late nineteenth century to protect women, but not men, from the hazards of the workplace, protective legislation everywhere utilized gender, but not always in the same ways. In Western European nations, debates around such legislation . . . invariably occurred at the intersection of issues of national self-interest with those of women's roles in the family. Thus, Denmark chose to restrict women's work at night in order to claim a position for itself among the civilized nations of the world. Austria, influenced by the power of the Catholic Church in the political process, curbed married women's work; Switzerland and the Netherlands repeatedly expanded restrictions on women out of a desire to preserve particular kinds of family forms thought necessary to national well-being and self-sufficiency; Australia differentiated between the sexes in order to preserve a self-image of justice and equity to families. Much of this legislation made statements about national values while maintaining and institutionalizing ritual forms of behavior in the family and workplace. . . .[9]

If the key ideas for the social policy changes of the 1930s came, as Daniel Rodgers persuasively argues, from Europe, the policy makers . . . who conceived some of the core pieces of United States social provision drew on their own sense of national memory to produce programs that sustained already-existing national images.[10] They utilized a rhetoric of American continuity that explicitly distanced itself from the European experience and incorporated Jeffersonian ideas of nation and citizenship to provide the boundaries within which policy makers disagreed. These ideas had emotional as well as historical resonance. Rooted in conceptions of an active citizenship and broad civic participation, they required economic independence as the single most important criterion for

---

[9]Wikander, Kessler-Harris, and Lewis, eds., *Protecting Women*, 1–27; Anna-Birte Ravn, "'Lagging Far Behind All Civilized Nations': The Debate over Protective Labor Legislation for Women in Denmark, 1899–1913," ibid., 210–34; Margarete Grandner, "Special Labor Protection for Women in Austria, 1860–1918," ibid., 150–87; Regina Wecker, "Equality for Men? Factory Laws, Protective Legislation for Women in Switzerland, and the Swiss Effort for International Protection," ibid., 63–90; Ulla Jansz, "Women or Workers? The 1889 Labor Law and the Debate on Protective Labor Legislation in the Netherlands," ibid., 188–209; Howe, "A Paradise for Working Men but Not Working Women."

[10]Daniel Rodgers, *Atlantic Crossings: Social Politics in a Progressive Age* (Cambridge, Mass., 1998), 409–84; a similar argument was made by Daniel Levine, *Poverty and Society: The Growth of the American Welfare State in International Comparison* (New Brunswick, 1988), 167–80; and see Kathryn Kish Sklar, Anja Schuler, and Susan Strasser, *Social Justice Feminists in the United States and Germany: A Dialogue in Documents, 1885–1933* (Ithaca, 1998).

democratic political life. . . . It assumed a mutual respect made possible by the idea that even the most ordinary men (unlike married women and slaves) owned property in their own labor. In theory at least, men's relationship to work embodied their capacity to exercise independent judgment and to command the respect required to participate in the polity. Early nineteenth-century skilled workers, like their brothers a century later, believed not only that paid labor would provide a putative independence but that it would lead the way to the relative self-sufficiency that constituted the essence of untrammeled political participation.

Of course, these ideas were both deeply racialized and deeply gendered. If in the nineteenth century their moral authority rested on their power to distance themselves from symbolic and actual slavery by setting dignified terms of labor, in the twentieth, racial identification still restricted or opened paths into practical self-sufficiency. And if the nineteenth century concept of free labor embodied a conception of male prerogatives rooted in an ordered and comfortable family life that relied on female labor at home, in the twentieth, the idea of a male-headed family still regulated a wide array of political and economic alternatives including access to education, jobs, and ultimately individual self-sufficiency.[11] At the time of the New Deal, the tangible privileges of whiteness and the more elusive notion of domestic spheres for women still encrusted the putatively universal ideas of Jeffersonian individualism, liberty, freedom, and citizenship that served as rallying cries for national unity.

While legislatures and the judiciary had agreed by 1930 that women owned property in their own labor, they continued to insist that the state held an important stake in women's family roles and could therefore regulate women's labor. . . . Many activist women subscribed to this view, including Edith and Grace Abbott, Katherine Lenroot, Rose Schneiderman, Mary Dewson, and others deeply involved in the policy decisions of the 1930s. Similarly, policy makers like . . . Paul Douglas, and the architects of the Social Security Act of 1935 believed that the vitality of the male head of household was central to preserving democracy. Neither the family roles of African Americans nor the democratic participation of black men particularly concerned white leaders.[12] These dismaying limits suggest a public imagination that restricted important tropes of American freedom, including economic liberty, individualism, and economic competition, largely to the province of white males. . . . African American leaders

[11]C. B. McPherson, *The Political Theory of Possessive Individualism: Hobbes to Locke* (London, 1962). For the development of these ideas among workers, see Sean Wilentz, *Chants Democratic: New York City and the Rise of the American Working Class, 1788–1850* (New York, 1984). The best exploration of free labor is still Eric Foner, *Free Soil, Free Labor, Free Men: The Ideology of the Republican Party before the Civil War* (New York, 1970); and see Jonathan Glickstein, *Concepts of Free Labor in Antebellum America* (New Haven, 1991), 1–22; and Robert Steinfeld, *The Invention of Free Labor: The Employment Relation in English and American Law and Culture, 1350–1870* (Chapel Hill, 1991), 147–72. For the gendered content of these ideas at the turn of the century, see Alice Kessler-Harris, *A Woman's Wage: Historical Meanings and Social Consequences* (Lexington, Ky., 1990), 33–56.

[12]Abraham Epstein discounted the African American community as a force: Abraham Epstein, *Insecurity. A Challenge to America: A Study of Social Security in the United States and Abroad* (New York, 1936), 24.

discovered that [these tropes of American imagination] effectively restricted the possibilities of a social policy that could sustain the economic freedom of women or men of color and . . . rendered alternatives politically implausible if not invisible. Thus idealized images of national values framed access to the benefits of citizenship in exclusionary ways.

By melding old understandings of nation with new efforts to seek public well-being, an ideology of gender managed to protect the independence of white male household heads at the cost of women's autonomy in the family. But this required a continuing reinforcement of male prerogatives at work. In most European countries, social insurance provided benefits earned as a right of citizenship or residence, paid for out of general revenues to those who qualified; it was meant for those in need, not tied to individual contributions through taxes. Germany had had health insurance for workers since 1884, as had Austria, Hungary, Norway, and Luxembourg since the end of the nineteenth century. By 1911, Germany, Britain, and Austria were among the countries that had comprehensive programs that covered such things as work accidents, health care, and maternity costs and provided security against old age and disability for men and women. All these programs incorporated relatively broad coverage that invoked some sense of government responsibility for the hazards of industrial life. . . . All envisaged a more active role for government in sustaining the quality of life through death, old age, and illness and in improving conditions of employment, as well as a commitment to reeducate and train workers for available jobs.

Gendered economic assumptions led American policy makers to opt for programs tied to wage work rather than to citizenship "rights." The choice reflected a desire to encourage participation in the marketplace and reward individual effort. Their programs would preserve dignity by sharply distinguishing relief . . . to those in need from entitlements to those who had earned benefits. . . . Direct contributions to benefit programs from individuals or their employers would sustain the dignity of recipients and testify to their self-sufficiency. At first, only contributors would benefit. Neither all work nor all workers deserved protection. In what emerged as the American model of social insurance, "rights," dignity, and liberty would be understood as prerogatives of generally white male heads of families, the distinction made palatable by tying it to the kind of work one did. . . .

A bitter set of arguments over the issue of old-age insurance tells us something of the origins of the penchant for attaching benefits to work and not to citizenship.[13] The Committee on Economic Security (CES), set up by President Franklin D. Roosevelt in the summer of 1934 to develop comprehensive recommendations for short- and long-term relief of want, consisted of half a dozen cabinet members, chaired by Secretary of Labor Frances Perkins. Recommendations were offered to

---

[13]For the political trajectory of these debates, see Roy Lubove, *The Struggle for Social Security: 1900–1935* (Cambridge, Mass., 1968); Martha Derthick, *Policymaking for Social Security* (Washington, D.C., 1979); Arthur Altmeyer, *The Formative Years of Social Security* (Madison, 1966); and Edwin E. Witte, *The Development of the Social Security Act* (Madison, 1963).

it by an Advisory Council, which in turn relied on technical committees. The work of all these people was overseen by Executive Director Edwin Witte, who had trained at Wisconsin with the influential economist John Commons. Among the people who helped draft the Social Security Act (SSA), chairing the technical committee on old-age security was a Berkeley economist and professor of law named Barbara Nachtrieb Armstrong. Armstrong, a California native, had, in the course of nearly two decades at Berkeley, become an expert on European social insurance systems with a special interest in newly imagined systems of unemployment insurance. . . .

. . . Her recently published book *Insuring the Essentials* (1932) brought her an invitation to Washington in the summer of 1934. . . . She was then, by her own account, an unknown quantity. . . .[14] Almost from the beginning, Edwin Witte . . . must have regretted the appointment. A fiery and combative champion of social insurance, Armstrong imagined that the charitable old-age assistance programs to which Perkins and Witte were at first wedded were too limited in scope. She much preferred some of the European-type schemes where, as in Sweden, social insurance, paid for out of general revenues, redistributed income to the unemployed and the aged as needed. . . . To be effective, she believed, any system had to be national in scope, not state-based. . . . To reduce her influence, so they thought, Perkins and Witte assigned her to head the task force on old-age security . . . an issue that was far less important to them than unemployment insurance.

Armstrong's strongest ally on the Old Age Insurance subcommittee, and the man who would help steer the Social Security Act through Congress, was the Princeton University economist and industrial relations expert J. Douglas Brown. Brown, an experienced consultant to corporate welfare programs, was a known quantity, trusted and liked by some of the other players, including Witte. He also got along well with Armstrong and shared her faith in social insurance. . . . They were convinced that insurance would provide a permanent solution to poverty in old age and that it . . . would successfully encourage older people to retire from jobs in a way that reserved the dignity of the insured. They devised what became known as the contributory model with the dignity of breadwinners in mind.

Measuring "dignity" by the relationship of contributions to benefits, Armstrong and Brown developed a proposal (close to the one that passed) that incorporated a flat payroll tax, evenly divided between employer and employee and capped at a level that reflected median wages. Unlike some of the European plans, it had little redistributional value. Rather, benefits were meant to reflect individual contributions plus interest, and a lump-sum death benefit would guarantee to return contributions to the families of workers who died before collecting anything. The plan departed from European examples sufficiently to satisfy legislators of the

[14]Barbara Nachtrieb Armstrong, *Insuring the Essentials: Minimum Wage, plus Social Insurance—a Living Wage Program* (New York, 1932). Barbara Nachtrieb Armstrong interview by Peter A. Corning, Dec. 19, 1965, transcript, pp. 30, 34, 38, Columbia University Oral History Research Collection (Butler Library, Columbia University, New York).

independence of recipients and to conserve images of workers as self-sufficient males. This was exactly its intent.... Armstrong ... [noted,] "If we hadn't made those insured people contributors—pay regularly toward their insurance so that they would think of it as theirs, they would have no protection against the politicians who periodically would wish to reduce their benefits or even eliminate them."[15]

Armstrong and Brown willingly accommodated the demands of politics (including those of racial bias) to their goal. Dignity did not require including workers whose relationships to work produced marginal standards of living. Armstrong left out domestic and agricultural labor (thus omitting two-thirds of all black women workers) because, she said, no one could effectively collect their contributions. Yet her European expertise had already exposed her to effective stamp systems that worked well for casual workers in many countries.... [Armstrong and Brown's] proposal also excluded workers in educational institutions, nonprofits, retail sales, and government offices (all heavily female), as well as casual labor. Together these exclusions omitted more than three-quarters of all female wage earners from coverage and about 87 percent of African American women workers.

Even these compromises did not convince Witte that old-age insurance was a high priority. His resistance irritated Armstrong enormously. She considered him a limited man, mocked him to other members of her committee, and made end runs around him politically.... When Witte would not bend on the principle of a nationally administered contributory social insurance program she took her fight to the public ... leaking the proposal to the press. These daring strategies proved enormously successful. Business members of the Advisory Council (like the members of Congress who voted for the bill) loved the idea of an insurance program that could not be tagged as charity and preserved dignity, especially one on a national scale. Testifying before Congress, Marion Folsom of the Eastman Kodak Co. argued that the worker "doesn't look upon it as a tax. He looks upon it just the same as he would paying his own insurance, and of course it's a right."[16]

To European minds, the idea of a regressive tax to fund a relatively narrow social insurance scheme appears to be a constraint on the rights of the excluded rather than a benefit for the included. But in the United States, the continuing discussion over old-age insurance suggests that the rights offered to selected workers as well as the powerful defense of individual dignity for the included played a role in the bill's conception and final passage. Brown, writing shortly after the bill's passage, noted, with some reservations, that it was what

---

[15]Later J. Douglas Brown added, "We felt benefit as a matter of right was far more to be preferred than one for which there would be a needs test." J. Douglas Brown interview by Peter A. Corning, Feb. 5, 1965, transcript, pp. 2, 23, Columbia University Oral History Research Collection. Armstrong interview, 275–76.

[16]For her account of the press incident, see Armstrong interview, transcript, pp. 87, 154, 164. Marion B. Folsom interview by Peter A. Corning, June 19, 1965, transcript, p. 53, Columbia University Oral History Research Collection. Brown interview, transcript, p. 21.

distinguished the American from the British system. . . . Relying on wages as the measure of insurance benefits helped affirm the Americanness of the American worker, creating the impression that workers had "paid for" their own pensions. Dividing insurance from assistance confirmed what Brown described as "the American philosophy that an *individual*—and not the *social system*—determines his economic status." At the same time, including everyone within certain job categories, no matter at what income, satisfied the democratic instinct for not discriminating on the basis of financial status. "The percentage contribution concept, the degree of graduation, the coverage of everyone and so on were essentially American concepts."[17] To be sure, the job categories included were relentlessly white and male, and these factors account for the fact that though Old Age Insurance offered not a drop of relief from the depression . . . [and] depended on a highly regressive taxation system, the program had instant appeal among much of the public.[18] Its attraction suggests neither its novelty nor its uniqueness, but its affirmation of a cherished American ideal. Legislators, businessmen, and ultimately policy makers and much of the general public believed that a program rooted in male dignity would work.

. . . If these assumptions produced some of the major drawbacks in the program, particularly its racial and gendered exclusions, its regressive taxation, its high reserves, and its utterly inadequate benefits, they also produced its major accomplishment: preserving the language of rights while providing collective economic security to many white male American workers.

The coda to this story occurs just a few years later when, faced with correcting some of the flaws, including having to deal with an enormous revenue surplus that was already building, the Senate convened an advisory committee to recommend changes. It appointed J. Douglas Brown as chair and included some of the same business leaders who had participated in the earlier deliberations. During more than a year and a half of deliberations, the advisory council resisted heavy pressure from African American groups to expand coverage to the previously excluded, especially domestic and agricultural workers. Instead, in deference to the dignity of working men who were breadwinners and in an effort to provide more adequate return for their contributions, it chose to give more money to men with wives and to support their surviving children and aged widows. The resolution solidified wavering public support and affirmed the old-age insurance program's position as the girder of provident working men and the families dependent on them.[19]

---

[17]J. Douglas Brown, "British Precedent and American Old Age Insurance," *American Labor Legislation Review* 27 (March 1937), 19, 20. Brown interview, transcript, p. 63.

[18]The racial exclusion was not invisible to leaders of the African American community, though that of women was. See Mary Poole, "Securing Race and Ensuring Dependence: The Social Security Act of 1935" (Ph.D. diss., Rutgers University, forthcoming).

[19]This story is told in Alice Kessler-Harris, "'Designing Women and Old Fools': The Construction of the Social Security Amendments of 1939," in *U.S. History as Women's History*, ed. Linda Kerber, Alice Kessler-Harris, and Kathryn Kish Sklar (Chapel Hill, 1995), 87–106.

... Historians of maternalism have often noted that the Social Security Act offered widowed, divorced, or deserted mothers support for their minor children, providing a mother's allowance that substituted a new dependence on the state for failed family provision. In return for giving up certain liberties, it provided means-tested aid that required the generally female caregiver to prove that she did not work for pay. These benefits were easily won ... [most reformers] fully supported government commitment to relief for poor women and children rather than reform for all. The results appear to constitute what some have called a two-track system in which women, neglected by social insurance, benefitted from needs-based aid on the ground of their mothering roles. . . . Maternalists who advocated these provisions ... saw them as ensuring that the federal government would participate in nurturing children and commit itself to giving relief from destitution while it simultaneously encouraged male breadwinning. Their vision did not differ in significant ways from those of policy makers who advocated extended protections of liberty for male family heads.

The same could not be said for unemployment insurance, whose trajectory clarifies how gender-bound conceptions of work participated in reshaping notions of liberty. Unemployment insurance was, by all accounts, the most contested issue in the Social Security Act of 1935. . . . Produced out of arguments over whether it should be federal or state-based, it emerged in the end as an unsatisfactory hodgepodge of ... [programs] that covered less than half the work force with an inconsistent panoply of rules that differed from state to state. Neither universal in scope nor adequate in terms of relief, it was developed with almost no input from the organized trade union movement. . . .

As finally enacted, the unemployment provision of the Social Security Act amalgamated the heart of two competing plans, each proposed by industrial relations activists and their supporters. They earned organized labor's support by sharply distinguishing themselves from comparable European programs. American unemployment insurance would cover relatively small categories of contributing workers and employers, rather than the population at large. Its rates were predicated on the belief that responsibility for reducing unemployment lay in the hands of employers, not the government. In contrast to European industrial states, which envisaged an active role for government in improving conditions of employment, as well as a commitment to reeducate and train workers for available jobs, John Commons, architect of one proposal, imagined a far narrower governmental jurisdiction. He believed that employers could be held accountable for their own workers and that assessing contributions according to employers' rates of unemployment would encourage them to participate in regularizing employment. In Commons's vision (and in that of his students who became the architects of New Deal legislation), requiring employers to contribute to a fund to compensate workers according to their success in preventing unemployment would serve as a whip to persuade business to prevent unemployment. Failing that, it would carry workers through temporary economic dislocations, for which employers were said to be responsible. . . .

The context of the conversation around unemployment insurance ensured that gender (the claims of male workers to a liberty and freedom that embodied their commitment to manhood) would play a large role in the shape of the legislation that emerged. At some cost, Bryce Stewart, chair of the Technical Committee on Unemployment Insurance, who had been involved in some of the early experiments with trade union unemployment insurance and who was a friend and former colleague of J. Douglas Brown's, tried to write into the committee's recommendations a commitment to pooled funds outside of employer control. His failure led him to resign the committee's chair. In his absence, the Technical Committee produced an awkward amalgam of . . . plans . . . which reflected the labor movement's concerns for protecting the liberties of its members. As passed, unemployment compensation may have subjected the worker to the state authority he resisted, but it did so, like old-age insurance, as a matter of "right" rather than of need.

Prevailing values obscured the gendered mechanisms built into the contribution, eligibility, and state-generated provisions of the law. Only relatively large, producing businesses (where most women did not work) that could regularize employment were expected to participate. Few saw any fault with this because women were presumed to be secondary workers whose families would provide economic backstop. African Americans of both sexes and most white women, who lacked the opportunity to earn wages on the same basis as white men, almost immediately found these particular rights of citizenship inaccessible. With regard to African Americans, this was seen then . . . as an unfortunate bow to southern politics.[20] With regard to women, it was quite deliberate. Epstein, citing the 88 percent of married women whom the 1930 census declared to have earned no wages, put it this way: "The American standard assumes a normal family of man, wife, and two or three children, with the father fully able to provide for them out of his own income. This standard presupposes no supplementary earnings from either the wife or young children. . . the wife is a homemaker rather than a wage-earner. . . . The needs of these families must be considered paramount."[21] Inevitably, the resolution demeaned the rights of the excluded, placing them in an inferior position as far as the social rights of citizenship were concerned.

[Passage of the Social Security Act of 1935 with unemployment insurance provisions] . . . resolved the enormous tension produced by a competing set of ideas . . . that closely resembled the seamless systems then beginning to emerge in Europe. Formally known as the Workers Unemployment and Social Insurance Bill and generally referred to as the Lundeen bill, in 1934 and 1935 it proposed unemployment and old-age insurance "for all workers, including all wage earners, all salaried workers, farmers, professional workers, and the self-employed." It guaranteed compensation equal to average earnings, and in no

---

[20]Quadagno, *Transformation of Old Age Security*; Harvard Sitkoff, *A New Deal for Blacks: The Emergence of Civil Rights as a National Issue* (New York, 1978), 21–50.

[21]Epstein, *Insecurity*, 101.

case less than a "minimum standard of living."[22] It prohibited discrimination because of age, sex, race, or color, and it specifically included those who worked part time and in agricultural and domestic or professional work. It covered lost wages due to maternity, sickness, accident, and old age. And it provided allowances for mothers of children under eighteen with no male support. Costs were to be borne, not by payroll taxes, but by the federal government out of general revenues.[23]

The bill was drafted with the help of Mary Van Kleeck, one of the women reformers who had moved to the left during the depression and who led the charge against unemployment proposals that covered only "a specified group of beneficiaries who join in establishing these reserves."[24] The Lundeen bill, with its tempting offer of general revenues to fund government-sponsored social insurance, had been favorably reviewed by the House Committee on Labor and reported out to the House in spring 1934. Supported by many old-style progressives as well as socialists and communists, its promise of government subsidy not connected to work terrified more traditional legislators as well as labor leaders committed to the idea of benefits as earned rights. Van Kleeck, in contrast, deplored "rules and regulations... which exclude all those not involved in the contributions.[25]

But supporters of Lundeen were tarred as un-American, derogatorily identified with communists, and dismissed for their attachment to European models. Representative Claude Pepper, one of the legislators who had helped steer the Social Security Act through Congress, captured the perceived distinctions between the two proposals and the palpable relief offered by the act's careful compromise. Mustering all the resources that memory could accumulate, he told the assembled delegates of the American Federation of Labor in 1936 that the... [Social Security Act] preserved their linkages to democracy along with their well-being. The Social Security Act, he triumphantly explained, resolved one aspect of an important question: "How may the

---

[22]U.S. Congress, Senate, Committee on Education and Labor, *Social Insurance, Hearings on S. 3475*, 74 Cong., 2 sess., April 14, 1936, p. 2. The progress of the bill can be traced in Casebeer, "Workers' Unemployment Insurance Bill," 231–59; the rationale for the bill and the final text can be found in the hearings, cited above, as well as in Mary Van Kleeck, "The Case for H.R. 7598," typescript, Nov. 14, 1934, folder 534, box 28, Mary Van Kleeck Collection (Sophia Smith Archives, Smith College, Northampton, Mass.). This was apparently prepared for the *New Masses* but, as far as I can tell, was never published.

[23]Casebeer, "Workers' Unemployment Insurance Bill," 232.

[24]Van Kleeck, "Case for H.R. 7598," 7.

[25]Still, even within the labor movement the Lundeen bill had many champions, including two of the large female unions (the Amalgamated Clothing Workers of America and the International Ladies' Garment Workers Union), the Textile Workers Union, the United Mine Workers of America, and the Mine, Mill, and Smelter Workers Union. Van Kleeck, "Case for H.R. 7598," 7; see also Mary Van Kleeck, "Security for Americans, V: The Workers' Bill for Unemployment and Social Insurance," *New Republic* 81 (Dec. 12, 1934), 123. Witte attributed the defeat of this bill to the labor movement, writing "Thanks to labor's clear denunciation, the 'thunder' for this measure never became more than a tinpan disharmony, which fooled scarcely anyone": Witte, "Organized Labor and Social Security," 255.

national conscience concern itself about the welfare of the individual man or woman without at the same time breaking down in the spiritual fabric of that individual that which is characteristically American-American initiative, enterprise and self reliance." . . .[26]

No single factor explains the construction of the particular social provisions for which the United States has become widely known. Yet the spirit that shaped them emerged from a vision of nation rooted in nineteenth-century ideas of independence and liberty. To implement new policies, their architects melded them into a world view familiar to Americans and responsive to their visions of national meaning. They produced a deeply gendered set of social policies that preserved the liberties and freedoms that seemed so important to national identity—with all its racial content. Deeply enmeshed in ideas about work, these liberties reflected the gendered world from which they came and perpetuated its perspectives. A transnational perspective, and one that problematizes the gendered imagination, immediately discerns the parochialism in their image.

If social programs in the United States have contributed little to building an idea of nation with a capacious shared sense of social justice, their shortcomings and putative failures have helped to promote the virtues of individual responsibility. These attitudes have been more or less consistent. "Ask not what your country can do for you—ask what you can do for your country," said John F. Kennedy in 1961, neatly reminding me, as a still relatively new immigrant, that I was in a nation where collective responsibility flowed from individuals to government, rather than the reverse. New reminders are everywhere. In the past decade or so, the American model of freewheeling capitalism has been widely admired, its assumptions that market institutions could best care for the public good repeatedly emulated and sometimes imposed by institutions of international finance. The United States has taken the lead in promoting this stance. The 1996 Personal Responsibility Act meted out harsh discipline to adult recipients of government aid, holding them personally liable for their poverty. In 1998–1999, a debate over old-age insurance threatens to privatize all or some of what is arguably the most successful government entitlement program. The idea of nation that justifies these policies certainly preexisted the 1930s, but in reframing old ideas to accommodate the depression crisis, it institutionalized the boundaries of the possible.[27]

It was all very well to have economic security, Claude Pepper told his labor audience, but never could "an American citizen . . . fall so low that he shall be satisfied to sit on his front porch and wait for an agent of any government to come and tell him when and where and how he shall look for a job . . . and define for

---

[26]American Federation of Labor, *Report of the Proceedings of the Fifty-Sixth Annual Convention*, Tampa, Florida, Nov. 16, 1936, p. 5.

[27]John F. Kennedy, Jan. 20, 1961, inaugural address in David Burner, *John F Kennedy and a New Generation* (Glenview, 1988), 58. The slogan perfectly suited the idealism of antiwar protesters and civil rights activists of the 1960s, and it also served the purposes of Wall Street brokers of the 1980s and 1990s.

him the scope or the character of his ambitions." Max Weber put it this way: "Not ideas but interests—material and ideal—directly govern men's conduct. Yet very frequently the 'world images' that have been created by 'ideas' have, like switchmen, determined the tracks along which action has been pushed by the dynamic of interest."[28]

As Weber warned, American conceptions of social insurance were haunted by world images. Pepper had asked, how were American "initiative, enterprise, and self-reliance" to be saved in the face of the clamor for government intervention to halt destitution? He shared with his House colleagues and with most Americans the conviction that these were the qualities that had "made this nation the enviable empire upon the pages of all history." And, like others, he was convinced that any program "must and shall preserve the spirit of Americanism, the same spirit that actuated those pioneer forefathers of ours.[29] His nostalgic invocation may not have been understood by many—but the shared commitment to preserving cherished American values was. At issue in the effort to transform American provision were such cherished values as human dignity and the rights of citizenship, liberty, and independence. Gendered sensibilities nurtured all these ideals, none applied in quite the same way to women as to men, and each provided a piece of the boundary of what was possible in a legislative agenda.

---

[28]American Federation of Labor, Report of the Proceedings, 1936, p. 5. Max Weber quoted in Rogers Brubaker, Citizenship and Nationhood in France and Germany (Cambridge, Mass., 1992), 17.

[29]American Federation of Labor, Report of the Proceedings, 1936, p. 5.

Alice Kessler-Harris

I started out as a labor historian with an interest in the formation of trade unions among immigrant workers. The women's liberation movement inspired me to turn my attention to women workers, in and outside unions. I wrote several articles and three books on this subject before I turned my attention to gender. *Women Have Always Worked* (1981), *Out to Work: A History of Wage-Earning Women in the United States* (1982), and *A Woman's Wage: Historical Meanings and Social Consequences* (1990), were the products of this period. When I began to work on the book that became *In Pursuit of Equity: Women, Men, and the Quest for Economic Citizenship in Twentieth Century America* (2001), I tried to explore how deeply embedded ideas about gender shaped social policy in ways that defined ideals of fairness, constrained women's aspirations, and undermined women's equality. My research in this regard is reflected in the article in this volume. The arc of some of my work is reflected in the essays collected in *Gendering Labor History* (2007). Fuelled by a long-standing fascination with America's most controversial (and perhaps most radical) female playwright, I took a brief detour into biography that resulted in the publication of *A Difficult Woman: The Challenging Life and Times of Lillian Hellman* (2012). I have now embarked on a new project: an exploration of the history of mothering in its relationship to wage work.

QUESTIONS FOR CONSIDERATION

1. What does Kessler-Harris mean when, quoting Homi Babha, she describes the nation as a "cultural construction?"
2. According to Kessler-Harris, how did Americans' ideology of individualism shape national identity? How was gender used by Americans to shape national identity? How was race likewise used?
3. In what way did American individualistic identity shape New Deal policies during the 1930s? How were these policies defined as opposed to European models? In what ways did gender and race shape these New Deal policies?
4. Describe why the Workers Unemployment and Social Insurance Bill, also referred to as the Lundeen Bill, failed to become law in the late 1930s.
5. Describe how American dominant conceptions of the individual shaped the context in which New Deal reforms were instituted. To what extent were these self-conceptions a continuation of traditional American identity? To what extent were they a change? Refer to at least one article you have already read in this volume to help you answer this question.

CHAPTER EIGHT

❧

"Speaking of Annihilation": Mobilizing for War against Human and Insect Enemies, 1914–1945[1]

Edmund P. Russell III

In 1944 and 1945, two periodicals with very different audiences published similar images. Both showed half-human, half-insect creatures, talked of the "annihilation" of these vermin, and touted modern technology as the means to accomplish that end. One piece, a cartoon in the United States Marines' magazine *Leatherneck*, showed a creature labeled "Louseous Japanicas" and said its "breeding grounds around the Tokyo area . . . must be completely annihilated." (See figure 8.1.) A month after the cartoon appeared, the United States began mass incendiary bombings of Japanese cities, followed by the atomic blasts that leveled Hiroshima and Nagasaki. Although the *Leatherneck* cartoon was surely intended to be humorous and hyperbolic, calls for annihilation of human enemies had, by the end of the war, become realistic.

So too with insect enemies. The second cartoon, an advertisement in a chemical industry journal, promoted perfumes to eliminate insecticide odors. (See figure 8.2.) Tapping the rhetoric that pervaded World War II, the text began, "Speaking of annihilation." The accompanying image showed three creatures with insect bodies, each with a stereotypical head representing a national enemy. The Italian creature lay on its back, an allusion to Allied victory over the Italian army. The German and Japanese creatures remained standing, as guns blasted all three with chemical clouds. Like human enemies, the advertisement implied, insect enemies could and should be annihilated. That possibility, too, had come within reach by the end of World War II. The Allies killed disease-bearing lice and mosquitoes over wide areas using a powerful new insecticide called DDT (dichlorodiphenyltrichloroethane), and entomologists called for the extermination of entire species.

Most Americans welcomed technology that brought "total victory" over national and natural enemies. They felt grateful for a bomb that saved the lives of

---

[1]Interested students are encouraged to read this essay in the original form. Edmund P. Russell, "'Speaking of Annihilation': Mobilizing for War against Human and Insect Enemies, 1914–1945," *The Journal of American History* 82, no. 4 (March 1996), 1505–29.

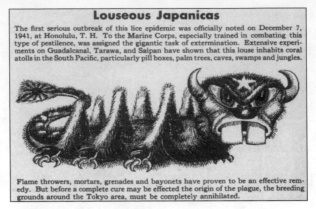

Louseous Japanicas

The first serious outbreak of this lice epidemic was officially noted on December 7, 1941, at Honolulu, T. H. To the Marine Corps, especially trained in combating this type of pestilence, was assigned the gigantic task of extermination. Extensive experiments on Guadalcanal, Tarawa, and Saipan have shown that this louse inhabits coral atolls in the South Pacific, particularly pill boxes, palm trees, caves, swamps and jungles.

Flame throwers, mortars, grenades and bayonets have proven to be an effective remedy. But before a complete cure may be effected the origin of the plague, the breeding grounds around the Tokyo area, must be completely annihilated.

Figure 8.1
In 1945, United States Marine Sgt. Fred Lasswell praised efforts to annihilate "Louseous Japanicas." Fred Lasswell, "Bugs Every Marine Should Know," *Leatherneck* 28 (March 1945), 37. Printed with permission of *Leatherneck* Magazine.

American soldiers and for a chemical that enabled people to "bomb" insect pests. As time passed, however, many came to wonder whether human beings had struck a Faustian bargain. Did "weapons of mass destruction" threaten, rather than promote, human welfare? Opponents of chemical and nuclear weapons thought so. Had the ability of human beings to conquer nature surpassed some limit, threatening not only human well-being but the planet itself? After Rachel Carson published *Silent Spring* in 1962, many feared that DDT exemplified this threat.[2]

Although war and concerns about the impact of human beings on the environment have been among the most important forces shaping the twentieth century, scholars have tended to analyze these issues separately. . . .[3] The tendency to separate war from environmental change (or military from civilian affairs)

---

[2]Rachel Carson, *Silent Spring* (New York, 1962).

[3]Peter Paret, "The New Military History," *Parameters* 21 (Autumn 1991), 10–18; William H. McNeill, *The Pursuit of Power: Technology, Armed Force, and Society Since A.D. 1000* (Chicago, 1982); Carolyn Merchant, ed., *Major Problems in American Environmental History* (Lexington, Mass., 1993); Jeffrey K. Stine and Joel A. Tarr, "Technology and the Environment: The Historians' Challenge," *Environmental History Review* 18 (Spring 1994), 1–7; Merritt Roe Smith, ed., *Military Enterprise and Technological Change: Perspectives on the American Experience* (Cambridge, Mass., 1985); Barton C. Hacker, "Military Institutions, Weapons, and Social Change: Toward a New History of Military Technology," *Technology and Culture* 35 (no. 4, 1994), 768–834; Elaine Tyler May, *Homeward Bound: American Families in the Cold War Era* (New York, 1988); and Paul Boyer, *By the Bomb's Early Light: American Thought and Culture at the Dawn of the Atomic Age* (New York, 1985); Susan D. Lanier-Graham, *The Ecology of War: Environmental Impacts of Weaponry and Warfare* (New York, 1993); Seth Shulman, *The Threat at Home: Confronting the Toxic Legacy of the U.S. Military* (Boston, 1992); J. P. Robinson, *The Effects of Weapons on Ecosystems* (Oxford, 1979); Arthur H. Westing and Malvern Lumsden, *Threat of Modern Warfare to Man and His Environment: An Annotated Bibliography Prepared under the Auspices of the International Peace Research Association* (Paris, 1979); Avner Offer, *The First World War: An Agrarian Interpretation* (Oxford, Eng., 1989); and Alfred W. Crosby, *Ecological Imperialism: The Biological Expansion of Europe, 900–1900* (New York, 1986).

has deep roots. Isaiah's metaphor, "They shall beat their swords into plowshares," suggests that people have long seen one of the most important ways they change the environment—agriculture—as the opposite of war. . . .[4]

Historians of insecticides have shown, however, that efforts to control human and natural enemies have not proceeded independently. Between them, Emory Cushing, Vincent Dethier, Thomas Dunlap, and John Perkins have pointed out that manufacturing of explosives in World War I produced a by-product called PDB (paradichlorobenzene), which entomologists then developed into an insecticide; that entomologists often used military metaphors; that World War II stimulated development of DDT; and that some insecticides were related to nerve gases. Historians of chemical weapons, too, have noted this last point.[5]

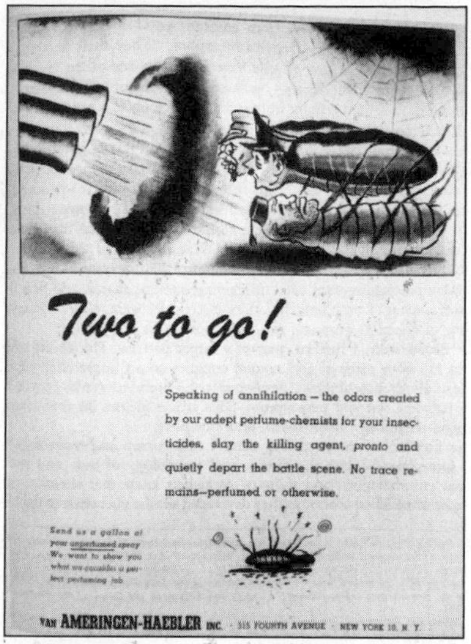

These events were, I believe, part of a larger pattern. The ability of human

Figure 8.2
This 1944 advertisement, which appeared in a journal that served the National Association of Insecticide and Disinfectant Manufacturers, took it for granted that national and insect enemies required annihilation. Reprinted from *Soap and Sanitary Chemicals* (April 1944), 92.

beings to kill both national and natural enemies on an unprecedented scale, as well as fears about those abilities, developed in the twentieth century partly because of links between war and pest control. This article focuses on three such links: science and technology, institutions, and metaphor.

In the first half of the twentieth century, the *science and technology* of pest control sometimes became the science and technology of war, and vice versa. Chemists, entomologists, and military researchers knew that chemicals toxic to one species often killed others, so they developed similar chemicals to fight human and insect enemies. They also developed similar methods of dispersing chemicals to poison both.

---

[4]Isa. 2:4; Joseph A. Wildermuth to editor, *Washington Post Book World*, Feb. 20, 1994, p. 14. See also Keith Thomas, *Man and the Natural World: A History of the Modern Sensibility* (New York, 1983).

[5]John H. Perkins, *Insects, Experts, and the Insecticide Crisis: The Quest for New Pest Management Strategies* (New York, 1982), 4–10; John H. Perkins, "Reshaping Technology in Wartime: The Effect of Military Goals on Entomological Research and Insect-Control Practices," *Technology and Culture* 19 (no. 2, 1978), 169–86; Thomas R. Dunlap, *DDT: Scientists, Citizens, and Public Policy* (Princeton, 1981), 36–37, 59–63; Emory C. Cushing, *History of Entomology in World War II* (Washington, D.C., 1957); V. G. Dethier, *Man's Plague? Insects and Agriculture* (Princeton, 1976), 112; Stockholm International Peace Research Institute, *The Problem of Chemical and Biological Warfare: A Study of the Historical, Technical, Military, Legal, and Political Aspects of CBW, and Possible Disarmament Measures*, vol. I: *The Rise of CB Weapons* (New York, 1971), 70–75.

Ideas and hardware moved between civilian and military spheres partly because of *institutional* links. The two world wars stimulated nations to mobilize civilian and military institutions to achieve military victory. They also catalyzed the founding of new organizations that coordinated civilian and military efforts. Peace also catalyzed links among institutions. When guns fell silent on battlefields, military and civilian institutions worked together to apply military ideas and technology to farm fields as a way to survive and meet their institutional goals.

Shared *metaphors* helped military and civilian institutions shape and express the way people experienced both war and nature.[6] As figures 8.1 and 8.2 show, publicists described war as pest control, pest control as war, and the two endeavors as similar. On the one hand, describing war as pest control transformed participation in war from a potentially troubling moral issue to a moral virtue. Comparing chemical weapons to insecticides made it easier to portray poison gas as natural and humane. (Ironically, opponents of poison gas used the same metaphor to argue that chemical warfare was inhumane because it treated human beings like insects.) On the other hand, describing pest control as war helped entomologists portray nature as a battlefield, elevate the status of their profession, and mobilize resources.

. . . Since people had previously imagined (and sometimes succeeded in) annihilating enemies, what set the twentieth century apart? The *scale* on which people could plan and carry out killing stands out. Technology, industry, and governments grew large enough to enable us to wage "total war"—not just against armies, but against insects and civilians. People could plan, carry out, and (even when it did not come to pass) fear annihilation on a breathtaking scale across geographic and phylar boundaries. Zygmunt Bauman has suggested that modernity aimed to make the world into a garden in which some organisms belonged and from which others, which did not belong, were extirpated. The story told here complements his argument. Warfare resembled gardening, gardening resembled warfare, and both were attempts to shape the world to long-standing human visions.[7]

This article explores only some aspects of the topic. It focuses more on alliances among institutions than on conflicts, more on institutional politics than on economics, more on harms than on benefits, and more on similarities than on differences. Noting similarities does not mean equating. In World War II, for example, Germans, Americans, propagandists, and entomologists all talked of annihilating enemies. However, the actions of the United States and entomologists

---

[6]I use the term *metaphor* to include simile, analogy, and imagery. On the role of metaphor in thought and communication, see David E. Leary, "Psyche's Muse: The Role of Metaphor in the History of Psychology," in *Metaphors in the History of Psychology*, ed. David E. Leary (New York, 1990), 1–78; George Lakoff and Mark Johnson, *Metaphors We Live By* (Chicago, 1980); and Mary B. Hesse, *Models and Analogies in Science* (Notre Dame, 1966).

[7]*Oxford English Dictionary*, 2d ed., s.v. "Exterminate"; Zygmunt Bauman, *Modernity and the Holocaust* (Ithaca, 1989); Craig M. Cameron, *American Samurai: Myth, Imagination, and the Conduct of Battle in the First Marine Division, 1941–1951* (New York, 1994); and Michael S. Sherry, *The Rise of American Air Power: The Creation of Armageddon* (New Haven, 1987).

differed in critical moral ways from those of Germany and of the architects of the horrors of the Holocaust.

This story prompts two reflections about the ways we write history. First, we often talk about the impact of one aspect of life (war, science, politics) on another (the state, culture, the environment). This framework tells us a great deal, but is it complete? Few forces are monolithic, and two-way interactions may be more common than one-way impacts. War changed the natural environment, and the environment changed war. Metaphors shaped human understanding of the material world, and the material world shaped metaphors. Second, we may tend to tell stories of progress *or* decline, but life is a mixture of the two.[8] For some people insecticides and chemical weapons were blessings; for others they were curses; and for some they were both. The world gets both better and worse, and we have yet to exterminate either good or evil.

WORLD WAR I: CHEMISTRY AND WAR, 1914–1918

On April 22, 1915, Germany initiated a new chapter in the evolution of war. That day, Allied troops huddled in trenches near Ypres, France, found themselves enveloped in a greenish yellow cloud of chlorine gas released by German troops. Allied soldiers futilely tried to outrun the cloud, which reportedly killed 5,000 soldiers and injured 10,000 more. German military leaders lost the initial advantage when they failed to mount a large-scale attack, but they succeeded in demonstrating the military power that flowed from knowledge and control of nature.[9]

Knowledge about nature came in many forms, including scientific understanding of molecules, and Germany's preeminence in chemistry underpinned its initial success with chemical weapons. This preeminence depended . . . on the brilliance of civilian scientists such as Fritz Haber. . . .[10] Other nations followed Germany's lead in turning civilian science and industry to military research and production. . . . In the United States, the National Research Council (an arm of the National Academy of Sciences) organized academic, industrial, and governmental scientists to work on offensive and defensive aspects of poison gases. In 1918 the United States Army incorporated this mammoth civilian enterprise into its new Chemical Warfare Service. Other nations created similar organizations,

---

[8]Eugene D. Genovese, *Roll, Jordan, Roll: The World the Slaves Made* (New York, 1974); and James C. Scott, *Weapons of the Weak: Everyday Forms of Peasant Resistance* (New Haven, 1985); William Cronon, "A Place for Stories: Nature, History, and Narrative," *Journal of American History* 78 (March 1992), 1347–76.

[9]Hugh R. Slotten, "Humane Chemistry or Scientific Barbarism? American Responses to World War I Poison Gas, 1915–1930," *Journal of American History* 77 (Sept. 1990), 476–98; Robert Harris and Jeremy Paxman, *A Higher Form of Killing: The Secret Story of Chemical and Biological Warfare* (New York, 1982); L. F. Haber, *The Poisonous Cloud: Chemical Warfare in the First World War* (Oxford, 1986); and Daniel Patrick Jones, "The Role of Chemists in Research on War Gases in the United States during World War I" (Ph.D. diss., University of Wisconsin, 1969).

[10]Harris and Paxman, *Higher Form of Killing*, 9–11.

and tons of poison gases wafted across Europe. By the end of the war, gas report-edly had killed 90,000 people and caused 1.3 million casualties. Observers dubbed World War I "the chemist's war." . . .[11]

Chemical warriors . . . relied on compounds already known to kill organ-isms, including insects. French soldiers . . . at the battle of the Somme in 1916 . . . fired artillery shells containing hydrogen cyanide. Since the nineteenth century, farmers and entomologists had used hydrogen cyanide to fumigate in-sects in orchards and buildings. Arsenic, too, made its way from farm fields to battlefields. In the United States, the Chemical Warfare Service turned a third of the country's arsenic supply into the poison gas diphenylchloroarsine, causing shortages of arsenical insecticides used to kill orchard pests.[12]

War prompted scientists not only to convert insecticidal chemicals into chemical weapons but also to reverse the process. Lice, which sometimes carried deadly typhus, infested American troops in France. Military and civilian re-searchers alike hoped that war gases might offer a way to conquer this plague of war. In a collaborative experiment, researchers from the Chemical Warfare Service and the Bureau of Entomology of the United States Department of Agriculture tested four chemical weapons on lice. They hoped to find "a gas which can be placed in a chamber and be experienced safely for a short period of time by men wearing gas masks and which in this time will kill all cooties and their nits."[13]

These experiments stimulated tests of other chemical weapons as insecti-cides. The Chemical Warfare Service, the Bureau of Entomology, and other agen-cies of the Department of Agriculture researched the efficacy of war gases against dozens of species of insects. Most of the gases fell short, but chloropicrin, [a] compound that chemical warfare had lifted from obscurity, killed insects effec-tively. Chloropicrin harmed civilian exterminators as readily as enemy soldiers, of course, but entomologists found it less dangerous (as a tear gas, chloropicrin had good "warning properties") or more effective than other fumigants. The battlefields of Europe approximated, albeit unintentionally, laboratory experi-ments on a massive scale, and entomologists took note. *American Miller* maga-zine reported that the "scarcity of insect pests around Rheims is attributed to the

---

[11]Rexmond C. Cochrane, *The National Academy of Sciences: The First Hundred Years, 1863–1963* (Washington, D.C., 1978), 209, 231–36; Leo P. Brophy, Wyndham D. Miles, and Rexmond C. Cochrane, *The Chemical Warfare Service: From Laboratory to Field* (Washington, D.C., 1959), 1–27; W. A. Noyes Jr., "Preface," in *Chemistry: A History of the Chemistry Components of the National Defense Research Committee, 1940–1946*, ed. W. A. Noyes Jr. (Boston, 1948), xv–xvi; and Harris and Paxman, *Higher Form of Killing*, 22–23, 34.

[12]Haber, *Poisonous Cloud*, 62–63, 117–18; Brophy, Miles, and Cochrane, *Chemical Warfare Service*, 55–56; Haynes, *American Chemical Industry*, III, 111–12; L. 0. Howard, "Entomology and the War," *Scientific Monthly* 8 (Jan.–June 1919), 109–17; and Dunlap, *DDT*, 20.

[13]W. Dwight Pierce to L. 0. Howard, n.d., Correspondence on Body Lice, Vermin, Cooties, in Army, Tests and Recommendations 1918, Correspondence and Reports Relating to a Study of Body Lice 1918, Records of the Bureau of Entomology and Plant Quarantine, RG 7 (Washington National Records Center, Suitland, Md.); "Report on Experiments Conducted on October 16, 1918, Testing the Effect of Certain Toxic Gases on Body Lice and Their Eggs," ibid.

use of poisonous gases in that region during the World War," and French researchers tested chloropicrin as an insecticide on grain in closed rooms.[14]

While scientists researched ways to use pest control technology in war, soldiers and publicists in World War I, like their predecessors in previous wars, described military enemies as animals, including insect pests. A British soldier, for example, described German soldiers as running around like "disturbed earwigs under a rotten tree stump." By dehumanizing enemies, animal metaphors reduced the sense of guilt about killing human beings in battle. The "lower" the phylum, the lower the sense of guilt, and few phyla ranked lower than insects. Moreover, Europeans had long regarded nature, defined as everything on earth other than humans and their creations, as something that human beings not only could but should conquer. Describing war as an exercise in control of nature helped define war as not just morally permissible, but morally necessary.[15]

While soldiers found insect metaphors useful in minimizing the significance of killing human beings, entomologists found war metaphors useful in elevating the significance of killing insects. L. O. Howard, chief of the Bureau of Entomology, for example, described his bureau as waging "warfare against insect life." Military rhetoric was not new to science. Francis Bacon had described science as an antagonist of nature, and Darwinian rhetoric had portrayed nature as a giant battlefield. But such rhetoric took on added resonance in wartime. It implied that insects threatened the nation much as human armies did, associated scientific activity with patriotic national priorities, imbued the Bureau of Entomology with the prestige of the armed forces, and provided a rallying cry to mobilize resources against nonhuman threats.[16]

"PEACEFUL WAR" IN THE UNITED STATES, 1919-1939

Links between military and civilian endeavors forged in World War I bent, but did not always break, after the Treaty of Versailles. In the United States, the Bureau of Entomology and the Chemical Warfare Service continued to borrow

---

[14]"Killing Weevils with Chloropicrin," abstract, in Roark, *Bibliography of Chloropicrin*, 3. The Bureau of Chemistry, the Bureau of Plant Industry, and the Federal Horticultural Board helped conduct research at Chemical Warfare Service laboratories at American University. "The Chemical Warfare Service in Peace," n.d., file 029.0611: Articles and Speeches-Peacetime Activities, Station Series, 1942–1945, Security Classified, Records of the Chemical Warfare Service, U.S. Army, RG 175 (Washington National Records Center); I. E. Neifert and G. L. Garrison, *Experiments on the Toxic Action of Certain Gases on Insects, Seeds, and Fungi* (Washington, D.C., 1920); Haynes, *American Chemical Industry*, III, 111.

[15]Paul Fussell, *The Great War and Modern Memory* (New York, 1975), 77; Sam Keen, *Faces of the Enemy: Reflections of the Hostile Imagination* (San Francisco, 1986), 60–64; Peter Paret, Beth Irwin Lewis, and Paul Paret, *Persuasive Images: Posters of War and Revolution from the Hoover Institution Archives* (Princeton, 1992); and J. Glenn Gray, *The Warriors: Reflections on Men in Battle* (New York, 1970); Roderick Nash, *Wilderness and the American Mind* (New Haven, 1982), 27.

[16]Howard, "Entomology and the War," 117; Carolyn Merchant, *The Death of Nature: Women, Ecology, and the Scientific Revolution* (San Francisco, 1980); and Dunlap, *DDT*, 36–37; JoAnne Brown, *The Definition of a Profession: The Authority of Metaphor in the History of Intelligence Testing, 1890–1930* (Princeton, 1992).

each other's technology and metaphors, a process facilitated by explicit collaboration. On the other side of the Atlantic Ocean, Germany surged ahead in the search for new chemical weapons by uniting research on poison gases and insecticides. Out of these alliances came technology that shaped campaigns against both human beings and insects in World War II.

For L. O. Howard of the Bureau of Entomology, the cessation of the war in Europe set the stage for escalating "the war against insects." . . . Howard['s] 1921 address . . . [t]itled "The War against Insects," . . . sounded like propaganda from the just-completed war in Europe. Ignoring the benefits insects provided—which he had praised earlier in his career—Howard portrayed his enemy in only one dimension. Quoting Maurice Maeterlinck, Howard said that insects seemed to have a quality born of "another planet, more monstrous, more energetic, more insensate, more atrocious, more infernal than ours." How was the nation to protect itself from this threat? Federal entomologists, "a force of four hundred trained men," fought a "defensive and offensive campaign" against these hordes.[17]

AMBUSHED ARMY

Figure 8.3
Old Testament writers described insects as invading armies, and subsequent generations updated the metaphor. In 1938, an advertisement for a chemical company suggested that rifle-toting insects stood no chance against snipers spraying scentless insecticides. Reprinted from *Soap and Sanitary Chemicals* 14 (Feb. 1938), 80.

With this speech, Howard moved military metaphors—which had jostled with public health metaphors in entomological discourse—to the center of his agency's public rhetoric. Other entomologists repeated Howard's warning that insects threatened human survival. Chemical companies, too, called on martial and cultural traditions to promote their products. (See figure 8.3.) As Thomas Dunlap has suggested, it is difficult to resist the idea that the appeal of insecticides arose partly from their promise of victory over, rather than coexistence with, insect enemies.[18]

Howard could not have asked for a better symbol of "the war on insects" than the airplane, the technology that epitomized martial glory in World War I. The text of Howard's "War against

---

[17]L. O. Howard, "The War against Insects: The Insecticide Chemist and Biologist in the Mitigation of Plant Pests," *Chemical Age* 30 (no. 1, 1922), 5–6; Howard, "Entomology and the War," 109, 117.

[18]L. O. Howard, *The Insect Menace* (New York, 1931), ix; Howard, "U.S. Wages Insect War"; R. C. Roark, "Household Insecticides," *Soap and Sanitary Chemicals* 11 (Nov. 1935), 117 (emphasis added); Dunlap, *DDT*, 37; Sharon E. Kingsland, *Modeling Nature: Episodes in the History of Population Ecology* (Chicago, 1985), 12–17; C. L. Marlatt, *The Principal Insect Enemies of Growing Wheat* (Washington, D.C., 1908); and W. D. Hunter, *The Boll Weevil Problem, with Special Reference to Means of Reducing Damage* (Washington, D.C., 1909).

Insects" speech appeared in *Chemical Age* with a photograph of an airplane dusting a farm with insecticides. . . . Three days after Howard's talk, entomologist J. S. Houser announced that, in collaboration with Army Air Service researchers, he had converted a military airplane to disperse insecticides.[19]

Chemical warfare may have inspired this development. *McClure's Magazine* reported that a colonel returning from France to his job as an Ohio entomologist "knew that near the close of the war preparations were being made to sprinkle poison gas and liquid fire by airplane on soldiers in the trenches and he thought something like this could probably be used against caterpillars." *The New York Times* suggested a more mundane origin of the idea, saying that birds inspired aerial dispersal. Whatever the inspiration, the availability of military airplanes and the willingness of the Army Air Service to work on this technique made aerial dispersal of insecticides feasible. . . .[20]

Collaboration between military and civilian institutions also transferred airplanes from experimental farms to commercial agriculture. In March 1923, acting Secretary of War Dwight F. Davis declared that the United States Army should do whatever possible to help crop-dusting "in a commercial way." The Huff-Daland Corporation, which built experimental planes for the air service, sent representatives to a Bureau of Entomology laboratory in 1923 to work on a special dusting plane. . . . Before long, commercial crop dusters became important symbols of wars on insects, especially on the boll weevil.[21]

Despite Howard's predictions . . . most chemical weapons did not prove immediately impressive in fighting insects. Howard told the 1924 meeting of the Entomological Society of America that postwar collaboration between the Chemical Warfare Service and the Bureau of Entomology had produced mountains of data of "undoubted value," but the Chemical Warfare Service was keeping almost all of the results secret. But in 1931 Howard laconically reported that the experiments were "not promising, on account of the resultant damage to vegetation," which ended the Bureau of Entomology's public discussion of the war gas experiments. The exception was chloropicrin, which became a popular fumigant for clothing, households, and grain elevators.[22]

The disappointing results did not derive from lack of effort. For its own reasons, the Chemical Warfare Service devoted resources in the 1920s to the

[19]Eldon W. Downs and George F. Lemmer, "Origins of Aerial Crop Dusting," *Agricultural History* 39 (July 1965), 123–35, esp. 126.

[20]Corley McDarment, "The Use of Airplanes to Destroy the Boll Weevil," *McClure's Magazine* 57 (Aug. 1924), 90–102, esp. 91–92; Downs and Lemmer, "Origins of Aerial Crop Dusting," 124, 127.

[21]Ina L. Hawes and Rose Eisenberg, eds., *Bibliography on Aviation and Economic Entomology* (Washington, D.C., 1947), 8–9; Downs and Lemmer, "Origins of Aerial Crop Dusting," 130–32, esp. 130; Douglas Helms, "Technological Methods for Boll Weevil Control," *Agricultural History* 53 (Oct. 1979), 286–99.

[22]L. O. Howard, "The Needs of the World as to Entomology," *Smithsonian Institution Annual Report*, 1925 (Washington, D.C., 1925), 355–72, esp. 370; Roark, *Bibliography of Chloropicrin*; Howard, *Insect Menace*, 283.

search for insecticidal uses of war gases. Because poison gases had symbolized, for many, the brutality and senselessness of modern warfare, post–World War I peace movements focused much of their energy on chemical weapons. International conventions twice almost banned use of chemical weapons in the 1920s, and even within the United States Army powerful individuals wanted to eliminate the Chemical Warfare Service and to transfer its responsibilities to other units.[23]

The Chemical Warfare Service and its allies responded by emphasizing the humanity of poison gas (which killed a smaller proportion of casualties than did bullets and bombs) and the civilian uses of war gases, including their use as insecticides. Borrowing a metaphor from Isaiah, the journal *Chemical Warfare* reported in 1922 that chemical warriors had beaten "the sword into the plowshare." By emphasizing agricultural uses of war gases, the service tried to reverse its image from agent of war to agent of peace. According to the *Pittsburgh Gazette Times*, Amos Fries, chief of the Chemical Warfare Service, described his agency as doing "peace work principally." Since conquest of nature had long been seen as a morally uncontroversial endeavor, insecticide projects provided an ideal way to place chemical warfare in a more positive light. An article in *Chemical Warfare*, for example, stated, "Efficient offensive warfare must be developed against animal, bird and insect life." . . .[24]

One of the most heavily publicized "swords into plowshares" projects involved the search, in collaboration with the Bureau of Entomology and state experiment stations, for insecticides to kill the boll weevil. For seven years, the Chemical Warfare Service held out hope for a solution to "the boll weevil problem, the curse of the cotton states of the South," to the public and Congress. In the end, however, it had little to show. In 1926, H. W. Walker and J. E. Mills of the Chemical Warfare Service reported that toxic gases were "ineffective against the weevil due to its apparent ability to suspend breathing more or less at will."[25]

Although of little use to farmers, the research project did help the Chemical Warfare Service. The advantages grew partly out the service's ability to conduct military research while publicizing civilian applications. Substances toxic to insects stood a good chance of being toxic to human beings, and the Chemical Warfare Service could learn about the physiology of poisoning in human beings by studying the effects of chemicals on insects. The Chemical Warfare Service

---

[23]Frederic J. Brown, *Chemical Warfare: A Study in Restraints* (Westport, 1968), 52–96; Daniel P. Jones, "From Military to Civilian Technology: The Introduction of Tear Gas for Civil Riot Control," *Technology and Culture* 19 (no. 2, 1978), 151–68.

[24]"Chemical Warfare Making Swords into Plowshares," *Chemical Warfare* 8 (no. 2, 1922), 2–5, esp. 2; "Its Greater Service to Peace: From *Gazette Times*, Pittsburgh, Pa., November 24, 1924," ibid., 11 (no. 2, 1925), 22; "Chemical Warfare: Editorial in 'Army and Navy Register,' January 7, 1922," ibid., 8 (no. 1, 1922), 20–21, esp. 20.

[25]Amos A. Fries, "Chemical Warfare Inspires Peace," ibid., 6 (no. 5, 1921), 3–4, esp. 3. See also Amos A. Fries, "Chemical Warfare and Its Relation to Art and Industry," ibid., 7 (no. 4, 1921), 2–8, esp. 6–7. H. W. Walker and J. E. Mills, "Progress Report of Work of the Chemical Warfare Service on the Boll Weevil *Anthonomus Grandis*," *Journal of Economic Entomology* 19 (Aug. 1926), 600–601.

lauded this side of the boll weevil investigations in its 1927 report, saying that the project had *"extended our knowledge of the fundamental facts concerning the toxicity of compounds* which will prove beneficial to certain investigations undertaken with a view to the *solution of specific Chemical Warfare problems."*[26]

Similarly, projects on aerial dispersal of insecticides helped develop aerial dispersal of poison gases, which chemical warriors expected to be a prominent feature of future wars. A 1921 pamphlet issued under the auspices of the National Research Council predicted, "Armed with such [poisonous] liquids and solids the airman of the next war will not need a machine gun or even bombs to attack the enemy underneath.... All he need do is to attach a sprayer to the tail of his machine and rain down poison on the earth beneath as the farmer kills the bugs on his potato field."[27]

Insecticide projects allowed the Chemical Warfare Service not only to equate chemical weapons and insecticides but also to portray the targets of those chemicals—human beings and insects—as similar. Fries made this comparison explicit in 1922 when he said "that the human pest is the worst of all pests to handle." Others saw parallels between gassing insects and gassing human beings but resisted the implication that such similarities were desirable. A 1921 piece in the *New York Herald* criticized a report of potential use of poison gas against moonshiners, saying, "In the great war the world saw too much of human beings killed or tortured with poison gas.... Ordinary killing is bad enough, but that man should treat his fellow as he treats a rat or a cockroach is inherently repugnant to all from whom decent instincts have not fled."[28]

The Chemical Warfare Service's projects on insecticides and other civilian applications for war gases faded away in the late 1920s.... Although neither the Chemical Warfare Service nor the Bureau of Entomology discovered powerful new chemicals in the 1920s, they made heavy use of each other's metaphors. Portraying insect control as war built up the practical significance of entomology, while portraying war as insect control played down the political and moral issues associated with chemical weapons.

MOBILIZATION IN GERMANY, 1935–1939

In Germany, too, researchers in the interwar period saw the value of linking research on insecticides and chemical weapons. But while heavy publicity and meager results marked the American efforts, the opposite held true in Germany.

---

[26]H. W. Walker, "A Brief Resume of the Chemical Warfare Service Boll Weevil Investigation," *Chemical Warfare* 13 (no. 12, 1927), 231–37, esp. 233. Emphasis added.

[27]"Chemistry and War: The Following Was Printed in a Pamphlet Issued under the Auspices of the National Research Council," ibid., 6 (no. 6, 1921), 13–15, esp. 14; Brophy, Miles, and Cochrane, *Chemical Warfare Service*, 32.

[28]Amos A. Fries, "Address before Chemical Industries Exposition, New York City," Sept. 12, 1922, file 029.0611: Articles & Speeches-Peacetime Activities, Station Series, 1942–1945, Security Classified, Records of the Chemical Warfare Service, U.S. Army. On the piece in the *New York Herald*, see "Not Poison Gas!," *Chemical Warfare* 9 (no. 2, 1921), 22.

Out of a laboratory in the giant chemical combine I. G. Farben came little publicity and big discoveries, including a new family of chemicals called organophosphates with tremendous lethality to insects and human beings.

The difference in outcomes arose largely from differences in attitudes toward mobilization. While Americans struggled with the legacy of World War I—Congress went so far as to hold hearings on whether corporations stimulated the war in order to boost profits—and the economic distress of the Great Depression, Germany prepared its civilians and industry for war. In 1936 Adolf Hitler ordered the armed forces to be ready for war within four years. Politicians used poison gas and gas-dispersing airplanes as icons of the threat posed by other nations, and drills with gas masks reinforced the need for discipline and technology to protect the nation.[29]

Similarly, the central government mobilized chemical technology to protect the nation from insect enemies. In 1937, the German government mandated that farmers use insecticides. Unfortunately for this program, Germany imported most of its insecticides. The country's reliance on expensive imports stimulated the German chemical industry to search for cheaper synthetic insecticides.[30]

The giant German chemical combine I.G. Farben developed a working relationship with the Nazi leadership and became involved in the chemical warfare program. In November 1936, I.G. Farben officers urged the military economic staff to produce and stockpile chemical weapons. Poison gas, they argued, could determine the outcome of the next war if it were used against *civilian* populations, who would be panic-stricken and find "every door-handle, every fence, every paving stone a weapon of the enemy." I.G. Farben officials thought Germans were too disciplined and technically equipped to collapse should an enemy retaliate.[31]

The search for new insecticides and poison gases came together in the laboratory of I.G. Farben's Gerhard Schrader. In fact, *all* German chemical laboratories became de facto parts of the country's chemical warfare program in 1935, when the central government mandated the reporting of all toxic substances. . . . When Schrader sprayed chemicals on insects, he was in fact screening chemical weapons. Schrader began with a compound, chloroethyl alcohol, known to be toxic to human beings and dogs, varied the atoms on the molecule, and screened the resulting compounds on insects. A series of substitutions led him to a little-studied family of compounds called organophosphates,

[29] Rolf-Dieter Müller, "World Power Status through the Use of Poison Gas? German Preparations for Chemical Warfare, 1919–1945," in *The German Military in the Age of Total War*, ed. Wilhelm Deist (Dover, N.H., 1985), 171–209, esp. 183; Peter Fritzsche, "Machine Dreams: Airmindedness and the Reinvention of Germany," *American Historical Review* 98 (June 1993), 685–709.

[30] "Chemicals—Use of Agricultural Insecticides Compulsory in Germany," *Commerce Reports*, May 1, 1937, p. 354; A. Buxtorf and M. Spindler, *Fifteen Years of Geigy Pest Control* (Basel, 1954), 8.

[31] Müller, "World Power Status through the Use of Poison Gas?," 184–86, esp. 186; Peter Hayes, *Industry and Ideology: IG Farben in the Nazi Era* (New York, 1987), xvii.

which killed insects effectively. Schrader and a colleague patented the generic blueprint of the molecule in 1939.[32]

Few people knew about this patent, for it was declared "top secret." The basic molecule constituted the basis not only for new insecticides but also for highly lethal new nerve gases. On December 23, 1936, Schrader had attached cyanide to his basic organophosphate molecule. The compound killed plant lice at a concentration of only 1 part per 200,000. When inhaled in small doses, it also killed human beings. I.G. Farben patented the substance in February 1937 and sent a sample to the chemical warfare section of the Army Weapons Office in May. . . .[33]

In 1938, Schrader found a related compound whose potential "as a toxic war substance" he judged to be "astonishingly high." On animals, the substance tested ten times as toxic as tabun [the first nerve gas he named]. Schrader dubbed it sarin. Other nerve gases followed. Through his superiors at I.G. Farben, Schrader reported between one and two hundred highly toxic compounds to the government in the late 1930s and early 1940s. . . .[34]

At the same time that Schrader's work demonstrated biochemical similarities between human beings and insects, Nazi propagandists promoted metaphorical links between human and insect enemies. Nineteenth-century German theologians had described Jews as "vermin, spiders, swarms of locusts, leeches, giant parasite growths, poisonous worms." Nazis capitalized on such long-standing metaphors, with Hitler calling Jews a "pestilence," "typical parasites," and "carriers of bacilli worse than Black Death." As Nazis grew in power, so did their propaganda. Joseph Goebbels said that "since the flea is not a pleasant animal we are not obliged to keep it, protect it and let it prosper so that it may prick and torture us, but our duty is rather to exterminate it. Likewise with the Jew." Metaphor and "reality" blurred in Nazi rhetoric: Jews were to be exterminated as deliberately, and literally, as insects.[35]

---

[32]Combined Intelligence Objectives Subcommittee, "A New Group of War Gases, No. 23-7," n.d., p. 7, Library Project Files 1946-1951, Records of Assistant Chief of Staff (G-2) Intelligence, Administrative Division, U.S. Army, RG 319 (Washington National Records Center); British Intelligence Objectives Subcommittee, "The Development of New Insecticides, Report No. 714 (Revised)," n.d., pp. 13-14, 21-24, ibid.

[33]Harris and Paxman, *Higher Form of Killing*, 57; Stockholm International Peace Research Institute, *Problem of Chemical and Biological Warfare* I, 71-72; British Intelligence Objectives Subcommittee, "Development of New Insecticides," 23; Robert L. Metcalf, "The Impact of Organophosphorous Insecticides upon Basic and Applied Science," *Bulletin of the Entomological Society of America* 5 (1959), 3-15.

[34]Gerhard Schrader worked with Eberhard Gross, who did toxicology testing. Gross forwarded results to Heinrich Hoerlein, director of I. G. Elberfeld, who forwarded them to Berlin. Combined Intelligence Objectives Subcommittee, "A New Group of War Gases, No. 23-7," pp. 3-7; Harris and Paxman, *Higher Form of Killing*, 58-59, esp. 58.

[35]C. C. Aronsfeld, *The Text of the Holocaust: A Study of the Nazis' Extermination Propaganda: 1919-1945* (Marblehead, 1985), 2, 12.

WORLD WAR II: WAR ON HUMAN BEINGS
AND INSECTS, 1940–1945

World War II, scientific discoveries, and a massive bureaucracy offered Nazi Germany the chance to put the rhetoric of extermination into practice on a massive scale. Heinrich Himmler organized SS troops to begin mass slaughter when German armies conquered Poland, and Germany set up the first extermination center at Chelmno, Poland, in the fall of 1939. Himmler's troops relied on carbon monoxide from the exhaust of vans to gas the first victims, and the center became efficient enough to kill 1,000 people per day. When Himmler ordered Commander Rudolf Hess to begin gassing Jews at Auschwitz in June 1941, Hess set up similar gas chambers, but he found carbon monoxide too slow.[36]

Greater efficiency came about when the SS began using technology more closely suited to its rhetoric. Hess later said that fumigation of insects in the concentration camp inspired him to try gas on prisoners in the fall of 1941, and that he used crystals of an insecticide, Zyklon B, left by an extermination company, for the first experiments on human beings. Zyklon B was hydrocyanic acid, one of the substances called an "insecticide" in civilian settings and a "chemical weapon" in military settings. During World War I, the compound had been used for both purposes; Germany had developed hydrocyanic acid to kill lice that transmitted typhus and used it to fumigate submarines, barracks, and prison camps. Hess first tested Zyklon B on Soviet prisoners of war.[37]

The "fit" between insecticide technology and Nazi "extermination" rhetoric did not escape notice. When the manager of the insecticide manufacturer asked the SS procurement officer the purpose of Zyklon B shipments, he learned that the insecticide would be used to "exterminate criminals, incurable patients, and inferior human beings." Much of the company's 1943 sales of Zyklon B went to Auschwitz, where members of the SS crowded human victims into "shower rooms," then climbed onto the roof and released Zyklon B into the chambers below. According to a Nuremberg prosecutor, a chemical firm called Degesch (which stood for German vermin-combating corporation) shipped enough Zyklon B to Auschwitz to kill millions of human beings.[38]

[36]Joseph Borkin, *The Crime and Punishment of I. G. Farben* (New York, 1978), 121–22; Gerald Fleming, *Hitler and the Final Solution* (Berkeley, 1984); and Michael R. Marrus, ed., *The Nazi Holocaust: Historical Articles on the Destruction of European Jews*, vol. III: *The "Final Solution".' The Implementation of Mass Murder* (Westport, 1989); Bartov, *Hitler's Army. Soldiers, Nazis, and War in the Third Reich* (New York, 1991); Gerald Reitlinger, *The Final Solution: The Attempt to Exterminate the Jews of Europe, 1939–1945* (Northvale, 1987); and Yehuda Bauer, *A History of the Holocaust* (New York, 1982).

[37]Reitlinger, *Final Solution*, 146. Zyklon B was tested on 500 Russian prisoners of war in August 1941, according to Borkin, *Crime and Punishment of I. G. Farben*, 121–22. Zyklon B was first tested on "about 850 Soviet prisoners of war and sick inmates in September 1941," according to Hayes, *Industry and Ideology*, 362.

[38]Josiah E. DuBois Jr., *The Devil's Chemists: 24 Conspirators of the International Farben Cartel Who Manufacture Wars* (Boston, 1952), 213–16, esp. 214; Borkin, *Crime and Punishment of I. G. Farben*, 123; See Hayes, *Industry and Ideology*, 361–62.

Indirectly, I.G. Farben supported and profited from the SS campaign against Jews.... I.G. Farben was linked to the horrors of the death camps.... Tabun and sarin, the nerve gases developed along with insecticides by Schrader, offered Germany new weapons of great but unmeasured power. Guinea pigs and white rats seemed inadequate for testing the effects of nerve gases on human beings, so, after ill-fated attempts with apes, experiments began, using concentration camp Jews.[39]

Some observers believed that metaphorical redefinition of human enemies as animals, including insects, also facilitated bloodletting in the Pacific theater. When describing Japanese soldiers and civilians, American propagandists and soldiers employed vermin metaphors more often than when describing Germans. Ernie Pyle noted this difference in 1945, when he visited the Pacific after seeing some of the worst fighting in Europe: "In Europe we felt our enemies, horrible and deadly as they were, were still people. But out here I gathered that the Japanese were looked upon as something subhuman and repulsive; the way some people feel about cockroaches or mice." Claire Chennault, a retired United States Army officer and adviser to the air force of Chiang Kai-shek, later said that in 1940 he had wanted to "burn out the industrial heart of the Empire with fire-bomb attacks on the teeming bamboo ant heaps of Honshu and Kyushu. " In *God Is My Co-Pilot*, Col. Robert Scott Jr. of the United States Army Air Force wrote that every time he killed a "Jap" he felt he "had stepped on another black-widow spider or scorpion."[40]

Why did Americans describe the Japanese as insects and other vermin? Historians have noted that Americans had previously feared a "yellow peril" and discriminated against Asians, and that in World War II they found the Japanese approach to war brutal and irrational. Japanese treatment of prisoners of war (symbolized by the Bataan death march) contributed to the view that the Japanese behaved in subhuman ways.[41]

Whatever the cause, seeing enemies as vermin must have made it seem "natural" to talk of extermination. Adm. William F. Halsey congratulated troops who captured Peleliu in 1944: "The sincere admiration of the entire Third Fleet is yours for the hill[-]blasting, cave[-]smashing extermination of 11,000 slant-eyed gophers." The novelist Herman Wouk, who experienced World War II aboard a destroyer in the South Pacific, later wrote:

> This cold-bloodedness, worthy of a horseman of Genghis Khan, was quite strange in a pleasant little fellow like Ensign Keith. Militarily, of course, it was an asset beyond price. Like most of the naval executioners at Kwajalein, he seemed to regard the enemy as a species of animal pest. From the grim and

---

[39]40 DuBois, *Devil's Chemists*, 213; Borkin, *Crime and Punishment of I. G. Farben*, 121, 132; Hayes, *Industry and Ideology*, 361–62.

[40]John W. Dower, *War without Mercy: Race and Power in the Pacific War* (New York, 1986). For Ernie Pyle's remark, see Cameron, *American Samurai*, 1; for Claire Chennault's and Robert Scott's, see Sherry, *Rise of American Air Power*, 101–2, 134.

[41]Dower, *War without Mercy*, 77–180; Cameron, *American Samurai*, 98–129.

desperate taciturnity with which the Japanese died, they seemed on their side to believe they were contending with an invasion of large armed ants. This obliviousness on both sides to the fact that the opponents were human beings may perhaps be cited as the key to the many massacres of the Pacific war.[42]

. . . . Combatants (except, probably, Japan) did not use gas against human enemies on battlefields in World War II. On the insect front, however, technology made it feasible to annihilate enemies. In 1939, a chemist at the Swiss chemical company Geigy had found that DDT killed insects at low doses for long periods and had low acute toxicity to humans. . . . Then World War II prompted the (re-named) United States Bureau of Entomology and Plant Quarantine to search for chemicals to protect soldiers from louse-borne typhus. Geigy gave a sample of DDT to the bureau in 1942, and entomologists found DDT powder ideal for kill-ing lice. With help from the War Production Board, Geigy and other companies began making DDT in the United States for the armed forces. After it helped quell a typhus outbreak in war-torn Naples in the winter of 1943–1944, DDT became known as the miracle chemical of World War II.[43]

The campaign against another insect-borne disease, malaria, revitalized links between insect control and chemical warfare. Entomologists at the Bureau of Entomology and Plant Quarantine found that DDT killed mosquitoes well, but the standard way to disperse insecticides from the air—as dusts—worked poorly with DDT. The entomologists then tried spraying DDT from the air as a liquid. This method was new to entomology, but not to chemical warfare. The Bureau of Entomology and Plant Quarantine began working with the United States Army Air Forces in 1943 to adapt chemical warfare tanks and nozzles to DDT. By 1945 the armed services could blanket "thousands of acres" with DDT using airplanes, from small combat planes to large transports. Chemical Warfare Service pilots and planes sprayed DDT to control mosquitoes in the malaria-ridden Pacific. As in other campaigns, propagandists unified images of insect and human enemies. One anti-malaria cartoon portrayed Japanese soldiers and mosquitoes as two as-pects of a common enemy, with mosquitoes causing eight times as many casual-ties as did Japanese soldiers.[44]

---

[42]Cameron, *American Samurai*, 1; Herman Wouk, *The Caine Mutiny* (Garden City, 1951), 240; *Washington Post*, May 16, 1995, p. C1.

[43]Reports charged that Japan used poison gas in China in the 1930s and 1940s. Brown, *Chemical Warfare*, 288–89; Harris and Paxman, *Higher Form of Killing*, 148–49; Jeffrey W. Legro, "Cooperation within Conflict: Submarines, Strategic Bombing, Chemical Warfare, and Restraint in World War II" (Ph.D. diss., University of California, Los Angeles, 1992); Stockholm International Peace Research Institute, *Problem of Chemical and Biological Warfare*, I, 147–57; Victor Froelicher, "The Story of DDT," *Soap and Sanitary Chemicals* (July 1944), 115; E. F. Knipling, "Insect Control Investigations of the Orlando, Fla., Laboratory during World War II," in *Annual Report of the Board of Regents of the Smithsonian Institution*, 1948 (Washington, D.C., 1948), 331–48, esp. 335–37; R. C. Roark to P. N. Annand, Jan. 6, 1945, History of Developments-Bureau of Entomology and Plant Quarantine-World War 2, 1945, History of Defense and War Activities, 1941–50, Correspondence and Reports, Records of the Bureau of Entomology and Plant Quarantine; "Publications," *Soap and Sanitary Chemicals* (May 1944), 107; and Dunlap, *DDT*, 62.

[44]Knipling, "Insect Control Investigations," 338; Brooks E. Kleber and Dale Birdsell, *The Chemical Warfare Service: Chemicals in Combat* (Washington, D.C., 1966), 319; P. A. Harper, E. T.

Military success against insect enemies during World War II inspired entomologists to call for similar wars on insects at home. E. O. Essig used his December 1944 presidential address to the American Association of Economic Entomologists to call for "An All Out Entomological Program." Noting that the world had never been so conscious of insect control as during World War II, Essig urged that entomologists seize "the great opportunities" and create "a new day" for entomology. He thought one of the "most promising prospects" was "the strong emphasis being placed on the complete extermination of not only newly introduced pests but also those of long standing in the country."[45]

Science News Letter summarized Essig's talk as calling for "Total war against man's insect enemies, with the avowed object of total extermination instead of mere 'control.'" ... *Science News Letter* emphasized that DDT was a "powerful agent in these *postwar wars* to make crops less costly and personal life safer, more comfortable." *Popular Mechanics* also thought that the home front would become more like a battlefront. In an article titled "Our Next World War—Against Insects," it reported that "Uncle Sam, fighting one World War, is preparing for the next—and this one will be a long and bitter battle to crush the creeping, wriggling, flying, burrowing billions whose numbers and depredations baffle human comprehension."[46]

Publicists for chemical companies showed no doubt that DDT would bring enormous benefits to civilians, but entomologists tempered their hopes with concern. They believed DDT was appropriate on battlefronts, where risks of insect-borne diseases ran high, and they hoped that DDT could be used in agriculture. But they found that DDT could create as well as solve problems, by killing off predators and parasites that normally kept pests under control. ... A naval medical officer reported that the first use of DDT in the Pacific had led to "complete destruction of plant and animal life."[47]

Lisansky, and B. E. Sasse, "Malaria and Other Insect-Borne Diseases in the South Pacific Campaign," *American Journal of Tropical Medicine*, Supplement 27 (no. 3, 1947), 1–67, esp. 36; Office of Scientific Research and Development Committee on Insect and Rodent Control and the National Academy of Science-National Research Council Coordinating Committee on Insect Control; Leo Finkelstein and C. G. Schmitt, *History of Research and Development of the Chemical Warfare Service in World War II (1 July 1940–31 December 1945)*, vol. XIX, pt. 1: *Insecticides, Miticides, and Rodenticides* (Army Chemical Center, Edgewood, Md., 1949), 26–27.

[45]E. O. Essig, "An All Out Entomological Program," *Journal of Economic Entomology* 38 (Feb. 1945), 1–8, esp. 6, 8.

[46]"Total Insect War Urged," *Science News Letter*, Jan. 6, 1945, p. 5 (emphasis added); "Our Next World War—Against Insects," *Popular Mechanics* 81 (April 1944), 66–70, esp. 67.

[47]Subcommittee on Dispersal, Minutes of the Fourth Meeting, Feb. 18–19, 1946, p. 18, Miscellaneous Minutes and Conferences, Insect Control, Committee on Insect Control (OSRD), Minutes (Bulletins) and Reports (Drawer 7), Committees on Military Medicine, Division of Medical Sciences, 1940–1945, Records of the National Research Council (National Academy of Sciences Archives, Washington, D.C.); Frederick S. Philips, "Medical Division Report No. 13, A Review of the Biological Properties and Insecticidal Applications of DDT," Nov. 22, 1944, p. 2, USA Typhus Commission-DDT- General, USA Typhus Commission, Records of the Army Surgeon General, RG 112 (Washington National Records Center).

Worries found expression in metaphors that echoed criticisms of chemical warfare. Col. J. W. Scharff, a British malariologist who praised the role of DDT in protecting troops from malaria, complained, "DDT is such a crude and powerful weapon that I cannot help regarding the routine use of this material from the air with . . . horror and aversion." The nature writer Edwin Way Teale shared Scharff's distress: "Given sufficient insecticide, airplanes and lackwit officials after the war, and we will be off with yelps of joy on a crusade against all the insects." Teale was sure of the result of this "bug-blitz binge": a "conservation headache of historic magnitude." The Bureau of Entomology and Plant Quarantine's H. H. Stage and C. F. W. Muesebeck fretted, "Biological deserts may be produced by heavy treatments of DDT and these would be, of course, highly undesirable."[48]

Although federal entomologists thought it premature to recommend DDT for unrestricted civilian use, no peacetime government agency had the authority to keep DDT off the market. On August 1, 1945, the War Production Board allowed manufacturers to sell DDT, once military needs were met, without restriction. The United States dropped an atomic bomb on Hiroshima five days later, then another on Nagasaki, and Japan surrendered. (A woman from Milwaukee used an animal metaphor to express her wish that destruction had been more thorough: "When one sets out to destroy vermin, does one try to leave a few alive in the nest? Certainly not!") The War Production Board soon lifted all restrictions on DDT sales. Declaring that "the war against winged pests was under way," *Time* magazine announced DDT's release for civilian use on the same page where it published photographs of the first atomic explosion.[49]

A postwar "insecticide revolution" began, with DDT and its relatives leading the way. Meanwhile, intelligence teams combing through records of the German chemical industry uncovered Schrader's work on organophosphates. They publicized information about insecticides while keeping secret news of the closely related nerve gases. Even as organophosphates opened a new chapter in the history of chemical weaponry, such organophosphates as parathion joined DDT in

---

[48]Special Joint Meeting of the Army Committee for Insect and Rodent Control and the Office of Scientific Research and Development, Insect Control Committee, Minutes, Jan. 12, 1945, p. 7, Report 39, OSRD Insect Control Committee Reports, vol. 1, Minutes (Bulletins) and Reports (Drawer 7), Committees on Military Medicine, Division of Medical Sciences, 1940–1945, Records of the National Research Council; Edwin Way Teale, "DDT," *Nature Magazine* 38 (March 1945), 120; H. H. Stage and C. F. W. Muesebeck, "Insects Killed by DDT Aerial Spraying in Panama," July 1, 1945, p. 1, National Research Council Insect Control Committee Report 108, OSRD Insect Control Committee Reports-Numbered-vol. 2, Minutes (Bulletins) and Reports (Drawer 7), Committees on Military Medicine, Division of Medical Sciences, 1940–1945, Records of the National Research Council.

[49]"WPB Lifts Restrictions on DDT," *Soap and Sanitary Chemicals* (Aug. 1945), 125; "DDT Insecticides Rushed on Market," ibid. (Sept. 1945), 124A-C; DDT Producers Industry Advisory Committee Meeting Summary, July 25, 1945, pp. 3–4, file 535.61105, Policy Documentation File, Records of the War Production Board, RG 179 (National Archives, Washington, D.C.); Leonie M. Cole to editor, *Milwaukee Journal*, Aug. 16, 1945, quoted in Boyer, *By the Bomb's Early Light*, 185; "War on Insects," *Time*, Aug. 27, 1945, p. 65.

revolutionizing pest control in agriculture. Sales of insecticides soared, replacing earlier methods of pest control that relied on preventing insect attacks.[50]

The rhetoric of war pervaded this revolution. On the first anniversary of the bombing of Hiroshima, Rohm & Haas, which earlier had compared "Japs" to flies, used a full-page photograph of a mushroom cloud to publicize DDT. Industrial Management Corporation sold a war-developed technology for dispersing DDT called "bug bombs" (forerunners of aerosol cans). The name of the DDT bomb, "Insect-O-Blitz," alluded to the German term for fast, mechanized warfare and to bombing of English cities. As *Modern Packaging* noted, "The Bug Bomb derives its name both from its devastating effect on insect life and its appearance." Coupled with DDT, this new weapon promised to play a central role in the "postwar wars" on insects: "One malaria authority has stated that, given sufficient aerosol bombs and unlimited funds, he can wipe malaria off the earth within 20 years after the war." In its advertisement for DDT, S. B. Penick & Company called for women to join a domestic version of World War II, "the continued battle of the home front."[51]

CONCLUSION

Publicists for S. B. Penick and other advertisers surely saw their cries for a "battle of the home front" as metaphorical. Human beings waged "real" war against each other, after all, not against bugs. But the frequent use of military metaphors in insecticide advertisements, like the use of insect metaphors in warfare, highlighted similarities in ways that human beings dealt with two-legged and six-legged enemies in the first half of the twentieth century.

Wars on human and insect enemies both focused on enemies, and especially enemies that did not respect *boundaries*. Once erected, international borders, fencerows, and the walls of homes created the rights of citizens, farmers, and homeowners to protect their land and homes against "invading" enemies—including, ironically, some longtime residents. In Europe, Nazis blamed Jews for almost all of the nation's ills, deported them, and killed them. The United States confined American citizens of Japanese ancestry to concentration camps. American farmers referred to insects in fields as "trespassers," even though most insects had arrived long before the farmers.[52] The emphasis on protection against

---

[50]Thomas R. Dunlap, "The Triumph of Chemical Pesticides in Insect Control, 1890–1920," *Environmental Review* 1 (no. 5, 1978), 38–47; Perkins, *Insects, Experts, and the Insecticide Crisis*, 11–13; Metcalf, "Impact of Organophosphorous Insecticides." There are two versions of the official British report on Gerhard Schrader's research, with the nerve gas information censored from the "revised" version. British Intelligence Objectives Subcommittee, "Development of New Insecticides." On intelligence teams, see John Gimbel, *Science, Technology, and Reparations: Exploitation and Plunder in Postwar Germany* (Stanford, 1990).

[51]Rohm & Haas, "Fastest Action," advertisement, *Soap and Sanitary Chemicals* (Aug. 1946), 134; Industrial Management Corporation, "Insect-O-Blitz," advertisement, ibid. (Dec. 1946), 146; "Bug Bomb," *Modern Packaging* 18 (Oct. 1944), 98–102, esp. 98.

[52]U.S. Entomological Commission, *First Annual Report of the United States Entomological Commission for the Year 1877 Relating to the Rocky Mountain Locust* (Washington, D.C., 1878), 115.

outsiders helps explain the popularity of extermination, or driving beyond boundaries, as a term for dealing with both human and insect enemies.

Like physical structures, mental divisions between human beings and nature created useful boundaries, especially because one could move human beings and animals from one side of the boundary to the other. Describing insects as national enemies elevated them from the category of *nuisance* to that of national threat. This was not always an exaggeration. In the Pacific, for example, malaria-carrying mosquitoes caused more casualties than did enemy soldiers, making them important dangers for armies. Movement of people into the category of *animal* had consequences of far more horrifying significance. Wouk emphasized that the ability to redefine a human being as an insect was an "asset beyond price" in a military setting, but an asset that resulted in "massacres." And Nazis surely knew exactly what they were doing when they used "extermination" to describe their campaign against Jews.

Not coincidentally, human beings developed similar technologies to kill human and insect enemies. In many cases, farmers and armies used identical chemicals (chloropicrin and hydrogen cyanide) to kill their enemies. In others, closely related chemicals (arsenicals and organophosphates) served both purposes. For chemical warriors, at least, these similarities came as no surprise. William Porter, chief of the Chemical Warfare Service, noted in 1944, "The fundamental biological principles of poisoning Japanese, insects, rats, bacteria and cancer are essentially the same."[53]

The development of common technologies relied on alliances, usually organized by nation-states, between civilian and military institutions. In the United States, the Bureau of Entomology collaborated intermittently with the Chemical Warfare Service from World War I through World War II. In Germany, I.G. Farben conducted research for the German army. The world wars forged especially close links between military and scientific institutions, and the effort to maintain such links became a hallmark of the post–World War II era. . . .

The rhetoric of exterminating or annihilating enemies—whether insect or human—antedated the twentieth century. The first half of this century, however, saw the development of technology and institutions that enabled nations to kill enemies with chemical compounds more quickly, and over a wider area, than ever before. In practice, insecticides found far wider use than did chemical weapons, but chemicals played a central role in extermination of human beings in the Holocaust. . . .[54]

Similar in some ways, Germany and the United States were in contrast in others. In the 1930s, they differed in their commitment to mobilization, which contributed to Germany's success in finding new chemical weapons. During

---

[53]William N. Porter to Vannevar Bush, Sept. 30, 1944, file 710, Office of Scientific Research and Development, Miscellaneous Series, 1942–1945, Records of the Chemical Warfare Service, United States Army.

[54]Chemical weapons continue to be feared as weapons of mass destruction, and efforts to eliminate them continue. See *The Washington Post*, Jan. 14, 1993, p. A24.

World War II, Nazi Germany employed chemicals on a horrific scale to exterminate human beings but had little success with new insecticides. The United States, on the other hand, did not use chemical weapons to kill human beings in World War II (except accidentally) and did not make genocide a national policy. It did develop an effective new insecticide (DDT).[55]

By the end of World War II, then, lines between human and insect enemies, military and civilian institutions, and military and civilian technology had all been blurred. Annihilation of national and natural enemies had become realistic on a large scale, a reality both comforting and disturbing to people who lived in the post–World War II era. The twin insecurities raised by military and civilian technology illustrated that war and environmental change were not separate endeavors, but rather related aspects of life in the twentieth century.

---

[55]In 1943, German airplanes attacked an American ship in the harbor at Bari, Italy. Mustard gas in the ship's hold escaped and killed about 1,000 Americans and Italians. Institute of Medicine, *Veterans at Risk: The Health Effects of Mustard Gas and Lewisite* (Washington, D.C., 1993), 43–44.

Edmund P. Russell

I study the history of people's interactions with their environments. My article in this volume provides an example of how primary research shapes the ideas of historians. I began with the question, Why did chemical insecticides displace other methods of pest control in agriculture after World War II? I expected the answer would be civilian science and economics, but archival research uncovered evidence that chemical warfare accelerated development of pesticides. I did not expect to write about images and metaphors, but research in industry journals led me to the advertisements in the article. They convinced me that ideas about nature shaped ideas about war, and ideas about war shaped ideas about nature. For more on these topics, please see *War and Nature: Fighting Humans and Insects with Chemicals from World War I to Silent Spring* (2001).

I was fortunate to take AP US History from Mr. Virgil Beckman, who had us read and write about a different book by a historian each week. It was demanding but exciting to understand how historians produced the knowledge that later appeared in textbooks. I love history because it helps me understand aspects of our world that would otherwise remain mysterious. Lately, I have been exploring ways in which people have shaped their history by altering the traits of non-human populations. My book on this topic is *Evolutionary History: Uniting History and Biology to Understand Life on Earth* (2011). I am the Hall Professor of US History at the University of Kansas.

QUESTIONS FOR CONSIDERATION

1. According to Russell, historians have "tended to analyze [war and the environment] separately." How do the cartoons described at the beginning of the article show that these two themes had been wrongly separated?

2. For Russell, how did "metaphors" serve to symbolize the way twentieth-century Americans came to understand both wars against national enemies and wars against environmental pests?

3. Compare the application of metaphors for enemies both human and environmental during World War I. What were some similarities and differences? In what way did World War I serve as a laboratory for experiments with these metaphors of annihilation?

4. Describe in what ways these war metaphors continued to work during the years of "peace" between 1919 and 1939.

5. Compare the uses of vermin metaphors in both Germany and the United States in the nineteenth century. How had these metaphors changed by the twentieth century?

6. Describe DDT's transformation from military necessity to environmental pesticide. What concerns did government and military officials have with the domestic use of DDT? How did the metaphors of vermin undermine these concerns?

7. Russell also claims that preconceived "boundaries" helped fuel the use of chemicals both militarily and domestically. Explain his reasoning. How did government and private institutions help define these boundaries?

CHAPTER NINE

Strategy, Diplomacy, and the Cold War: The United States, Turkey, and NATO, 1945–1952[1]

Melvyn P. Leffler

On March 12, 1947, President Harry S. Truman appeared before a joint session of Congress and made one of the most momentous addresses of the postwar era. Requesting $400 million in aid for Greece and Turkey, he emphasized that a "fateful hour" had arrived and that nations had to "choose between alternative ways of life." The United States, Truman insisted, had to support "free peoples who are resisting attempted subjugation by armed minorities or by outside pressures." Greece, of course, was then beleaguered by civil war. Turkey, while enjoying remarkable internal stability, supposedly was subject to pressure from the Soviet Union, a constant war of nerves, and the prospect of outright Soviet aggression. Undersecretary of State Dean G. Acheson warned that if the United States did not act, three continents could fall prey to Soviet domination.[2]

The international situation, of course, was far more complex than that described by Truman or Acheson. The president and his closest advisers simplified international realities in order to generate public support for unprecedented peacetime foreign-policy initiatives.[3] Many scholars have demonstrated that the Greek civil war did not fall neatly into the category of Soviet

---

[1]Interested students are encouraged to read this essay in the original form. Melvyn P. Leffler, "Strategy, Diplomacy, and the Cold War: The United States, Turkey, and NATO, 1945–1952," *The Journal of American History* 71, no. 4 (March 1985), 807–25.

[2]*Public Papers of the Presidents of the United States: Harry S. Truman, 1947* (Washington, D.C., 1963, 178–79; Dean Acheson, *Present at the Creation: My Years in the State Department* (New York, 1969), 219; Joseph M. Jones, *Fifteen Weeks* (February 21–June 5, 1947) (New York, 1955), 39–198.

[3]President Harry S. Truman said that he confronted "the greatest selling job ever facing a President." Dean Acheson admitted: "No time was left for measured appraisal." Matthew J. Connelly, notes on cabinet meeting, March 7, 1947, box 1, Matthew J. Connelly Papers (Harry S. Truman Library, Independence, Mo.); Acheson, *Present at the Creation*, 219.

aggression–American response. Developments in Turkey, however, have received far less attention.[4]

The purpose of this article is to examine the policy of the United States toward Turkey in the postwar era, to elucidate United States policy makers' assessments of Soviet intentions toward Turkey, and to explain the reasons for and the consequences of Turkey's inclusion in the Truman Doctrine. Rather than expecting an imminent Soviet attack on Turkey, United States officials sought to take advantage of a favorable opportunity to enhance the strategic interests of the United States in the Middle East and the eastern Mediterranean. Assistance under the Truman Doctrine was designed to improve the military capabilities of both Turkey and the United States to wage war against the Soviet Union should conflict unexpectedly erupt. . . . United States officials . . . soon found that their investment in Turkey might be wasted and their hopes for strategic gain unrealized if they did not accept more binding commitments in the form of Turkey's admission into the North Atlantic Treaty Organization (NATO). This article, then, underscores the important and often unexplained role of strategic imperatives in the shaping of foreign-policy actions and alliance relationships. More indirectly, it seeks to stimulate a reconsideration of how the relationship between the United States and Turkey might have interacted with other variables to escalate tensions during the formative years of the Cold War.

In the immediate aftermath of World War II, United States policy makers did not believe that Soviet leaders intended to use force to achieve their goals vis-à-vis Turkey. . . . Foreign Service officers such as George F. Kennan and Elbridge Durbrow and strategic planners such as Gen. George A. Lincoln . . . maintained

---

[4]Lawrence S. Wittner, *American Intervention in Greece, 1943–1949* (New York, 1982); John R. Oneal, *Foreign Policy Making in Times of Crisis* (Columbus, 1982), 137–215; George Martin Alexander, *The Prelude to the Truman Doctrine: British Policy in Greece, 1944–1947* (New York, 1982); John O. Iatrides, *Revolt in Athens: The Greek Communist "Second Round," 1944–1945* (Princeton, 1972); C. M. Woodhouse, *The Struggle for Greece, 1941–1949* (London, 1976); Daniel Yergin, *Shattered Peace: The Origins of the Cold War and the National Security State* (Boston, 1977), 233–35; John Lewis Gaddis, *The United States and the Origins of the Cold War, 1941–1947* (New York, 1972), 336–52; Thomas G. Paterson, *Soviet-American Confrontation: Postwar Reconstruction and the Origins of the Cold War* (Baltimore, 1973), 174–206; Joyce Kolko and Gabriel Kolko, *The Limits of Power: The World and United States Foreign Policy, 1945–1954* (New York, 1972), 242–45, 336–46; George Kirk, *The Middle East, 1945–1950* (London, 1954), 21–56; John C. Campbell, *Defense of the Middle East: Problems of American Policy* (New York, 1958), 154–82; and George Lenczowski, *Soviet Advances in the Middle East* (Washington, D.C., 1972), 37–49; Bruce Robellet Kuniholm, *The Origins of the Cold War in the Near East: Great Power Conflict and Diplomacy in Iran, Turkey, and Greece* (Princeton, 1980); Harry N. Howard, *Turkey, the Straits and U.S. Policy* (Baltimore, 1974); Anthony R. De Luca, "Soviet-American Politics and the Turkish Straits," *Political Science Quarterly* 92 (Fall 1977), 503–24; David J. Alvarez, *Bureaucracy and Cold War Diplomacy: The United States and Turkey, 1943–1946* (Thessaloniki, 1980); J. Garry Clifford, "President Truman and Peter the Great's Will," *Diplomatic History* 4 (Fall 1980), 371–85.

that Soviet leaders felt too weak to engage in military aggression and thereby to risk a general war. . . .[5]

When the Soviets finally raised the issue of the [Dardenelle] straits in a formal diplomatic note in August 1946, the furor engendered in Washington was out of proportion to the diplomatic event. Edwin C. Wilson, the United States ambassador to Turkey, interpreted the Soviet proposals, including a request for joint defense of the Dardanelles, as a smoke screen for destroying Turkey's independence. Wilson acknowledged, however, that the Soviet note itself was not threatening in tone. Nor were Turkish officials particularly alarmed. They did not expect a Soviet attack, and they had anticipated a more bellicose Soviet diplomatic initiative. Moreover, they considered the second Soviet note, circulated in September, even milder and more restrained. The Soviet quest for bases in the Dardanelles, in fact, was similar to ongoing United States efforts to negotiate base rights in Iceland, Greenland, Panama, the Azores, and the western Pacific. Several months earlier Loy W. Henderson, the director of Near Eastern and African Affairs in the State Department, had emphasized precisely this point when he had advised against raising a formal objection to Soviet requests of Turkey.[6]

What supposedly distinguished Soviet actions toward Turkey was Soviet bellicosity. Diplomats and historians often have focused on Soviet troop movements to support their contention that the Soviets were preparing or threatening to use force to dominate Turkey. On March 18, 1946, for example, in a frequently cited dispatch, Ambassador Wilson informed Washington of new Soviet troop dispositions and suggested that the Soviets might soon be in a position to strike at Turkey. In the most recent and widely acclaimed analysis of developments in the Near East, Bruce Robellet Kuniholm fully accepts Wilson's appraisal of Soviet actions and intentions.[7]

---

[5]Expanded draft of letter from Secretary of War to Secretary of State, "U.S. Position re Soviet Proposals on Kiel Canal and Dardanelles," July 8, 1945, sec. 1-A, ABC 093 Kiel (6 July 1945), Records of the War Department General and Special Staffs, RG 165 (National Archives); George A. Lincoln to Stanley D. Embick, July 7, 1945, ibid.; Lincoln to John E. Hull, April 11, 1945, OPD 336 TS, ibid.; Joint Chiefs of Staff [JCS] 1418/1, enclosure "B," JCS to Secretary of State, July 30, 1945, CCS 092 (7-10-45), Records of the Joint Chiefs of Staff, RG 218 (National Archives); JCS 1641, "U.S. Security Interests in the Eastern Mediterranean," March 10–13, 1946, sec. 6, CCS 092 USSR (3-27-45), ibid.; *Foreign Relations of the United States, 1946* (11 vols., Washington, D.C., 1969–1972), VII, 840–42; George F. Kennan to Secretary of State, March 17, 1946, box 63, George M. Elsey Papers (Harry S. Truman Library); Elbridge Durbrow to Secretary of State, Aug. 5, 1946, file 761.67/8-546, Records of the Department of State, RG 59 (National Archives).

[6]*Foreign Relations of the United States, 1946*, VII, 827–29, 835, 837, 859, 860, 867–68, 869; Thomas T. Handy to Dwight D. Eisenhower, Aug. 15, 1946, P&O 092 TS, Records of the United States Army Staff, RG319 (National Archives); JCS 1704/1, "Military Implications of the Current Turkish Situation," Aug. 24, 1946, sec. 1, CCS 092 (8-22-46), Records of the Joint Chiefs of Staff; Loy W. Henderson to H. Freeman Matthews, Jan. 30, 1946, box 17, Lot 54D394, Records of the Department of State.

[7]*Foreign Relations of the United States, 1946*, VII, 818–19; Kuniholm, *Origins of the Cold War in the Near East*, 316–17, 356.

There is, however, considerable reason to question that view of Soviet behavior and to reassess the motivations behind subsequent actions of the United States. Throughout late 1945 and 1946, for example, United States officials received intelligence that Soviet troops were being withdrawn in substantial numbers from eastern and southeastern Europe. Although troop rotations and maneuvers did occur, those actions were considered normal. In October 1945 a report from the joint intelligence subcommittee in London emphasized that there was no appreciable buildup of troops in Bulgaria and no concentration of aircraft, either in Bulgaria or in the Caucasus, capable of sustaining a Soviet attack on Turkey. In late December 1945 United States Army intelligence reported that stories of Soviet troop concentrations in Bulgaria had been alarmist. . . . Indeed, at the very time that Wilson sent his alarming dispatch on March 18, warning of impending Soviet aggression, both the Turkish prime minister and the secretary-general of the Turkish Foreign Office were discounting that possibility. According to United States intelligence, between May and September 1946, Soviet troops in Europe decreased from about 2 million men to about 1.5 million; within the Soviet Union, from about 5 million to 2.7 million. During the crisis of August 1946, Gen. Hoyt S. Vandenberg, director of the Central Intelligence Group, reassured President Truman that there were no unusual Soviet troop concentrations, troop movements, or supply buildups.[8]

Why, then, were United States officials so exercised by Soviet policy toward Turkey? Although they did not expect the Soviets to apply military force, policy makers worried that the Soviet demand for bases in the Dardanelles might be a ruse for the eventual projection of Soviet power into the eastern Mediterranean and the Near East. Bases in the straits, United States military experts argued, would not suffice to keep the waterway open in wartime against modern air power; hence, the Soviets were likely to seek additional bases in the Aegean and the eastern Mediterranean. If Soviet influence expanded in that region, vital British petroleum supplies and communication networks might be jeopardized. And if the British Empire disintegrated, Soviet prospects for gaining control of Eurasia would be greatly enhanced, and the United States might be left vulnerable and exposed. At a meeting with the president on August 15, 1946, Acting Secretary of State Acheson, Secretary of the Navy James V. Forrestal, Assistant Secretary of War Kenneth C. Royall, and top military leaders

---

[8]Carl Espe, memoranda, 1946, A8, box 106, series V, Strategic Plans Division (Naval Historical Center, Washington Navy Yard); JIC (45) 289 (0) (FINAL), Report by Joint Intelligence Subcommittee, "The Russian Threat to Turkey," Oct. 6, 1945, ABC 092 USSR (15 November 1944), Records of the War Department General and Special Staffs; Joint Intelligence Committee, "Russian Troop Movements in South East Europe and Persia," May 15, 1946, ibid.; Military Intelligence Division, "Review of Europe, Russia, and the Middle East," Dec. 26, 1945, sec. 2, OPD 350.05 TS, ibid.; John Weckerling to Deputy Chief of Staff, March 19, 1946, ibid.; SACMED AFHQ, Caserta, Italy, to War Department, March 9, 1946, box 1, Leahy Papers, Records of the Joint Chiefs of Staff; William M. Robertson to War Department, June 13, 1946, ibid.; Hoyt S. Vandenberg, memorandum for the President, Aug. 24, 1946, box 249, President's secretary's file, Truman Papers; Wilson to Secretary of State, March 19, 1946, file 761.67/3-1946, Records of the Department of State.

presented those arguments and urged resistance to Soviet demands. Truman fully concurred with their advice.[9]

The decision to encourage Turkish opposition to Soviet overtures constituted part of the overall toughening of United States policy toward the Soviet Union during 1946. Truman began the year determined to stop babying the Soviets; in his "long" telegram in February, Kennan laid out an elaborate rationale for resisting Soviet pressure; during the Iranian crisis in the spring, United States officials learned that if they assumed a determined posture, the Soviets would back down. . . .[10]

During the summer the president asked Clark M. Clifford, one of his assistants in the White House, to write a paper outlining Soviet violations of international commitments. Clifford and George M. Elsey, another White House aide, took the opportunity to consult with all the leading members of the administration, including top military officers, and to write a comprehensive report calling for the global containment of Soviet influence. The rapid, decisive, and unanimous accord to stiffen Turkish resistance to Soviet demands reflected a consensus that new initiatives had to be taken to shore up United States influence in areas of vital importance.[11]

Top officials suspected, however, that the American public would not understand the strategic importance of Turkey. At their August meeting with the president, Royall and Forrestal emphasized the importance of properly briefing the press. Shortly thereafter, Royall informed Secretary of War Robert P. Patterson that Acheson was ready to discuss means "of conditioning the public mind." Exactly what was done is uncertain, but the news media did begin to explain to the attentive public that the dispute over the straits was assuming central importance in the overall rivalry between the Soviet Union and the United States. For example, *Time* noted that the Soviet proposals on the Dardanelles, coupled with Bulgaria's request for part of Thrace, represented the Soviet Union's effort to gain access to the Aegean, to seal off the straits, and to threaten Greece and Turkey. At the same time, the *Saturday Evening Post* reproached left-wingers, isolationists, and appeasers for their indifference to the Soviet Union's ominous attempt to exclude the shipping of other nations from the Black Sea. *United States News*, quoting administration officials, reported that the Soviet goal was to gain control of the eastern Mediterranean, to secure access to oil in the Middle East, and to establish a "flanking position on India and China."[12]

---

[9]*Foreign Relations of the United States, 1946*, VII, 840–58.

[10]Robert L. Messer, *The End of an Alliance: James F. Byrnes, Roosevelt, Truman, and the Origins of the Cold War* (Chapel Hill, 1982), 137–94; Oneal, *Foreign Policy Making*, 68–136; Clifford, "President Truman and Peter the Great's Will."

[11]Arthur Krock, *Memoirs: Sixty Years on the Firing Line* (New York, 1968), 421–82; box 63, Elsey Papers; boxes 14, 15, Clark M. Clifford Papers (Harry S. Truman Library).

[12]Walter Millis, ed., *The Forrestal Diaries* (New York, 1951), 191–92; Kenneth C. Royall to Robert P. Patterson, n.d. [mid-August 1946], box 9, general decimal file, Robert P. Patterson Papers, Records of the Office of the Secretary of War, RG 107 (National Archives); *Time*, Sept. 2, 1946, p. 22; "Our Left Wingers Go Isolationist," *Saturday Evening Post*, Oct. 12, 1946, p. 160; "U.S. Stand on Dardanelles: High Stakes in the Middle East," *United States News*, Aug. 30, 1946, pp. 16–17.

What top officials did not tell the press and what the media did not explain were the precise strategic calculations that underlay United States determination to contain Soviet influence in the Near East. Indeed, on the very day that Acheson, Forrestal, and Royall met with Truman, military planners on the Joint War Plans Committee were putting the final touches on a strategic study, known as "Griddle," that emphasized the importance of Turkey as a base for Allied operations against the Soviet Union should war unexpectedly erupt. . . .[13]

In fact, despite the rhetoric about the Soviet expansionist thrust southward, military analysts and civilian officials acknowledged that Soviet demands on Turkey had a substantial defensive component. "Soviet pressure in the Middle East," concluded the Joint Chiefs of Staff (JCS) in March 1946, "has for its primary objective the protection of the vital Ploesti, Kharkov and Baku areas." Three months later, in a comprehensive assessment of Soviet intentions in the Middle East, British intelligence emphasized Soviet efforts to move the center of Soviet industry eastward, to safeguard the Caucasian oil fields, and to protect the development of Soviet resources from prospective attack. In their report to the president, Clifford and Elsey also noted that "the Near East is an area of great strategic interest to the Soviet Union because of the shift of Soviet industry to southeastern Russia, within range of air attack from much of the Near East." And in November 1946, in a still more detailed assessment of the region, United States war planners stressed that the Soviet Union wanted to control the eastern Mediterranean and Persian Gulf areas in order "to deny them as possible enemy air, sea, and ground offensive bases. By this increase in the depth of her southerly territorial border, the Soviets would greatly increase the security of their vital areas from air attack and from seizure by ground forces."[14]

It was this very vulnerability that United States strategic planners hoped to capitalize on. In fact, United States interest in Turkey accelerated as war planners began to develop a strategic concept for the postwar era and as overall United States-Soviet relations deteriorated sharply in early 1946. . . . With regard to a prospective war with the Soviet Union, the aim was "to oppose, as far as possible, Russian advances beyond her own borders and to obtain such strategic positions as are required to destroy her war potential rather than to overrun the USSR." Later in the autumn of 1945, the first efforts were made to define Soviet industrial-urban centers of critical strategic importance. In order of priority, planners focused on oil-producing centers in the Caucasus and in Rumania and, secondarily, on industrial complexes in the Urals, Ukraine, Upper Silesia and

---

[13]Joint War Plans Committee [JWPC] 467/1, Aug. 15, 1946, sec. 11, CCS 092 USSR (3-27-45), Records of the Joint Chiefs of Staff. See also citations in footnote 16.

[14]JCS 1641/1, "U.S. Security Interests in the Eastern Mediterranean," March 10, 1946, sec. 6, CCS 092 USSR (3-27-45), Records of the Joint Chiefs of Staff; JWPC 475/1, "Strategic Study of the Area between the Alps and the Himalayas," Nov. 2, 1946, sec. 3, pt. 1, CCS 381 USSR (3-2-46), ibid.; Joint Intelligence Committee [of the British Staff Mission], Memorandum for Information No. 223, "Russia's Strategic Interests and Intentions in the Middle East," June 28, 1946, sec. 1-C, ABC 336 Russia (22 August 1943), Records of the War Department General and Special Staffs; Krock, *Memoirs*, 434.

Czechoslovakia, Moscow, and Mukden areas. "Destruction by air of the Cauca-sian and Ploesti oil fields and the Ukraine and Ural industrial centers would prevent Soviet prosecution of war."[15]

Turkey's special role emerged in March 1946 when, during the Iranian crisis, State Department officials pressed military planners to define more clearly the importance of Turkey and when strategic analysts were forced to come to terms with the effects of Western Europe's military weakness and the United States' rapid demobilization. Assuming that Soviet troops would easily overrun all of Western Europe and that United States forces would be evacuated from the con-tinent, the utilization of air power took on more significance than ever before. Turkey was seen as a key to the effective application of air power.[16] During the spring and summer of 1946, prior to the Soviet note on the straits, strategic plan-ners decided that other than Great Britain, the Cairo-Suez area was the most desirable place on the globe from which to launch an air attack against Soviet targets. Should war erupt, Turkey's great importance would be that it provide a cushion, absorbing the initial Soviet blow and deterring Soviet advances, while the United States prepared to undertake the counteroffensive, particularly from the Cairo-Suez area. . . . By the time of the August 1946 crisis, it was evident to high-level civilian policy makers, not just to military planners, that "Turkey must be preserved for reasons of Middle East strategy" as well as to prevent the falling of other dominoes in Western Europe and in the Far East.[17]

While State Department officials labored over an answer to the Soviet note on the Dardanelles, military planners insisted that "every practicable measure

[15]Joint Planning Staff [JPS] 744/3, "Strategic Concept and Plan for the Employment of United States Armed Forces," Sept. 14, 1945, sec. 1, CCS 381 (5-13-45), Records of the Joint Chiefs of Staff; Joint Intelligence Staff [JIS] 80/8, "Strategic Vulnerability of Russia to a Limited Air Attack," Oct. 25, 1945, sec. 2, CCS 092 USSR (3-27-45), ibid.; JIS 226/2, "Areas Vital to Soviet War Effort," Feb. 12, 1946, sec. 5, ibid.; JIS 226/3, "Areas Vital to Soviet War Effort," March 4, 1946, ibid.

[16]Byrnes to JCS, March 6, 1946, sec. 5, CCS 092 USSR (3-27-45), ibid.; memo for the Joint Staff Planners, March 8, 1946, ibid.; JCS 1641/1, "U.S. Security Interests in the Eastern Mediterranean," March 10, 1946, sec. 6, ibid.; JPS 789, "Concept of Operations for Pincher," enclosure "B," sec. 1, CCS 381 USSR (3-2-46), ibid.; JWPC 453, "Disposition of Occupation Forces in Europe and the Far East in the Event of Hostilities in Europe, and the Importance of Certain Areas of Eurasia," March 27, 1946, sec. 5, CCS 092 USSR (3-27-45), ibid.; Operations Division, "Adequate Governmental Machin-ery to Handle Foreign Affairs," March 13, 1946, P&O 092 TS, Records of the United States Army Staff; meeting of the Secretaries of State, War, and Navy, March 6, 1946, box 3, safe file, Patterson Papers.

[17]JPS 789/1, appendix "B," April 13, 1946, sec. 1, CCS 381 USSR (3-2-46), Records of the Joint Chiefs of Staff; Pincher plans and discussions on JWPC 432 series, April–July 1946, sec. 2, ibid.; JCS 1704/1, "Military Implications of the Current Turkish Situation," Aug. 24, 1946, sec. 1, CCS 092 (8-22-46), ibid.; S.W.D., memorandum for the record, June 12, 1946, P&O 092 TS, Records of the United States Army Staff; Patterson to Truman, July 27, 1946, ibid.; Lincoln, memorandum for the record, April 16, 1946, sec. 1-C, ABC 336 Russia (22 August 1943), Records of the War Department General and Special Staffs; James McCormack, memorandum for Charles H. Bonesteel, April 20, 1946, sec. 1-A, ABC 093 Kiel (6 July 1945), ibid.; H.C.P., memorandum for Patterson, April 22, 1946, box 1, safe file, Patterson Papers; "Possible Program in Connection with Turkey," Aug. 15, 1946, box 9, general decimal file, ibid.; Richard L. Conolly interview, 1960, transcript, pp. 293–303, Columbia Oral History Collection (Butler Library, Columbia University, New York City).

should be undertaken to permit the utilization of Turkey as a base for Allied operations in the event of war with the USSR." If war occurred Turkey could slow down a Soviet advance to Suez and North Africa, attack Soviet oil resources, provide fighter cover for bombers heading toward Moscow, bottle up Soviet submarines in the Black Sea, destroy Soviet shipping, and launch a possible ground offensive into the Soviet heartland. It was indispensable, then, to encourage Turkey to resist Soviet demands in peacetime and to thwart Soviet advances in wartime. Accordingly, military planners began advocating the allocation of military assistance to Turkey, including fighter aircraft, automatic weapons, ammunition, and small arms. They believed that previous studies had exaggerated Soviet logistic capabilities and that Turkey could mount an effective resistance, especially if provided with aid prior to hostilities. With that in mind, initial United States Army Air Force plans for launching a strategic offensive assumed the deployment to the Cairo-Suez area of three heavy bomber groups and the commencement of sustained conventional bombing of Soviet Russia from that location within 120 days after the onset of hostilities. On January 14, 1947, Adm. Forrest Sherman made a detailed presentation of those evolving strategic concepts to President Truman.[18]

By early 1947 almost all civilian and military officials agreed on the need to furnish military assistance to Turkey.... Nevertheless, United States policy makers had considerable difficulty making their case for aid to Turkey. Turkey was not experiencing dire economic conditions, nor was it facing financial stringencies. The Soviets had not recently exerted pressure on Turkey, nor did American officials expect an imminent attack. Hence, the most effective argument that could be made in public was that the Turkish military establishment constituted a serious burden on the Turkish economy; that burden had to be eased to ensure that the Turks would not acquiesce to Soviet demands. During executive sessions of the Committee on Foreign Relations, however, senators' skepticism about whether the Turkish crisis constituted an emergency compelled Acheson to acknowledge the strategic motivations behind the United States initiative. Similar questions forced Ambassador Wilson to answer so frankly that his testimony had to be stricken even from the executive hearings. In his classic, personal account of the period, Joseph M. Jones acknowledges that "the strategic importance of Turkey ranked high in discussions within the executive branch and in discussions with congressional leaders. They were, however, consciously played down in the President's message, in the public sessions of the congressional

---

[18]JWPC 467/1, "Griddle," Aug. 15, 1946, sec. 11, CCS 092 USSR (3-27-45), Records of the Joint Chiefs of Staff; Joint Logistic Plans Committee [JLPC] 35/23, "Request for Logistic Information relative to Turkey," Oct. 10. 1946, sec. 12, pt. 1, ibid.; JWPC 475/1, "Strategic Study of the Area between the Alps and the Himalayas," Nov. 2, 1946, sec. 3, CCS 381 USSR (3-2-46),ibid.; JCS 1704/1, "Military Implications of the Current Turkish Situation," Aug. 24, 1946, sec. 1, CCS 092 (8-22-46), ibid.; A. R. Pefley to Op-30, Aug. 21, 1946, box 68, series III, Strategic Plans Division; "Air Plan for Makefast," n.d., sec. 3, ABC 381 USSR (2 March 1946), Records of the War Department General and Special Staffs; Forrest P. Sherman, "Presentation to the President," Jan. 14, 1947, box 2, Forrest P. Sherman Papers (Naval Historical Center).

committees, and in the public approach generally." That long-term strategic calculations rather than short-term expectations of Soviet aggression prompted concern with Turkey was evident several months later when United States officials supported a partial demobilization of Turkish forces because "no immediate danger of an armed clash between Turkey and Russia" was foreseen.[19]

Although planned Soviet aggression was not anticipated, war could erupt as a result of a miscalculation in a diplomatic crisis. Accordingly, under the auspices of the Truman Doctrine, United States officials designed the aid program to enhance the fighting capabilities of the Turkish army, air force, and navy, to help build strategic roads, and to restock Turkish arsenals and war reserves. . . .[20] United States military advisers hoped that the Turkish army would play a key role in retarding a Soviet land offensive in the Middle East should war occur, thereby affording time for the United States and Great Britain to activate and utilize bases in the Cairo-Suez region. . . . Recognizing that Turkish forces could not hold . . . United States military assistance sought to provide the Turkish army with the mobility and logistical capability to fall back gradually . . . and to make a final, large-scale stand in southern Turkey in the Iskenderon pocket. Much of the road construction undertaken in Turkey with United States funds was designed to facilitate that strategy. From the military perspective, a concentrated Turkish defense in the Iskenderon area was a key to maintaining access to Middle Eastern oil as well as to defending vital strategic airports and communication facilities in Egypt.[21]

---

[19]Henderson, memorandum, "'Aid to Turkey," Nov. 24, 1946, EF-70, series 1, Records of the Politico-Military Division; *Foreign Relations of the United States, 1946*, VII, 921–22; *Foreign Relations of the United States, 1947*, V, 61–62, 90–91, 95, 364–65; Wilson to Secretary of State, Feb. 26, 1947, file 761.67/2-2647, Records of the Department of State; LeBreton to Henderson, Oct. 8, 1947, file 867.20/10-447, ibid.; "Summary of Costs of U.S. Assistance to Greece and Turkey until 30 June 1948," n.d. [early March 1947], box 65, Elsey Papers; Lincoln to Secretary of War, March 12, 1947, box 1, general subject file, Howard C. Petersen Papers, Records of the Office of the Secretary of War; U.S. Congress, Senate, Committee on Foreign Relations, *Legislative Origins of the Truman Doctrine: Hearings Held in Executive Session before the Committee on Foreign Relations* (Washington, D.C., 1973), 7–10, 48–53, 55–61, 84, 105; Jones, *Fifteen Weeks*, 162.

[20]Minutes of the Executive Committee, Turkish General Staff/U.S. Mission, May 27–July 10, 1947, file 867.20/7-1047, Records of the Department of State; Wilson to Secretary of State, Jan. 30, 1948, file 867.20/1-3048, ibid.; *Foreign Relations of the United States, 1947*, V, 233–36; "Call for Estimates, FY 1950, MAP," Sept. 23, 1949, P&O 092 Europe TS, Records of the United States Army Staff; Joint American Military Mission for Aid to Turkey [JAMMAT], "Major Items of Equipment: Aid to Turkey Program," March 1952, box 56, Records of the Assistant Secretary of Defense, International Security Affairs, Office of the Secretary of Defense, RG 330 (National Archives).

[21]Central Intelligence Agency, "The Current Situation in Turkey," Oct. 20, 1947, box 254, President's secretary's file, Truman Papers; Joint Strategic Plans Committee [JSPC] 868/1, "Guidance for the Coordinator, Armed Forces Groups, American Mission for Aid to Turkey [AMAT]," March 26, 1948, P&O 091 Turkey TS, Records of the United States Army Staff; Chief of Staff, U.S. Army, memorandum, "Turkish and Iranian Military Effort in War," Feb. 25, 1950, 381 Middle East TS, ibid.; Robert B. Carney, memorandum for Secretary of Defense, Sept. 29, 1948, CD 2-2-5, box 4, Records of the Office of the Secretary of Defense; Subcommittee for the Near and Middle East, memorandum for the State-Army-Navy-Air Force Coordinating Committee, Dec. 15, 1948, box 134, TS file, Records of the State-War-Navy Coordinating Committee [SWNCC], RG 353 (National Archives).

From air bases in Turkey, fighter bombers and attack planes could not only aid Turkish ground forces inside Turkey but also interdict Soviet troops moving through Iran and Iraq toward Persian Gulf oil or sweeping widely toward Cairo-Suez. . . . During 1948, for example, the United States transferred over 180 F-47s, 30 B-26s, and 86 C-47s. Smaller numbers of jet fighters began arriving in 1950 and 1951. At the same time, the United States placed a great deal of stress on re-constructing and resurfacing Turkish airfields at places such as Bandirma and Diyarbakir. As a result, Turkey began to develop the capability to attack vital Soviet petroleum resources in Rumania and in the Caucasus; Ploesti and Baku, for example, came within range of the F-47s and the B-26s. Even more important, the rehabilitation of Turkish airfields and the construction of new ones at Adana, for example, meant that if war erupted, the United States would be able to bring in its own B-29s to bomb the Soviet Union. . . .[22]

United States assistance to the Turkish navy aimed primarily at enhancing Turkey's ability to close the Dardanelles and to prevent Soviet submarines from entering the Mediterranean. The United States also wanted to help the Turkish navy plan the defense of the Bosporus and develop the capability of destroying Soviet Black Sea shipping. But the latter mission also was within the purview of the United States Navy. Aircraft from United States carriers would leapfrog to Turkish air bases, refuel, and attack oil cargoes on Soviet ships in the Black Sea. To achieve that capability, Admiral Conolly, with the support of the secretary of defense, sought funds for the storage of aviation gas in Turkey.[23]

Throughout the period 1947-1950, United States military planners were eager to use assistance as a lever to bring Turkish military planning into line with United States desires. . . . United States Air Force advisers, frustrated by the de-fensive mentality of Turkish officers, wanted to use Turkey's air assets to attack

[22]Ambassador's Report on Aid to Turkey, July 15, 1947, Annex D, Part Three, P&O 091 Turkey, Records of the United States Army Staff; Chief of Staff, U.S. Army, memorandum, "Turkish and Iranian Military Effort in War," Feb. 25, 1950, 381 Middle East TS, ibid.; "Proposal for Continuing Aid to the Turkish Air Force," appended to Wilds to Robert A. Lovett, Jan. 23, 1948, file 867.20/1-2348, Records of the Department of State; John H. Ohly to Llewellyn E. Thompson, Nov. 22, 1949, box 1, Lot 484, ibid.; USTAP Report No. 29, March 12, 1949, file 867.00/5-1249, ibid.; Stuart Syming-ton to James V. Forrestal, March 9, 1948, CD 6-2-38, box 35, Records of the Office of the Secretary of Defense; Lyman L. Lemnitzer to James H. Burns, March 6, 1950, CD 6-2-46, box 23, ibid.; National Security Council [NSC] 42, "U.S. Objectives with Respect to Greece and Turkey to Counter Soviet Threats to U.S. Security," March 4, 1949, Records of the National Security Council, RG 273 (National Archives); Foreign Relations of the United States, 1950 (7 vols., Washington, D.C., 1976–1980), V, 1234, 1250; Foreign Relations of the United States, 1951 (6 vols., Washington, D.C., 1977–1983), V, 1124–25.

[23]JCS 1704/8, enclosure "A," memorandum for the Coordinator, Armed Forces Group, AMAT; n.d. [Sept. 1948], P&O 091 Turkey TS, Records of the United States Army Staff; J. R. D., memo for the record, Feb. 18, 1949, ibid.; Ray T. Maddocks, memorandum for Horace L. McBride, March 1, 1949, ibid.; Louis Denfeld, memorandum for JCS, Aug. 9, 1948, JJ7, box 245, Strategic Plans Divi-sion; E. T. Wooldridge, memorandum for Op-03, Jan. 10, 1949, A19, box 251, ibid.; Elliott B. Strauss, memorandum for Op-30, June 17, 1949, A14, box 249, ibid.; JCS 1887/20, Carney to CNO, Jan. 30, 1951, sec. 4, CCS 381 Eastern Mediterranean and Middle East Area [EMMEA] (11-19-47), Records of the Joint Chiefs of Staff; Forrestal, memorandum for the NSC, n.d. [early 1949], CD 19-2-21, box 92, Records of the Office of the Secretary of Defense.

enemy airfields, refineries, and communication and rail centers in Bulgaria, Rumania, and the Caucasus. United States officers also were uncertain whether Turkey would permit their use of its airfields. In order to clarify matters and to achieve United States goals, Arthur W. Radford, the vice chief of naval operations, Admiral Conolly, and other military officers desired to institutionalize strategic coordination with Turkey.[24]

State Department officials, however, would not permit formal strategic collaboration without prior treaty commitments. During 1948–1949 the formation of the NATO alliance riveted American attention on Western Europe and unexpectedly reoriented United States strategic priorities. In July 1948 Undersecretary of State Robert A. Lovett told the Turkish ambassador that Americans "must be careful not to over-extend ourselves. We lack sufficient financial and economic resources simultaneously to finance the economic recovery of Europe, to furnish arms and equipment to all individual countries or groups of countries which request them, and to build up our own military strength." When Acheson assumed the office of secretary of state, he reiterated those views. The United States, he maintained, was assuming unprecedented obligations in Western Europe; those commitments had to be worked out in all their complexity before the United States could offer additional guarantees elsewhere. Throughout 1949 Acheson repeatedly rebuffed Turkish pleas to be included in the alliance.[25]

Toiling over the problem of meeting expanding commitments with extremely circumscribed resources, stemming from budgetary restrictions, the JCS vigorously supported Acheson's desire to limit the alliance and to give priority to assistance to Western Europe. United States war planners were overwhelmed by the difficulties of figuring out how to defend Western Europe. They modified emergency war plans and placed a much greater emphasis on defense of the western Mediterranean and the launching of the strategic offensive primarily from Great Britain. Had a war erupted in 1949 or 1950, the United States would not have had the means to aid Turkey directly or even to secure Cairo-Suez. Defense

---

[24]Foreign Relations of the United States, 1950, V, 1249–50; McBride to Director, Plans and Operations Division, May 18, 1948, P&O 091 Turkey TS, Records of the United States Army Staff; J.R.D., memorandum for the Record, Feb. 18, 1949, ibid.; JCS 1704/7, McBride, memorandum for the JCS, Feb. 19, 1948, ibid.; JSPC 868/1, Guidance for the Coordinator, Armed Forces Groups, AMAT, March 26, 1948, ibid.; Chief of Staff, U.S. Army, memorandum, n.d. [Feb. 25, 1950], 381 ME TS, ibid.; A. D. Struble, memo for CNO, Oct. 4, 1948, A19, box 244, Strategic Plans Division; Carney, memorandum for Op-03, March 22, 1949, EF, box 252, ibid.; Strauss, memorandum for Op-30, March 25, 1949, ibid.; C. V. Johnson, memorandum for Op-30, Sept. 16, 1949, A8, box 249, ibid.; Carney to Struble, March 31, 1949, A16-1, ibid.; CNO, memorandum, March 13, 1950, sec. 1, CCS 337 (2-20-50), Records of the Joint Chiefs of Staff; JCS 2105 series, "Proposed Positions to Be Taken in Conversations with Political and Military Authorities of Near and Middle East Countries," Feb.–April 1950, ibid.; Arthur W. Radford to Richard L. Conolly, Jan. 17, 1949, drawer 1, safe A, Arthur W. Radford Papers (Naval Historical Center).

[25]Foreign Relations of the United States, 1948 (9 vols., Washington, D.C., 1972–1975), III, 197, IV, 84–85, 114–15, 148–49, 172–73, 214; Foreign Relations of the United States, 1949 (9 vols., Washington, D.C., 1974–1978), IV, 120, 177–78, 234–35, 243–44, 270–71, 359–60, VI, 1647–53, 1656–57; Foreign Relations of the United States, 1950, V, 1238–40.

of the Middle East, although recognized as critically important, was assigned to Great Britain despite that nation's limited capabilities. . . .[26]

Turkish officials, however, were offended by rebuffs to their requests for concrete military guarantees and for inclusion in the NATO alliance. Ambassador Wilson feared that the Turkish government might conclude that the United States was downgrading the importance of Turkey and might adopt a more neutral posture. The Central Intelligence Agency (CIA) agreed that Turkey felt exposed and vulnerable. The great imponderable, then, was what Turkey would do if a Soviet attack took place beyond Turkey's borders. The United States air attaché emphasized to naval planners that Turkey would resist if attacked but otherwise would attempt to remain neutral. In March 1950 Admiral Conolly beseeched Sherman, now chief of naval operations, to get the JCS to support an alliance with Turkey. "It is of utmost importance," Conolly wrote,

> to engage Turkey's certain participation [in a war]. Although it can be assumed that Turkey would fight if attacked it is almost as certain that Turkey would not fight if not attacked and very probable that USSR would not immediately attack Turkey. It would therefore be greatly to our national interest considering money we have spent on her military establishment to have Turkey bound to us formally by mutual defense treaty, to include an engagement for her to go to war in case of attack upon her own territory or upon or through any neighboring contiguous state.[27]

In the spring of 1950, however, neither State Department officials nor the JCS were ready to make commitments to Turkey. . . . The outbreak of the Korean War initially intensified those views. Faced with the emergency in the Far East, [and] fearing a full-scale war in Europe . . . policy makers did not wish to incur commitments that might embroil the United States in another localized conflict and sap the nation's strength.[28]

The real dilemma for the United States was to find a means to ensure the availability of Turkey's strategic assets to the West without extending commitments that might be both beyond the capabilities of the United States and disproportionate to the advantages that might accrue from a formal alliance. . . . But to rebuff Turkey completely risked the loss of a key prospective ally in wartime.

---

[26]*Foreign Relations of the United States, 1949*, I, 285–87; *Foreign Relations of the United States, 1951*, V, 36–37; JCS 2105 series cited in footnote 23; JCS 2105/2, Report by the Joint Strategic Survey Committee, March 17, 1950, sec. 1, CCS 337 (2-20-50), Records of the joint Chiefs of Staff. For the evolution of United States war plans from 1948 to 1950, see especially the JCS 1844 series, secs. 10-45, CCS 381 USSR (3-2-46), ibid.; and documents in secs. 1, 2, CCS 381 EMMEA (11-19-47), ibid.

[27]Joseph C. Satterthwaite to Secretary of State, March 31, 1949, file 711.67/3-3149, Records of the Department of State; Robertson to George McGhee, July 26, 1949, box 1, Lot 484, ibid.; Central Intelligence Agency, "Review of the World Situation," April 20, 1949, box 206, President's secretary's file, Truman Papers; Johnson, memorandum to Op-30, Sept. 16, 1949, A8, box 249, Strategic Plans Division; Conolly to CNO, March 9, 1950, box 6, Sherman Papers.

[28]JCS 2105/6, enclosure "B," Office of Near Eastern and African Affairs, Department of State, "Regional Security Arrangements in the Mediterranean and Near Eastern Areas," April 18, 1950, sec. 1, CCS 337 (2-20-50), Records of the Joint Chiefs of Staff; *Foreign Relations of the United States, 1950*, I, 353–57, 376–87, III, 975–76, 1218, V, 153–57.

Hence, the JCS concluded that the United States ought to try "to obtain the ben-efits of Turk and Greek participation in the North Atlantic Treaty Organization and at the same time minimize the disadvantages thereof by according to these two nations an associate status—such a status would permit their representatives to participate in coordinated planning against Soviet aggression." Acheson pre-sented this position to the British and the French in September 1950. Shortly thereafter, the Defense Committee of the North Atlantic Council voted to invite Turkey and Greece to coordinate their military planning with appropriate NATO commanders.[29]

The Turkish government immediately agreed but again expressed disap-pointment in not securing full membership. When Assistant Secretary of State George C. McGhee visited Turkey in February 1951, President Celal Bayar emphasized that he was affronted by NATO's refusal to offer full membership to Turkey, especially in view of Turkey's direct military contribution in Korea. Speaking bluntly, President Bayar told McGhee that Turkey was unhappy with its status and sought reciprocal guarantees; Turkey would not be content with any-thing less. . . . McGhee wired the State Department that "there is reason to be-lieve that Turkey will veer towards a policy of neutralism, which will always have a strong basic appeal; and, until a commitment is extended to Turkey, there is no assurance that Turkey will declare war unless it is attacked. In order to assure Turkey's immediate co-belligerency, utilization in collective security action of the military potential which Turkey is building, and immediate United States and Allied utilization of Turkish bases . . . a commitment on the part of United States is required." At about the same time, Henry S. Villard, of the Policy Plan-ning Staff, urged Paul H. Nitze, the staff's director, to focus attention on meeting Turkey's desire for security guarantees. In general, State Department officials believed that new United States initiatives in the Middle East could and ought to be taken because the military buildup in the United States already had reached significant proportions, organizational progress had been achieved in Western Europe, and "the chances of the Middle East remaining tranquilly on the side of the West without some practical evidence of Western interest have greatly declined."[30]

United States defense officials, however, remained ambivalent. While the JCS still feared any agreement that might imply the commitment of forces to the region in the event of hostilities, Adm. Robert B. Carney, commander in chief of United States forces in the Mediterranean, urged officials to reexamine the question of security commitments to Turkey. Carney agreed with McGhee's

[29]JCS to Secretary of Defense, Sept. 9, 1950, box 1, Lot 484, Records of the Department of State; *Foreign Relations of the United States, 1950*, III, 1218-20, 1284–85; Matthews to Burns, Oct. 3, 1950, CD 092.3 NATO-Defense Committee, box 184, Records of the Office of the Secretary of Defense; Paul H. Nitze to Philip Jessup, Aug. 14, 1950, box 1, Lot 484, Records of the Department of State; JCS to Secretary of Defense, Sept. 9, 1950, ibid.

[30]Memorandum of conversation, Feb. 12, 1951, CD 092.3 NATO-GEN, box 243, Records of the Office of the Secretary of Defense; *Foreign Relations of the United States, 1950*, V, 1321; *Foreign Rela-tions of the United States, 1951*, V, 4–11, esp. 8, 21–27, 51–76, esp. 52, 1117–19.

assessment of the situation, feared Turkish neutrality, and sought substantial military aid "predicated on the Turkish capacity for great resistance and the possibility of generating some limited Turkish offensive." At NATO headquarters a separate study, conducted under the authority of Vice Adm. Jerauld Wright, also stressed that there was a "real danger" of Turkish neutrality "stemming from the Turks' gnawing feeling of frustration and isolation." And at the end of February 1951, the CIA completed the coordination of a new National Intelligence Estimate (NIE) of "Turkey's Position in the East-West Struggle." Emphasizing Turkey's strong antipathy to the Soviet Union as well as Turkey's desire to facilitate a Western victory should war erupt elsewhere, the NIE nevertheless noted that "the commitment of Turkish troops or the provision of Turkish bases would . . . be contingent upon a firm assurance of U.S. armed support in event of Soviet attack."[31]

Fear of Turkey's neutrality, then, played a decisive role in compelling another appraisal of Turkey's relationship to NATO. Officials in the State Department, not those in the Defense Department, continued to be the most vigorous proponents of expanding military assistance and commitments throughout the Middle East. In their view, the forces of nationalism and neutralism were making headway, partly because of a pervasive feeling of insecurity. Military assistance would help strengthen United States influence on existing governments; security guarantees to Turkey would bolster confidence in that country, the linchpin of efforts to defend the Middle East. When Secretary Acheson asked the Defense Department to reconsider Turkey's admission into NATO, he emphasized that a security arrangement might induce Turkey to undertake certain measures that would redound to the military advantage of the entire anti-Soviet coalition. He specifically alluded to the peacetime mining of the straits that the Navy Department had been advocating for several months. A security agreement also would facilitate conclusion of an agreement on the use of forward air bases in Turkey. Fearing the loss of those opportunities, McGhee summed up the view of the State Department when he returned from the Middle East and met with the JCS. He emphasized that "there is a real danger that the Turks will choose neutrality if they cannot obtain a security commitment. We cannot be sure that we will have Turkey as an ally unless we extend a security commitment."[32]

In May 1951 the JCS finally decided to accede to an expansion of United States commitments. Military officers recognized the critical role Turkey could play in protecting the West's southern flank in Europe, in diverting large numbers of Soviet troops to the Turkish theater, and in facilitating defense of the Mediterranean and the Middle East. If the Soviets decided to sweep around

---

[31]*Foreign Relations of the United States, 1951*, V, 27–42, 103–4, 113–18, 1118, 1119–26, esp. 1120; JCS 2009/12, "Factors Involving the Inclusion of Greece and Turkey as Full Members of the North Atlantic Treaty Organization," March 16, 1951, sec. 1, CCS 337 (2-20-50), Records of the Joint Chiefs of Staff.

[32]*Foreign Relations of the United States, 1951*, III, 501–505, V, 4–11, 21–42, 80–83, 113–20, esp. 117; memorandum for the Secretary of Defense, Feb. 27, 1951, CD 092 Turkey, box 236, Records of the Office of the Secretary of Defense.

Turkey through Iran and Iraq and if Turkey opted for neutrality, military planners recognized that the West would have great difficulty closing the straits to Soviet submarines, protecting NATO's lines of communication in the Mediterranean, and destroying Soviet shipping in the Black Sea. Even more disillusioning was the prospect of wasting the millions of dollars that had been spent on the construction of airfields in Turkey. With that in mind, the army chief of staff circulated a memorandum to the other chiefs underscoring the importance of readying Turkish airports for use by heavy bombers and jet fighters and urging the consummation of a commitment by treaty with Turkey. Cognizant that United States capabilities had been expanding rapidly, the JCS now endorsed Turkey's inclusion in NATO. The National Security Council formally adopted that position in May 1951. During the following summer and autumn, United States officials persuaded NATO allies to admit Turkey and Greece into the alliance.[33]

From the time of the Truman Doctrine until Turkey's entry into NATO, strategic considerations exerted an important influence on the course of United States policy toward Turkey. Turkey became first the object of assistance from and then the formal ally of the United States, not because of the expectation of any imminent Soviet attack on Turkey, but because of Turkey's potential utility in waging war, protecting air bases, and safeguarding Middle Eastern oil resources. In March 1951, as had been the case in March 1947, United States officials realized that the Soviet threat to Turkey was "relatively quiescent." Soviet policy seemed ominous in other areas of the world, however, and if hostilities erupted elsewhere, United States war planners wanted to use Turkish facilities and manpower to neutralize the Soviet submarine threat in the Mediterranean, to tie up large numbers of Soviet troops, and to launch air attacks on vital Soviet petroleum resources. Estimates that Soviet air defenses in the south were meager and ineffective were added inducements to establish a strategic air base in the region.[34]

What effect did all of this have on relations between the United States and the Soviet Union? From the middle of 1947, the Soviets bitterly condemned United States military assistance to Turkey. Soviet diplomats insisted that the United States was undertaking aggressive action and establishing bases from

---

[33]JCS 1704/49, memorandum by the Chief of Staff, U.S. Army, May 1, 1951, sec. 53, CCS 092 (8-22-46), Records of the Joint Chiefs of Staff; "Summary Views and Bases for Joint Chiefs of Staff Position on Security Arrangements for Greece and Turkey," n.d. [April 1951], CD 092.3 NATO, box 243, Records of the Office of the Secretary of Defense; *Foreign Relations of the United States, 1951*, V, 1148–62; *Foreign Relations of the United States, 1951*, III, 479–85, 505–6, 551–55, 558, 567, 569–71, 574–613, 621–32, 661–63, 669, 678–81, 744, 1265–67, 1302.

[34]JCS 2009/12, "Factors Involving the Inclusion of Greece and Turkey as Full Members of the North Atlantic Treaty Organization," March 16, 1951, sec. 1, CCS 337 (2-20-50), Records of the Joint Chiefs of Staff. For the situation in March 1947, see citation in footnote 18; JCS 1952/1, Chief of Staff, United States Air Force, memorandum, Dec. 21, 1948, sec. 1, CCS 373 (10-23-48), Records of the Joint Chiefs of Staff; Op-32 to General Board, May 12, 1948, 425 (serial 315), Records of the General Board (Naval Historical Center).

which attacks on the Soviet Union could be launched easily and effectively.[35] United States war plans and military-assistance programs demonstrate that Soviet military planners had reason to worry about the ramifications of United States aid to Turkey. A major object of United States policy was to enhance Turkey's military capabilities and, if military conflict occurred, to integrate those capabilities into the war effort. This is not to say or even to intimate that the United States was planning aggressive war. But if war broke out as a result of a miscalculation in a diplomatic crisis—and that was considered the most probable cause of war—then Turkey would play an important role in American offensive as well as defensive actions.

The Soviets had cause to worry about developments in Turkey; just as the United States feared Soviet inroads in Cuba in 1962. The difference, of course, was that in 1962 the United States had the military wherewithal to stop the emergence of an offensive threat on its southern border. In 1947–1948 the Soviets had no such power. Although they had exerted rather little pressure on Turkey, they now had to contemplate the development of a more modern military infrastructure in Turkey, to grapple with the latent ability of the United States to project power from the Middle East, and to deal with the global geopolitical policy inherent in the Truman Doctrine. That challenge, along with other concurrent developments, may well have served to intensify their suspicions of United States intentions and to magnify their sense of weakness.[36]

A study of American policy toward Turkey in the aftermath of World War II highlights the role of strategic imperatives both in the expansion of United States global interests and in the formation of the nation's alliance system. It also helps to elucidate the matrix of considerations that accelerated distrust between the Soviet Union and the United States and generated the Cold War.

---

[35]Wilson to Secretary of State, July 29, 1947, file 861.20267/7-2947, Records of the Department of State; Smith to Secretary of State, Aug. 2, 1947, file 867.00/8-247, ibid.; Wilson to Secretary of State, Sept. 11, 1947, file 861.20267/8-2947, ibid.; Bursley to Secretary of State, Nov. 18, Nov. 25, 1947, file 861.20267/11-1847, 10-3147, ibid.; Wilson to Secretary of State, Dec. 1, 1947, file 761.67/11-2147, ibid.; Smith to Secretary of State, April 30, 1948, file 861.20267/4-3048, ibid.; *Foreign Relations of the United States, 1950*, IV, 1254–55; [Nikita S. Krushchev], Krushchev Remembers, ed. Edward Crankshaw and Strobe Talbott (Boston, 1970), 494, 514.

[36]William O. McCagg, Jr., *Stalin Embattled, 1943–1948* (Detroit, 1978); William Taubman, *Stalin's American Policy: From Entente to Detente to Cold War* (New York, 1982), esp. 128–92.

Melvyn P. Leffler

I have always been most interested in exploring the sources, motives, and goals of US foreign policy. In my first book on US policy toward France and Western Europe after World War I, I wanted to explore whether economic interests inspired US policymakers in the 1920s and to explain why the United States did not incur strategic commitments to help bring about European stability after World War I. Subsequently, I sought to explain the origins of the Cold War and examined whether geopolitical, ideological, economic, or strategic factors prompted US actions. Once I explored the beginnings of the Cold War, I wanted to explain how it came to an end because, like almost everyone else of my generation, I did not expect the Cold War to end in my lifetime. In that book, *For the Soul of Mankind: The United States, the Soviet Union, and the Cold War* (2008), I looked closely at the role of key individuals, like Ronald Reagan and Mikhail Gorbachev. Right now, I am continuing this intellectual journey in my explorations of US foreign policy after the attack on 9/11 and in my efforts to explain why the United States went to war in Iraq in 2003.

QUESTIONS FOR CONSIDERATION

1. Leffler claims that "The international situation . . . was far more complex than that described by [President] Truman or [Undersecretary of State] Acheson." Describe some of this complexity regarding Soviet relations with Turkey before the announcement of the Truman Doctrine.
2. What claims did the Truman Administration make to the American public to convince them of a Soviet threat in Turkey? According to Leffler, what was the real reason for Soviet interests in the region?
3. Why, according to Leffler, did the Truman Administration officials want Turkey to reject Soviet peace overtures?
4. How did Turkey use US strategic interests in the region to successfully lobby for its inclusion in NATO? How did the Soviet Union interpret Turkey's inclusion in NATO?
5. To what extent did US relations with Turkey between 1947 and 1951 represent a continuation of American foreign policy since the nineteenth and early twentieth century? In what ways did it represent a change in US foreign policy?

CHAPTER TEN

❧

Crabgrass-Roots Politics: Race, Rights, and the Reaction against Liberalism in the Urban North, 1940–1964[1]

Thomas J. Sugrue

The dominant narratives of twentieth-century United States history depict the rise of a triumphant liberal state, shaped by the hopeful marriage of government and expertise and validated by a "liberal consensus" of workers, corporations, southerners and northerners, whites and blacks, Catholics and Jews. Conservative critics of the state have remained on the fringes of historiography, as Alan Brinkley has recently argued, a "largely neglected part of the story of twentieth-century America." One of the unexamined ironies of recent American history is that the most influential critics of the liberal state came neither from the ranks of the Republicans nor from . . . radical rightist organizations . . . nor from the ranks of Communists and socialists. The most vocal—and ultimately the farthest-reaching challenge to liberalism—came from within the New Deal coalition itself. Southern whites, whether die-hard Democrats or disaffected Dixiecrats, constrained New Deal liberalism from its inception. Corporate leaders and business unionists limited the possibilities for social democratic reform in the workplace. Their stories are well known. But crucial to the fate of liberalism and antiliberalism in the mid-twentieth-century United States were northern, urban whites. They were the backbone of the New Deal coalition; their political views and their votes limited the possibilities of liberal reform in the mid-twentieth century and constrained the leading liberal social movement, the extension of civil rights and liberties to African Americans.[2]

---

[1]Interested students are encouraged to read this essay in the original form. Thomas J. Sugrue, "Crabgrass-Roots Politics: Race, Rights, and the Reaction against Liberalism in the Urban North, 1940–1964," *The Journal of American History* 82, no. 2 (Sept. 1995), 551–78.

[2]Alan Brinkley, "The Problem of American Conservatism," *American Historical Review* 99 (April 1994), 410; Michael Kazin, "The Grass-Roots Right: New Histories of U. S. Conservatism in the Twentieth Century," ibid., 97 (Feb. 1992), 136–55; James C. Cobb and Michael Namorato, eds., *The New Deal and the South* (Jackson, 1984); Numan V. Bartley, *From Thurmond to Wallace: Political Tendencies in Georgia, 1948–1968* (Baltimore, 1970); Jill Quadagno, "From Old Age Assistance to Supplemental Security Income: The Political Economy of Relief in the South, 1935–1972," in *The Politics of Social Policy in the United States*, ed. Margaret Weir, Ann Shola Orloff, and Theda Skocpol

The New Deal may have been, as Lizabeth Cohen and others have argued, a unifying moment in American political history, at least in the urban North. Industrial workers discovered common political goals in the Democratic party, . . . and expressed their grievances through an inclusive language of Americanism. Yet beneath the seeming unity of the New Deal order were unresolved questions of racial identity and racial politics. Eating away at the "liberal consensus," just as it reached its postwar apotheosis, was a newly assertive working-class whiteness.[3] As early as the 1940s, white politicians in the urban North began to identify the hot-button issues that motivated urban working-class and middle-class white voters. In the crucible of postwar northern cities undergoing profound racial and economic transformation, they fashioned a new politics that combined racial antipathy with a growing skepticism about liberalism. The white rebellion against the New Deal had its origins in the urban politics of the 1940s and 1950s. The local politics of race and housing in the aftermath of World War II fostered a grass-roots rebellion against liberalism and seriously limited the social democratic and egalitarian possibilities of the New Deal order.

POSTWAR DETROIT

. . . The values, ideals, and social movements that formed the political world of the mid-twentieth century can be seen most clearly . . . at the local level, where political and social history intersected in the day-to-day lives of ordinary Americans. An examination of post–World War II Detroit, Michigan, offers insights into the travails of liberalism at the grass-roots level. Dominated by a blue-collar work force, heavily unionized, and predominantly Catholic, Detroit was a stronghold of the Democratic party, a bastion of support for New Deal liberalism. Detroit workers—both white and black—benefited tremendously from New Deal programs. By providing temporary work during the Great Depression, the Works Progress Administration cemented the loyalty of the unemployed of all races to the New Deal. The National Labor Relations Act of 1935 facilitated unionization, which brought tangible gains to Detroit's blue-collar population. By the 1940s Detroit's heavily unionized work force commanded high wages and generous benefits. In addition, federal housing subsidies, under the aegis of the Home

(Princeton, 1988), 235–64; and Bruce J. Schulman, *From Cotton Belt to Sunbelt: Federal Policy, Economic Development, and the Transformation of the South, 1938–1980* (New York, 1991); Nelson Lichtenstein, "From Corporatism to Collective Bargaining: Organized Labor and the Eclipse of Social Democracy in the Postwar Era," in *The Rise and Fall of the New Deal Order, 1930–1980*, ed. Steve Fraser and Gary Gerstle (Princeton, 1989), 122–52; and Elizabeth A. Fones-Wolf, *Selling Free Enterprise: The Business Assault on Labor and Liberalism, 1945–60* (Urbana, 1994).

[3]Lizabeth Cohen, *Making a New Deal: Industrial Workers in Chicago, 1919–1939* (New York, 1990); Gary Gerstle, *Working-Class Americanism: The Politics of Labor in a Textile City, 1920–1960* (New York, 1989); Gary Gerstle, "Working-Class Racism: Broaden the Focus," *International Labor and Working-Class History* 44 (Fall 1993), 33–40; Bruce Nelson, "Class, Race, and Democracy in the CIO: The 'New' Labor History Meets the 'Wages of Whiteness,'" *International Review of Social History* 41 (1996), 407–20; David Roediger, *Towards the Abolition of Whiteness: Essays on Race, Politics, and Working Class History* (London, 1994).

Owners' Loan Corporation, the Federal Housing Administration, and the Veterans Administration, protected homeowners from foreclosure and made home ownership possible for much of the city's working class.

Detroit's voters turned out in droves for Democratic presidential candidates in every election after 1932, most prominently supporting Franklin D. Roosevelt, whose portrait graced working-class clubs, bars, and homes throughout the city. . . . Only once after 1932 did Detroiters fail to rally behind the Democratic candidate for governor. But just as support for the New Deal reached its zenith at the state and national levels, social and demographic changes began to erode support for the liberal agenda in Detroit.[4]

The Second Great Migration of southern blacks to the city set into motion political tremors. . . . The city's black population increased by over five hundred thousand between 1940 and 1970, growing from 9 percent of the city's population in 1940 to 45 percent in 1970. Aspiring black workers, many of whom found stable and relatively high-paying employment in the city's defense and automobile industries, began to look for housing outside Detroit's small and crowded inner-city area, which had held most of the city's African American population in 1940. In the postwar decades, the city's racial geography changed dramatically. Upwardly mobile blacks sought better housing in predominantly white sections of the city. . . . Between 1940 and 1960, the first African Americans moved into 110 previously white census tracts.[5]

In the wake of this influx of blacks, racial tensions mounted. World War II brought a wave of hate strikes against black defense workers, a riot at the site of the Sojourner Truth Homes, a public housing project for blacks, and the 1943 race riot, the bloodiest civil disorder in the United States since the draft uprisings of the Civil War. . . . Race relations in the period after World War II were not tranquil. . . .[6]

---

[4]Melvin G. Holli, ed., *Detroit* (New York, 1976), 274.

[5]U.S. Department of Commerce, Bureau of the Census, *U.S. Census of Population and Housing, 1940, Census Tract Statistics for Detroit, Michigan and Adjacent Area* (Washington, D.C., 1942), table 1; U.S. Department of Commerce, Bureau of the Census, *U. S. Census of Population, 1950, Census Tract Statistics, Detroit, Michigan and Adjacent Area* (Washington, D.C., 1952), table 1; U.S. Department of Commerce, Bureau of the Census, *U.S. Censuses of Population and Housing, 1960, Census Tracts, Detroit, Michigan Standard Metropolitan Statistical Area*, Final Report PHC(1)-40 (Washington, D.C., 1962), table P-1.

[6]Dominic J. Capeci Jr., *Race Relations in Wartime Detroit: The Sojourner Truth Housing Controversy of 1942* (Philadelphia, 1984); August Meier and Elliott Rudwick, *Black Detroit and the Rise of the UAW* (New York, 1979), 192–97; Nelson Lichtenstein, *Labor's War at Home: The CIO in World War II* (New York, 1982); Martin Glaberman, *Wartime Strikes: The Struggle against the Nonstrike Pledge in the UAW during World War II* (Detroit, 1980); Harvard Sitkoff, "The Detroit Race Riot of 1943," *Michigan History*, 53 (Fall 1969), 183–206; Alan Clive, *State of War: Michigan in World War II* (Ann Arbor, 1979), 157–62; Alfred McClung Lee and Norman Daymond Humphrey, *Race Riot* (New York, 1943); Robert Shogan and Tom Craig, *The Detroit Race Riot: A Study in Violence* (Philadelphia, 1964); B. J. Widick, *Detroit: City of Race and Class Violence* (Chicago, 1972), 99–112; Dominic J. Capeci Jr. and Martha Wilkerson, *Layered Violence: The Detroit Rioters of 1943* (Jackson, 1991).

Postwar Detroit was not unique in its history of racial tension. The post–World War II decades witnessed a profound transformation in the politics, urban geography, and economies of dozens of northern industrial cities. Urban whites responded to the influx of millions of black migrants to their cities in the 1940s, 1950s, and 1960s by redefining urban geography and urban politics in starkly racial terms. In Chicago and Cicero, Illinois, working-class whites rioted in the 1940s and 1950s to oppose the construction of public housing in their neighborhoods. . . . And in the postwar period, white Philadelphians and Cincinnatians attacked blacks who moved into previously all-white enclaves and resisted efforts to integrate the housing market. Countless whites retreated to suburbs or neighborhoods on the periphery of cities where they excluded blacks by federally sanctioned redlining, real estate steering, and restrictive zoning laws.[7]

While the racial demography of Detroit was changing, the economy of the Motor City and other older industrial centers began to decline. On the surface, Detroit seemed an embodiment of the postwar affluent society. Detroit's workers . . . were among the best paid in the country. They used their relatively high wages, along with federal mortgage subsidies, to purchase or build modest single-family houses on Detroit's sprawling northeast and northwest sides. The proportion of homes in the city that were occupied by their owners rose from 39.2 percent in 1940 to 54.1 percent in 1960. Yet the working-class hold on affluence was tenuous. . . . Beginning in the early 1950s, the industrial bases of almost every major city in the North began to atrophy, and Detroit was no exception. Large and small companies relocated outside cities to suburban and rural areas, reduced the number of workers in newly automated plants, and closed dozens of central city factories altogether. Between 1954 and 1960, Detroit lost more than eighty thousand manufacturing jobs. The vagaries of the economy jeopardized workers' most significant asset, usually their only substantial investment—their homes.[8]

---

[7]Arnold R. Hirsch, *Making the Second Ghetto: Race and Housing in Chicago, 1940–1960* (New York, 1983), 40–99; Arnold R. Hirsch, "Massive Resistance in the Urban North: Trumbull Park, Chicago, 1953–1966," *Journal of American History* 82 (Sept. 1995), 522–50; John F. Bauman, *Public Housing, Race, and Renewal: Urban Planning in Philadelphia, 1920–1974* (Philadelphia, 1987), 160–64; Kenneth S. Baer, "Whitman: A Study of Race, Class, and Postwar Public Housing Opposition" (senior honors thesis, University of Pennsylvania, 1994); Charles F. Casey-Leininger, "Making the Second Ghetto in Cincinnati: Avondale, 1925–1970," in *Race and the City: Work, Community, and Protest in Cincinnati, 1820–1970*, ed. Henry Louis Taylor Jr. (Urbana, 1993), 239–40, 247–48; Kenneth T. Jackson, *Crabgrass Frontier: The Suburbanization of the United States* (New York, 1985), esp. 190–218; Patricia Burgess Stach, "Deed Restrictions and Subdivision Development in Columbus, Ohio, 1900–1970," *Journal of Urban History* 15 (Nov. 1988), 42–68.

[8]U.S. Department of Commerce, Bureau of the Census, *U.S. Census of Population and Housing, 1940, Population and Housing Statistics for Census Tracts: Detroit, Michigan and Adjacent Area* (Washington, D.C., 1942), table 4; Bureau of the Census, *U.S. Censuses of Population andHousing, 1960, Census Tracts, Detroit, Michigan Standard Metropolitan Statistical Area*, table H-I; Thomas J. Sugrue, "The Structures of Urban Poverty: The Reorganization of Space and Work in Three Periods of American History," in *The "Underclass" Debate: Views from History*, ed. Michael B. Katz (Princeton, 1993), 100–117; John Kasarda, "Urban Change and Minority Opportunities," in *The New Urban Reality*, ed. Paul E. Peterson (Washington, D.C., 1985), 43–47, esp. tables 1 and 2.

The simultaneous black migration and economic dislocation in postwar Detroit created a sense of crisis among the city's white homeowners. As they endured layoffs, plant closings, and downsizing, some working-class home- owners feared that they would lose their homes to foreclosure. . . . In a compre- hensive survey of Detroit residents conducted in 1951, the Wayne University sociologist Arthur Kornhauser found that white Detroiters ranked housing needs as the most pressing problem in the city. Home ownership required a significant financial sacrifice for Detroit residents: the most frequent complaint (voiced by 32 percent of respondents) was that the cost of housing was too high.[9]

The issues of race and housing were inseparable in the minds of many white Detroiters. Homeowners feared, above all, that an influx of blacks would imperil their precarious economic security. A self-described "average American house- wife" wrote: "What about us, who cannot afford to move to a better location and are surrounded by colored? . . . Most of us invested our life's savings in property and now we are in constant fear that the neighbor will sell its property to people of different race." Kornhauser found that race relations followed a close second in Detroiters' ranking of the city's most pressing problems. Only 18 percent of white respondents from all over the city expressed "favorable" views toward the "full acceptance of Negroes," and 54 percent expressed "unfavorable" attitudes toward integration. When asked to discuss ways in which race relations "were not as good as they should be," 27 percent of white respondents mentioned "Negroes moving into white neighborhoods." Among white respondents 22 percent answered that the "Negro has too many rights and privileges; too much power; too much inter- mingling." Another 14 percent mentioned "Negroes' undesirable characteristics." Only 14 percent mentioned discrimination as a problem in race relations.[10]

Whites in Kornhauser's sample regularly spoke of the "colored problem" or the "Negro problem." In their responses to open-ended questions, Kornhauser's informants made clear what they meant by the "colored problem." "Eighty percent of [blacks] are animals," stated one white respondent. "If they keep them all in the right place there wouldn't be any trouble," responded another. . . . When asked "What do you feel ought to be done about relations between Negroes and whites in Detroit?" a remarkable 68 percent of white respondents called for some form of racial segregation—56 percent of whites surveyed advocated residential segrega- tion. Many cited the Jim Crow South as a model for successful race relations. . . .[11]

---

[9]"Open Letter to Henry Ford II," *Ford Facts*, Sept. 15, 1951; Arthur Kornhauser, *Detroit as the People See It: A Survey of Attitudes in an Industrial City* (Detroit, 1952), 68–69, 75, 77–82. Korn- hauser's team interviewed 593 adult men and women randomly selected from all sections of the city. On the survey's methodology, see ibid., 189–96.

[10]"Integration Statement," anonymous letter [c. mid-1950s], box 9, part I, Metropolitan Detroit Council of Churches Collection (Archives of Labor and Urban Affairs); Kornhauser, *Detroit as the People See It*, 95.

[11]The term "colored problem" was used most frequently by whites to describe Black movement into their neighborhoods; Property Owners Association, flyer, 1945, box 66, Civil Rights Congress of Michigan Collection (Archives of Labor and Urban Affairs); and the newsletter of the Courville

In reaction to the postwar transformation of the city, Detroit's whites began fashioning a politics of defensive localism that focused on threats to property and neighborhood. They directed their political energy toward the two groups they believed were the agents of change: blacks and their liberal allies. Acting on their perception of the threat of the black newcomers to their stability, economic status, and political power, many of Detroit's working- and middle-class whites banded together in exclusive neighborhood organizations, in what became one of the largest grass-roots movements in the city's history. By moving the politics of race, home ownership, and neighborhood to center stage, they reshaped urban politics in the 1940s and 1950s and set in motion the forces that would eventually reconfigure national politics.[12]

Between 1943 and 1965, whites throughout Detroit founded at least 192 neighborhood organizations, variously called "civic associations," "protective associations," "improvement associations," and "homeowners' associations." . . . The surviving records of homeowners' associations do not, unfortunately, permit a

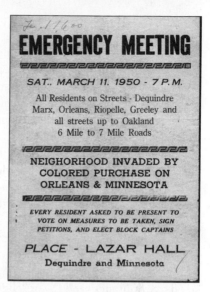

Photo 10.1
Flyer announcing neighborhood association meeting to prevent African Americans from moving into a predominantly white neighborhood on Detroit's east side, March 1950. Folder 25-107, box 25, part III, Detroit Commission on Community Relationships Collection, Archives of Labor and Urban Affairs. Printed with permission of the Archives of Labor and Urban Affairs, Walter P. Reuther Library, Wayne State University, Detroit, Michigan.

close analysis of their membership. . . . It is clear that no single ethnic group dominated most neighborhood associations. . . . Letters . . . seldom referred to national heritage or religious background. Organizational newsletters and neighborhood newspapers never used ethnic modifiers or monikers to describe neighborhood association members—they reserved ethnic nomenclature for "the colored" and Asians (and occasionally Jews). . . . Members of homeowners' and neighborhood groups shared a common bond of whiteness and Americanness—a

District Improvement Association, *Action!*, Feb. 15, 1948, attached to Mayor's Interracial Committee, Minutes, April 5, 1948, box 10, part I, Detroit Commission on Community Relations Collection, ibid. Kornhauser, *Detroit as the People See It*, 85, 185, 100. There was virtually complete residential segregation in Detroit when Kornhauser conducted his survey. Karl E. Taeuber and Alma F. Taeuber, *Negroes in Cities: Residential Segregation and Neighborhood Change* (Chicago, 1965), 39.

[12]I borrow the term "defensive localism" from Margaret Weir, "Urban Poverty and Defensive Localism," *Dissent* 41 (Summer 1994), 337–42.

bond that they asserted forcefully at public meetings and in correspondence with public officials.[13]

Neighborhood associations had a long history in cities such as Detroit. Real estate developers had originally created them to enforce restrictive covenants and, later, zoning laws. . . . During and after World War II, these organizations grew rapidly in number and influence. Increasingly, they existed solely to wage battles against proposed public housing sites and against blacks moving into their neighborhoods. . . . Beginning in the 1940s, the threat of a black influx became the *raison d'être* of community groups. One new group, the Northwest Civic Association, called its founding meeting "So YOU will have firsthand information on the colored situation in this area," and it invited "ALL interested in maintaining Property Values in the NORTHWEST section of Detroit." The Courville District Improvement Association gathered residents of a northeast Detroit neighborhood to combat the "influx of colored people" into the area and rallied supporters with its provocatively entitled newsletter, *Action!* . . . Members of the San Benardo Improvement Association pledged to keep their neighborhood free of "undesirables"—or "Niggers"—as several who eschewed euphemism shouted at the group's first meeting. . . .[14]

As the racial demography of Detroit changed, neighborhood groups demarcated racial boundaries with great precision and, abetted by federal agencies and private real estate agents, divided cities into strictly enforced racial territories. From the 1940s through the 1960s, white urban dwellers fiercely defended their

---

[13]On the ethnic heterogeneity of Detroit neighborhoods, see Olivier Zunz, *The Changing Face of Inequality: Urbanization, Industrial Development, and Immigrants in Detroit, 1880–1920* (Chicago, 1982), 340–51; Hirsch, *Making the Second Ghetto*, 81–84; see letters to Mayor Edward Jeffries, regarding the Algonquin Street and Oakwood defense housing projects, Housing Commission Folder, box 3, Detroit Archives -Mayor's Papers, 1945 (Burton Historical Collection, Detroit Public Library, Detroit, Mich.); Exhibit A, Oct. 22, 1948, pp. 1–2, attached to Charles H. Houston to Charles S. Johnson et al., memorandum, Michigan: *Swanson v. Hayden* Folder, box B133, group II, NAACP Papers (Manuscript Division, Library of Congress, Washington, D.C.); newsletter of the Greater Detroit Neighbors Association-Unit No. 2, *Neighborhood Informer* (Dec. 1949), 2, folder 4-19, box 4, UAW, Community Action Program Collection (Archives of Labor and Urban Affairs); "Demonstrations Protesting Negro Occupancy of Homes, September 1, 1945–September 1, 1946: Memorandum J," p. 31, box 3, part I, Detroit Commission on Community Relations Collection; K. Anderson to Herbert Schultz, Oct. 17, 1958, South Lakewood Area Association Papers, 1955–1960 (Burton Historical Collection); Chronological Index of Cases, 1951 (51-31) and (51-58), box 13, Detroit Commission on Community Relations Collection; Detroit Police Department Special Investigation Bureau, Summary of Racial Activities, April 30, 1956–May 17, 1956, folder A2-26, box 38, Detroit Urban League Papers (Michigan Historical Collections, Bentley Library, University of Michigan, Ann Arbor); Capeci and Wilkerson, *Layered Violence*; and John M. Hartigan Jr., "Cultural Constructions of Whiteness: Racial and Class Formations in Detroit" (Ph.D. diss., University of California, Santa Cruz, 1995).

[14]"OPEN MEETING . . . for Owners and Tenants," poster, [c. 1945], Property Owners Association Folder, box 66, Civil Rights Congress of Michigan Collection; *Action!*, Feb. 15, 1948, p. 2; Guyton Home Owners' Association and Connor-East Home Owners' Association, leaflets, 1957–1960 Folder, South Lakewood Area Association Papers; Richard J. Peck, Community Services Department, Detroit Urban League, "Summary of Known Improvement Association Activity in Past Two Years, 1955–1957," box 2, Pre-1960, Community Organization 1950s Vertical File (Archives of Labor and Urban Affairs); *Southwest Detroiter*, May 11, 1950, Housing Commission Folder, box 5, Detroit Archives-Mayors' Papers, 1950.

turf. They referred to the black migration in military terms: they spoke of "invasions" and "penetration" and plotted strategies of "resistance." White neighborhoods became "battlegrounds" where residents struggled to preserve segregated housing. Homeowners' associations helped whites to "defend" their homes and "protect" their property.[15]

Their militancy was more than rhetorical. As a former Detroit race relations official remarked of the postwar period, the city "did a lot of firefighting in those days." White Detroiters instigated over two hundred incidents against blacks attempting to move into formerly all-white neighborhoods, including mass demonstrations, picketing, effigy burning, window breaking, arson, vandalism, and physical attacks. . . . A potent mixture of fear and anger animated whites who violently defended their neighborhoods. All but the most liberal whites who lived along the city's racial frontier believed that they had only two choices. They could flee, as vast numbers of white urbanites did, or they could hold their ground and fight.[16]

. . . The movement of a single black family to a white block fueled panic. Real estate brokers canvassed door to door in areas bordering black neighborhoods warning fearful white homeowners that if they did not sell quickly, the value of their houses would plummet. Realtors created a climate of fear by ostentatiously showing houses to black families, waiting a day or two for rumors to spread throughout the neighborhood, and then inundating residents with leaflets and phone calls urging them to sell. One broker paid a black woman to walk her baby down an all-white block, to spark fears that "Negroes [were] 'taking over' this block or area" and that the residents "had best sell now while there was still a chance of obtaining a good price." Such sales tactics . . . were remarkably effective. Whites living just beyond "racially transitional" neighborhoods witnessed rapid black movement into nearby areas. They feared that without concerted action, their neighborhoods would turn over just as quickly.[17]

White Detroiters also looked beyond transitional neighborhoods to the "slum," a place that confirmed their greatest fears. Whites saw in the neighborhoods to which blacks had been confined in the center city area a grim prophecy of their neighborhoods' futures. They focused on places like Paradise Valley, Detroit's first major ghetto, which housed two-thirds of the city's black

---

[15]*Neighborhood Informer* (Dec. 1949), 1, 3, folder 4-19, box 4, UAW, Community Action Program Collection; "Emergency Meeting, March 11, 1950," handbill, folder 25-107, box 25, part III, Detroit Commission on Community Relations Collection; Ruritan Park Civic Association, "Dear Neighbor," folder 25-101, ibid.

[16]John G. Feild interview by Katherine Shannon, Dec. 28, 1967, transcript, p. 11, Civil Rights Documentation Project (Moorland-Spingarn Research Center, Howard University Library, Washington, D.C.). The finding guide and interview transcript mistakenly spell Feild as Fields; Thomas J. Sugrue, "The Origins of the Urban Crisis: Race, Industrial Decline, and Housing in Detroit, 1940–1960" (Ph.D. diss., Harvard University, 1992), 208–78.

[17]Mel Ravitz, "Preparing Neighborhoods for Change," July 13, 1956, folder A8-1, box 44, Detroit Urban League Papers; William Price, "Scare Selling in a Bi-Racial Housing Market," June 11, 1957, ibid.; "Incident Report," July 6, 1950, folder 50-23, box 6, Detroit Commission on Community Relations Collection; Mary Czechowski to Mayor Albert Cobo, Oct. 8, 1950, folder 50-57, box 7, ibid.

population during World War II. Housing in Paradise Valley consisted mainly of run-down rental units, most built in the 1860s and 1870s, owned by absentee white landlords. . . . Whites feared the incursion of a "lower-class element" into their neighborhoods.[18]

To white Detroiters, the wretched conditions in Paradise Valley . . . were the fault of irresponsible blacks, not of greedy landlords or neglectful city officials. Wherever blacks lived, whites believed, neighborhoods inevitably deteriorated. "Let us keep out the slums," admonished one east-side homeowners' group. . . . A northwest-side neighborhood association poster played on white residents' fears of the crime that, they believed, would accompany racial change: "Home Owners Can You Afford to . . . Have your children exposed to gangster operated skid row saloons? Pornographic pictures and literature? Gamblers and prostitution? You Face These Issues Now!"[19]

The most commonly expressed fear was not of "riotous living" or crime, but of racial intermingling. Black "penetration" of white neighborhoods posed a fundamental challenge to white racial identity. Again and again, neighborhood groups and letter writers referred to the perils of rapacious black sexuality and race mixing. . . . As one opponent of a proposed Negro housing project stated: "We firmly believe in the God-given equality of man. He did not give us the right to choose our brothers . . . but he did give us the right to choose the people we sleep with." Newspaper accounts ominously warned of the threat of miscegenation. . . . Neighborhood defense became . . . a battle for the preservation of white womanhood. Men had a duty, as the Courville District Improvement Association admonished, to "pitch for your civic rights and the protection of your women."[20]

The prevention of interracial residential and sexual contact was not just a masculine responsibility. Women also policed the boundaries of race and sex . . . [in] demonstrations led by women against Edward Brock. Brock, the white owner of two houses on Detroit's lower west side, had sold them to black families in 1948. Groups of ten to twenty-five women, many pushing baby strollers, gathered at Brock's workplace every day for a week, carrying hand-painted

---

[18]Detroit Housing Commission and Work Projects Administration, *Real Property Survey of Detroit, Michigan* (Detroit, 1939), II, III, maps and data for Area K; Sugrue, "Origins of the Urban Crisis," 316–17. Gloster Current, "Paradise Valley: A Famous and Colorful Part of Detroit as Seen through the Eyes of an Insider," *Detroit* (June 1946), 32, 34.

[19]Outer-Van Dyke Home Owners' Association, "Dear Neighbor" [1948], folder 25-94, box 25, part III, Detroit Commission on Community Relations Collection; interview with Six Mile Road-Riopelle area neighbors in Incident Report, Aug. 30, 1954, folder A7-13, box 43, Detroit Urban League Papers; Longview Home Owners Association, poster, n.d., Housing-Homeowners Ordinance-Friendly Folder, box 10, part I, Metropolitan Detroit Council of Churches Collection. Ellipsis in original.

[20]Alex Csanyi and family to Jeffries, Feb. 20, 1945, Housing Commission 1945 Folder, box 3, Detroit Archives- Mayors' Papers 1945. Ellipsis in original. *Home Gazette*, Oct. 25, 1945, Charles Hill Papers (Archives of Labor and Urban Affairs); Gloster Current, "The Detroit Elections: A Problem in Reconversion," *Crisis* 52 (Nov. 1945), 319–21; *Action!*, Feb. 15, 1948, p. 2; Elaine Tyler May, "Cold War, Warm Hearth: Politics and the Family in Postwar America," in *Rise and Fall of the New Deal Order*, ed. Fraser and Gerstle, 153–81.

signs that read: "My home is my castle, I will die defending it"; "The Lord separated the races, why should Constable Brock mix them"; "We don't want to mix"; and "Ed Brock sold to colored in white neighborhood." . . . Replete with the symbols of motherhood and family, these protests touched a deep, sympathetic nerve among onlookers, many of whom saw black movement into a neighborhood as a threat to virtuous womanhood, innocent childhood, and the sanctity of the home.[21]

"RIGHTS," HOUSING, AND POLITICS

Neighborhood associations resorted to pickets, harassment, and violence in the days and weeks of desperation that followed black "invasions" of their neighborhoods. More commonly, however, they relied on traditional political means—the ballot box, constituent letters, and testimony at city hearings—to stem racial change. Neighborhood associations became the most powerful force in postwar Detroit politics. They backed conservative politicians who opposed public housing, tax increases, and racial integration. Their members turned out in huge numbers on election day. . . . Issues of race and home ownership dominated local politics in postwar Detroit. White homeowners forged an extraordinarily well-organized grass-roots conservative coalition in local politics, constrained public housing policy, and thwarted attempts to integrate the private housing market.

Perhaps the issue that most visibly galvanized neighborhood groups was the threat of "socialized housing," especially government-sponsored developments for low-income blacks. Public housing became the first significant wedge between white voters and New Deal liberalism in Detroit. Federal officials made public housing a centerpiece of New Deal social policy, beginning with the Federal Public Housing Act in 1937 and culminating in the Taft-Ellender-Wagner Housing Act of 1949. New Deal and Fair Deal legislation allocated over a billion dollars in federal resources to provide shelter for the poorest Americans. . . .[22]

---

[21]Attachment to letter, Miss James, Detroit Branch NAACP, to George Schermer, Aug. 23, 1948, folder 48-125A, box 5, part I, Detroit Commission on Community Relations Collection. See photographs and description in "Constable Sells Home to Negro-Picketed," *Michigan Chronicle*, Aug. 21, 1948; "Three Families Move into Homes on Harrison As Police Stand By to Prevent Violence," ibid., Aug. 28, 1948; and "Mayor Guarantees Protection for Negro Home-Owner," *Detroit Tribune*, Aug. 28, 1948; "Memorandum J," p. 31, attached to "Demonstrations, 1945–1946," folder 47-54, box 4, part I, Detroit Commission on Community Relations Collection; "Case Report: Case No. 54," ibid.; George Schermer, "Report of Incident, Subject: Neighborhood Protest to Sale of House on 13933 Maine Street," June 23, 1947, ibid.; Schermer to John F. Ballenger, commissioner, Department of Police, June 23, 1947, ibid.; John Feild to Director, "Neighborhood Protest to Sale of House on 13933 Maine Street," memo, June 1947, ibid.; "Police Action Averts Riot," *Pittsburgh Courier* (Detroit edition),June 28, 1947; and "White Neighbors Threaten Negroes Moving into Home," *Michigan Chronicle*, June 28, 1947; *Pittsburgh Courier* (Detroit edition), June 18, 1955; Sylvie Murray, "Suburban Citizens: Domesticity and Community Politics in Queens, New York, 1945–1960" (Ph.D. diss., Yale University, 1994); Hirsch, *Making the Second Ghetto*, 195–96.

[22]Robert Moore Fisher, *Twenty Years of Public Housing: Economic Aspects of the Federal Program* (New York, 1959); Richard O. Davies, *Housing Reform during the Truman Administration* (Columbia, Mo., 1966).

Photo 10.2
Sign protesting plans to open the Soujourner Truth Homes, a public housing project on Detroit's northeast side, to African Americans, February 1942. Photograph by Arthur Siegel, Office of War Information. Courtesy Prints and Photos Division, Library of Congress.

White Detroiters, however, vehemently opposed public housing during and after World War II, largely on racial grounds. Between 1942 and 1950 neighborhood associations resisted public housing proposed for outlying white sections of the city, and they succeeded in preventing the building of almost all the projects.

In 1942 whites in northeast Detroit tried unsuccessfully to prevent black occupancy of the Sojourner Truth defense housing project, and whites and blacks battled on the streets when the first black families arrived at the site. In 1944 whites living near the site of a proposed temporary wartime project for blacks, on Algonquin Street, flooded city officials with angry petitions. In 1944 and 1945, residents of suburban Dearborn and Ecorse, cooperating with the Ford Motor Company, had prevented the construction of public housing in their communities, and white Detroiters in the Oakwood district in southwest Detroit blocked the construction of a public housing project for blacks in their neighborhood. In 1948 and 1949, neighborhood group members packed city plan commission and common council hearings on proposals to locate twelve public housing projects on sites on Detroit's periphery. They won a mayoral veto of all outlying public housing projects in 1950. Through intensive lobbying efforts, they succeeded in restricting Detroit's public housing to neighborhoods with sizable African American populations.[23]

In the battles over public housing in the 1940s, neighborhood groups fashioned a potent political language of rights, a language that they refined and extended in the 1950s and 1960s. As one observer noted, "the white population has come to believe that it has a vested, exclusive, and permanent 'right' to certain districts." Civic associations cast their demands for racially segregated neighborhoods in terms of entitlement and victimization. Homeowners' groups were by no means alone in couching their political demands in the language of rights. They were part of a New Deal–inspired rights revolution that empowered other groups, including African Americans, trade union members, and military

---

[23]On Dearborn and Ecorse, see Dearborn Press, Nov. 22, 1944; Detroit Times, May 24, 1945; Detroit News, May 15, 1945; and David L. Good, Orvie: The Dictator of Dearborn: The Rise and Reign of Orville L. Hubbard (Detroit, 1989), 142; Detroit News, Feb. 16, 28, March 20, 1945.

veterans, to use rights talk to express their political discontent and their political vision.[24]

The notion of the white entitlement to a home in a racially homogeneous neighborhood was firmly rooted in New Deal housing policy. Supporters of the Home Owners' Loan Corporation (HOLC) and the Federal Housing Administration (FHA) argued that national security and self-preservation required the stability of private home ownership. President Franklin Delano Roosevelt frequently alluded to the ideal of a nation of free homeowners in his speeches, and he included the right to a decent home in his 1944 "Second Bill of Rights." This New Deal rhetoric touched a deep nerve among white Detroiters who . . . with government-backed mortgages and loans . . . were able to attain the dream of property ownership with relative ease. . . . The FHA and HOLC's insistence that mortgages and loans be restricted to racially homogeneous neighborhoods also resonated strongly with Detroit's homeowners. They came to expect a vigilant government to protect their segregated neighborhoods. . . .[25]

The experience of World War II solidified white Detroiters' belief in their right to racially homogeneous neighborhoods. Flyers produced by neighborhood improvement associations couched the grievances of whites struggling against public housing in the language of Americanism and wartime patriotism. In the immediate aftermath of World War II, petitioners highlighted the theme of wartime sacrifice, appealing to the sentiments that undergirded federal entitlements for returning veterans. In 1945 Michael J. Harbulak, who opposed the construction of a public housing project in his neighborhood, Oakwood, wrote: "Our boys are fighting in Europe, Asia, and Africa to keep those people off our soil. If when these boys return they should become refugees who have to give up their homes because their own neighborhood with the help of our city fathers had been invade[d] and occupied by the Africans, it would be a shame which our city fathers could not outlive." Testifying against public housing, Louis J. Borolo, president of the Oakwood Blue Jackets Athletic Club, appealed to the city council using the patriotic language that many of his neighbors had used in their petition

---

[24]Sidney M. Milkis, *The President and the Parties: The Transformation of the American Party System Since the New Deal* (New York, 1993), esp. 41–43, 48–50; and Alan Brinkley, *The End of Reform: New Deal Liberalism in Recession and War* (New York, 1995), 10–11, 164–70; Rogers M. Smith, "Rights," in *A Companion to American Thought*, ed. Richard Wightman Fox and James Kloppenberg (Oxford, Eng., 1995); and Mary Ann Glendon, *Rights Talk: The Impoverishment of Political Discourse* (New York, 1991).

[25]Franklin Delano Roosevelt, "Message to Congress on the State of the Union," Jan. 11, 1944, in *The Public Papers and Addresses of Franklin D. Roosevelt*, vol. XIII: *Victory and the Threshold of Peace, 1944–45* (New York, 1950), 41; Henry Lee Moon, "Danger in Detroit," *Crisis* 53 (Jan. 1946), 28; Seven Mile-Fenelon Improvement Association, "WE DEMAND OUR RIGHTS," poster, Property Owners Association Folder, box 66, Civil Rights Congress of Michigan Collection; Ronald Tobey, Charles Wetherell, and Jay Brigham, "Moving Out and Settling In: Residential Mobility, Home Owning, and the Public Enframing of Citizenship, 1921–1950," *American Historical Review* 95 (Dec. 1990), 1395–1422, esp. 1415–20; and Cohen, *Making a New Deal*, 272–77; Zunz, *Changing Face of Inequality*, 129–76; Kenneth T. Jackson, "Race, Ethnicity, and Real Estate Appraisal: The Home Owners Loan Corporation and the Federal Housing Administration," *Journal of Urban History* 6 (Aug. 1980), 419–52.

letters. "There are 1,500 blue stars in the windows of homes of that neighborhood," he testified. "Those stars represent soldiers waiting to come back to the same neighborhood they left." Acknowledging the "moral and legal right" of blacks to adequate housing, he nonetheless contended that "we have established a prior right to a neighborhood which we have built up through the years—a neighborhood which is entirely white and which we want kept white."[26]

"Homeowners' rights" was a malleable concept that derived its power from its imprecision. Some whites described their rights in humble "bootstraps" terms. They had acquired property and earned their rights through hard work and responsible citizenship. Homeowners' rights were, in this view, a reward for sacrifice and duty. Others drew from an idiosyncratic reading of the Declaration of Independence and Bill of Rights to justify their neighborhood defensiveness. Public housing for blacks in a white neighborhood was a violation of white "rights" to "peace and happyness." Some defined homeowners' rights as an extension of their constitutional right of freedom of assembly. They had a right to choose their associates. That right would be infringed if their neighborhoods were racially mixed.[27]

In an era of growing civil rights consciousness, many white letter writers and petitioners made grudging acknowledgements of racial equality. . . . Rights for blacks were acceptable in the abstract, as long as blacks remained in their own neighborhoods and kept to themselves. But many whites believed that civil rights for blacks were won only at the expense of white rights. . . .[28]

In the crucible of Detroit's racial and economic transformation, not all rights were equal. Neighborhood groups criticized public housing as a handout to the undeserving poor, who demanded rights without bearing the burden of responsibilities. . . . An opponent of public housing noted in 1949 that "taxpayers and home-owning groups are rising in wrath against subsidizing homes." Why should government compel hardworking whites to pay for housing for the poor? And why should it "force" white neighborhoods to accept housing for poor blacks?[29]

. . . Detroit's whites began to view public housing as "Negro housing," and they grew increasingly skeptical of the federal agenda that called for the provision of shelter for America's poor. Erosion of support for public housing on

---

[26]MichaelJ. Harbulak to Jeffries, Feb. 21, 1945, Housing Commission 1945 Folder, box 3, Detroit Archives- Mayors' Papers 1945; "Negro Homes Vote Delayed," *Detroit News*, March 9, 1945; *Current*, "Detroit Elections," 325. See also *Action!*, March 15, 1948; Gerstle, *Working-Class Americanism*; Gary Gerstle, "The Working Class Goes to War," *Mid-America* 75 (Oct. 1993), 303–22; Michael Kazin and Steven J. Ross, "America's Labor Day: The Dilemma of a Workers' Celebration," *Journal of American History* 78 (March 1992), 1294–1323; and James R. Barrett, "Americanization from the Bottom Up: Immigration and the Remaking of the Working Class in the United States, 1880–1930," ibid., 79 (Dec. 1992), 996–1020.

[27]Harbulak to Jeffries, Feb. 21, 1945, Housing Commission 1945 Folder, box 3, Detroit Archives-Mayors' Papers 1945.

[28]Mr. and Mrs. Fred Pressato to Jeffries, March 6, 1945, ibid.; William Leuffen to Jeffries, March 6, 1945, Housing / Bi-Racial Letters Folder, ibid.; John Watson to Jeffries, March 6, 1945, ibid.

[29]The remarks appear in an editorial, *Brightmoor Journal*, Oct. 27, 1949; *Action!*, March 15, 1948, p. 2.

grounds of race also eroded support for New Deal programs more generally. One astute observer noted in 1946:

> In the field of housing, there has tended to develop a tie-up in our thinking between Negroes and government. Public housing and housing for Negroes is synonymous or nearly so in the minds of many people. This is bad for public housing and bad for Negroes. Many people are concerned about government interference of all kinds. This tends to create a separation in their minds between themselves and "the government."[30]

Alienated Detroit whites increasingly directed their animus against local public officials, whom they saw as active agents in the transformation of their neighborhoods. "We must stop the wasting of the taxpayers' money on public housing, or any other wasteful planning," warned a west-side chapter of the National Association of Community Councils in 1945. In the same year, a "Group of Taxpayers" complained to the city of the "insurmountable tax, housing, hospitalization and social problems facing taxpayers" because of the influx of "colored" moving to the city to collect welfare benefits denied them in the South. Equally blameworthy were the black poor who depended on government assistance and the bureaucrats who fostered that dependence through social welfare programs. . . . Speaking for the neighborhood associations that he advocated, Karl H. Smith, a local realtor, praised groups who fought "unjust tax levies for the benefit of shiftless drifters who have not the guts to want to own a home of their own."[31]

As domestic anticommunism rose to political prominence, neighborhood groups began to articulate their concerns in McCarthyite terms. A growing number of white Detroiters believed in a conspiracy of government bureaucrats, many influenced by communism or socialism (terms used interchangeably), who misused tax dollars to fund experiments in social engineering for the benefit of pressure groups. In so doing, the government repudiated property rights and democratic principles. Behind the scenes was a cabal of public housing officials, city planning committees, civil rights groups, labor activists, and socialist agitators who worked to defraud honest taxpayers and destroy the city.

Homeowners' groups and sympathetic politicians used McCarthyite rhetoric against liberal politicians and advocates of public housing and open housing. . . . Many whites believed that a sinister conspiracy was afoot. In their minds, the issues of race, left-wing politics, and government action became inextricably linked. Public housing projects were part of the conspiratorial effort of well-placed

---

[30]"Fourth Meeting of the Speaker's Study Group of Intercultural Affairs," Feb. 4, 1946, p. 2, Interracial Resolutions / Intercultural Council Folder, box 74, Citizens Housing and Planning Council Papers (Burton Historical Collection).

[31]"Join the Fight," flyer, Nov. 1945, folder 20-37, box 20, part III, Detroit Commission on Community Relations Collection; "A Group of Taxpayers" to the councilmen of the City of Detroit, April 12, 1945, Common Council Folder, box 23, Citizens Housing and Planning Council Papers; "Survey of Racial and Religious Conflict Forces in Detroit," Sept. 30, 1943, box 71, Civil Rights Congress of Michigan Collection.

Communists and Communist sympathizers in the government to destroy traditional American values through a carefully calculated policy of racial and class struggle. Floyd McGriff, the editor of a chain of northwest-side neighborhood newspapers, warned that . . . reds in the city government planned to "move the slum-area residents into city-built housing projects in Northwest Detroit" and "to force pioneering families to move out." Open housing was the product of a "leftist political brigade" that had as its mission "political activity to provide colored persons with homes they cannot afford to live in." Small neighborhood struggles against the "black invasion" and against public housing were really skirmishes in a larger battle against communism itself.[32]

The pro-homeowner and anti-integrationist sentiments unleashed by public housing debates had a profound impact on local mayoral elections. The political career of Detroit mayor Edward Jeffries (1941–1947) revealed the power of crabgrass-roots politics and the fragility of liberalism in Detroit. Jeffries was first elected mayor in 1941 as a New Dealer, prolabor and racially liberal. He garnered the endorsements of labor unions and civil rights groups and swept both black and white working-class precincts. After the wartime riots and hate strikes and the emergence of a powerful homeowners' movement, Jeffries refashioned his racial politics. He combined red-baiting and race-baiting in his successful reelection bid in 1945 against the liberal candidate . . . Richard Frankensteen. In a campaign laden with racial innuendo, [Jeffries] flooded neighborhoods on the northwest and northeast sides with literature highlighting Frankensteen's ties to black organizations. Handbills reading . . . "Negroes Can Live Anywhere with Frankensteen Mayor. Negroes—Do Your Duty Nov. 6" were widely distributed in white neighborhoods during the election. Jeffries supporters sounded the ominous warning that Frankensteen was a "red" who, if elected, would encourage "racial invasions" of white neighborhoods. . . .[33] The black journalist Henry Lee Moon, writing in the National Association for the Advancement of Colored People (NAACP) monthly *Crisis*, accused Jeffries of appealing "to our more refined fascists, the big money interests and the precarious middle class whose sole inalienable possession is a white skin." Racial appeals bolstered the flagging Jeffries campaign and gave him a comfortable margin. . . . On the local level, the link between black and red was a clever strategy for attracting white Democrats, suspicious of liberalism and its capacity for equalitarian political and social rhetoric.[34]

---

[32]*Brightmoor Journal*, Feb. 3, May 12, Jan. 12, 1950, April 21, 1966. See also *Action!*, March 15, 1948; Floyd McGriff Papers (Michigan Historical Collections).

[33]Capeci, *Race Relations in Wartime Detroit*, 17-27. Handbills, folder 3-8, box 3, Donald Marsh Papers (University Archives, Wayne State University, Detroit, Mich.); "The 1945 Mayoral Campaign-National Lawyers Guild," Jan. 10, 1946, attached to Gloster Current to Thurgood Marshall, memo, Racial Tension Detroit, Mich., 1944–46 Folder, box A505, group II, National Association for the Advancement of Colored People Papers; "Mayor Jeffries Is Against Mixed Housing," flyer, Politics, Michigan, 1945–1953 Folder, box A475, ibid.

[34]"White Neighborhoods Again in Peril: Frankensteen Policy Up On Housing Negroes Here," *Home Gazette*, Oct. 11, 1945, clipping, Clippings File, Hill Papers; Moon, "Danger in Detroit," 12.

The political tensions over race and housing came to a head in the mayoral election of 1949. The liberal common council member George Edwards faced the conservative city treasurer, Albert Cobo. Edwards, a one-time UAW activist, former public housing administrator, and New Deal Democrat, was the political antithesis of Cobo, a corporate executive, real estate investor, and Republican. Cobo focused his campaign on the issues of race and public housing. Armed with the endorsement of most white neighborhood improvement associations, Cobo swept the largely white precincts on the northeast and northwest sides, where voters were especially concerned about the threat of public housing. The distinction between Cobo and Edwards was crystal clear. Cobo adamantly opposed "Negro invasions" and public housing, whereas Councilman Edwards had consistently championed the right of blacks to decent housing anywhere in the city and had regularly voted for proposals to locate public housing in outlying areas.[35]

Liberal leaders were baffled that the conservative Cobo had beaten the pro-labor Edwards in a heavily Democratic city and that Cobo did particularly well among union voters. . . . A west-side [UAW] coordinator explained the seeming paradox of union support for Cobo: "I think in these municipal elections we are dealing with people who have a middle class mentality. Even in our own UAW, the member is either buying a home, owns a home, or is going to buy one. I don't know whether we can ever make up this difficulty." The problem was that "George was beaten by the housing program."[36]

The 1949 election revealed the conflict between the politics of home and the politics of workplace, a conflict exacerbated by racial tensions in rapidly changing neighborhoods. . . . Racial fears and neighborhood defensiveness made the political unity of home and workplace impossible. East-side UAW shop stewards, many of whom were open Cobo supporters, told one UAW Political Action Committee organizer that "the Union is okay in the shop but when they buy a home they forget about it. You can tell them anything they want to but as long as they think their property is going down, it is different." . . . The combination of racial resentment and homeowners' politics that defeated Edwards dimmed future hopes for the triumph of labor liberalism on the local level in Detroit.[37]

---

[35]Melvin G. Holli and Peter d'A. Jones, *Biographical Dictionary of American Mayors, 1820–1980: Big City Mayors* (Westport, 1981), 69–70; *Detroit News*, Oct. 31, 1947, clipping, folder 10-4, box 10, UAW, Research Department Collection (Archives of Labor and Urban Affairs); "Biographical Data, George Edwards," Vertical File-Biography, ibid. *Brightmoor Journal*, Sept. 22, 1949; newsletter of the Outer-Van Dyke Home Owners Association, *"Hi" Neighbor*, 1 (Nov. 1949), copy, folder 5-5, box 5, UAW, Community Action Program Department Collection; *Detroit News*, Nov. 8, 1949; Coles interview, 17.

[36]"West Side Coordinators Meeting, Wednesday, November 16, 1949," notes, folder 62-11, box 62, UAW, Political Action Committee-Roy Reuther Collection.

[37]"East Side Meeting, Thursday November 17, 9:00 a.m.," notes, p. 6, folder 62-13, box 62, ibid; David Greenstone, "A Report on the Politics of Detroit," unpublished paper, Harvard University, 1961 (Purdy-Kresge Library, Wayne State University); Kevin G. Boyle, "Politics and Principle: The United Automobile Workers and American Labor-Liberalism, 1948–1968" (Ph.D. diss., University of Michigan, Ann Arbor, 1991), 94–100; Ira Katznelson, *City Trenches: Urban Politics and the Patterning of Class in the United States* (New York, 1981); Kevin G. Boyle, "'There Are No Union Sorrows That the Union Can't Heal': The Struggle for Racial Equality in the United Automobile

The new Cobo administration was sympathetic to neighborhood associations. Cobo offered prominent housing and city plan commission appointments to movement leaders. He established an advisory council of civic groups and regularly addressed neighborhood improvement association meetings. In his first weeks of office, he vetoed eight proposed public housing sites in outlying, predominantly white sections of the city.... Orville Tenaglia, the southwest Detroit community leader who had fought public housing throughout the 1940s, wrote Cobo that "we who have come to look upon this community as 'our home,' living with people of our 'own kind,' do most humbly . . . thank you for the courageous stand you have taken" on the housing issue. With the support of grateful home-owners' groups, Republican Cobo won reelection easily in 1951, 1953, and 1955. By advocating and defending "homeowners' rights," he brought the majority of Detroit's whites into a powerful, bipartisan antiliberal coalition.[38]

CIVIL RIGHTS AND "CIVIL WRONGS"

The neighborhood movement's monopoly on Detroit politics was short-lived. Huge numbers of white Detroiters fled the city for the booming suburbs in the 1950s. Detroit's white population fell by more than 23 percent in the 1950s, while its African American population rose by more than 180,000, to nearly one-third of the city's population. By the mid-1950s, blacks had become an increasingly large bloc of voters in Detroit, electing black candidates to citywide offices for the first time and providing a crucial swing vote in many local elections. As black electoral power grew, homeowners' associations lost their stranglehold on the city government and struggled for power against an emerging alliance uniting blacks and a small but vocal population of liberal white activists....[39]

As the racial balance of power in Detroit began to change, civil rights organizations found a new voice and began to challenge the conservative politics of neighborhood associations.... In the early and mid-1950s . . . a coalition of labor activists, religious groups, and African American organizations directed their energies toward racial integration and open housing. They found a powerful ally in the Detroit Mayor's Interracial Committee (MIC), which had been founded

Workers, 1940–1960," *Labor History* 36 (Winter 1995), 5–23; Bruce Nelson, "Race Relations in the Mill: Steelworkers and Civil Rights, 1950–1965," paper delivered at the conference "Toward a History of the 1960s," Madison, Wisconsin, April 1993 (in Thomas J. Sugrue's possession).

[38]On Albert Cobo's appointments, see box 2, Detroit Archives-Mayors' Papers 1951. Detroit Housing Commission, "Monthly Report," Dec. 1949, 1–2, Detroit Housing Commission Folder, box 2, Detroit Archives-Mayors' Papers 1950; Detroit City Plan Commission, Minutes, vol. 16 (1950–1951), 44, Detroit City Plan Commission Collection (Burton Historical Collection); *Detroit Free Press*, March 14, 1950; Orville Tenaglia to Cobo, March 28, 1950, Civic Associations Folder, box 2, Detroit Archives–Mayors' Papers 1950; "Degree of Voting in Detroit Primary," Sept. 11, 1951, folder 62-25, box 62, UAW, Political Action Committee— Roy Reuther Collection.

[39]Greenstone, "Report on the Politics of Detroit," 68; Dudley W. Buffa, *Union Power and American Democracy: The UAW and the Democratic Party, 1935–1972* (Ann Arbor, 1984), 140–41; James Q. Wilson, *Negro Politics: The Search for Leadership* (New York, 1960), 28–30; and Sidney Fine, *Violence in the Model City: The Cavanagh Administration, Race Relations, and the Detroit Riot of 1967* (Ann Arbor, 1988), 3, 6, 16.

after the race riot of 1943 to monitor racial tension in the city and to advocate civil rights reform. Dominated by liberal whites and blacks close to civil rights organizations, the MIC consistently opposed segregation in public housing and other facilities, worked to abolish restrictive covenants, and investigated incidents of racial conflict in the city. . . .[40]

Empowered by the conservative climate of the Cobo administration, neighborhood improvement associations targeted the city's race relations agency. . . .[41] The anti-MIC campaign combined an anti-civil rights stance with antibureaucratic and antitax sentiments. Neighborhood group representatives charged that the MIC wrongfully used public funds to assist civil rights organizations. C. Katherine Rentschler, a member of the Warrendale Improvement Association and chair of Home-Owner Civic and Improvement Associations, accused the "watchdog commission" of "using our TAX MONEY to create agitation." . . . The campaign against the Mayor's Interracial Committee met with success: in 1953, Mayor Cobo restructured the MIC, purged its most liberal members, and appointed two prominent white neighborhood association members to the board. . . .[42]

Even with the temporary defeat of their ally in city government, civil rights groups continued to battle for open housing in Detroit throughout the 1950s. Inspired by the United States Supreme Court's 1948 ruling in *Shelley v. Kraemer* that racially restrictive covenants were legally unenforceable, they launched a campaign to integrate Detroit's neighborhoods. At first their attempts were primarily educational. . . . By the late 1950s, open housing groups moved beyond advocacy to political action. In the mid-1950s, they lobbied the Federal Housing Administration and Home Owners' Loan Corporation to allow blacks to purchase foreclosed houses in white neighborhoods. In 1959, they persuaded the Michigan Department of State to revoke the licenses of real estate brokers who refused to support open housing.[43]

[40]Robert Korstad and Nelson Lichtenstein, "Opportunities Found and Lost: Labor, Radicals, and the Early Civil Rights Movement," *Journal of American History* 75 (Dec. 1988), 786–811. *Brightmoor Journal*, April 20, 1950.

[41]*Brightmoor Journal*, April 5, 1951; Ralph Smith to Cobo, March 23, 1950, Civic Associations Folder, box 2, Detroit Archives–Mayors' Papers 1950.

[42]Home-Owner Civic and Improvement Associations, "Memorandum to Home-Owner Presidents," March 13, 1953, Civic Associations Folder, box 1, Detroit Archives-Mayors' Papers 1953; C. Katherine Rentschler, "Request to Abolish the Present Mayor's Interracial Committee and to Refrain from Authorizing the Proposed Commission on Community Relations," April 7, 1953, ibid.; C. Katherine Rentschler to Detroit Common Council, Aug. 17, 1953, ibid.; *Detroit Focus* (March–April 1954), folder 8-1, box 8, Detroit Urban League Papers; "Statement of the Detroit Branch NAACP Board of Directors Regarding the City of Detroit Commission on Community Relations," Feb. 22, 1954, ibid.; Detroit Urban League, Board of Directors, Minutes of Special Meeting, Jan. 27, 1954, folder 11-18, box 11, ibid.; Cobo to Father John E. Coogan, Jan. 18, 1954, Freedom Agenda Folder, box 71, Citizens Housing and Planning Council Papers.

[43]*Shelley v. Kraemer*, 334 U.S. 1 (1948); William H. Boone, "Major Unmet Goals that Suggest Continuing Attention," March 9, 1956, folder A2-16, box 38, Detroit Urban League Papers; UAW Legal Department to Thomas Kavanagh, Michigan Attorney General, Draft of letter, July 18, 1956, folder A2-17,ibid; Housing Folder, box 10, part I, Metropolitan Detroit Council of Churches Collection; Rose Kleinman Papers (Michigan Historical Collections); and Rose Kleinman Papers (Archives of Labor and Urban Affairs).

As civil rights groups began to agitate for open housing, neighborhood groups began a counterattack. The Federated Property Owners of Detroit, an umbrella organization of neighborhood protective associations, lambasted those who breached the now unenforceable racial covenants. "Property owners violating these principles have larceny in their hearts. They are worse than outlaw hoodlums who hold you up and steal your money. They have blood on their hands for having cut deep into their hearts and homelife." . . . Throughout the 1950s, neighborhood groups pressured "block-busting" real estate agents who sold homes to blacks in predominantly white neighborhoods, petitioned the city government to preserve racially segregated areas, and harassed black newcomers to formerly all-white blocks.[44]

In the early 1960s, the struggle between civil rights and homeowners' rights culminated at the ballot box. At the urging of civil rights groups, the city council drafted and passed a mild Fair Housing Practices Ordinance that . . . prohibited references to race in real estate ads. Open housing groups, however, drafted a stronger ordinance that would outlaw all discrimination in real estate transactions.[45] In response, neighborhood groups proposed a "Homeowners' Rights Ordinance" that would preserve their "rights" to segregated neighborhoods. The competing ordinances pitted blacks, white racial liberals, and civil rights groups against a solidly white, bipartisan, antiliberal coalition.

Leading the anti-open housing movement was Thomas Poindexter, a founder of the Greater Detroit Homeowners' Council. Poindexter, an unsuccessful labor-liberal candidate for the city council in the 1950s, abandoned liberalism in the early 1960s and adopted crabgrass-roots politics with all the fervor of a convert. In August 1963, he testified on behalf of "99 percent of Detroit white residents" to the United States Senate Committee on Commerce (invited by Dixiecrat senator Strom Thurmond) against Kennedy administration civil rights legislation. Poindexter warned that "when integration strikes a previously all-white neighborhood . . . there will be an immediate rise in crime and violence . . . of vice, of prostitution, of gambling and dope." With a "general lowering of the moral standards," racially mixed neighborhoods "will succumb to blight and decay, and the residents will suffer the loss of their homes and savings."[46]

---

[44]*Michigan Chronicle*, Dec. 4, 1948; Eastside Civic Council, Meeting announcement, May 24, 1948, Restrictive Covenants Folder, box 66, Civil Rights Congress of Michigan Papers; "Report on Ruritan Park Civic Association Meetings, September 20, 1956 and November 29, 1956," folder A7-13, box 43, Detroit Urban League Papers; Detroit Commission on Community Relations, Minutes, March 17, 1958, pp. 4–6, Minutes-Jan.–March 1958 Folder, box 2, part IV, Detroit Commission on Community Relations Collection; "Racial Appeals in Primary Election," Aug. 18, 1958, folder 13-28, box 13, part III, ibid.

[45]*Detroit News*, July 14, 1963; Mayor Jerome P. Cavanagh, Statement, Sept. 26, 1963, folder A18-11, box 54, Detroit Urban League Papers; Detroit Commission on Community Relations, Annual Report, 1963, box 2, Kleinman Papers (Archives of Labor and Urban Affairs).

[46]*Ford Facts*, July 10, 1954; Detroit Free Press, Nov. 3, 1963, Nov. 27, 1964; U.S. Congress, Senate, Committee on Commerce, *Civil Rights—Public Accommodations Hearings*, 88 Cong., 1 sess., Aug. 1, 1963, part 2, esp. pp. 1085, 1088.

... Many whites directed a populist rage against both civil rights organizations and their allegedly well-off white supporters. "The hypocrites who scream about the homeowners' refusal to be dictated to by pressure groups and who advocate open housing," wrote one angry woman, "are the very ones who live in ultraexclusive neighborhoods." ... The open housing movement, in their view, elevated minority rights over the rights of the majority. "You can't ram people down people's throats," argued another angry white Detroiter who opposed open housing.[47]

Drawing from the rights rhetoric of the neighborhood movement, the Homeowners' Rights Ordinance pledged to protect the individual's "right to privacy," the "right to choose his own friends and associates," "the right to freedom from interference with his property by public authorities attempting to give special privileges to any group," the "right to maintain what in his opinion are congenial surroundings for himself, his family, and his tenants," and the "right" to choose a real estate broker and tenants and home buyers "for his own reasons." More was at stake than the preservation of rights, for, Poindexter contended, the ordinance would stop "the spread of crime, disease, and neighborhood blight" and the takeover of the city by "persons living on public assistance."[48]

Supporters of the Homeowners' Rights Ordinance quickly collected over forty-four thousand signatures to put it on the 1964 primary ballot.... On Detroit's northeast side, more than two thousand volunteers assisted the campaign. The campaign was remarkably successful.... The ordinance passed by a 55-to-45 margin. In the city's two largest, predominantly white wards, the ordinance passed by a 2-to-1 margin; it lost by nearly 4-to-1 in predominantly African American wards in the inner city.[49] Poindexter capped his efforts by winning a seat on the Common Council, the top vote getter in a thirty-six-candidate field. Although he called himself a "moderate liberal," Poindexter built a base of support among working-class Democrats and middle-class Republicans alike.[50]

---

[47]4Annual Meeting of the Butzel-Guest Property Owners' Association, Housing-Michigan, Detroit, 1956–1964 Folder, box A160, group III, NAACP Papers; Glenna Stalcup to *Detroit News*, Jan. 11, 1965; Ronald P. Formisano, *Boston against Busing: Race, Class, and Ethnicity in the 1960s and 1970s* (Chapel Hill, 1991); and James R. Ralph Jr., *Northern Protest: Martin Luther King, Jr., Chicago, and the Civil Rights Movement* (Cambridge, Mass., 1993), 114–30. Anonymous letter, n.d., Civil Rights Activity Folder, box 9, part I, Metropolitan Detroit Council of Churches Collection; Albert Nahat to *Detroit News*, May 28, 1964.

[48]"Exhibit of Petition, Ordinance, and Ballot Proposed by Greater Detroit Homeowner's Council," Housing-Homeowners' Ordinance-Friendly Statements Folder, box 10, Metropolitan Detroit Council of Churches Collection; *Detroit News*, July 1, July 14, 1963; "Home Owners Ordinance," transcript of WBTM discussion with Thomas Poindexter and Leonard Gordon [c. summer 1964], NAACP v. Detroit-Background Material Folder, box 59, group III (Legal Department Cases), NAACP Papers.

[49]*Michigan Chronicle*, Sept. 12, 1964; East Side Shopper, Sept. 12, 1964; *Detroit Daily Press*, Sept. 3, 1964. "Primary Election Results, City of Detroit," Sept. 1, 1964, *NAACP v. Detroit*-Background Material Folder, box 59, group III (Legal Department Cases), NAACP Papers.

[50]*Detroit Daily Press*, Sept. 3, 1964; ibid., Nov. 11, 1964.

The Homeowners' Rights Ordinance was declared unconstitutional by the Wayne County District Court in 1965 and never implemented. But the language of home-owners' rights remained potent long after the campaign. In the mid-1960s, stalwart northern Democratic voters turned out in cheering crowds of thousands at rallies for Gov. George C. Wallace of Alabama, who derided civil rights, open housing, welfare spending, urban crime, and big government. . . . The politician whose most famous declaration was "Segregation now, segregation forever" found a receptive audience among supposedly liberal northern urban voters. He won the 1972 Michigan Democratic primary, sweeping every predominantly white ward in Detroit. Wallace found some of his most fervent support on Detroit's northwest and northeast sides, the remaining bastions of homeowners' association activity in a city that was 45 percent African American. Following the lead of Wallace, Richard M. Nixon and Spiro Agnew repudiated their party's moderate position on civil rights and wooed disaffected urban and southern white Democrats. They swept predominantly white precincts in Detroit in 1968 and 1972.[51]

The timing of the New Right insurgency gives credence to the thesis of many recent commentators that the Democratic party made a grievous political error in the 1960s by ignoring the needs of white working-class and middle-class voters, in favor of the demands of the civil rights movement, black militants, the counterculture, and the "undeserving" poor. "The close identification of the Democratic party with the cause of racial justice," argues Allen J. Matusow, "did it special injury." Jonathan Rieder contends that the 1960s rebellion of the "silent majority" was in part a response to "certain structural limitations of liberal reform," especially "black demands" that "ran up against the limits of liberalism." Wallace's meteoric rise seems to sustain the argument of Thomas Byrne Edsall and Mary D. Edsall that the Alabama independent "captured the central political dilemma of racial liberalism and the Democratic party: the inability of Democrats to provide a political home for those whites who felt they were paying—unwillingly—the largest 'costs' in the struggle to achieve an integrated society."[52]

The Edsalls, Rieder, and Matusow, although they correctly emphasize the importance of white discontent as a national political force, err in their overemphasis

---

[51]*New York Times*, Oct. 6, 1968, p. 75; ibid., May 18, 1972, p. 36; Election Returns, Wayne County, Michigan, Primary Election 1972, microfilm (Office of the Wayne County Clerk, City-County Building, Detroit, Mich.).

[52]Allen J. Matusow, *The Unraveling of America: A History of Liberalism in the 1960s* (New York, 1984), 438; Jonathan Rieder, "The Rise of the 'Silent Majority,'" in *Rise and Fall of the New Deal Order*, ed. Fraser and Gerstle, 254; Thomas Byrne Edsall and Mary D. Edsall, *Chain Reaction: The Impact of Race, Rights, and Taxes on American Politics* (New York, 1991), 77; Frederick F. Siegel, *The Troubled Journey: From Pearl Harbor to Ronald Reagan* (New York, 1983), esp. 152–215; Jim Sleeper, *The Closest of Strangers: Liberalism and the Politics of Race in New York City* (New York, 1990); Jonathan Rieder, *Canarsie: The Jews and Italians of Brooklyn against Liberalism* (Cambridge, Mass., 1985); and Edward G. Carmines and James A. Stimson, *Issue Evolution: Race and the Transformation of American Politics* (Princeton, 1989); James R. Grossman, "Traditional Politics or the Politics of Tradition?," *Reviews in American History* 21 (Sept. 1993), 533–38; Adolph Reed and Julian Bond, "Equality: Why We Can't Wait," *Nation*, Dec. 9, 1991, pp. 723–37; and Adolph Reed, "Review: Race and the Disruption of the New Deal Coalition," *Urban Affairs Quarterly* 27 (Dec. 1991), 326–33.

on the role of the Great Society and the sixties rebellions in the rise of the "silent majority. "To view the defection of whites from Democratic ranks simply as a reaction to the War on Poverty and the civil rights and black Power movements ignores racial cleavages that shaped the local politics of the North well before the tumult of the 1960s. Urban antiliberalism had deep roots in a simmering politics of race and neighborhood defensiveness that divided northern cities well before Wallace began his first speaking tours in the snowbelt, well before Lyndon B. Johnson signed the Civil Rights Act of 1964, well before the long, hot summers of Watts, Harlem, Chicago, Newark, and Detroit, and well before affirmative action and busing began to dominate the civil rights agenda.

The view of postwar urban politics from Detroit (and from other cities) shows the importance of the politics of race and neighborhood in constraining liberal social reform. From the 1940s through the 1960s, Detroit whites fashioned a language of discontent directed toward public officials, blacks, and liberal reformers who supported public housing and open housing. The rhetoric of George Wallace, Richard M. Nixon, Spiro Agnew, and Ronald Reagan was familiar to the whites who supported candidates such as Edward Jeffries, Albert Cobo, and Thomas Poindexter."[53]

The "silent majority" did not emerge de novo from the alleged failures of liberalism in the 1960s; it was not the unique product of the white rejection of the Great Society. Instead it was the culmination of more than two decades of simmering white discontent and extensive antiliberal political organization. The problem of white backlash in the urban North is longer-lived and far more intractable than recent analyses would suggest. Until we have a greater understanding of the deeply entrenched politics of race in the urban North, our understanding of politics in the contemporary United States will be truncated, and our solutions to the problems of the nation's divided metropolises inadequate.

---

[53]Arnold R. Hirsch, "Chicago: The Cook County Democratic Organization and the Dilemma of Race, 1931–1987," in *Snowbelt Cities: Metropolitan Politics in the Northeast and Midwest Since World War II*, ed. Richard M. Bernard (Bloomington, 1988), 63–90; Richard M. Bernard, "Milwaukee: The Death and Life of a Midwestern Metropolis," ibid., esp. 173–75; Michael Kazin, *The Populist Persuasion: An American History* (New York, 1995), 221–66.

Thomas Sugrue

I am a twentieth-century American historian, with strong interests in modern European (especially British and French) history. I became interested in history during my senior year of high school, when I took an AP history course with Mr. Gerry Moynihan. He was especially interested in colonial history and assigned books and articles on the cutting edge of the field. When I was in college at Columbia, my interests shifted forward to modern American history, with special attention to race, politics, and American cities. I spent two years at King's College, Cambridge, where I studied modern British social, economic, and political history, and earned my Ph.D. at Harvard. I have written books on the struggle for civil rights in the North, on race and inequality and postwar Detroit, and the way in which race in the twentieth century shaped Barack Obama's career as a community organizer, attorney, professor, and presidential candidate. The research in this article can also be found in my book *The Origins of the Urban Crisis: Race and Inequality in Postwar Detroit,* which was awarded the Bancroft Prize for American History. As a modern American historian, I spend a lot of time thinking about how the past shapes our society, politics, and public policy today. I have spent most of my career at the University of Pennsylvania, where I am the David Boies Professor of History and Sociology. In the fall of 2015, I will be joining the faculty at New York University.

QUESTIONS FOR CONSIDERATION

1. According to Sugrue, who within the "New Deal coalition" ultimately revolted against the "consensus" of the 1940s and 1950s? How did economic factors and racial tensions fuel this revolt?

2. Sugrue argues that these Detroiters claimed a "shared a common bond of whiteness and Americanness." How did this claim prove useful in their attempt to maintain the racial exclusivity of Detroit neighborhoods? What other tactics did white Detroiters use to maintain this racial exclusivity?

3. Describe the ways in which white Detroiters used poorer black neighborhoods to justify their racial exclusivity, and later, their flight from the city itself. How did the real estate industry in Detroit help fuel white fears of integration?

4. Describe the process by which liberal reforms came to be perceived after 1945 in racial terms.

5. How did the politics of race transform the rhetoric of local politicians like Detroit mayor Edward Jeffries? How did this change in political rhetoric affect other local political races, like that between George Edwards and Albert Cobo?

6. According to Sugrue, "Many whites directed a populist rage against both civil rights organizations and their allegedly well-off white supporters." In what ways does this represent a continuation of racial politics in the United States, and in what ways does it represent a change? Refer to at least one article you previously read in this volume to support your response.

7. Sugrue claims that conservative politics in the late twentieth century were the "culmination of more than two decades of simmering white discontent and extensive antiliberal political organization." What evidence does he provide for this claim? What evidence could be used to contradict this claim? Feel free to consult your textbook or class notes to help you answer this question.

CHAPTER ELEVEN

From Hash House to Family Restaurant: The Transformation of the Diner and Post–World War II Consumer Culture[1]

Andrew Hurley

George Yonko was a regular patron of the small diner across the street from the Continental Foundry and Machine factory in East Chicago, Indiana. Yonko worked in the factory's machine tool shop during World War II, and every evening at the end of their shift, he and some buddies stopped at the diner for a hamburger. After the war, Yonko noticed an abandoned dining car beside Route 6 in Gary. Aware that this thoroughfare carried hundreds of workers to and from Gary's steel mills each day, Yonko bought the dining car and prepared to develop a business that would replicate his old haunt in East Chicago. It was the archetypical workingman's diner. With a very limited menu that featured chili, hamburgers, french fries, soup, pie, coffee, and milk shakes, the Chuck Wagon Diner quickly developed a regular following among shift workers from the steel mills and people from the neighborhood. . . . The overwhelming majority of the customers were men.[2]

Business was so good that within seven years, Yonko decided to trade in his tiny wooden lunch car for a larger stainless steel unit. He was shrewd enough to realize that to make the new operation profitable he would be wise to diversify his clientele by catering to the burgeoning family market. Observation persuaded him that this was a reasonable proposition. Although most customers at his roadside diner were steelworkers, some patronage came from men and women returning from the movies or other social outings at night. These observations were buttressed by American Restaurant Association seminars he

---

[1]Interested students are encouraged to read this essay in the original form. Andrew Hurley, "From Hash House to Family Restaurant: The Transformation of the Diner and Post–World War II Consumer Culture," *The Journal of American History* 83, 4 (March 1997), 1282–1308.

[2]George Yonko interview by Andrew Hurley, May 23, 1994, transcript, pp. 1–2 (in Andrew Hurley's possession).

attended, where he learned about the nationwide trend toward families' dining out together.

Once Yonko purchased the steel unit, he took aggressive steps to attract and keep new customers. First, Yonko relocated his business on a larger lot that could accommodate automobile parking. Next, he posted billboards along the major highways within a seventy-five-mile radius of his diner, hoping to attract families traveling through Gary on their summer vacations. Yonko expanded his menu to accommodate women and children, introducing special kiddie menus and lighter fare, including salads. Discovering that his new patrons shunned the counter in favor of the booths and tables, Yonko remodeled. Within several years, he dismantled the original counter and added dining room annexes that featured table service. In making these changes, Yonko had created a new consumer space that not only reflected the changing preferences of his customers but also promoted new types of consumer behavior and social interaction.

This article will trace the transformation of an American consumer institution, the diner, from a male, working-class eatery to a middle-income family restaurant, from the perspective of people such as George Yonko. The people who built and owned diners in the years following World War II adapted their trade to dramatic changes in American society—changes that influenced how people spent their money and how they ate their meals. Widespread affluence, massive population movement from city to suburb, a loosening of ethnic affiliations, and unusually high rates of marriage and birth altered people's interrelationships and gave rise to new patterns of behavior. To run successful businesses, diner builders and owners had to read the demographic trends accurately and to anticipate ways to redirect and expand people's engagement in the consumer market. Indeed, as they decided where to put their establishments, how to market their product, what foods to offer, how to allocate interior space, and whom to privilege with access, diner manufacturers and proprietors helped reconfigure the social contours of postwar consumer culture. . . . By locating my inquiry where producers met consumers across a counter, I intend to . . . [show] how post–World War II consumer culture evolved out of new rhythms of daily life and new tensions that surfaced along the borders of class, gender, race, ethnicity, and generation.

In transforming the diner, builders and proprietors created a borderland, a place where cultures intersected, clashed, and sometimes fused. Physically, postwar diners occupied a geographical space between inner-city ethnic neighborhoods and mass-produced suburbs. In social function and orientation, they straddled the worlds of blue-collar work and white-collar domesticity. Historically, they were transitional institutions, a temporal link between the corner saloon and the fast-food restaurant. Diners bridged the transition from a localized, socially fragmented culture of consumption to a more homogenized mass culture dominated by national and multinational corporations. How was this transition accomplished? The story of the postwar diner suggests some ways that purveyors of consumer commodities finessed and exploited emergent social dislocations in the drive to expand and diversify markets. In particular, it highlights the power of the domestic ideal to promote new and unfamiliar patterns of consumption.

This essay will focus on counter-service restaurants constructed in central-ized factories and distributed to independent entrepreneurs who operated them where and how they pleased. About twelve companies manufactured and sold pre-fabricated diners during the late 1940s. . . . Diners produced in those years exhibited remarkable similarity. . . . About six thousand such units did business in the United States in the years just after World War II, most in the East and the upper Midwest.

Prefabricated diners owed their origin to the horse-drawn lunch carts that prowled factory districts at night in the late nineteenth century, offering quick and cheap nourishment to industrial workers. After the turn of the century, when such lunch carts became stationary to accommodate more elaborate cook-ing facilities, operators placed them where industrial laborers predominated. Diners flourished during Prohibition, which eliminated their primary competi-tors, the saloons. They fared well during the depression because of their low prices; some establishments began to sell beer to dissuade patrons from return-ing to the saloons for lunch. By the 1940s, the diner had carved out a niche and had become a familiar sight in factory precincts, along high-volume highways where truckers hauled industrial goods from one city to another, and in down-town retail districts that supported many mechanics, craftsmen, and construc-tion workers.[3]

When World War II ended, most people in the diner industry expected that diners would continue to perform their established social function of serving cheap and hearty food to workingmen. Thus, diner architecture of the immedi-ate postwar years sacrificed aesthetics and comfort to durability, frugality, and speed. Because owners counted on rapid turnover from customers anxious to return quickly to the road or factory floor and because low overhead costs kept food prices down, few dining cars exceeded fifty feet in length or seventeen in width. The standard interior layout featured a long counter in front of a row of densely packed stools, although most models also included booths or tables lined against the front wall or packed tightly on one end. To expedite service, manufac-turers placed cooking facilities directly behind the counter; there was no need to hire waiters or waitresses to carry food from cook to customer. . . . Customers made their selections from signboards above the grill. Manufacturers favored stainless steel for both interiors and exteriors because it was sturdy and required little maintenance.

In catering to the culinary needs of industrial laborers, diners conformed to a consumer culture that bifurcated along class lines. Until the late 1940s, working-class families rarely took meals away from home unless they had to. For most of the first half of the twentieth century, there was little middle ground between the

---

[3]Richard J. S. Gutman, *American Diner: Then and Now* (New York, 1993), 12–112; Blake Ehrlich, "The Diner Puts on Airs," *Saturday Evening Post*, June 19, 1948, pp. 130–31; Jerry O'Mahony, Inc., *Facts and Figures That Will Interest You*, sales brochure, c. 1922, files of Peter Lepera (Georgia-Pacific Corporation, Jarratt, Va.); Kullman Dining Car Company, *Is This Your Opportunity?*, sales brochure, c. 1935, Diner Archives (Kullman Industries, Avenel, N.J.).

elegant dining rooms and tearooms that catered to a leisure class and the greasy spoons that slung hash for the masses. . . .[4]

As working-class institutions, diners were anchored in a culture that was still ethnically fragmented. The majority of diner builders, operators, and customers were immigrants or second-generation Americans. German, Irish, Italian, and Jewish families dominated the manufacturing end of the business; the same groups were well represented among the operators. Diner operators frequently attempted to secure customer loyalty by offering a generous selection of Old World dishes. Because many customers at the Club Car Diner in McKeesport, Pennsylvania, were eastern European immigrants who worked across the street at the U.S. Steel National Tube Works, owner Fred Jamison filled his menu with pierogies, goulash, stuffed cabbage, and halushki, a dish of fried cabbage, onions, and noodles. . . . Abe Kullman, who catered to a predominantly Jewish clientele in Newark, New Jersey, was famous for his potato pancakes; William Ramundo and Florian Walchak featured Hungarian-style stuffed cabbage at the State Diner in Bloomfield, New Jersey.[5]

While ethnic affiliations did much to bind diner builders, operators, and patrons in webs of loyalty, class remained the fundamental social category around which the diner oriented its appeal. As the historian Nelson Lichtenstein observed, the American working class entered the postwar era more homogenized than ever before. Participation in labor unions, the armed forces, public schools, and such class-based forms of mass leisure as bowling leagues and amusement parks provided blue-collar families with a unifying set of experiences, institutions, and aspirations. Diners contributed to this homogenizing trend. Because diners cultivated a constituency from varied ethnic backgrounds, they were sites of cultural amalgamation. Indeed, they fostered a male-oriented, working-class culture. Patronized by regular customers, diners were gathering places where men could banter—often in salty language—about sports, politics, and work. . . .[6]

---

[4]Harvey Levenstein, "Paradox of Plenty: A Social History of Eating in Modern America" (New York, 1993), 28, 45–47; *American Restaurant Magazine*, Market Analysis of the Restaurant Industry (Chicago, 1952), 1–2; Philip Langdon, *Orange Roofs, Golden Arches: The Architecture of American Chain Restaurants* (New York, 1986), 5–25; "Layouts for Locations," *Fountain & Fast Food Service* 49 (Oct. 1951), 33–35, 74.

[5]Don Bailey (owner, Summit Diner, Somerset, Pa.) interview by Hurley, July 2, 1993, transcript, p. 3 (in Hurley's possession); Mike Zappone (owner, Mr. Z's, Cleveland, Ohio) interview by Hurley, July 24, 1995, transcript, p. 1, ibid.; Harold Kullman interview by Hurley, June 1, 1994, transcript, p. 1, ibid.; Johnny Rogers, "State Diner Sets New Concept in City Diner–Restaurant Operation," *Fountain, Luncheonette, and Diner* 1 (June 1954), 16.

[6]Nelson Lichtenstein, "The Making of the Postwar Working Class: Cultural Pluralism and Social Structure in World War II" *Historian* 51 (Nov. 1988), 42–55. See also Cohen, *Making a New Deal*, 324–57; and Rosenzweig, *Eight Hours for What We Will*, 171–221. Yonko interview, 3. On menus, see Marvin Zelin (owner, Market Diner, New York, N.Y.) interview by Hurley, Dec. 29, 1982, transcript, p. 4 (in Hurley's possession); Alfred Welte (owner, Miss America Diner, Jersey City, N.J.) interview by Hurley, Jan. 7, 1983, transcript, p. 3, ibid; Lester Bammesberger (former owner, Lester's Diner, Cortland, N.Y.).

While informality, coarse language, and heavy food accounted for much of the diner's popularity among male wage earners, the same qualities repelled those who upheld standards of middle-class etiquette and respectability. Some older dining cars lacked toilet facilities, and the managers of some newer ones were indifferent to hygiene and cleanliness. Popular magazines and radio programs often portrayed diners as hovels, gambling dens, and magnets for the socially undesirable. . . . Many people associated all diners with such places as Steffie's Diner, a truck driver's rest stop in Gary, Indiana, that was regularly raided by the vice squad and ultimately shut down by the local health commissioner. . . .[7] Moreover, such attributes deterred women, regardless of their class background. . . . When one puzzled lunch car aficionado asked several female friends to explain their disdain for diners, they said the buildings looked dingy, the stools were uncomfortable, and the countermen were rude.[8]

By the late 1940s, operators had discovered that the traditional diner market was in deep trouble. Establishments in inner-city industrial districts suffered from a declining customer base as manufacturers relocated to suburbs where land was cheap and abundant. Moreover, many of the new manufacturing plants housed their own cafeterias. . . . Thus, many diners found their traditional customer base pulled from underneath them, and some went out of business. Sometimes entire cities were abandoned by the diner industry. Pat Fodero recalled that when he began working with his father at the Fodero Dining Car Company just after World War II, much of their business came from small northeastern cities with large blue-collar populations. By the 1950s, industrial flight from such towns as Trenton, New Jersey, and Gloucester, Massachusetts, devastated that market. Older industrial districts that still thrived were already saturated with diners, and they presented few opportunities

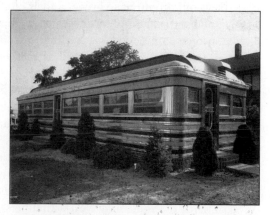

Photo 11.1
This diner, manufactured by the Fodero Dining Car Company during the 1940s, was typical of the compact units sold in the yards just after World War II. Printed with permission of the Diner Archives of Richard J. S. Gutman.

---

[7]"All Nite Diner," *Diner* 7 (Aug. 1948), 29; "Editorial: Correction, Please," ibid., 5. According to a 1949 survey, 19% of diners and lunch-counter restaurants lacked restrooms. See "An Objective Study of the Diner–Counter Service Restaurant Market," ibid., 8 (special supplement, 1949), 5. Newspaper clipping, *Gary Post-Tribune*, c. 1949, scrapbook, Philip Rosenbloom Collection (Calumet Regional Archives, Gary, Ind.).

[8]Ehrlich, "Diner Puts on Airs," 133; George H. Waltz Jr., "The Roadside Diners Are Rolling," *Coronet* 34 (Sept. 1953), 133; A. D. Wayne to editor, *Diner* 5 (Aug. 1946), 4.

for prospective operators. Manufacturers and aspiring operators began search-ing for alternative locations and customers.[9]

As they surveyed the market and observed changes in their clientele, they found reasons to be optimistic. If they read trade journals, they learned that Americans were eating away from home more than ever before. Restaurant patronage had grown sharply during the war, not only because people had more money to spend but also because busy work schedules and food shortages made domestic dining difficult. Many of the new restaurant customers were women who had entered the full-time labor force as machine operators, office workers, and retail clerks. Initially, market analysts expected that the return of peace and the exodus of women from the work force would resuscitate prewar dining pat-terns. The experts were wrong; Americans continued eating out in record num-bers. If some diners lost patronage, plenty of others, especially those located outside industrial districts, had more business than they could handle.[10]

Moreover, many proprietors were attracting a more diversified clientele than in prewar years. In addition to ladling goulash for hungry laborers and pouring coffee for tired truckers, countermen found themselves frying scrambled eggs for executives on their way to work, preparing sandwiches for female clerical work-ers on lunch breaks, and slicing pie for couples streaming out of nightclubs and movie theaters. Industry leaders were confident that if they took appropriate steps, they could continue to broaden their constituency, making inroads into a largely untapped market of businessmen, high school kids, young couples, and middle-income families. As one diner manufacturer informed prospective clients in a sales brochure, a $12 billion market awaited the operator who was willing to play "host to everyone."[11]

The most immediate decision confronting owners who wanted a slice of that market was where to do business. . . . Through the 1950s, most diner manufac-turers produced about 25 new diners each year, for an annual total of between 200 and 250 new diners for the whole industry.[12] Increasingly, however, the new diners found their way to unconventional locations: suburban shopping centers, well-heeled residential neighborhoods, seaside resorts, and small college towns. Several manufacturers decided that the time was right to pursue a national strat-egy, colonizing the South and West with diners. The Jerry O'Mahony Company, of Elizabeth, New Jersey, the nation's largest diner builder, opened a plant in St. Louis, Missouri, in 1952 to infiltrate the largely untapped West. By 1956, another

[9]American Restaurant Magazine, *Market Analysis of the Restaurant Industry*, 1; Pat Fodero interview by Hurley, Sept. 17, 1993, transcript, p. 4 (in Hurley's possession).

[10]"Nutrition . . . A Public Demand," *Diner* 5 (July 1946), 6; *American Restaurant Magazine*, Market Analysis of the Restaurant Industry, 1–4; A. J. Brady to editor, *Diner* 6 (Feb. 1947), 4.

[11]Mike Flynn, "I Just Got Back from Lunch," *Diner* 5 (Sept. 1946), 22; Ernie Gisin, "A La Carte," ibid. (Aug. 1946), 20; "Nutrition . . . A Public Demand," 6; Mountain View Diners, *A Modern Tribute to Good Taste*, sales brochure, c. 1949, p. 2, Diner Archives.

[12]Harold Kullman interview by Hurley, Jan. 5, 1983, transcript, p. 3 (in Hurley's possession); Jerry Manno interview by Hurley, Jan. 7, 1983, transcript, p. 3, ibid.; "The Diner Business," *Fortune* 46 (July 1952), 167; Ehrlich, "Diner Puts on Airs," 133.

New Jersey manufacturer, Mountain View Diners . . . had already shipped units to Louisiana, Washington, Arizona, Iowa, and Wisconsin. But most diner manufacturers hewed to a more conservative line, directing business to places where people were familiar with diners and where proprietors could hang on to older customers while they tried to attract new ones. . . .[13]

Over adventurous operators and builders frequently ran into trouble when they tried to place diners in unfamiliar territory. In the 1930s, exclusive suburbs and vacation resorts fought the intrusion of diners, and such opposition persisted through the 1960s. In April 1934 *The New York Times* reported that the Drake Road Neighborhood Association in Scarsdale, New York, an upscale suburb, was enraged by a bright yellow lunch wagon that had recently appeared in the center of town. Condemning the diner as an eyesore, detracting from their town's quaint, country village architecture, the angry homeowners insisted on its immediate removal. Elsewhere, town councils passed legislation to prevent such intrusions on the landscape. . . .[14]

Manufacturers steered new proprietors to safer locations where diners were not yet abundant but where people were already acquainted with them. A 1949 advice column in an industry trade journal counseled would-be proprietors to stick with rapidly growing blue-collar communities that contained a high proportion of high-income wage earners. Jerry Manno remembered that when his diner-manufacturing company scouted sites for potential customers in the early 1950s, it looked for suburban neighborhoods populated by second-generation Jewish Americans and Italian Americans. The response to such advice was a pronounced shift in diner geography as new diners gravitated to a zone of transition between inner-city neighborhoods and mass-produced suburbs: residential communities on the fringe of cities that were experiencing an influx of upwardly mobile, middle-income families of recent European extraction. . . .[15] In Baltimore, Maryland, Newark, New Jersey, and New York, New York, the picture was much the same; diners flourished in rapidly growing residential areas with a solid base of affluent blue-collar workers. . . .[16]

---

[13]On diner locations, see "Over the Counter," *Diner and Restaurant* 11 (Dec. 1952), 35. Jerry O'Mahony, Inc., fact sheet, Oct. 1952, p. 2 (American Diner Museum, Providence, R.I.); Mountain View Diners, Inc., "Offering Circular," June 20, 1956, p. 3, Diner Archives; Mountain View Diners, *A Modem Tribute to Good Taste*, 14.

[14]*The New York Times*, April 23, 1934, p. 18; Ehrlich, "Diner Puts on Airs."

[15]"Pick Your Spot Scientifically," *Diner* 8 (Feb. 1949), 15–16; Manno interview, 1. Another diner builder, Harold Kullman, confirmed that diners were most successful in these neighborhoods. Kullman interview, June 1, 1994, p. 2.

[16]U.S. Bureau of the Census, *U.S. Census of Population: 1950*, vol. II: *Characteristics of the Population*, pt. 30: *New Jersey* (Washington, D.C., 1952), 36, 80; U.S. Bureau of the Census, *U.S. Census of Population: 1960*, vol. I: *Characteristics of the Population*, pt. 32: *New Jersey* (Washington, D.C., 1963), 93, 198, 226, 254, 284; Bureau of the Census, *U.S. Census of Population: 1950*, III, 16–21, 35–39, 46–47; U.S. Bureau of the Census, *U.S. Censuses of Population and Housing: 1960, Census Tracts, Final Report PHC (1)–13* (Washington, D.C., 1962), 26–28, 40–41, 101, 113–14, 126–27, 151, 165–66, 174, 181–82.

Diner owners did not always shy away from white-collar areas. It was not uncommon to find new diners in white-collar areas where second- and third-generation Americans had recently leaped the collar line. After scouting locations for several years, the owners of the Claremont Diner selected a busy intersection in Verona, New Jersey, where they developed a following among the largely white-collar Jewish residents of the surrounding neighborhoods. . . .[17]

Within these transitional suburban neighborhoods, proprietors sought to maximize their access to customers by placing their units along busy commercial thoroughfares. Diner owners clearly expected to do business with local residents. . . . Directing his appeal to local homemakers, Roland Michel, who operated a diner across from an A&P supermarket, advertised that a "delicious meal or tempting snack" at the Cape Ann Diner was a perfect way to take a break from shopping chores. The real virtue of locating in a commercial strip, however, was that it enabled proprietors to tap into a virtually limitless metropolitan transient trade. A diner with a spacious parking lot and an eye-catching neon sign next to a highway entrance ramp, sports arena, regional airport, or string of budget motels was well positioned to complement its local business with vacationers, truckers, and motorists traveling to and from work. Joe Swingle probably knew as much about opportune locations as anyone in the business, having worked as a sales agent for the Fodero Dining Car Company for many years. When he purchased his own diner in 1953, he placed it on Route 22 in the rapidly growing suburb of Springfield, New Jersey. There he anticipated patronage not only from local residents but also from nearby factory and office workers and motorists on their way to and from New York City.[18]

Operators such as Swingle who hoped to cultivate a diversified clientele faced a daunting task. Satisfying the demands of customers with very different needs and sensibilities emerged as the primary challenge for the diner industry in the 1950s. The assumption that a working-class institution could be remolded to suit a more diversified clientele presupposed a cultural fluidity that people in the industry could not be sure existed. Moreover, doing business in transitional suburban neighborhoods bound owners and builders to an unpredictable constituency that was crossing all sorts of social borders and reevaluating its cultural expectations. Decisions about what features of the diner to retain and what to add would test entrepreneurs' capacity to gauge how far consumers might venture across unfamiliar cultural borders and to identify points where divergent cultures might converge.

---

[17]Bureau of the Census, *U.S. Censuses of Population and Housing: 1960, Census Tracts, Final Report PHC (1)–13*, pp. 26–28, 40–41, 101, 113–14, 126–27, 151, 165–66, 174, 181–82; U.S. Bureau of the Census, *U.S. Censuses of Population and Housing: 1960, Census Tracts, Final Report PHC (1)–104*, pt. 2 (Washington, D.C., 1962), 26, 31, 160, 165; Bureau of the Census, *U.S. Census of Population: 1960*, vol. I, pt. 32, pp. 232, 280; "They're Standing in Line for Hours at New Jersey's New Claremont Diner!," *Fountain, Luncheonette, and Diner* 1 (Nov. 1954), 15.

[18]"Godfrey Diner," 12; "Wednesday and Thursday . . . Michel's Cape Ann Diner Will Donate 10% to the G.H.S. football team for their Florida trip," newspaper clipping, c. 1955 (American Diner Museum); Albert S. Keshen, "A Diner Man's Diner," *Diner, Drive-In, and Restaurant* 13 (Jan. 1954), 11.

Photo 11.2
Note that all of the customers at the counter are men.
Even as diner owners reoriented their businesses to the
family trade, the counter remained a primarily male
preserve. Courtesy Prints and Photos Division, Library of Congress.

The chief strategy that the industry used to expand its market across social
and cultural borders was to repackage the diner as a middle-income family restaurant. In the lexicon of the trade, "family" replaced "workingman" as the basic
social unit to which the diner yoked its reputation. Proprietors went to elaborate
lengths to attract more families and to secure the loyalty of women and children
by making diners more pleasant, more comfortable, and, above all, more respectable. Indeed, efforts to transform the diner into a family institution were often
indistinguishable from efforts to upgrade the social cachet of eating in a diner. In
an era when middle-class status was synonymous with consumption rituals
organized around the nuclear household, domesticating the diner became the
key to attaining social respectability. Transforming the diner from an extension
of the factory floor to an extension of the suburban home would make the diner
acceptable, if not hospitable, to a wide range of potential clients.

To remake the diner as a family institution, proprietors must first lure families out of their homes at dinner time. . . . In addition to emphasizing the modest
cost of dining out, the advertisements usually played upon the theme of familial
obligations. Commercial dining was portrayed as an antidote to domestic drudgery and a catalyst for family cohesion. . . . Kintz Diner, in Fort Wayne, Indiana,
advertised its "special Sunday dinners" with the slogan: "Sure mother is a won-
derful cook. But what a treat it is for her to dine out at least once a week with the
family."[19]

These appeals rested on the assumption that temporary relief from domestic
duties would prove attractive to women, especially to the growing numbers of

---

[19]Clifford Edward Clark Jr., *The American Family Home*, 1800–1960 (Chapel Hill, 1986),
207–10; "Enjoy Life! Eat Out More Often," *American Restaurant Magazine* 34 (July 1950), 43; "Enjoy
Life!–Eat Out More Often," ibid., 35 (July 1951), 49.

Photo 11.3
The Peter Pan Diner in New Caster, Delaware, 1957. Its
ten-foot cutout of Peter Pan advertised the diner's family
atmosphere to passersby. Courtesy General Research Division,
The New York Public Library, Astor, Lenox and Tilden Foundations.

wives who held part- or full-time jobs during the 1950s to help finance families'
expanding consumer budgets. Roughly 30 to 40 percent of women who lived in
transitional suburban neighborhoods worked outside the home.[20] It was not only
working women, however, who welcomed dining away from home as a respite
from cooking and cleaning. . . . A 1959 study indicated . . . wives were twice as
likely as their husbands to suggest that the family eat a meal away from home.[21]
Thus a marketing strategy that targeted women without challenging conventional domestic roles made good sense.

So did strategies that targeted children. Presaging a tactic that underwrote
the McDonald's fast-food empire, some diner proprietors reasoned that if they
secured the loyalty of children, they would capture the patronage of doting parents as well. Among them was Bill Noller, who ran a diner in the resort community of Beach Haven, New Jersey, during the 1950s. He remembered, "We had
kiddie menus, adequate high chairs. No girls with a sour look on their face when
kids came in. We'd give kids a lollipop and a bib and make them feel at home." In
Butler, Pennsylvania, Herman Dight used plates depicting nursery rhyme characters to encourage children to eat all their food in order to see the drawings.
William Martindale targeted children by naming his Delaware establishment the
Peter Pan Diner and by erecting a ten-foot cutout of the fictional character on his

---

[20]U.S. Bureau of the Census, *U.S. Census of Population, 1950*, vol. III, ch. 4, pp. 16–21, 35–39,
46–47; ibid., ch. 42, pp. 20–29, 75–98; ibid., vol. II, pt. 30, pp. 36, 80; Bureau of the Census, *U.S.
Censuses of Population and Housing: 1960, Census Tracts, Final Report PHC (1)–13*, pp. 26–28,
40–41, 101, 113–14, 126–27, 151, 165–66, 174, 181–82; Bureau of the Census, *U.S. Censuses of Population and Housing: 1960, Census Tracts, Final Report, PHC (1)–15*, pp. 30–48, 252–70; Bureau of the
Census, *U.S. Census of Population: 1960*, vol. I, pt. 32, pp. 93, 198, 226, 254, 284.

[21]Kathy Corbett interview by Hurley, June 21, 1995, transcript, p. 2 (in Hurley's possession);
"Why Do They Eat Out?," *American Restaurant Magazine* 43 (May 1959), 212.

Photo 11.4
Inside the Peter Pan Diner, 1957, a waitress offers a
children's menu shaped like a Peter Pan character to a
family seated in a booth. Note the table-side jukebox,
which many proprietors installed to attract teenagers.
Courtesy General Research Division, The New York Public Library, Astor,
Lenox and Tilden Foundations.

roof. Martindale gave children colorful Peter Pan masks, with a children's menu
featuring meals named Tinker Bell, Never, Never Land, and Captain Hook on
the back.[22]

As the examples illustrate, transforming the diner into a family restaurant
required proprietors and builders to reconstruct the entire diner experience.
Incrementally, diner owners made innovations that meshed better with suburban rhythms, domestic norms, and the practical and psychological needs of
middle-income families. During the 1950s, proprietors relayed shifting consumer tastes to the builders, propelling a rapid evolution of diner architecture.

Within the diner, seating arrangements favored tables and booths over the
counter. Large upholstered booths, in particular, offered advantages over the
counter-and-stool arrangement for operators intent on attracting family groups
because they could accommodate four, five, or even six patrons at a time, and
because they offered privacy. . . .[23]

Diners relying on the family trade and on large groups also required more
space, not only because tables and booths took up more room but also because
families and customers who were socializing often lingered over their meals,
slowing turn-over. To handle the swelling volume, many proprietors added separate dining rooms to their units. In the first years after the war, several dining car
companies did a healthy business selling dining room annexes. Eventually, the

---

[22]Bill Noller interview by Hurley, Aug. 11, 1982, transcript, p. 4 (in Hurley's possession); "Diner
Host of Western Pennsylvania," *Diner and Restaurant* 11 (Nov. 1952), 18; "Martindale's Peter Pan
Diner," *Diner, Drive–In* 16 (April 1957), 26–29.

[23]Earle Hersman interview by Hurley, July 24, 1955, transcript, p. 1 (in Hurley's possession);
Chip Silverman, *Diner Guys* (New York, 1989), 29–30, 39.

builders constructed larger diners and offered dining room extensions as a standard option on their prefabricated units. By the late 1950s, manufacturers delivered diners that measured two thousand square feet and seated more than one hundred patrons at a time, most of them at private "family-sized" booths.[24]

In the 1950s proprietors also devoted attention to the ambience of their establishments. The cold, industrial look appropriate to an eatery functioning as an extension of the workplace seemed inappropriate to an institution trying to pass itself off as a dignified family restaurant. Charles Taxin extensively remodeled to attract new customers, especially families. His aim was to upgrade the "appearance and atmosphere," so that "customers would feel they were eating in a better quality restaurant." . . .[25]

As operators strove to provide a more pleasurable and comfortable dining experience, air conditioning emerged as a standard feature of diners in the 1950s. During the 1940s, most manufacturers simply placed electric fans in their units to facilitate air circulation. Operators who ran diners in hot climates, such as Harvey Hale, proprietor of the Park Terrace Grill in Clearwater, Florida, did not deem fans sufficient. In 1950, Hale installed two, twenty-ton air-conditioning units on his own, a move he later cited as the major reason why his became one of the first diners in Florida to succeed. In response to the growing demand for air conditioning, in Florida and other places where it grew uncomfortably hot, manufacturers began fitting diners with ductwork that would accommodate cooling equipment. By the early 1950s, some companies were installing air conditioning prior to shipment.[26]

These changes closely paralleled architectural trends in middle- and upper-income suburban homes. The materials that diner builders turned to in the 1950s—Formica, vinyl, and terrazzo—were also appearing in middle-class kitchens, foyers, and basements. . . . The expansive picture windows that provided visual continuity between the diner interior and the parking lot corresponded to the glass walls characteristic of the popular split-level and ranch-style homes. Although air conditioning remained a rarity in working-class homes, climate-controlled interiors were available to upper-income suburbanites.[27] By constructing diners of the latest materials, decorating them in the most up-to-date styles, and fitting them with the most modern equipment, proprietors established an

---

[24]This information was gleaned from the monthly "Over the Counter," column in Diner and its subsequent incarnations—Diner and Counter Restaurant; Diner and Restaurant; Diner, Drive-In; and Diner, Drive-In, and Restaurant—between 1946 and 1959. This column reported sales of new diners and dining room annexes with information about floor space and seating capacities. Sales brochures issued by diner builders contain comparable information. Kullman Dining Car Company, New Space Age Design, sales brochure, c. 1960, Diner Archives.

[25]"How Taxins Raised Prices," Diner, Drive-In 17 (Feb. 1958), 42–43; Johnny Rogers, "The Magic of the Mari-Nay Diner," Fountain, Luncheonette, and Diner 1 (Oct. 1954), 10.

[26]Worcester Diners, There's More Money in Worcester Diners, sales brochure, [1947], p. 5 (Worcester Public Library, Worcester, Mass.); "40 Years of Diners," Diner, Drive-In 16 (July 1957), 22–25; "Over the Counter," Diner and Restaurant 12 (Nov. 1953), 24.

[27]Gwendolyn Wright, Building the Dream: A Social History of Housing in America (New York, 1981), 249–54; Clark, American Family Home, 210–12.

aesthetic and even a technological link between public consumption and private home life, thereby assuring mothers and fathers that in visiting the diner they were not shirking familial responsibilities.

Perhaps the most dramatic change made by diner builders and owners in response to new consumer sensibilities was to move the grill from behind the counter to a separate kitchen behind the diner. As one veteran New York City operator recalled, "When the war ended, the desire to see food prepared in front of you decreased. . . . People didn't want greasy spoons. The griddleman was greasy."[28] Placing all cooking facilities in a back room removed the griddleman and his greasy operation from the customer's sight.

With cooking performed out of sight and increased seating at booths, someone had to carry food from kitchen to customer. Operators turned to women to wait on tables, a move that not only solved a practical problem but went a long way toward domesticating the diner. Waitresses helped dispel the notion that diners were all-male establishments. James Mears was ahead of his time when he opened his Deluxe Diner in New Jersey, in 1946. Not only did Mears anticipate the postwar consumer binge, unveiling what he claimed was the largest diner in the world, he also pioneered the use of female employees. As he explained to Diner magazine shortly after his grand opening, "Women belong in restaurants as waitresses, hostesses and cashiers. They give an atmosphere to your place which encourages the family trade."[29]

Catering to families and people from all walks of life also required changes in cuisine. Ernest Weber, a European-trained chef at the Village Diner in Tuckahoe, New York, spoke for many in the industry when he explained, "we have a fight on our hands to correct this impression . . . [that diners] are hash houses where most people grab a cup of coffee and gulp down a hamburger." To correct that impression, diners showcased more elaborate menus. Operators added salads and fountain drinks to bring in more women, children, and teenagers. Many also expanded the choices—adding steaks and seafood—to suit a clientele with an increasingly sophisticated palate. . . .[30]

To accommodate second- and third-generation Americans of varied ethnic backgrounds, suburban diners eliminated the most exotic ethnic foods from their menus. Although recent immigrants, particularly Greeks, continued to dominate the proprietary end of the business, they purposefully underplayed their ethnic roots in the effort to appeal to diverse suburban populations. . . . Angelo and Fanny Blentsen made a similar decision after emigrating from Greece and opening several diners in Virginia in the late 1950s and early 1960s. Although their Blue Star Diner might have catered to the sizable Greek community in Newport News, the Blentsens decided not to emphasize their native cuisine except to offer a Greek salad. Fanny Blentsen recalled that if friends or relatives requested a special

---

[28]Zelin interview, 2.

[29]"Completely Deluxe," *Diner* 6 (Jan. 1947), 11.

[30]"The Diner Goes to a Party," ibid., 5 (Nov. 1946), 11; Noller interview, 4–5.

Greek dish, she was happy to oblige. Otherwise, she served standard American fare: steaks, hamburgers, chicken, and seafood.[31]

Blentsen's decision to retain the Greek salad symbolized the advent of a more pluralistic American cuisine in the postwar era. The appearance of pasta and tomato sauce, albeit without heavy garlic and spices, on dinner tables across the country during the depression signaled middle-class Americans' willingness to accept food items that had once been considered exotic. The retention of selected ethnic items on suburban diner menus carried the trend forward into the postwar years. Fried chicken, hamburgers, steaks, seafood, and meat sandwiches became the common denominators in a uniform selection of foods, but it was not unusual to find kosher-style sandwiches, spaghetti and meatballs, and Greek salads listed alongside these old standbys, even where diners catered to eclectic audiences. . . .[32]

Proprietors retained certain elements to attract the continued patronage of factory workers and truckers. While counter space was incrementally sacrificed for more comfortable booth and table seating in the 1950s—some diner counters extended only half the length of the unit—no manufacturer entirely eliminated the counter-and-stool arrangement.[33]

Customer resistance prevented some proprietors from dismantling specific features of the working-class diner. When Harry Zelin opened his sixth Market Diner on the West Side of Manhattan in 1958, he wanted an up-to-date operation. So he dispensed with the traditional overhead signboards and relied exclusively on individualized menus. But the longshoremen and truckers who frequented the restaurant demanded that Zelin install the old-fashioned menu boards so the place "would be more like a diner." Afraid of losing significant business, Zelin complied. . . .[34]

Despite concerted and partly successful efforts to construct a more socially inclusive consumer venue, class, gender, and generational divisions did not dissolve in the diner. They continued to be a source of tension. While diner owners tended to tout their establishments as the epitome of democratic social interaction, the evidence indicates an uneasy integration of classes, sexes, and generations within diners. Customers diverged in the way they used the diner, and proprietors often encouraged social segregation within the diner as a way of mediating competing cultural standards and consumer needs.

By retaining the counter, even in a truncated form, proprietors preserved a male domain within the diner. While booth seating, lighter fares, and redecorated

---

[31]William H. Whyte Jr., *The Organization Man* (New York, 1956), 300; Bailey interview, 3; Fanny Blentsen interview by Hurley, Aug. 6, 1993, transcript, p. 1 (in Hurley's possession).

[32]Levenstein, *Paradox of Plenty*, 30; "Menu Exchange," *Diner, Drive-In* 14 (Sept. 1955), 26; "Menu Exchange," ibid., 15 (May 1956), 44; "Menu Exchange," ibid., 16 (March 1957), 29; postcard, Meadowbrook Diner, 1954, photocopy displayed on wall of Connie's Soul Food Kitchen, Indianapolis, Ind.

[33]"Trends in Diner Construction," *Diner and Counter Restaurant* 10 (Aug. 1951), 28–30; Phil DeRaffele interview by Hurley, June 30, 1994, transcript, p. 2 (in Hurley's possession).

[34]"'Truck Stop' in Manhattan," *Diner, Drive-In* 17 (March 1958), 37; Paterson Vehicle Company, *Quality Diners That Make Excellent Profits*, sales brochure, c. 1960, folder 2, series IV, box 1, Grinwis Collection (Passaic County Historical Society, Paterson, NJ.); "Jet Diner with Rocket Service," *Fountain, Luncheonette, and Diner* 1 (Nov. 1954), 24–25.

interiors increased female patronage substantially, with some proprietors reporting nearly even numbers of women and men, male customers monopolized the
counter stools. As the area where truckers and solitary workers preferred to con-
gregate, the counter remained the one place in the diner where one could still
engage in coarse banter and argue about an upcoming horse race. . . .[35]

Proprietors also carved out distinctive spaces for potentially unruly teenagers. The teenage market was a lucrative one, and the installation of jukeboxes and
soda fountains testified to proprietors' interest in capturing it. But a national
preoccupation with juvenile delinquency, fueled by the threatening music of
Elvis Presley and the defiant images of James Dean and Marlon Brando, raised
the possibility that diners might shed a disreputable working-class reputation for
an equally undesirable identification as hangouts for rebels without a cause.
Hence, some proprietors sequestered youths in separate dining sections. . . . To
the relief of many diner owners, the potential clash of generational cultures was
averted by disparate schedules. Teenagers tended to use diners just after school or
late at night, times when families were unlikely to stop in. . . .[36]

The clock also turned out to be a convenient tool for segregating diner
patrons by class. At noon and midnight, workers from the Curtiss-Wright plant
streamed into Doyle's Diner in Lodi, New Jersey, for quick lunches. In between,
however, Doyle's sold meals to neighborhood families. When Eunice Fischer, a
waitress at the Beach Haven Diner on the New Jersey coast, arrived for work at
5 A.M., the place swarmed with commercial fishermen wolfing down quick
breakfasts before heading out to sea. Only much later did vacationers from New
York and Philadelphia arrive for their morning meal. . . .[37]

However incomplete the blending of class, generational, and gender cultures
in the 1950s diner, it contrasted sharply with almost universal persistence of racial
segregation. Despite the potential market created by an expanding black middle
class and the growing number of African American travelers, before the 1960s
most road-side diners refused to admit black patrons. While segregation was
more pervasive in southern states where both law and custom underpinned Jim
Crow practices, it held in many mid-Atlantic and midwestern states as well. . . .[38]

---

[35]Welte interview, 2.

[36]Albert S. Keshen, "Capturing the School Lunch Trade," *Diner, Drive-In, and Restaurant* 13
(Oct. 1954), 20; C. Thomas, "The Little Chickadees," *Diner* 6 (Aug. 1947), 8; "How the Triangle
House Diner Quadrupled Sales," *Diner, Drive-In* 15 (Sept. 1955), 22–23; Henry Scarupa, "Director
by Default," *Baltimore Sun Magazine*, Aug. 9, 1981, p. 15.

[37]"Two Peak Periods Pull 1,500 Checks at Doyle's Diner, Lodi, NJ.," *Fountain, Luncheonette,
and Diner* 1 (July–Aug. 1954), 20–21; Eunice Fischer interview by Hurley, Aug. 11, 1982, transcript,
p. 5 (in Hurley's possession).

[38]Eunice Ramsey (waitress, Tastee Diner, Silver Spring, Md.) interview by Hurley, Aug. 5, 1993,
transcript, p. 1 (in Hurley's possession); Connie Smith (owner, Connie's Soul Food Kitchen, formerly Meadowbrook Diner, Indianapolis, Ind.) interview by Hurley, Aug. 20, 1993, transcript, p. 1,
ibid.; Blentsen interview, 2. On racial discrimination in other diners, see Brian Butko, "Seen Any
Good Diners Lately," *Pittsburgh History* 73 (Fall 1990), 105; and U.S. Congress, Senate, *A Bill to
Eliminate Discrimination in Public Accommodations Affecting Interstate Commerce*, 88 Cong., 1
sess., Aug. 1, 1963, pp. 1063–81.

Even where overt racial discrimination was not practiced, residential segregation effectively preserved diners as white institutions. Through the 1950s, suburbanization was primarily a white phenomenon; as diners migrated to the outskirts of cities, segregation did not require any formal policy of discrimination. The few African Americans who passed through such areas were extremely cautious about patronizing restaurants, unsure of how their appearance would be greeted. Hence, when the owners of the Club Car Diner opened a new establishment on one of Pittsburgh's suburban thoroughfares, they found little reason to institute a segregation policy because, as one manager put it, "Blacks would have been reluctant to walk into a place like that."[39]

The significance of the diner's transformation can be better appreciated in the context of a changing commercial dining industry. As restaurants with different historical origins converged on the middle-income family market, commercial dining formulas and styles were synthesized into a uniform standard. This was not good news for the diner industry; as the diner lost its distinctiveness, it also lost its competitive edge.

In the 1950s, diners faced increasing competition from a profusion of new restaurant types: family restaurant chains, California-style coffee shops, drive-ins, and, ultimately, fast-food outlets. These competing eateries shared many characteristics with the suburban diner, and such similarities intensified as their managers adopted comparable marketing strategies. But none carried the diner's burden of trying to shed a working-class heritage.

... Howard Johnson's gained its reputation as a purveyor of high-butterfat-content ice cream at New England seaside resorts during the 1920s and 1930s before branching out to key locations along the new interstate highways. Decorated in the style of a middle-class living room, the restaurant featured knotty-pine wall paneling, window curtains, and small table lamps. A neocolonial exterior paid homage to the nation's prerevolutionary heritage; its featured menu items—hot dogs and ice cream—were quintessentially American. With its uniformed waitresses, extensive soda fountain service, and unique architecture, Howard Johnson's became a familiar beacon to middle-class families on the road who wanted simple food in a homey yet dignified atmosphere.[40]

Drive-ins capitalized on America's love affair with the automobile, a consumer commodity widely associated with suburban affluence. Eating in one's car was as close as one could get to going out for a meal while remaining in the

---

[39]Of the 24 diners that opened in Queens, New York, whose locations could be ascertained, only 2 were in neighborhoods where more than 1% of the population was African American. In those two exceptional neighborhoods, African Americans constituted 6% and 7% of the population. Information on locations is from listings of new openings in the trade journals *Diner, Diner and Counter Restaurant, Diner and Restaurant, Diner, Drive- In,* and *Restaurant, and Diner, Drive–In* between 1946 and 1957. Bureau of the Census, *U.S. Census of Population: 1950,* vol. III, ch. 37, 101–40; Bailey interview, 3.

[40]Langdon, *Orange Roofs, Golden Arches,* 6–8, 46–55; Warren Belasco, "Toward a Culinary Common Denominator: The Rise of Howard Johnson's, 1925–1940," *Journal of American Culture* 2 (Fall 1979), 503–18.

comfort and privacy of one's own domestic setting. Many customers considered automobile dining more convenient and comfortable than the alternatives. . . .[41]

Finally there were the California-style coffee shops, such as Denny's and Bob's Big Boy, which were popular in Los Angeles in the 1940s and 1950s before they spread eastward. With flamboyant space-age architecture—panoramic windows, angled canopies, and zigzagging parapets—they spoke not only to a vision of technological progress but to a culture steeped in excess. Much like the national chains and the drive-ins, the California coffee shop placed a premium on cleanliness, comfort, and ambience.[42]

On the West Coast the early appearance of drive-ins and coffee shops sealed off the middle-income market and prevented diners from gaining a foothold. In the East, the diner industry responded to the competition by incorporating elements of other eateries into its designs. Builders finished their dining room annexes with knotty-pine wall paneling that bore a striking resemblance to Howard Johnson's wall treatment. . . . Reflecting the near obliteration of distinctions among eateries and the diner's trajectory, the industry's trade journal, once called *Diner*, became *Diner, Drive-In, and Restaurant* in 1954. . . .[43] Imitation may have temporarily staved off the diner's demise. . . .

As people became familiar with the national chains—a process propelled by national advertising campaigns and exclusive contracts for superhighway food service— . . . more people began to choose Howard Johnson's and, eventually, McDonald's. Diner sales dropped dramatically in the 1960s, and by the 1970s most of the major postwar diner builders had gone out of business. . . .[44] Virtually all the family chains—Howard Johnson's, Denny's, Big Boy's—provided counter service by the 1960s. Most of the major fast-food chains originated as drive-ins, becoming household names only after they incorporated the sit-down service of the diner and family restaurant. The menu boards that hang behind the order stations at McDonald's and Burger King are reminiscent of those once found in diners.

Ironically, by narrowing the cultural distance between blue-collar and white-collar dining milieus, diners may have paved the way for the triumph of the national chains. Franchised formulas emphasizing fast service, rock-bottom prices, informality, and attention to the needs of families enabled the fast-food chains to replicate much of what diners offered with even greater consistency and without any traces of a working-class lineage. Standardizing food and service in

---

[41]Langdon, *Orange Roofs, Golden Arches*, 59–77; *Gary Post-Tribune*, July 29, 1956, "Panorama" section, 4–5.

[42]Langdon, *Orange Roofs, Golden Arches*, 113–29; Alan Hess, *Googie: Fifties Coffee Shop Architecture* (San Francisco, 1985).

[43]"Over the Counter," *Diner and Restaurant* 12 (May 1953), 22; "Over the Counter," *Diner, Drive-In, and Restaurant* 13 (April 1954), 34; "Over the Counter," *Diner, Drive-In* 15 (June 1956), 60; "Over the Counter," ibid., 16 (May 1957), 72; advertisement for Kullman Dining Car Company, *Fountain, Luncheonette, and Diner* 2 (Jan. 1955), 23; Kullman Dining Car Company, *Complete Story of the Dining Car*, 7.

[44]Gutman, *American Diner*, 182–83.

addition to architecture, they offered an experience that was acceptable and familiar to patrons of diverse class backgrounds and, above all, identical from Maine to California. By introducing many Americans to this type of consumer experience, diner owners and builders may have sowed the seeds of their own demise.[45]

The creative center of postwar consumer culture was located along the social borders that diner builders and proprietors attempted to navigate as they sought to expand and redefine their market. The marketing strategies deployed by diner builders and owners paralleled efforts made by other manufacturers, advertisers, and retailers that had the effect of diffusing threatening social tensions because they oriented an expansive consumer culture around family obligations and the ideal of classless prosperity.

Certainly, the social dislocations wrought by World War II and the widespread postwar prosperity transfigured the structure of American society, creating a distinct culture of consumption with new loci of innovation and new boundaries of inclusion. An unprecedented convergence in Americans' income levels, family structures, and residential patterns made the borderlands of American society a potentially lucrative, if a precarious, place to do business. In the 1950s diners and other consumer products and services were developed and redeveloped to capture the purse strings of what contemporary marketing experts termed "the middle majority." It was no coincidence that the major highways extending from the metropolitan core to outlying regions emerged as the locus of cultural innovation. There, in the supermarkets, automobile showrooms, drive-in movie theaters, and fast-food franchises of the commercial strip, American consumers encountered the products and services that redefined mainstream consumer culture. And there retailers and manufacturers forged a new consumer culture that both finessed and exploited emerging and eroding social distinctions.

That new consumer culture was a family culture. As the historian Warren Susman noted, the 1950s was the era not just of the family restaurant but also of the family car, the family room, the family film, the family vacation, and the family-size carton. Consumer commodities gained legitimacy by their ability to fulfill family obligations and by their association with domestic settings. . . .[46]

The resurgence of the domestic ideal in the postwar era has generated a substantial literature, much of it seeking to explain the widespread adoption of the nuclear family pattern and renewed endorsement of Victorian sex roles within

---

[45]Max Boas and Steve Chain, *Big Mac: The Unauthorized Story of McDonald's* (New York, 1977); John F. Love, *McDonald's: Behind the Arches* (New York, 1986), 113–50; Stan Luxenberg, *Roadside Empires: How the Chains Franchised America* (New York, 1985); Langdon, *Orange Roofs, Golden Arches*, 89–109.

[46]Warren Susman with Edward Griffin, "Did Success Spoil the United States? Dual Representations in Postwar America," in *Recasting America: Culture and Politics in the Age of Cold War*, ed. Lary May (Chicago, 1989), 22; Karal Ann Marling, *As Seen on TV: The Visual Culture of Everyday Life in the 1950s* (Cambridge, Mass., 1994), 132, 136.

the nuclear family. According to Elaine Tyler May, the retreat to home and hearth was driven by externally produced anxieties; the self-contained home would contain fears about the atomic bomb, women's emancipation, consumer decadence, and sexual promiscuity.[47] Historians of the postwar family, however, have not fully appreciated how much those anxieties contributed to the domestication of public consumption, . . . [particularly fears of] women's political and economic emancipation and a volatile teen culture. For many middle-class women, the rise of a consumer society at the turn of the century had provided an entree into the public world. Because women were responsible for 80 percent of consumer expenditures, certain consumer spaces, notably the department store, evolved as female domains.[48] Political enfranchisement and heightened participation in the paid labor force portended an even greater independent presence in public life. At the same time, extended adolescence, automobility, and unprecedented levels of discretionary income liberated young people from parental authority. If it was no longer possible to confine women and teenagers to the home, why not domesticate the public realm or at least coat it with a veneer of domesticity? In a domesticated culture of consumption, men, women, and children would play out carefully prescribed and nonthreatening roles in which the higher cause would always be the family rather than the self. From this perspective, the 1950s appears less a time when Americans sought refuge in the suburban nuclear household than a time when an all-pervasive domestic ideal collapsed distinctions between private and public spheres.[49]

Historians have amply demonstrated the efforts of manufacturers, entrepreneurs, and advertisers to expand mass culture, taking cultural forms associated with particular social groups and making them more widely available. Usually this phenomenon has involved the filtering down of consumer commodities from the rich to the not-so-rich. What seems to be exceptional about the post–World War II years is the extent to which cultural forms with working-class origins percolated up into the middle majority mainstream. This reversal of the usual cultural flow was manifested every time a white-collar professional wore blue jeans, listened to rock 'n' roll music, joined a bowling league, set up a do-it-yourself workshop in the basement, or watched television in the evening.

[47]Betty Friedan, *The Feminine Mystique* (New York, 1963); Glen H. Elder, *Children of the Great Depression* (Chicago, 1974); Elaine Tyler May, *Homeward Bound. American Families in the Cold War Era* (New York, 1988); Arlene Skolnick, *Embattled Paradise: The American Family in an Age of Uncertainty* (New York, 1991), 49–74; Stephanie Coontz, *The Way We Never Were: American Families and the Nostalgia Trap* (New York, 1992), 23–41.

[48]Marchand, *Advertising the American Dream*, 167; William Leach, "Transformations in a Culture of Consumption: Women and Department Stores, 1890–1925," *Journal of American History* 74 (Sept. 1984), 319–42; Susan Porter Benson, *Counter Cultures: Saleswomen, Managers, and Customers in American Department Stores, 1890–1940* (Urbana, 1986).

[49]For a similar argument from the perspective of changes within the household, see Lynn Spigel, *Make Room for TV: Television and the Family Ideal in Postwar America* (Chicago, 1992).

(Television made its initial splash in low-income households, and programming was intended to conform to working- class sensibilities.)[50]

Often national corporations appropriated working-class cultural styles and then repackaged them for more middle-class audiences. Steve Chapple and Reebee Garofalo, George Lipsitz, and others have described how corporate-sponsored rock stars and record companies adulterated African American and working-class folk music traditions for the consumption of a white middle-class mass market. A voluminous literature describes Walt Disney's pioneering efforts to supplant tawdry amusement parks with antiseptic family theme parks for the middle class.[51] Contemplating McDonald's as a sanitized version of the diner delivered to a more diverse or a more middle-class audience shows corporate appropriation as a final step in a process that involved active participation by working-class consumers. Corporate appropriation of working-class cultural forms might have been less likely if working-class consumers had not already pushed their own institutions toward middle-class standards and if the purveyors of consumer goods and services, clustering in and creating places of social transition, had not already experimented with fusing cultural styles from different groups.

As the ultimate collapse of the diner industry indicates, cross-class fusion involved strains. Perhaps we can detect evidence of the anxieties associated with border crossings in the visual garishness of much mainstream postwar consumer culture. The flashy and often gaudy displays of abundance—the . . . superfluous ornamentation on cars and appliances, the mounds of whipped cream on pies in diner pastry display cases—may have served the psychological needs of working-class families anxious to assert social mobility through consumption.

Perhaps the anxieties unleashed by the uneasy integration of class cultures were also responsible for attempts to reinvigorate the color line by excluding African Americans from the suburbs that nourished the new mass culture. In the

---

[50]Thorstein Veblen, *The Theory of the Leisure Class: An Economic Study of Institutions* (New York, 1934), 84, 103–4. On the adoption of blue jeans in the middle class, see U.S. Department of Commerce, Business and Defense Services Administration, *Leisure and Work Clothing: Trends and Outlook* (Washington, 1961); Ed Cray, *Levi's* (Boston, 1978), 98–234; and Iain Finlayson, *Denim: An American Legend* (New York, 1990), 15–33. On the do-it-yourself craze, see "The Leisured Masses," *Business Week*, Sept. 12, 1953, pp. 142–45. On bowling, see Steven Riess, *City Games: The Evolution of American Urban Society and the Rise of Sports* (Urbana, 1991), 76–81. On rock 'n' roll as a fusion of white, black, and Latino working-class musical traditions, see George Lipsitz, "Land of a Thousand Dances," in *Recasting America*, ed. May, 267–84; George Lipsitz, *Class and Culture in America: "A Rainbow at Midnight"* (New York, 1981), 195–225; and George Lipsitz, *Time Passages: Collective Memory and American Popular Culture* (Minneapolis, 1990), 120–32. On television, see Spigel, *Make Room for TV*.

[51]Steve Chapple and Reebee Garofalo, *Rock 'n' Roll Is Here to Pay: The History and Politics of the Music Industry* (Chicago, 1977), esp. ch. 7; David Szatmary, *Rockin' in Time: A Social History of Rock-and-Roll* (Englewood Cliffs, 1991), 1–72; Charlie Gillett, *Sound of the City: The Rise of Rock and Roll* (New York, 1984), 3–65; David Koenig, *Mouse Tales: A Behind-the-Ears Look at Disneyland* (Irvine, 1994); Randy Bright, *Disneyland: An Inside Story* (New York, 1987); Al Griffin, "*Step Right Up Folks*" (Chicago, 1974), 214–22; John M. Findlay, *Magic Lands: Western Cityscapes and American Culture after 1940* (Berkeley, 1992), 52–116; Marling, *As Seen on TV*, 87–126.

1950s social psychologists observed that racial prejudice was strongest among groups experiencing rapid mobility, either upward or downward.[52] Whatever the underlying reasons, exclusion from the postwar suburbs and their institutions kept black Americans from fully participating in the new culture of consumption, regardless of their incomes. Even if segregation did not become more pervasive with the emergence of a more inclusive consumer culture in the 1950s, it became more conspicuous, at least to African Americans. Since prevailing political rhetoric yoked American identity to unrestrained consumption, such exclusion could be seen as a conspiracy by white Americans to deny the rights of citizenship to members of minority populations. Thus, exclusion from mainstream consumer culture would form an important, if often underappreciated, impetus for the civil rights and Black Power movements of the 1960s.

---

[52]Joseph Greenblum and Leonard I. Pearlin, "Vertical Mobility and Prejudice: A Socio-Psychological Analysis," in *Class, Status, and Power*, ed. Reinhard Bendix and Seymour Martin Lipset (Glencoe, 1953), 480–91.

Andrew Hurley

I am a professor of history at the University of Missouri-St. Louis, and I teach courses on the United States, Latin America, historical methods, and public history. My research interests revolve around the study of cities. I am fascinated with how places within cities—neighborhoods, factory districts, streets, rivers, parks—change their character over time and how those changes affect the quality of life for people who live and work in urban areas. I am currently conducting research on the transformation of industrial suburbs in the late twentieth century, a time when plant closings and job layoffs threatened the viability of communities that had long relied on manufacturing. My research explores the ways in which such communities adapted to new circumstances and tried to reinvent themselves in the context of a new information economy.

QUESTIONS FOR CONSIDERATION

1. Hurley characterizes diners as creating "a place where cultures intersected, clashed, and sometimes fused." What were some of the geographic, social, and economic elements of America that the diner brought together?
2. Who were the first patrons of the diners? What made the diner attractive to them?
3. What economic changes forced the transformation of diners? How did these economic changes reflect larger changes in American society during the years after World War II and the early 1950s?
4. According to Hurley, "[i]n the lexicon of the trade, 'family' replaced 'working-man' as the basic social unit to which the diner yoked its reputation." How did these changes in architecture reflect continuities and changes in American society in general?
5. Hurley describes the rise of the family diner as an example of "cultural forms with working-class origins percolat[ing] up into the middle majority mainstream." What are some other examples of this "percolation" described by Hurley?
6. How did this merging of class "cultural forms" reinforce, rather than break down, racial boundaries between white and black Americans?

CHAPTER TWELVE

Brown as a Cold War Case[1]

Mary L. Dudziak

"The United States Supreme Court has given a new definition to unAmerican-ism," Roscoe Drummond wrote in the European edition of the *New York Herald Tribune* on May 21, 1954, following the U.S. Supreme Court ruling in *Brown v. Board of Education*. "It has ruled that segregated public schools are un-Constitutional—and therefore un-American." The *Brown* decision was timely, he argued, "because it comes at a moment when our leadership of the free peoples demands the best . . . of what America is and can be." Drummond was not alone in calling segregation un-American. When the Topeka, Kansas, Board of Education, whose policies were before the Court in *Brown*, voted to abandon segregation before the Supreme Court ruling came down, a board member commented, "We feel that segregation is not an American practice." By 1954 many Americans had come to that conclusion about segregation, a widely practiced American institution.[2]

Hearing speakers in 1954 call segregation "un-American" helps situate the school segregation cases within their cultural context. It was during the first decade of the Cold War, the era of Sen. Joseph R. McCarthy, during the heyday of the House Committee on Un-American Activities, that *Brown* was decided. American history texts often cover the McCarthy era and the *Brown* case in separate passages alongside each other, as partners in chronology alone, rather than as part of the same story. The case may seem to sit uncomfortably in the trajectory of the legal history of the 1950s. During the McCarthy era, after all, individual rights were restricted, but in Brown, individual rights were powerfully expanded. The Supreme Court decided *Dennis v. United States* in 1951,

---

[1]Interested students are encouraged to read this essay in the original form. Mary L. Dudziak, "Brown as a Cold War Case," *The Journal of American History* 91, no. 1 (June 2004), 32–42.

[2]Roscoe Drummond, "Washington: The Supreme Court Confirms,"*New York Herald Tribune* (European ed., Paris), May 21, 1954, p. 4; *Brown v. Board of Education*, 347 U.S. 483 (1954); Mary L. Dudziak, "The Limits of Good Faith: Desegregation in Topeka, Kansas, 1950–1956," *Law and History Review* 5 (Fall 1987), 352.

upholding prosecution of members of the Communist party based on evidence that they read the writings of Karl Marx and Friedrich Engels and talked about them. The Court decided *Harisiades v. Shaughnessy* in 1952, upholding the deportation of immigrants for past Communist party membership. Those cases sit alongside a case thought to be a highlight of American constitutional history. How can *Brown* and the Cold War be understood as part of the same story, the same historical moment?[3]

The standard way American legal history texts treat *Brown* and the Cold War is illustrated by a leading coursebook, Melvin I. Urofsky and Paul Finkelman's *A March of Liberty*. This excellent text covers the Cold War in one chapter, with readings on *Dennis v. United States* and other anticommunist cases from the 1950s and related matters. Race is not mentioned at all in the Cold War chapter. The Supreme Court's race cases are discussed in the next chapter, entitled "The Struggle for Civil Rights," which covers the landmark cases leading up to *Brown*, the National Association for the Advancement of Colored People (NAACP) legal effort, and other developments in civil rights law. The federal government appears in the story of *Brown* in the form of the Supreme Court. The struggle is one by lawyers to change an unjust legal regime. Its denouement is the Court's simple opinion in *Brown*. That treatment is consistent with a consensus narrative in American lawbooks: *Brown* is a straightforward story of the triumph of a

---

[3]Ellen Schrecker, *Many Are the Crimes: McCarthyism in America* (Boston, 1998); Michal Belknap, *Cold War Political Justice: The Smith Act, the Communist Party, and American Civil Liberties* (Westport, 1978); *Dennis v. United States*, 341 U.S. 494 (1951); *Harisiades v. Shaughnessy*, 342 U.S. 580 (1952). The literature linking civil rights and foreign relations during the Cold War is well developed and growing. On foreign relations and civil rights reform, see Thomas Borstelmann, *The Cold War and the Color Line: American Race Relations in the Global Arena* (Cambridge, Mass., 2001); Mary L. Dudziak, *Cold War Civil Rights: Race and the Image of American Democracy* (Princeton, 2000); Philip A. Klinkner with Rogers M. Smith, *The Unsteady March: The Rise and Decline of Racial Equality in America* (Chicago, 1999); and Azza Salama Layton, *International Politics and Civil Rights Policies in the United States, 1941–1960* (Cambridge, Eng., 2000). On race and foreign relations, see, for example, Brenda Gayle Plummer, *Rising Wind: Black Americans and U.S. Foreign Affairs, 1935–1960* (Chapel Hill, 1996); Gerald Home, *Black and Red: W E. B. Du Bois and the Afro-American Response to the Cold War, 1944–1963* (Albany, 1986); Penny M. Von Eschen, *Race against Empire: Black Americans and Anticolonialism, 1937–1957* (Ithaca, 1997); Carol Anderson, *Eyes off the Prize: The United Nations and the African American Struggle for Human Rights, 1944–1955* (New York, 2003); Brenda Gayle Plummer, ed., *Window on Freedom: Race, Civil Rights, and Foreign Affairs, 1945–1988* (Chapel Hill, 2003); Michael L. Krenn, *Black Diplomacy: African Americans and the State Department, 1945–1969* (Armonk, 1999); and Michael L. Krenn, ed., *Race and U.S. Foreign Policy from the Colonial Period to the Present: A Collection of Essays* (5 vols., New York, 1998). International perspectives on other topics appear in the work of leading American legal historians. On U.S. law as an export, see Lawrence Friedman, *American Law in the Twentieth Century* (New Haven, 2002), 572–87. On the United Nations in the context of the legal history of New York, see William E. Nelson, *The Legalist Reformation: Law, Politics, and Ideology in New York, 1920–1980* (Chapel Hill, 2001), 369–73. For a new essay that incorporates the Cold War history of *Brown*, see William E. Nelson, "*Brown v. Board of Education* and the Jurisprudence of Legal Realism," *St. Louis University Law Review* 48 (forthcoming, 2004).

progressive Court and a progressive Constitution, after a hard-fought battle by lawyers and litigants.[4]

A dichotomous narrative about 1950s cases flows from this characterization: McCarthyism on one side and civil rights on the other. The anticommunist cases had to do with national security issues, after all, something apparently not at stake in the civil rights context. On closer reflection, however, that categorization will not hold up.

Among the elements left out of Urofsky and Finkelman's story of *Brown* is the role of the U.S. Justice Department, which filed amicus curiae (friend of the court) briefs in the cases leading up to *Brown* and in *Brown* itself. The Justice Department briefs gave only one reason for the government's participation in the cases: segregation harmed U.S. foreign relations. As the United States argued in the *Brown* amicus brief, "the existence of discrimination against minority groups in the United States has an adverse effect upon our relations with other countries. Racial discrimination furnishes grist for the Communist propaganda mills, and it raises doubts even among friendly nations as to the intensity of our devotion to the democratic faith." World attention to U.S. race discrimination was "growing in alarming proportions," and school segregation in particular was "singled out for hostile foreign comment." Because of this, Secretary of State Dean Acheson concluded in a statement quoted in the brief, race discrimination "remains a source of constant embarrassment to this Government in the day-to-day conduct of its foreign relations; and it jeopardizes the effective maintenance of our moral leadership of the free and democratic nations of the world." The secretary's argument was not speculative. U.S. State Department files from the period are full of reports from the field that racial problems in the United States harmed U.S. relations with particular nations and compromised the nation's Cold War objectives.[5]

Cold War concerns provided a motive beyond equality itself for the federal government, including the president and the courts, to act on civil rights when it did. But if we strip the story of the complications of the Cold War, what remains is a romantic tale of heroic litigants, lawyers, and judges who did the right thing. There was much heroism and sacrifice in civil rights history, but as Derrick A. Bell Jr. and others have argued for decades, the history of American civil rights reform is not a

---

[4]Melvin I. Urofsky and Paul Finkelman, *A March of Liberty: A Constitutional History of the United States*, vol. II: From the Founding to 1890 (New York, 1988), 773–92. The omission of race is especially curious in the Cold War chapter's discussion of the Bricker Amendment to the U.S. Constitution, proposed in 1952, which would have limited the enforcement of treaties within the United States. A central motivation was to make international human rights treaties unenforceable within the United States, lest they invalidate southern racial policies. Duane Tananbaum, *The Bricker Amendment Controversy: A Test of Eisenhower's Political Leadership* (Ithaca, 1988), 1–15. The best version of the standard history of *Brown* remains Richard Kluger, *Simple Justice: The History of Brown v. Board of Education and Black America's Struggle for Equality* (New York, 1976).

[5]Dudziak, *Cold War Civil Rights*, 80–81; Mary L. Dudziak, "Desegregation as a Cold War Imperative,"*Stanford Law Review* 41 (Nov. 1988), 61–120. Thousands of records on this topic can be found in Decimal File 811.411, Records of the Department of State, RG 59 (National Archives, Washington, D.C.). See generally Dudziak, *Cold War Civil Rights*; and Borstelmann, *Cold War and the Color Line*.

straightforward tale of a struggle for justice, but a complex story that includes self-interest and limited commitments. Nevertheless, the story of *Brown* as a struggle for simple justice is replayed throughout standard treatments of American law.[6]

Examining *Brown* as a Cold War case complicates this narrative. This essay will take up the question of how it affects the story to set *Brown* in the Cold War chapter of American legal history books and to examine the case in an international context. Contextualizing and internationalizing *Brown* does not simply provide new details to a preexisting narrative. Viewing *Brown* as a Cold War case helps us rethink the story itself.

The connections between *Brown* and the Cold War are so ubiquitous in the primary sources that it is more difficult to explain them away than to find a place for them in the historical narrative. In the American press, for example, *Brown* was called a "Blow to Communism." The *Pittsburgh Courier* said that *Brown* would "stun and silence America's Communist traducers behind the Iron Curtain. It will effectively impress upon millions of colored people in Asia and Africa the fact that idealism and social morality can and do prevail in the Unites States, regardless of race, creed or color." Sharing this concern, the *San Francisco Chronicle* suggested that the ruling's greatest impact would be "on South America, Africa and Asia," since it would restore the faith of their people in the justice of American democracy.[7]

Brown was also a major international story. The decision was on the front page in all the daily newspapers in India. Under the headline "A Great Decision," the *Hindustan Times* of New Delhi suggested that "American democracy stands to gain in strength and prestige from the unanimous ruling. . . . The practice of racial segregation in schools . . . has been a long-standing blot on American life and civilization." An editorial in the *West African Pilot*, published in Lagos, Nigeria, argued that the decision "is of particular significance and special

---

[6]Derrick A. Bell Jr., *"Brown v. Board of Education* and the Interest-Convergence Dilemma,"*Harvard Law Review* 93 (Jan. 1980), 518; Alan David Freeman, "Legitimizing Racial Discrimination Through Antidiscrimination Law: A Critical Review of Supreme Court Doctrine,"*Minnesota Law Review* 62 (July 1978), 1049–1119. On American legal scholars' reverence for *Brown*, see Laura Kalman, *The Strange Career of Legal Liberalism* (New Haven, 1999). The narrative that treats *Brown* as separate from the Cold War has been resilient and is prominent in works by leading scholars. See Kermit L. Hall, *The Magic Mirror: Law in American History* (New York, 1989), 322–24; and David P Currie, *The Constitution in the Supreme Court: The Second Century, 1888–1986* (Chicago, 1990), 377–85. There are other important debates about the role and importance of *Brown*, centering particularly on whether the Court's rulings actually desegregated schools, whether judicial action was legitimate or antidemocratic, and whether *Brown* rested on sound constitutional interpretation. See Lucas A. Powe Jr., *The Warren Court and American Politics* (Cambridge, Mass., 2000); James T. Patterson, *Brown v. Board of Education: A Civil Rights Milestone and Its Troubled History* (New York, 2001); Robert J. Cottrol, Raymond T. Diamond, and Leland B. Ware, *Brown v. Board of Education: Caste, Culture, and Constitution* (Lawrence, 2003); and Jack M. Balkin, ed., *What Brown v. Board of Education Should Have Said: America's Top Legal Experts Rewrite America's Landmark Civil Rights Decision* (New York, 2001).

[7]The *New York Herald Tribune* and *Pittsburgh Courier* quoted in *The New York Times*, May 18, 1954, p. 2; *San Francisco Chronicle*, May 18, 1954, p. 18.

interest to Africans and people of African descent throughout the world." According to the paper:

> It is no secret that America is today hailed as leader of the democratic world. This carries with it a great deal of moral responsibility. Firstly, it entails that the American concept and practice of democracy within its own territories should acknowledge the necessity of equal opportunity for all citizens, no matter the racial origin. Secondly, it implies that the United States should set an example for all other nations by taking the lead in removing from its national life all signs and traces of racial intolerance, arrogance or discrimination for which it criticises some other nations. The paper argued that American actions, because they had global impact, could affect racial policies in other nations.

The *West African Pilot* asserted that abolishing racism in the United States "would be the greatest possible assurance of America's good faith and sincerity towards the establishment of a true world-wide democracy."[8]

A writer for the Australian *Sydney Morning Herald* echoed much of the world's press.

> To-day's thinking on the civil rights of Negroes in America is a product of the changes that have occurred as a consequence of two world wars. In the attempt to exert international leadership in a context with world Communism, the United States has been severely handicapped by what the non-white race have felt about the treatment of Negroes in America. The most powerful item of propaganda avail- able to Communists has been the alleged second-class citizenship of more than 15 million of these Americans.... To-day... the U.S. Supreme Court's decision should go a long way toward dissipating the validity of the Communist contention that Western concepts of democracy are hypocritical.[9]

The international impact of *Brown* was followed by civil rights activists in the United States. The NAACP had a keen interest in the international reaction to *Brown*. The organization's 1954 annual report argued that "it was not the NAACP alone which benefited" from the decision. It had "lessened" the "pressures of world opinion" and "eased""the burdened conscience of the United States" because "steady progress towards integration undermined the charge of hypocrisy, so often and so effectively leveled against our country whenever our

---

[8]Donald D. Kennedy to Walter White, Oct. 12, 1954, Folder: Supreme Court-School Case-Foreign Press—June–Dec. 1954, box A619, General Office Files, Group II, National Association for the Advancement of Colored People Papers (Manuscript Division, Library of Congress, Washington, D.C.); "A Great Decision,"*Hindustan Times* (New Delhi), May 20, 1954, Folder: Supreme Court-School Case-Foreign Press-1952-May 1954, ibid.; *West African Pilot* (Lagos), May 22, 1954, p. 2. Referring to an architect of apartheid in South Africa, the *West African Pilot* editorial suggested that "Dr. Malan would think twice before pursuing his racialist policy any further if America abolished all signs of racial discrimination in her own land." On the United States and South Africa, see Thomas Borstelmann, *Apartheid's Reluctant Uncle: The United States and Southern Africa in the Early Cold War* (New York, 1993).

[9]*Sydney Morning Herald*, May 22, 1954, p. 3. U.S. press coverage of *Brown* also emphasized the Cold War impact of the case. See Dudziak, *Cold War Civil Rights*, 107–12.

national leaders espouse human freedom." Walter White, the organization's executive secretary, sought details of the international press reaction and wrote to American ambassadors in at least thirteen nations inquiring about evidence of "increased faith in the American democratic process and in the United States itself" flowing from the *Brown* decision. Showing that an NAACP case aided American international prestige served two important interests. First, it gave civil rights activists important leverage. The argument that social change aided U.S. foreign relations could be used to further the NAACP's social change agenda. Second, showing that NAACP efforts enhanced American international prestige helped the NAACP argue that its work promoted, rather than undermined, the nation's Cold War interests. During the Cold War, when civil rights activists were red-baited as subversives, that could help the organization weather criticism.[10]

In response to his queries, White received evidence of the broad international reaction to the decision. For example, Clare Boothe Luce, the U.S. ambassador to Italy, wrote that "the Court's decision and the events following it have been watched with great interest by Italian public opinion. On balance, I think the result has been, not only to give Italians a fresh reminder of the meaning of American democracy, but also to cut the ground from under the anti-American propaganda put out by the Communists on this point." In Israel, U.S. Ambassador Francis H. Russell suggested that "the Supreme Court decision has done much to strengthen belief in the essential democracy of American life." There was little in the Soviet press because, the U.S. ambassador to the Soviet Union thought, *Brown* "so obviously contradicts Communist propaganda." *Izvestia* saw the case as an example of the United States' "demagogic gestures intended for export." Noting the delay in implementing desegregation authorized by the *Brown* opinion, the paper suggested that "the decision of the U.S. Supreme Court has a purely masking character and that it was taken only for propaganda purposes."[11]

The U.S. government worked to foster a positive overall international reaction to *Brown*. "You may imagine what good use we are making of the decision here in

[10]*The Year of the Great Decision: NAACP Annual Report, 46th Year, 1954* (New York, 1955), 3, K—Printed Matter, box K1, Group II, NAACP Papers; White to Horace A. Hildreth, Sept. 16, 1954, Folder: Supreme Court—School Case—Foreign Press—June–Dec. 1954, box A619, General Office Files, ibid.; Doug McAdam, *Political Process and the Development of Black Insurgency, 1930–1970* (Chicago, 1982); Doug McAdam et al., eds., *Comparative Perspectives on Social Movements: Political Opportunities, Mobilizing Structures, and Cultural Framings* (New York, 1996); Manning Marable, *Race, Reform, and Rebellion: The Second Reconstruction in Black America, 1945–1982* (Jackson, 1984), 12–42; Gerald Home, *Communist Front? The Civil Rights Congress, 1946–1956* (Rutherford, 1988); Anderson, *Eyes off the Prize*.

[11]Clare Boothe Luce to White, Sept. 24, 1954, Folder: Supreme Court—School Case—Foreign Press—June–Dec. 1954, box A619, General Office Files, Group II, NAACP Papers; Francis H. Russell to White, Oct. 18, 1954, ibid.; Charles E. Bohlen to White, Oct. 9, 1954, ibid.; S. Kondrashov, "Judges and Governors: International Notes,"*Izvestia*, June 23, 1954 (U.S. Embassy translation), ibid.

India," the U.S. ambassador to India, George V. Allen, wrote to Walter White. The United States Information Service (USIS) in India circulated a press release calling the decision "another milestone in the American Negro's steady progress toward full equality as a citizen." Immediately after *Brown* was decided, the Voice of America broadcast the news to the world. When school began in fall 1954, the USIS planned to show a film in ninety countries depicting white and African American students going to school together in Baltimore, Maryland.[12]

The role of American diplomats was not restricted to efforts to play up the ruling after the fact. When the U.S. government filed an amicus brief in *Brown* supporting the NAACP position, it relied on State Department materials on the impact of American racism on U.S. foreign relations. The Justice Department presented those arguments to a Court familiar with them. But evidence of American justices' concern about the global impact of American race discrimination will not generally be found in Supreme Court case files, a traditional source for legal history research. Instead, it can be found in justices' letters, speeches, foreign travel files, and personal files. For example, when Justice William O. Douglas traveled to India in 1950, the first question he was asked was, "Why does America tolerate the lynching of Negroes?" In his book *Strange Lands and Friendly People*, Douglas wrote that he had learned from his travels that "the attitude of the United States toward its colored minorities is a powerful factor in our relations with India." Chief Justice Earl Warren echoed Douglas's concerns about international perceptions of the United States in a 1954 speech to the American Bar Association. "Our American system like all others is on trial both at home and abroad," he suggested. "The way it works, the manner in which it solves the problems of our day; the extent to which we maintain the spirit of our Constitution with its Bill of Rights, will in the long run do more to make it both secure and the object of adulation than the number of hydrogen bombs we stockpile." Because of his role in *Brown*, Warren became an effective ambassador for American democracy overseas. When he traveled to India in 1956, substituting for President Dwight D. Eisenhower, Warren was introduced at Delhi University as a man who needed no introduction, for he "rose to fame in 28 minutes of that Monday afternoon as he read out his momentous decision outlawing racial segregation in American public schools." When Warren traveled to Moscow in 1959, the first question he was asked was about race discrimination in the United States. In the summer of 1963, when the Kennedy administration was gravely concerned about the impact of American civil rights problems on U.S. foreign

---

[12]For George V. Allen's statement to White, see the quotation in Mr. Ivy to White, June 4, 1954, ibid.; "Ban on School Segregation Another Milestone in Negro Progress," United States Information Service, India, May 21, 1954, Folder: Supreme Court—School Case—Foreign Press—1952-May 1954, ibid.; "U.S. Makes Film of Negro, White Mixed Schools: World Showing," *London Daily Telegraph*, Sept. 10, 1954, Clippings, Folder: Supreme Court—School Case—Foreign Press—June–Dec. 1954, ibid.

affairs, Warren traveled to Africa, a region of particular concern, and addressed progress in American race relations in a speech in Kenya.[13]

The *Brown* decision came as a relief to the State Department. Although the ranks of American diplomats would remain overwhelmingly white for many years, promoting an image of racial integration and equality in America had been an important objective. American racial progress was a regular feature of American propaganda in the years before *Brown*. The United States responded to widespread international criticism of American racism with an effort to construct a counternarrative of American racial progress. That narrative was captured in the pamphlet *The Negro in American Life*, which was published in many languages and distributed around the world. The pamphlet argued that the great change in the United States from the 1850s to 1950 was evidence of the superiority of democracy as a system of government. The nation's history of slavery was therefore not avoided in American propaganda, but embraced. If the nation had progressed from a base line of enslavement of African Americans to a free, if still not quite equal, society in a mere hundred years, then democracy, it was argued, was a system of government that facilitated such progress. Not accomplished by "dictatorial fiat," which the pamphlet suggested was characteristic of Communism, gradual progress was presented as a superior form of social change, and American democracy as a superior form of government. The history of racism in the United States, a liability in the Cold War, was thus reinterpreted into a strategic asset. The story of race in America became a story of the supremacy of democracy over Communism. In the face of continuing racial problems in the early 1950s, U.S. propaganda insisted that racism was not a fundamental national value, and that it was going away. *Brown* therefore served as an important reinforcement of the State Department's arguments about the nature of the U.S. Constitution and the inevitable character of American racial progress.[14]

For all the excitement about *Brown*, what was the decision's impact? *Brown* was an unusual case, departing from the normal rule in American law that where a right has been violated, there is a remedy. The 1954 decision postponed consideration of remedies for one year. Then, in *Brown v. Board of Education (II)* in 1955, the Court suggested that the "private interests" of the plaintiffs in

---

[13]William O. Douglas, *Strange Lands and Friendly People* (New York, 1951), 296; Dudziak, *Cold War Civil Rights*, 104–5. On Earl Warren's speech to the American Bar Association, see *The New York Times*, Aug. 20, 1954, Clippings (microfilm: reel 42), Papers of the United States Information Agency (John F Kennedy Library, Boston, Mass.). "Chief Justice Warren in India,"*Baltimore Sun*, Oct. 1, 1956, India 1956 Correspondence, Clippings, Photographs (Folder No. 1), box 56, Foreign File, Personal Papers, Earl Warren Papers (Manuscript Division, Library of Congress); Dudziak, *Cold War Civil Rights*, 105–6, 108–9; "Warren Still Talks Politics," *Montgomery Alabama Journal*, Aug. 20, 1959, Folder: Germany—1959 Speeches—Clippings—Pamphlets (Folder No. 2), box 57, Foreign File, Personal Papers, Warren Papers; United States Information Service, "Text of Speech by U.S. Chief Justice Earl Warren at Gloucester Hall, on July 25, 1963," Folder: Kenya—1963, box 60, ibid.; Berl Bernhard interview by Mary L. Dudziak, July 2003, audiotape (in Mary L. Dudziak's possession).

[14]Krenn, *Black Diplomacy*; Plummer, *Rising Wind*, 269–73; *The Negro in American Life* (c. 1950), folder 503, box 112, series II, Chester Bowles Papers (Manuscripts and Archives, Yale University Library, New Haven, Conn.); Dudziak, *Cold War Civil Rights*, 107–12.

desegregated schools must be balanced against the "public interest" in accomplishing desegregation in an orderly manner. As a result, desegregation should proceed "with all deliberate speed." Segregated school districts were not yet required to integrate. The named plaintiffs in the cases were not granted the right to attend a desegregated school, at least for the time being.[15]

In the consensus narrative about *Brown*, the Court's delay in ordering a remedy is often seen as a statesmanlike effort to avoid racial conflict. The debate focuses on whether the Court's judgment on how to avoid conflict was correct, and on how conflict shaped continuing desegregation efforts. But it is also true that actual desegregation in southern schools was not essential to address international concerns about the nature of a government whose constitution appeared to accommodate segregation. The next major school segregation crisis—in Little Rock, Arkansas, in 1957—illustrates that point. The Little Rock crisis was worldwide news. President Eisenhower's decision to send federal troops to ensure that nine African American students could attend Central High School won praise in the international press. It served as evidence that the U.S. federal government was behind *Brown*, even if some state governments were recalcitrant. However, Arkansas eventually responded to the Little Rock crisis with a complex "pupil placement law" that established procedures for determining whether a child could change schools. The discretion granted to school authorities under such placement laws ensured that much segregation could be accomplished bureaucratically. Although the international press covered U.S. civil rights with care, when challenges were brought to pupil placement laws in southern states and the U.S. Supreme Court upheld the laws, newspapers that had followed the Little Rock crisis in detail did not cover those decisions. By bureaucratizing segregation, southern states had brought it below the radar of international opinion. The abstract principle of *Brown* seemed to be the thing needed to maintain American prestige. In that sense, *Brown* and the Little Rock crises successfully protected the image of American democracy, even if they did not actually desegregate schools.[16]

---

[15]*Brown v. Board of Education (Brown II),* 349 U.S. 294 (1955).

[16]On desegregation after *Brown I* and *Brown II,* see, for example, Urofsky and Finkelman, *March of Liberty,* II, 785–91; Jennifer Hochschild, *The New American Dilemma* (New Haven, 1984); Gerald Rosenberg, *The Hollow Hope: Can Courts Bring About Social Change? American Politics and Political Economy* (Chicago, 1991), 70–71; Michael J. Klarman, "How *Brown* Changed Race Relations: The Backlash Thesis," *Journal of American History* 81 (June 1994), 81–118; Michael J. Klarman, "*Brown*, Racial Change, and the Civil Rights Movement," *Virginia Law Review* 80 (Feb. 1994), 7–150; Patterson, Brown v. Board of Education, 118–28; L. A. Powe Jr., "The Supreme Court, Social Change, and Legal Scholarship: A Review Essay," *Stanford Law Review* 44 (July 1992), 1615–41; and Peter H. Schuck, "Public Law Litigation and Social Reform: A Book Review of Hollow Hope and Rebellious Lawyering,"*Yale Law Journal* 102 (May 1993), 1763–86. Dwight D. Eisenhower, *The White House Years: Waging Peace, 1956–1961* (Garden City, 1965), 162; Dudziak, *Cold War Civil Rights,* 118–26, 133–37, 148–51; Mary L. Dudziak, "The Little Rock Crisis and Foreign Affairs: Race, Resistance, and the Image of American Democracy," *Southern California Law Review* 70 (Sept. 1997), 1641–1716; Cary Fraser, "Crossing the Color Line in Little Rock: The Eisenhower Administration and the Dilemma of Race for American Foreign Policy," *Diplomatic History* 24 (Spring 2000), 233–64; Azza Salama Layton, "International Pressure and the U.S. Government's Response to Little Rock," *Arkansas Historical Quarterly* 56 (Autumn 1997), 257–72.

For its objective of managing the nation's international prestige, the U.S. government got what it needed in *Brown* and Little Rock. Iconic cases set the image of American race relations in the international press. Continuing inequality in local communities could be explained away as a by-product of American federalism and one that would inevitably fade away in the inexorable march of progress made possible by American constitutionalism. It was, at least, a story that worked in U.S. propaganda, a narrative maintained by the U.S. government through the difficult years of the 1960s, when the civil rights movement kept American racism in the world press.[17]

Although *Brown* is still held up as a high point in American legal history, the case ultimately came under assault. In a 2001 collection of essays in which prominent legal scholars rewrote the Court's opinion, Derrick Bell wrote a dissent, arguing that in *Brown* the Court overestimated the power of law to achieve social change and underestimated the pervasiveness of racism. In spite of criticism, *Brown* remains an icon, a symbol of the promise of law. Isolating *Brown* from its international context helps sustain an argument that what happened in *Brown* was accomplished by litigants, lawyers, and judges within the boundaries of the American legal system. Domesticating the case elevates the role of the legal system as an engine of progressive social change. Law was put to much good use during the civil rights era. But examining the broader forces producing legal change helps us see *Brown's* historical contingency. *Brown* was the product of converging domestic and international developments, rather than an inevitable product of legal progress.[18]

Historians and legal scholars might raise important objections to the Cold War narrative of *Brown*. By drawing attention to the impact of *Brown* on U.S. foreign relations, an international frame might seem to take the story out of the streets and local communities where school desegregation struggles played out and to encourage an outdated, top-down approach to writing history. Scholarship on race and foreign relations has relied in part on government records and has examined the role of elites in managing the impact on foreign affairs of civil rights in America. Such work should not, however, be seen as in opposition to grass-roots history. In his important book, *I've Got the Light of Freedom*, Charles M. Payne eloquently argued against a "homogenized" narrative of civil rights history. The work of Payne, John Dittmer, and others illuminates the way attention to local struggles reshapes the narrative of civil rights history. Attention to the impact of civil rights on foreign affairs is another route away from a homogenized history. Local and transnational histories can also work together. It was only because of the "local people" who shouldered the work of organizing at the grass roots that civil rights conflicts in American communities resonated around the world.

---

[17]Dudziak, *Cold War Civil Rights*, 140–48.

[18]Derrick A. Bell, "Bell, J., Dissenting," in *What* Brown v. Board of Education *Should Have Said*, ed. Balkin, 185–200; Hugh Davis Graham, *The Civil Rights Era: Origins and Development of National Policy, 1960–1972* (New York, 1990). For a discussion of legal scholarship on *Brown* as evidence of law as a progressive force, see Kalman, *Strange Career of Legal Liberalism*.

The local civil rights struggles inspired independence movements in other nations, just as U.S. civil rights activists developed their ideas in part in response to developments overseas. The U.S. civil rights movement had an impact on American international prestige, giving civil rights activists important leverage at home.[19]

Another objection might be that interpreting *Brown*, a constitutional landmark, as in part a product of the Cold War might lend support to a domestic version of Cold War triumphalism in which the case becomes evidence the Cold War was good for the country. That objection cannot be maintained if the limits of *Brown* and the full impact of the Cold War on the civil rights movement are taken into account. In *Cold War Civil Rights*, I did not argue, as has sometimes been suggested, that the Cold War was "good" for the civil rights movement. Cold War–era red-baiting of activists harmed the movement and destroyed lives. Instead, I argue that while the Cold War narrowed acceptable civil rights discourse and led to sanctions against individuals who stepped outside those narrow bounds, within them it gave the movement important and effective leverage. It opened an opportunity for what Derrick Bell has called a "convergence of interest" between the U.S. government and the movement. The Cold War simultaneously harmed the movement and created an opportunity for limited reform.[20]

Legal scholars might object to viewing *Brown* alongside *Dennis* as a Cold War case because that is not how legal thinking is organized. We put cases dealing with one doctrine (the equal protection clause) in one category and cases dealing with a separate doctrine (the First Amendment) in another. We "shepardize" cases, taking one strand out of the law and pulling it to examine what is attached. That is how lawyers identify a relevant line of cases that matter to a legal argument. It is also the way law is learned. Our courses and our casebooks are largely organized according to such doctrinal categories. From that perspective, *Brown* is an equal protection case, and *Dennis* a First Amendment case. They are different topics and belong in different chapters.

While categorizing cases this way might be good when writing a brief, it is important for legal historians to work against our very ways of learning law when they construct barriers that interfere with our ability to see connections across categories. In *Dennis*, the anticommunist case, for example, lacking hard evidence of the harm of Communist party actions, Justice Felix Frankfurter's concurring opinion argued that the Court should take "judicial notice" of the threat of

[19]Charles M. Payne, *I've Got the Light of Freedom: The Organizing Tradition and the Mississippi Freedom Struggle* (Berkeley, 1995); John Dittmer, *Local People: The Struggle for Civil Rights in Mississippi* (Urbana, 1994); Von Eschen, *Race against Empire*; James Forman, *The Making of Black Revolutionaries: A Personal Account* (New York, 1972); Yvette Richards, *Maida Springer: Pan-Africanist and International Labor Leader* (Pittsburgh, 2000); Gerald Horne, *Race Woman: The Lives of Shirley Graham DuBois* (New York, 2000); James Meriwether, *Proudly We Can Be Africans: Black Americans and Africa, 1935–1961* (Chapel Hill, 2002).

[20]Bell, "*Brown v. Board of Education* and the Interest-Convergence Dilemma," 518. On the damaging impact of the Cold War on civil rights activists, see, for example, Home, *Communist Front?*; Martin Duberman, *Paul Robeson* (New York, 1989); Timothy B. Tyson, *Radio Free Dixie: Robert E Williams and the Roots of Black Power* (Chapel Hill, 2001); and Kenneth O'Reilly, *Racial Matters: The FBI's Secret File on Black America, 1960–1972* (New York, 1991).

Communism. The authority he cited was not case law, but an article in the *New York Times Magazine*.[21] He thought that the Court should act in part on the basis of what the justices knew about the world they inhabited. In their world, he thought, Communism and domestic subversion were serious threats. Having discussed that issue in *Dennis* and having faced it in other Cold War–related cases, members of the Court could not simply have forgotten about it when they read the Justice Department's warning about the impact of *Brown* on foreign affairs. Although the two cases address different constitutional arguments, the justices brought the same understanding of their world to their work on any of the cases they considered.

This is a long way of saying that *Brown* belongs in the Cold War chapter of American legal history. Seeing *Brown* as a Cold War case does not simply acknowledge the evidence all over the historical record. It also helps us to see in *Brown* an important element to look for elsewhere. Once the United States took on the role of a world leader and argued that its system of government was a model for the world, the world took an interest in American justice. Struggles over rights in American law had international as well as domestic implications. During *Brown's* anniversary year, rather than shoring up the boundary between the domestic and the foreign and safeguarding the consensus narrative, we might examine other border points where the domestic and the foreign become intertwined, other moments when judicial moorings in domestic affairs shifted when moved by international currents.[22] As we face new questions about the nation's role in the world in our own day, there is surely no better time to let the world into American legal history.

---

[21]*Dennis v. United States*, 341 U.S. at 553–57 (Frankfurter, J., concurring). Felix Frankfurter quoted from George E Kennan, "Where Do You Stand on Communism?,"*New York Times Magazine*, May 27, 1951, p. 7.

[22]On a contemporary example of the impact of international affairs on domestic law, see Christopher Eisgruber and Lawrence Sager, "Civil Liberties in the Dragon's Domain: Negotiating the Blurred Boundary between Domestic Law and Foreign Law after 9/11," in *September 11 in History: A Watershed Moment?*, ed. Mary L. Dudziak (Durham, 2003), 163–79; and John Strawson, ed., *Law after Ground Zero* (London, 2002).

Mary Dudziak

My writing often stems from being puzzled about something. My first book came out of wondering how to reconcile *Brown v. Board of Education* with McCarthyism in the 1950s, since racial equality expanded at the same time that other rights were under assault. How could these things have happened at the same time? My essay in this volume provides an answer. Curiosity about American lawyers and legal ideas outside U.S. borders led to my book on Thurgood Marshall's work in Kenya during the 1960s. Puzzling over the way people talked about "wartime" after 9/11 led me to write a book on wartime as a kind of time. Nowadays, I am provoked by ongoing war and militarization, so I am writing a book that asks why we seem to be perpetually at war when most Americans pay little attention to it—and whether these two things are related to each other. I am a legal scholar and a historian because I believe that history is essential to understanding law, politics, and social change.

QUESTIONS FOR CONSIDERATION

1. Dudziak argues that traditionally, McCarthyism and the *Brown* decision are interpreted as disconnected events, though both happened within the same context. What evidence does Dudziak use to claim that both McCarthyism and the *Brown* decision were in fact connected by the Cold War?
2. Characterize the international reaction to the *Brown* decision. In what ways was this reaction advantageous to American Cold War policy?
3. How did American policymakers use the idea of "racial progress" to counteract accusations of America's longstanding racist policies?
4. After *Brown*, how did Southern school authorities generally maintain their segregated school systems "below the radar" of international opinion?
5. Dudziak suggests, "rather than shoring up the boundary between the domestic and the foreign . . . we might examine other border points where the domestic and the foreign become intertwined, other moments when judicial moorings in domestic affairs shifted when moved by international currents." What is another example in this volume where domestic affairs became intertwined with international affairs?

CHAPTER THIRTEEN

❦

The Dialectics of Repression: The Los Angeles Police Department and the Chicano Movement, 1968–1971[1]

Edward J. Escobar

On August 29, 1970, the largest protest demonstration ever mounted by people of Mexican descent living in the United States took place in the Mexican-American barrio of East Los Angeles. Organized by a committee headed by former University of California, Los Angeles (UCLA), student body president and antiwar activist Rosalío Muñoz, the National Chicano Moratorium demonstration was designed to protest the disproportionately high numbers of Mexican-American casualties in the Vietnam War. Between twenty and thirty thousand people marched [through] the main shopping area in East Los Angeles, and congregated on a baseball field at Laguna Park. The day was warm and sunny, and whole families, from grandparents to young children, sat on the grass with plans to picnic, hear the speeches, and enjoy the accompanying music.[2]

A block away, however, deputies from the Los Angeles County Sheriff's Department, responding to a minor disturbance, declared the demonstration an unlawful assembly and ordered the park vacated. Before the mass of people had a chance to leave the park and, indeed, well before most people knew that police had ordered them to disperse, sheriff's deputies charged the crowd, shooting tear gas and beating fleeing demonstrators with nightsticks. Many people panicked as they were crushed against the fences and buses that surrounded the park. A large

---

[1]Interested students are encouraged to read this essay in the original form. Edward J. Escobar, "The Dialectics of Repression: The Los Angeles Police Department and the Chicano Movement, 1968–1971," *The Journal of American History* 79, no. 4 (March 1993), 1483–1514.

[2]*The Los Angeles Times*, Aug. 30, 1970, sec. 1, p. 1; ibid., Aug. 31, 1970, sec. 1, p. 1; ibid, Sept. 1, 1970, sec. 1, p. 1; ibid., Sept. 2, 1970; ibid., Sept. 3, 1970, sec. 1, p. 1; ibid, Sept. 16, 1970, sec. 1, p. 1; Raúl Ruiz interview by Edward J. Escobar, Jan. 8, 1988 (in Edward Escobar's possession); Diego Vigil interview by Escobar, Jan. 6, 1988, ibid; Celia Luna (Rodríguez) interview by Escobar, Jan. 18, 1988, ibid; Rosalho Muñoz interview by Escobar, Jan. 15, 1988, ibid; Rodolfo Acuña, *Occupied America: A History of Chicanos* (New York, 1988), 345–50; Armando Morales, *Ando Sangrando (I Am Bleeding): A Study of Mexican American-Police Conflict* (La Puente, 1972), 91–107; Rodolfo F. Acuña, *Community under Siege: A Chronicle of Chicanos East of the Los Angeles River, 1945–1975* (Los Angeles, 1984), 203–6.

Photo 13.1
Officer choking a Chicano during the riot that followed the
August 29, 1970, moratorium demonstration. Courtesy Raúl Ruiz.

contingent, however, turned against the line of deputies and fought pitched battles with them. As the angry crowd fled the park, many people . . . attacked passing patrol cars, broke windows, and set fire to several retail stores and police cars. *The Los Angeles Times* reported that by the end of the day police had arrested over one hundred people, forty were injured, and three lay dead or dying. One of the dead was journalist Rubén Salazar, a columnist for the *Times* and news director for Los Angeles's most popular Spanish-language television station, KMEX.[3]

Los Angeles County deputy sheriff Sgt. Thomas Wilson killed Salazar by shooting a tear gas projectile into the Silver Dollar Cafe, where Salazar sat drinking a beer. The 10-by-1½-inch projectile passed through a doorway covered only by a cloth curtain and went completely through Salazar's head. Salazar had arrived at the bar about a mile east of Laguna Park only minutes before, after covering the demonstration and the ensuing riot. Representatives of the Sheriff's Department claimed they had received a tip that a man with a gun had entered the Silver Dollar and that Wilson had shot the tear gas to flush out the armed man. The killing of Salazar, the Sheriff's Department maintained, was a tragic mistake. Many Mexican Americans, however, concluded that police had murdered Salazar because he was an articulate spokesman for the concerns of Mexican Americans and had given airtime on KMEX to militant critics of the police. Salazar became a martyr in the eyes of many Mexican Americans; activists would use the events of August 29 to politicize and organize the Los Angeles Mexican-American community.[4]

---

[3]*The Los Angeles Times*, Aug. 30, 1970, sec. 1, p. 1; ibid., Aug. 31, 1970, sec. 1, p. 1; ibid., Sept. 1, 1970, sec. 1, p. 1; ibid., Sept. 2, 1970; ibid., Sept. 3, 1970, sec. 1, p. 1; ibid., Sept. 16, 1970, sec. 1, p. 1; Ruiz interview; Vigil interview; Luna interview; Acuña, *Occupied America*, 345–50; Morales, *Ando Sangrando*, 91–107; Acuña, *Community under Siege*, 203–6.

[4]*The Los Angeles Times*, Aug. 30, 1970, sec. 1, p. 1; ibid., Aug. 31, 1970, sec. 1, p. 1; ibid., Sept. 1, 1970, sec. 1, p. 1; ibid, Sept. 4, 1970, sec. 1, pp. 2, 16; ibid., Sept. 5, 1970, sec. 1, p. 1; ibid, Sept. 6, 1970, sec. 1, p. 1; ibid., Sept. 11, 1970, sec. 1, p. 1; Muñoz interview.

Photo 13.2
Officer pointing a weapon into the Silver Dollar Cafe moments before Deputy Thomas Wilson shot and killed Rubén Salazar. Courtesy Raúl Ruiz.

The events of August 29, 1970—the Chicano Moratorium riot and the killing of Rubén Salazar—symbolized the rise of militant Mexican-American protest, official repression of that protest, and the Mexican-American response to police actions. For the previous three years, militant Mexican-American activists, who called themselves Chicanos, had waged a campaign to end discrimination against people of Mexican descent living in the United States. Nationally, this campaign comprised several smaller struggles, addressing issues such as farm workers' rights, land tenure, educational reform, political representation, the war in Vietnam, and "police brutality." Together, these various efforts became known as the Chicano movement.

Simultaneously, local law enforcement agencies, in particular the Los Angeles Police Department (LAPD), conducted their own campaign to destroy the Chicano movement in southern California. . . . First, police used their legal monopoly of the use of coercive force to harass, to intimidate, and, if possible, to arrest and prosecute individual activists and to suppress Chicano protest demonstrations with violence. Second, the LAPD infiltrated Chicano organizations, such as the Brown Berets and the National Chicano Moratorium Committee (NCMC), to gain information about their activities and to disrupt and destroy those organizations from within. Finally, the LAPD engaged in traditional red-baiting, labeling Chicano organizations and individual activists subversives and dupes of the Communist party in order to discredit them with the public. . . .

The LAPD's efforts, however, had mixed results. In a dialectical relationship, while the Los Angeles Police Department's tactics partially achieved the goal of undermining the Chicano movement, the police and their tactics became issues around which Chicano activists organized the community and increased the grassroots participation in movement activity. Moreover, as the police became more repressive, some Chicanos turned to organized violence to demonstrate their alienation from American society. Thus, police violence, rather than subduing Chicano movement activism, propelled that activism to a new level—a level that created a greater police problem than had originally existed. Most important, the conflict between the LAPD and the Chicano movement helped politicize Mexican Americans by making clearer their subordination, giving them an increased sense of ethnic identity, and arousing a greater determination to act collectively to overcome that subordination. These new attitudes led Chicanos to act with more determination and self-consciousness in voting, in litigating, and in developing new institutions that ultimately curtailed the power of the police to suppress legitimate protest.

The rise of the Chicano movement, the efforts of the LAPD to destroy the movement, and the Mexican-American community's response to those efforts all mirrored and were a part of a larger dynamic in American society in the late 1960s and early 1970s. While the Chicano movement developed in response to a historically unique set of grievances and generated distinctive solutions to those grievances, it emerged within and benefited from the broader currents of social protest that existed in the sixties. The black civil rights movement of the fifties and early sixties set the stage by focusing public attention on the issue of racial discrimination and legitimizing public protest as a way to combat discrimination. Native Americans, African Americans, Puerto Ricans, and Mexican Americans all took advantage of the favorable environment and developed broad-based social movements that demanded an end to racial discrimination. Women and gays, noting that they too had suffered from discrimination, also began agitating for equality. Movements launched by white college students and opponents of the Vietnam War also benefited from the general acceptance of protest.[5]

As each of the diverse protest movements developed new radical ideas and forms of protest, other movements borrowed them, selecting and redefining ideas and forms to fit their own experiences. . . . The Chicano movement emerged in the midst of demands for dramatic social and cultural changes—demands that eventually transformed much of American political culture but that also produced a hostile and often fierce reaction.[6]

In fact, political repression epitomized the late sixties as much as did political protest. Law enforcement agencies, from the Federal Bureau of Investigation

[5]David J. Garrow, *Bearing the Cross: Martin Luther King, Jr, and the Southern Christian Leadership Conference* (New York, 1986); Taylor Branch, *Parting the Waters: America in the King Years, 1954–1963* (New York, 1989); Clayborne Carson, *In Struggle: SNCC and the Black Awakening of the 1960s* (Cambridge, Mass., 1981). Félix M. Padilla, *Puerto Rican Chicago* (Notre Dame, 1987); Acuña, *Occupied America*, 307–62; Juan Gómez-Quiñones, *Chicano Politics: Reality and Promise, 1940–1990* (Albuquerque, 1990); Carlos Muñoz, Jr., *Youth, Identity, Power. The Chicano Movement* (New York, 1989); Gerald Paul Rosen, *Political Ideology and the Chicano Movement: A Study of the Political Ideology of Activists in the Chicano Movement* (San Francisco, 1975); Juan Gómez-Quiñones, *Mexican Students Por la Raza: The Chicano Student Movement in Southern California, 1967–1977* (Santa Barbara, 1978); Nancy Woloch, *Women and the American Experience* (New York, 1984), 479–528; Sara Evans, *Personal Politics: The Roots of Women's Liberation in the Civil Rights Movement and the New Left* (New York, 1979); John D'Emilio, *Sexual Politics, Sexual Communities: The Making of a Homosexual Minority in the United States, 1940–1970* (Chicago, 1983); Todd Gitlin, *The Sixties: Years of Hope, Days of Rage* (New York, 1987).

[6]Carson, *In Struggle*, 215–28, 265–86; Gitlin, *Sixties*, 242–60, 285–304, 362–76. See also D'Emilio, *Sexual Politics*, 197–239; Maulana Karenga, *Introduction to Black Studies* (Los Angeles, 1982), 247–50; Abdul Alkalimat and Associates, *Introduction to Afro-American Studies: A Peoples College Primer* (Chicago, 1973), 291–315.

(FBI) to municipal police departments, attempted to limit, undermine, and even destroy the various protest movements. The methods that they used to achieve these goals paralleled those used by the LAPD against the Chicano movement: red-baiting, harassment and arrest of activists, infiltration and disruption of movement organizations, and violence. . . .[7]

Mexican Americans' dialectical response to police repression also fit the pattern set in other movements: that is, police repression ultimately transformed movements and politicized whole populations. . . . The Black Panther Party for Self-Defense developed precisely to protect the African-American community from police abuse, and the violent repression of the Panthers led to the formation of the Congressional Black Caucus in the United States House of Representatives. . . . Similarly, on June 27, 1969, homosexuals in New York City responded to yet another police raid on a gay bar with several nights of rioting. The Stonewall riot (named after the bar the police raided) turned what had been an accommodationist, almost apologetic homophile movement into the aggressive and highly effective gay power movement that has revolutionized laws regarding sexual preferences. . . .[8]

This essay expands the historical analysis of militant protest and official repression in the sixties by focusing on Mexican Americans and by examining the effects of the conflict both on the Chicano movement and, more broadly, on the Mexican-American community. Specifically, this paper argues that while police were using violence and intimidation against the movement, Chicanos were using the issues of political harassment and police brutality to increase participation in their movement. Police repression not only invigorated the Chicano movement but also helped politicize and empower the Mexican-American community.

In the 1960s Mexican Americans were the nation's second largest and its fastest- growing minority group. . . . Historically, Mexican Americans [had] suffered from racial discrimination . . . [and] by the 1960s, . . . found themselves in a situation similar to that of blacks in the United States. In California, for example, blacks had a higher unemployment rate, lower income, and faced greater housing discrimination than Mexican Americans. Mexican Americans, on the other hand, had lower levels of educational attainment and experienced more rigid occupational stratification and more dilapidated housing. In addition, Mexican

[7]Gary T. Marx, "Thoughts on a Neglected Category of Social Movement Participant: The Agent Provocateur and the Informant," *American Journal of Sociology* 80 (Sept. 1974), 402–42; David J. Garrow, *The FBI and Martin Luther King, Jr* (New York, 1981); Kenneth O'Reilly, *"Racial Matters": The FBI's Secret File on Black America, 1960–1972* (New York, 1989), 125–55, 261–353; Churchill and Vander Wall, *Agents of Repression*, 37–99; Gitlin, *Sixties*, 244, 314, 317–40, 350–51, 378; Frank Donner, *Protectors of Privilege: Red Squads and Police Repression in Urban America* (Berkeley, 1990); and Frank J. Donner, *The Age of Surveillance: The Aims and Methods of America's Political Intelligence System* (New York, 1981).

[8]Churchill and Vander Wall, *Agents of Repression*; Henry Hampton and Steve Fayer, *Voices of Freedom: An Oral History of the Civil Rights Movement from the 1950s through the 1980s* (New York, 1990); Gitlin, *Sixties*, 249–56, 285; D'Emilio, *Sexual Politics*, 231–39.

Americans had even less political representation than African Americans. . . .[9] The Mexican-American community, in particular, the generation that came of age in the 1940s and 1950s, fought for equality. . . . They . . . worked together to end discriminatory practices in three distinct ways: by engaging in liberal politics in order to end the most offensive forms of anti-Mexican discrimination; by declaring Mexican Americans part of the white race and therefore worthy of equality; and by adopting a pluralistic vision of American society in which they could maintain aspects of their Mexican culture but still be integrated into the mainstream of American life. This generation thus saw Mexican-American progress in terms of partial and gradual acculturation, integration, and individual mobility. . . .[10]

The Chicano movement of the late sixties challenged many of the previous generation's assumptions and tactics. It consisted primarily of young people of high school and college age who had grown frustrated with the sluggish pace of traditional reform politics. Like the militants of the Black Power movement that they emulated, Chicanos (a previously pejorative term adopted by young Mexican Americans to establish and define their own identity) found American culture inherently racist and corrupt. They developed the nationalist concept of *chicanismo* to signal that they rejected assimilation. They declared that as a result of their Mexican ancestry and their experiences in the Southwest, they had an identity and heritage that they intended to keep intact. Moreover, Chicanos declared themselves a nonwhite minority in solidarity with other oppressed racial groups throughout the world. Like members of other nonwhite racial groups, they saw themselves as victims of white racism and argued Chicanos could achieve equality only through collective social and economic empowerment. Finally, unlike the previous generation of Mexican-American activists who eschewed the direct action, civil disobedience tactics of the black civil rights movement, many Chicanos believed that solely through militant, confrontational means could they force white institutions to redress their grievances. . . .[11]

Movement organizations communicated their message to the larger Mexican-American community through the Chicano media. In Los Angeles, newspapers such as *La Raza* provided information and an analysis of it that Mexican Americans found nowhere else. By fostering the concept of *chicanismo* and by being openly and even stridently critical of American institutions, these newspapers

[9]Leo Grebler, Joan W. Moore, and Ralph C. Guzmán, *The Mexican-American People: The Nation's Second Largest Minority* (New York, 1970), 106, 142–289; Fernando J. Guerra, "Ethnic Officeholders in Los Angeles County," *Sociology and Social Research* 71 (Jan. 1987), 89–94.

[10]Mario T. Garcia, *Mexican Americans*, 15–22; Muñoz, *Youth, Identity, Power*, 19–44; Gómez-Quiñones, *Chicano Politics*, 31–99; Mario Barrera, *Beyond Aztán: Ethnic Autonomy in Comparative Perspective* (Notre Dame, 1988), 21–31.

[11]Muñoz, *Youth, Identity, Power*, 47–64, 75–91; Gómez-Quiñones, *Chicano Politics*, 101–5, 118–24, 141–46; Gómez-Quiñones, *Mexican Students Porla Raza*, 11–35; Barerra, *Beyond Aztlán*, 33–44; Rosen, *Political Ideology and the Chicano Movement*, 52–67, 80–84, 89–90, 104–19; Acuña, *Occupied America*, 307–11, 317–20, 324–27, 332–42, 354–56; Gutierrez, "Sin Fronteras?" 11–16.

created a Chicano counterideology. That ideology celebrated Chicanos' culture and identity; declared them an oppressed minority; identified as their oppressors institutions such as the educational system, the Catholic church, the business community, and, in particular, the police; and demanded an end to racial discrimination. . . .[12]

. . . The Chicano movement had four general goals: to maintain pride in Mexican Americans' cultural identity; to foster a political understanding that Mexican Americans were an oppressed and exploited minority group; to use the ethnic pride and the sense of exploitation to forge a political movement through which Chicanos would empower themselves; and, finally, to force white society to end the discriminatory practices that restricted Chicanos' lives. Although Chicanos often used provocative rhetoric and engaged in confrontational politics, the basic goal of the Chicano movement—gaining equality for Chicanos *within* American society—was essentially reformist, not revolutionary.

Despite the Chicano movement's reformist agenda, Los Angeles police officials used their intelligence capabilities, along with . . . violence, to subvert and destroy the movement. . . . The LAPD defined intelligence broadly as gathering "information about organizations and persons whose plans or activities may influence the police posture or performance," and police officials explained their intelligence operations as intended only to protect the public from riots and terrorism.[13]

The LAPD's activities against the Chicano movement, however, went far beyond mere intelligence gathering, as police agents engaged in criminal activity themselves in order to disrupt and destroy the movement. . . . Agents often concoct phony information, provoke a group to commit crimes, or commit crimes themselves in order to disrupt an organization or provide testimony in court. . . .[14]

. . . Occasional unguarded remarks by LAPD officials reveal that catching criminals was not necessarily the department's first priority. The future police chief Edward M. Davis, for example, at a staff meeting in 1969, recommended using intelligence work to conduct "psychological warfare" against the LAPD's critics. Since the LAPD's intelligence efforts did not result in a single successful prosecution of a major Chicano movement figure, the primary intent of the repression was probably silencing the department's enemies.[15]

Undermining social protest movements also coincided with the LAPD's conservative ideology. That ideology, which had been developing since the late nineteenth century, became institutionalized during the administration of Police

---

[12]Acuña, *Community under Siege*; Rosen, *Political Ideology and the Chicano Movement*, 74–75.

[13]Los Angeles Police Department, Public Disorder Intelligence Division, "LAPD Public Disorder Intelligence Accomplishments," typescript, 1977, box 92854, Chief of Police General Files (Los Angeles City Records Center, Los Angeles, Calif.).

[14]Marx, "Thoughts on a Neglected Category of Social Movement Participant," 419–24.

[15]Ibid, 436; Los Angeles Police Department, Staff Meeting, Minutes, Jan. 20, 1969, box 38166, Chief of Police General Files.

Chief William H. Parker, who headed the department from 1950 to 1966. As an architect of the police professionalism movement, Parker transformed the LAPD into the model for professional big city police. . . . Police autonomy stood at the heart of police professionalism, and Parker saw gaining independence from political control as his greatest achievement. . . . Parker used that independence to build a police department that reflected his own views of strict authoritarianism and strident anticommunism. He saw it as the LAPD's role to protect the hardworking middle class from those who would steal their just rewards. Thus he viewed with great alarm the social movements that engulfed the United States during the sixties. Finally, Parker believed that police constituted the "thin blue line" that stood between civilized society and chaos, arguing that "the very existence of the Nation hinged on its ability to support its law enforcement agencies. For Parker, then, and for the police administrators across the country who admired him, critics of the police were, by their very nature, disloyal and un-American; and during the sixties, in police circles the adjective *antipolice* became a noun and synonymous with subversion.[16]

In addition to the police's ideological bias against social protest, their experience with the Black Power movement predisposed them to hostility toward the Chicano movement. . . . FBI director Hoover labeled the Panthers "the greatest threat to the internal security of the Country" and launched the famous COINTELPRO against that organization. This operation sought to destroy militant groups such as the Panthers by whatever means necessary, from the use of *agents provocateurs* to political assassination. Local police departments worked hand in hand with the FBI, and at a meeting convened by the National Commission on Civil Disorders in November 1967, police chiefs from across the nation developed a plan to establish their own intelligence capability to stop the growth of militant organizations. At that meeting Police Chief Thomas Reddin of Los Angeles articulated his department's . . . analysis of the Black Power movement. "The present Negro movement," Reddin declared, "is just as subversive as the past Communist movement or just as dangerous as the organized crime movement." Furthermore, since he regarded all protest demonstrations as potential sources of riots, Reddin concluded police should always be ready to employ massive force against demonstrators. He proclaimed that in preventing urban riots police should engage in "overkill—kill the butterfly with a sledge hammer." Reddin's sledge-hammer and Davis's psychological warfare became the LAPD's favorite tools against Chicano activists.[17]

From the moment Chicanos began protesting against police misconduct, law enforcement agencies responded by using . . . force to harass and intimidate

---

[16]Joseph Gerald Woods, "The Progressives and the Police: Urban Reform and the Professionalization of the Los Angeles Police" (Ph.D. diss., University of California, Los Angeles, 1973), 417–511; Manion Forum, "Anarchy Imminent: Local Police Hobbled in Efforts to Stem Crime" (interview with Los Angeles Police Chief William H. Parker), May 30, 1965, box 35318, Chief of Police General Files.

[17]O'Reilly, *"Racial Matters,"* 290. U.S. Commission on Civil Disorders, typescript, Nov. 2, 1967, box 38, Urban Policy Research Institute Papers; see Donner, *Age of Surveillance,* 126–230.

Chicano activists and organizations. In December 1967 a group called Young Chicanos for Community Action (YCCA) picketed the East Los Angeles sheriff's substation to protest cases of police brutality. *La Raza* reported that in retaliation sheriff's deputies began stopping and searching people who entered the YCCA meeting place at the Piranya Coffee House in East Los Angeles and arresting underage coffeehouse patrons for curfew violations. *La Raza* pointed out that the curfew arrests were illegal since those arrested were inside a building, not loitering on the streets as the ordinance specified. Partly in response to the police harassment, the YCCA the next month changed its name to the Brown Berets and adopted a much more militant posture.[18]

The events that spurred local police to even more repressive measures were the March 1968 student walkouts, when over ten thousand East Los Angeles Chicano high school students walked out of their classes to protest the inferior education they received. Organized by [United Mexican American Students] (UMAS), Brown Berets, and other activists, the students demanded the same facilities, textbooks, and supplies as students in predominantly white schools; curriculum changes to include Chicano history and culture; more Mexican-American teachers, counselors, and administrators; and amnesty for students and teachers who participated in the walkouts.[19]

. . . At Lincoln High School, where the protests began on March 1, administrators [initially] allowed the students to leave the school grounds. When the walkouts started spreading to other predominantly Mexican-American schools, officials from the Los Angeles City School District and the LAPD took a harder line. At Roosevelt High School on March 5, administrators locked the gates that surrounded the school to prevent striking students from leaving, and LAPD squad cars massed around the campus to intimidate the strikers. The students, however, climbed over the fences, and the police presence provoked minor violence (some students threw bottles at passing police cars). The police retaliated by attacking the demonstrators, peaceful or not, and arresting anyone who came to their aid. A newspaper that developed from the walkouts, *Chicano Student News*, described in detail how two Chicano teenagers were "jumped by four full grown armed policemen, beaten to the ground and held with a club to the neck." The LAPD attempted to justify its actions and discredit the student protests by claiming that Communists had participated in and influenced the walkouts.[20]

The walkouts dramatically altered the relationship between Chicanos and the LAPD. Both Chicano activists and police officials agreed that the level of violence in contacts between Chicanos and officers rose after the spring of 1968.

---

[18]*La Raza*, Dec. 25, 1967, Jan. 15, 1968; Rosen, *Political Ideology and the Chicano Movement*, 73.

[19]*Chicano Student News*, March 15, 1968; Muñoz, *Youth, Identity, Power*, 171–74; Acuña, *Occupied America*, 356; Gómez-Quiñones, *Chicago Politics*, 101–53; Gómez-Quiñones, *Mexican Students PorIa Raza*, 26–35; Rosen, *Political Ideology and the Chicano Movement*, 68–101, 139–40.

[20]*Inside Eastside*, March 29, 1968; *La Raza*, March 31, 1968; Ruiz interview; Commander Clifford J. Shannon, Press Release, April 30, 1968, box 38166, Chief of Police General Files.

Chicanos charged that the increase resulted from police attempts to intimidate movement activists; police officials believed the movement caused Chicanos to be more combative toward police officers. Whatever the cause, after March 1968 Chicano movement newspapers and community organizations paid increased attention to charges of police harassment and brutality.[21]

The Chicano press gave particular attention to two cases of police brutality. One was the beating by the LAPD of Jesús Domínguez, a member of the Educational Issues Coordinating Committee, a group organized by parents to support their children during the walkouts. According to *La Raza*, "at least 15 policemen jumped at him, hitting him with clubs and fists and kicking him while he was already handcuffed and on the pavement." Domínguez's injuries were so serious that he underwent brain surgery. In the other case, publicized by *Inside Eastside*, LAPD officers beat thirteen-year-old Salvador Barba, breaking two vertebrae and causing head injuries that required forty stitches.[22]

. . . Chicanos argued that the beatings were politically motivated and invoked them to organize the community . . . and created organizations to assist the victims of official misconduct. To provide legal assistance for the Domínguez family, the EICC developed a subcommittee that held rallies, hired lawyers, and organized fund-raising dances, which became large community events. Eventually, that subcommittee, led by Celia Luna (then known as Celia Rodriguez), institutionalized itself as the Barrio Defense Committee (BDC) and gave similar assistance to other victims of police abuse.[23]

An even more effective rallying point for Chicano organizers was the prosecution of individuals involved in Chicano protest activity. . . . At the end of May 1968, District Attorney Evelle Younger gained indictments against thirteen of the walkout organizers. Chicanos reacted with outrage. Although authorities developed no evidence that anyone did anything more serious than disturb the peace, the grand jury indicted the thirteen for conspiracy to commit a misdemeanor; such conspiracy was a felony and carried with it a long prison term. . . . Chicanos instituted a 200-person picket around LAPD headquarters the day after the arrests. On the following day, 2,000 people demonstrated at the same, the largest Mexican-American demonstration in the city's history. . . . The official response to the walkouts, instead of inhibiting Chicano protest, had provoked increased activity and had raised the issue of police repression of Chicano political activism.[24]

---

[21]United States Commission on Civil Rights, *California Advisory Committee, Police-Community Relations in East Los Angeles, California: A Report of the California State Advisory to the United States Commission on Civil Rights* ([Los Angeles], 1970), 19–20.

[22]Luna interview; *La Raza*, Oct. 15, 1968, Nov.–Dec. 1969; *Inside Eastside*, Nov. 18, 1968; *Chicano Student Movement*, Nov. 1968; *La Raza*, June 1969; U.S. Commission on Civil Rights, *Mexican Americans and the Administration of Justice in the Southwest* (Washington, D.C., 1970), 4–5.

[23]*Inside Eastside*, Nov. 18, Dec. 23, 1968; *Chicano Student Movement*, Nov. 1968; *La Raza*, Dec. 1969; Luna interview.

[24]*Inside Eastside*, April 26, 1968; *La Raza*, June 7, 1968; *Chicano Student News*, June 12, 1968; and *Inside Eastside*, June 10, 1968.

Police officials, however, also responded to the walkouts in more subtle, less public ways by establishing an intelligence network within the Chicano community. At its least significant level, the network gathered information on Chicano movement activity from public sources. More destructive was the planting of police officers or civilian agents within Chicano organizations. . . . Both the presence of informers and the belief in their presence sowed debilitating distrust within movement organizations. Finally, the infiltrators often did not confine their activities to information gathering. . . . In their roles as infiltrators, both civilian agents and police officers sworn to enforce the law allowed, instigated, and engaged in illegal activity.[25]

During the two years after the walkouts, the Brown Berets were a favorite target of LAPD agents. In a celebrated case, LAPD Officer Fernando Sumaya, who had infiltrated the organization, testified before a grand jury that Brown Berets had started fires at the Biltmore Hotel during a May 1969 speech by Gov. Ronald Reagan. In the subsequent trials, Sumaya claimed that Berets Carlos Montes and Ralph Ramírez set the blazes, but the defendants gave vivid testimony that Sumaya himself started the fires in order to entrap them. The juries apparently found the Berets' testimony convincing, for they acquitted the defendants on all charges. . . .[26]

LAPD officials worried that the charges of police brutality and political repression publicized by the Chicano press were having an impact on the Mexican-American community. . . . An internal LAPD document expressed fear that this "type of garbage [reporting] . . . may well contribute to the rise is assaults on police officials." Publications such as *La Raza*, . . . the LAPD intelligence summary concluded, "do nothing put preach and foment hate of minorities toward whites and in particular, law enforcement. It would be beneficial if some of these publications could be forced to stop publication or at least, control the biased and unfounded reports they print." . . .[27]

In the last days of 1969 and the first eight months of 1970, tension and violence between Chicanos and police increased. On Christmas Eve 1969, officers beat members of Católicos Por La Raza for demonstrating in front of Saint Basil Church to protest the Catholic Church's neglect of the Mexican-American community. In February the National Chicano Moratorium Committee held a march in a driving rain to protest the Vietnam War. . . . Early in March Chicano students at Roosevelt High School again walked out of school to protest educational policies. This time the LAPD responded with immediate and intimidating violence. Television cameras showed police beating protestors with nightsticks and

---

[25]Los Angeles Police Department, "Intelligence Summary," Jan. 1, 1969–Dec. 7, 1969, box 74284, Chief of Police General Files; Luna interview.

[26]Carlos Montes interview by Escobar, Jan. 9, 1989 (in Escobar's possession); *California v. Carlos Montes*, No. A 244906 and No. A 408717, California Superior Court Department No. 132, Reporters' Transcript of Proceedings, Feb. 9 to April 26, 1979, 653–82; *The Los Angeles Times*, Aug. 10, Aug. 20, Aug. 21, Aug. 24, 1971, May 18, 1972.

[27]Los Angeles Police Department, "Intelligence Summary," July 30, 1969, box 74284, Chief of Police General Files.

dragging young Mexican-American girls across the high school campus by their hair. Such spectacles frightened and angered the Mexican-American community. KMEX, the Spanish-language television station, interviewed one mother who said that she had kept her boy home from school because she feared the police would kill him. In the aftermath of the demonstrations, the Barrio Defense Committee attracted more than a thousand people to a meeting to plan ways of counteracting the police actions. The LAPD reacted hostilely to the negative publicity. An article in the *Los Angeles Times* by Rubén Salazar that criticized LAPD Chief Edward Davis's cavalier attitude toward Chicano concerns about the events at Roosevelt infuriated the chief and his associates. Davis's personal assistant, Lt. Bob Walter, promised that his boss would tear "the hide right off [Salazar's] back," and the department opened an intelligence file on the journalist. . . .[28]

The publication in March 1970 of the United States Civil Rights Commission report *Mexican Americans and the Administration of Justice in the Southwest* reinforced many of the charges Chicanos had been making about the Los Angeles police. Nationally, the report found "evidence of widespread . . . police misconduct against Mexican Americans" and specifically cited police for using "excessive . . . violence against Mexican Americans" and for interfering with legitimate Chicano political activity. By including and documenting the Domínguez and Barba cases as examples of LAPD misconduct, the report encouraged Chicanos to increase their criticism of the department. Salazar, for example, wrote that the report gave credibility to Brown Beret prime minister David Sánchez's statement that "to Anglos justice means *just us*."[29]

The tensions and violence between Chicanos and police continued throughout the spring and summer of 1970. . . . During July the violence turned deadly. On the seventeenth, while searching for a murder suspect, LAPD Sgt. Frank Gaines without warning kicked in the door of an apartment in a skid row hotel where five undocumented Mexican workers lived. Within seconds of entering the apartment, Gaines shot through a closed door at the end of a hallway, killing Guillermo Sánchez. Other police officers stationed outside the building shot and killed Guillermo's cousin, Beltrán Sánchez, as . . . [he] climbed out of a window. The Barrio Defense Committee condemned the killings and staged a mock funeral procession from the skid row hotel to police headquarters at Parker Center. The killings received wide coverage in the Chicano and mainstream

---

[28]Luna interview. Católicos Por la Raza (newspaper), Jan. 1970; Muñoz interview; *The Los Angeles Times*, n.d., box 49, Urban Policy Research Institute Papers;ibid., March 11, 1970; Theodora Jacobs to Edward M. Davis, March 10, 1970, box 66024, Chief of Police General Files; Mrs. C. López to Ernest E. Debs, March 16, 1970, ibid; LAPD, transcript of KMEX newscast, March 11, 1970, box 38156, ibid.; Luna interview; *The Los Angeles Times*, March 13, 1970; Bob Walter to Davis, March 13, 1970; box 38156, Chief of Police General Files; Davis to Nick Williams, March 13, 1970, ibid.; LAPD, press release, March 13, 1970, ibid; anon., March 18, 1870, ibid.

[29]U.S. Commission on Civil Rights, *Mexican Americans and the Administration of Justice in the Southwest*, 2–26; *The Los Angeles Times*, May 1, 1970.

press and made police brutality an issue to be addressed at the upcoming National Chicano Moratorium demonstration.[30]

That August 29 demonstration turned violent and tragic. The demonstration became a riot when the owner of a liquor store . . . [near] Laguna Park called the Sheriff's Department to complain that teenagers had stolen cold drinks. . . . Deputies responded in squad cars with their sirens and lights blazing. The young people who allegedly stole the drinks ran off toward the park and the demonstration. The deputies followed and were met with rocks and bottles from the perimeter of the park. Monitors attempted to quell the disturbance and pleaded with the youngsters to cease the violence and with the deputies to leave the scene. The Sheriff's Department instead declared the demonstration an unlawful assembly and attempted to disperse the crowd with tear gas and nightsticks. The ensuing violence lasted for several hours and resulted in three deaths, including that of Rubén Salazar.[31]

If the moratorium riot shocked the city, the killing of Salazar outraged Chicanos. Many Chicanos believed that police had murdered Salazar because he was an articulate spokesman for Mexican Americans. After ten years of working as a foreign correspondent for *The Los Angeles Times*, Salazar returned to Los Angeles in 1969 and began writing news stories and a weekly column on issues related to Mexican Americans. In April 1970 he became news director for Los Angeles's most popular Spanish-language television station, KMEX. For the *Times*, Salazar wrote articles aimed primarily at white readers explaining and often supporting the Chicano movement. Occasionally, he wrote articles critical of the police and sufficiently angered the LAPD that the department opened an intelligence file on him. . . .[32]

Police seemed especially concerned with Salazar's role as news director at KMEX. Salazar gave airtime to people and organizations the LAPD considered subversive. . . . Salazar repeatedly gave representatives of the Brown Berets, the Barrio Defense Committee, and *La Raza* newspaper airtime to publicize and interpret the LAPD killing of the Sánchez cousins. According to the historian Rodolfo Acuña, the LAPD responded by sending officers to visit Salazar. These officers "ordered him to tone down his television coverage" because "he was inciting the people". . . . According to Acuña, the officers concluded by telling Salazar "they would get him if he continued his coverage." . . . Guillermo Restrepo, Salazar's cameraman, recalled that on the day of his death Salazar acted as if someone was following him and told Restrepo he was "scared." Restrepo observed that since Salazar had served in Vietnam, the Dominican

[30]*The Los Angeles Times*, July 18, 1970; Los Angeles Police Department, Robbery-Homicide Division Report of Officer-Involved Shooting, July 28, 1970, box 38162, Chief of Police General Files; Luna interview, Muñoz interview.

[31]*The Los Angeles Times*, Aug. 30, 1970, sec. 1, p. 1; ibid., Aug. 31, 1970, sec. 1, p. 1; ibid., Sept. 1, 1970, sec. 1, p. 1; ibid., Sept. 2, 1970; ibid., Sept. 3, 1970, sec. 1, p. 1; ibid., Sept. 16, 1970, sec. 1, p. 1; Ruiz interview; Vigil interview; Luna interview; Acuña, *Occupied America*, 345–50; Morales, *Ando Sangrando*, 91–107.

[32]*The Los Angeles Times*, Sept. 1, 1970; ibid., Sept. 3, 1970, sec. 1, p. 3; Luna interview; memorandum, March 18, 1970, box 38156, Chief of Police General Files.

Republic, and Mexico City amid much greater violence, he doubted Salazar feared the relatively minor violence of the moratorium riot.[33]

Mexican Americans of various political persuasions refused to believe that Salazar's death at the hands of Deputy Wilson was an accident, as Los Angeles County Sheriff Peter Pitchess claimed. The Chicano attorney Oscar Acosta called Salazar's death a "political murder, plain and simple," and the traditionally moderate League of United Latin American Citizens accused the Sheriff's Department of "wanton murder." Protestors from the NCMC demonstrated in front of the East Los Angeles Sheriff's Substation, chanting, "Who killed Salazar? Wilson! Who gave the orders? Pitchess!"[34]

The investigation that officials conducted left the circumstances of Salazar's death unclear. Representatives of the Sheriff's Department gave contradictory accounts of how Salazar died and of how the department's officers acted following the incident. At first, deputies reported that Salazar died of gunshot wounds and that officers entered the bar immediately after the shooting. Later, in what became the Sheriff's Department's official version, deputies claimed that the tear gas projectile killed Salazar and that they did not discover the body until several hours later.[35]

Various sources, however, immediately called the Sheriff's Department's story into question. The *Times* disclosed that the tear gas projectile that killed Salazar . . . was designed to capture "barricaded criminals" and could pierce the stucco wall of a house at less than one hundred feet. Photos taken by Chicano activist and journalist Raul Ruiz and eyewitness accounts show that, rather than trying to evacuate the building (the alleged reason for using tear gas), deputies forced people back into the Silver Dollar Cafe at gunpoint moments before the shooting. Witnesses at the official inquest also testified that Sergeant Wilson stood at the doorway holding a "miniature cannon" and opened the curtains to look inside the bar, thus seeing exactly where Salazar sat seconds before he fired the fatal shot. Finally, no one inside the bar had heard a warning before deputies fired the tear gas.[36]

The dramatic high point of the investigation came during the coroner's inquest, which local television stations broadcast live. Chicano observers charged that inquest judge Norman Pittluck conducted a cover-up. They accused him of allowing improper testimony that supported the Sheriff's Department's version of the event but impeaching the credibility of Chicano witnesses, such as Raul Ruiz. . . . Pittluck even instructed the seven-member inquest jury to find that Salazar had died "by accident"—a verdict that would almost certainly prevent any criminal prosecution Despite Pittluck's instruction, four of the seven jurors

---

[33]Luna interview; Ruiz interview; Muñoz interview; Acuña, *Occupied America*, 346; Manuel Ruiz, Jr., to Herman Sillas, Nov. 11, 1970, addendum 3, Manuel Ruiz, Jr., Papers (Special Collections, Stanford University Library, Stanford, Calif.); *The Los Angeles Times*, Sept. 22, 1970, sec. 1, p. 3.

[34]*The Los Angeles Times*, Sept. 4, 1970, sec. 1, pp. 2, 16; Muñoz interview.

[35]*The Los Angeles Times*, Aug. 30, sec. 1, p. 1; ibid, Aug. 31, 1970, sec. 1, p. 1.

[36]*The Los Angeles Times*, Sept. 1, 1970, sec. 1, p. 1; ibid., Sept. 4, 1970, sec. 1, p. 1; ibid., Sept. 19, 1970, sec. 1, p. 1; ibid., Sept. 20, 1970, sec. 1, p. 1; ibid., Sept. 21, 1970, sec. 1, p. 1; ibid., Sept. 22, 1970, sec. 1, p. 1; ibid., Sept. 23, 1970, sec. 1, p 1; ibid., Sept. 24, 1970, sec. 1, p. 1; ibid., Sept. 26, 1970, sec. 2, p. 10; ibid., Sept. 29, 1970, sec. 1, p. 1.

believed that the criminal investigation should proceed and found Salazar had died "at the hands of another." After the verdict was delivered, the three other jurors stated they too would have voted with the majority but felt compelled to comply with Pittluck's instructions.[37]

As many Chicanos had anticipated, District Attorney Evelle Younger refused to file any criminal charges. He stated that since three jurors on the inquest jury had voted for a "by accident" verdict, he doubted he could convince twelve jurors in a criminal trial that any crime had been committed. The *Times* pointed out that all the inquest jurors would have voted for the stronger verdict but that three felt compelled to follow Pittluck's erroneous instructions. When the United States Justice Department refused to enter the case, the criminal investigation into the killing ended.[38]

The killing of Rubén Salazar had profound consequences. First, as a writer for the *Times*, Salazar had been perhaps the most articulate spokesperson for Chicano concerns to the Anglo community. Second, and more important, as news director for KMEX, the main Spanish-language television station in Los Angeles, Salazar had provided airtime to Chicano community activists. By giving militants access to the airwaves, he furnished many Mexican Americans the type of information and an analysis of that information that could lead to their politicization or even radicalization. With Salazar dead, this alternative news source ceased to exist. The owners of KMEX, bowing to pressure from police and government officials, now refused Chicano activists access to the airwaves. For Chicanos, Salazar became a hero—a martyr who died for the cause of Chicano liberation and a symbol for those who fought ongoing repression.[39]

Despite the public outcry over the killing of Rubén Salazar, official harassment, intimidation, and violence against Chicanos increased after the August 29 moratorium demonstration and riot. The LAPD raised the level of its rhetoric. . . . Chief Davis issued a statement that the August 29 violence resulted from a decision by the Communist party to concentrate its efforts on the Mexican-American community. Davis claimed that "swimming pool Communists" exploited Chicanos as "prison fodder" in their attempts to overthrow the government of the United States. In the months that followed, Davis incessantly charged that the Brown Berets were "self-avowed Marxists" and that they engaged in "revolution on the installment plan."[40]

---

[37]*The Los Angeles Times*, Sept. 9, 1970, sec. 1, p. 1; ibid, Sept. 11, 1970, sec. 1, p. 1; ibid, Sept. 16, 1970, sec. 1, p. 3; ibid, Sept. 18, 1970, sec. 1, p. 3; ibid, Oct. 1, 1970, sec. 1, p. 3; ibid., Oct. 6, 1970, sec. 1, p. 1; ibid., Oct. 8, 1970; ibid, Sept. 15, 1970, sec. 1, p. 1; ibid., Oct. 6, 1970, sec. 1, p. 1.

[38]*The Los Angeles Times*, Oct. 15, 1970, sec. 1, p. 1; ibid., Dec. 19, 1973, sec. 1, p. 1.

[39]Ruiz interview; Luna interview; see Los Angeles Theatre Center, *An Anthology for the Play August 29* (Los Angeles, 1990).

[40]*The Los Angeles Times*, clipping, n.d., box 38158, Chief of Police General Files; Robert Kaiser, "Partial Transcript of Tape Recording of Interview of Chief Edward M. Davis," Jan. 20, 1971. Supplement, Urban Policy Research Institute Papers; statement by E. M. Davis in U.S. Senate Subcommittee on Internal Security, "Assaults on Law Enforcement Officers," Oct. 9, 1970, box 38162, Chief of Police General Files.

Photo 13.3
Chicanos marching toward Parker Center (Los Angeles Police
Department headquarters) during the January 9, 1971,
demonstration against LAPD repression. Courtesy Raúl Ruiz.

In addition, police increased the use of infiltrators and *agents provocateurs*. Frank Martínez, for example, infiltrated both the NCMC and the Brown Berets. He exhorted others to commit acts of violence and committed illegal acts himself. On November 4, 1970, Martinez brandished a weapon in front of the NCMC headquarters in full view of several LAPD squad cars. The police used his act as an excuse to storm the building, beat and arrest several occupants, and confiscate NCMC documents. Martinez later revealed that agents of the Treasury Department's Bureau of Alcohol, Tobacco, and Firearms, working in collaboration with the LAPD, had ordered him "to cause confusion, . . . to provoke incidents" in order "to eliminate" the Brown Berets and the NCMC. . . .[41]

In response, Chicano groups organized or took part in several demonstrations in the six months after August 29. On September 16 a contingent from the NCMC participated in the annual Mexican Independence Day parade. On January 9, 1971, Chicanos demonstrated in front of the LAPD's Hollenbeck Division station in East Los Angeles and then marched on LAPD headquarters to protest police attacks on the NCMC. Finally, on January 31, Chicanos again demonstrated to condemn police practices against activists. Each of these demonstrations ended in violence. The greatest violence occurred at the end of the January 31 demonstration when sheriff's deputies shot into a crowd of rock-throwing Chicanos, killing one and wounding thirty-five.[42]

[41]National Chicano Moratorium Committee, Press Release, Nov. 17, 1970, box 20, Bert Corona Papers (Special Collections, Stanford University Library); Muñoz interview; Citizens' Research and Investigation Committee and Louis Tackwood, *The Glass House Tapes: The Story of an Agent-Provocateur and the New Police Intelligence Complex* (New York, 1973), 137–39.

[42]Morales, Ando Sangrando, 107–20; Acuña, *Community under Siege*, 213–14; *The Los Angeles Times*, Sept. 17, 1970, sec. 1, p. 1; ibid, Jan. 10, 1971, sec. 1, p. 1; ibid., Feb. 1, 1971, sec. 1, p. 1; ibid., Feb. 2, 1971, sec. 2; ibid., Feb. 3, 1971, sec. 1, p. 1; ibid., Feb. 4, 1971, sec. 1.

Photo 13.4
January 31, 1971. Chicano moratorium demonstration
against police violence at Hazard Park in East Los Angeles.
Courtesy Raúl Ruiz.

The LAPD used intelligence from informers to try to prove that Chicanos had planned the violence. An agent, for example, reported that the Brown Berets had stockpiled weapons for the January 9 demonstration and that David Sánchez, prime minister of the Berets, boasted that the demonstration would end in a "bloodbath." Subsequent reports proved this information false and showed that the Berets wanted to keep the demonstration peaceful. Nevertheless, Chief Davis repeated the bloodbath story to the press to discredit the Berets.[43]

Davis's strategy ultimately succeeded, as the violence undermined support for future public protests in the white establishment and among some important elements within the movement itself and ultimately destroyed important movement organizations. The *Times*, for example, became decidedly hostile toward Chicano demonstrations after the January 9, 1971, protest in which Chicanos rioted outside the *Times* building. In the wake of the January 31, 1971, rally that again ended in street violence and death, Esteban Torres and Ed Aguirre, of the important Council on Mexican American Unity, declared that no more large-scale public demonstrations should take place. Rosalío Muñoz, the chair of the NCMC, bowed to this pressure. Having decided to hold no more public protests, the NCMC lost its reason for existence and subsequently withered away.[44]

---

[43]Los Angeles Police Department, "Intelligence Summary," Jan. 1, 1969–Dec. 7, 1969, box 74284, Chief of Police General Files; Los Angeles Police Department, Intelligence Report, Dec. 18, 1970, box 43986, ibid; Los Angeles Police Department, "Unconfirmed N.C.M.C. Demonstration Activity Scheduled for Saturday, January 9, 1971," n.d., ibid.; Kaiser, "Partial Transcript of Tape Recording of Interview of Chief Edward M. Davis."

[44]Morales, *Ando Sangrando*, 107–20; *The Los Angeles Times*, Jan. 10, 1971, sec. 1, p. 1; ibid., Feb. 1, 1971, sec. 1, p. 1; ibid., Feb. 2, 1971, sec. 2; ibid., Feb. 3, 1971, sec. 1, p. 1; ibid., Feb. 4, 1971, sec. 1, p. 1; Muñoz interview; Vigil interview; Luna interview; Kaiser, "Partial Transcript of Tape Recording of Interview of Chief Edward M. Davis."

Photo 13.5
Raúl Ruiz laying the Mexican flag on the body of a Chicano demonstrator killed by sheriff's deputies after the January 31, 1971, moratorium demonstration. Courtesy Raúl Ruiz.

The tensions created by the presence of police informers also took its toll on Chicano organizations. Celia Luna states that the organization she headed, the Barrio Defense Committee, eventually dissolved because the possible presence of informers not only made members suspect one another but also discouraged potential complainants from filing charges for fear of police reprisals. In 1972, thwarted by police harassment and racked with internal dissension, the Brown Berets officially disbanded.[45]

With legitimate forms of protest closed and with their organizations collapsing, some Chicanos turned to random violence to vent their frustrations. During 1971 a wave of bombings rocked Los Angeles; a group calling itself the Chicano Liberation Front (CLF) claimed responsibility for the attacks. The bombings began on January 29, 1971, when "a sophisticated and highly explosive device" exploded in the men's washroom in the federal building in downtown Los Angeles, killing an innocent bystander. . . . Over the next several months, the LAPD received hundreds of bomb threats (many against LAPD installations) and investigated scores of actual bombings. Except at the federal building, no one was injured.[46]

In a "Declaration" distributed in August 1971, the CLF justified its actions as a response to police repression. It argued that Chicanos had attempted to bring about change through peaceful means but had been met only with rejection from

[45]Luna interview; David Sánchez, *Expedition through Aztlán* (La Puente, 1978); Gómez-Quiñones, *Chicano Politics*, 120.

[46]56 Los Angeles Police Department, Criminal Conspiracy Section, Weekly Activities Report, Feb. 4, April 8, June 11, 1971, box 43988, Chief of Police General Files.

politicians and violence from the police. "We have been shot in the streets, shafted in the courts, drafted into the army, taken advantage of by corrupt politicians, and ignored by the Government," the CLF charged. "Now we scream YA BASTA!" Adopting "the liberating force of revolution" the CLF declared itself to be "in a state of war with the Fascist system that dares to control our lives" and promised to continue the attacks. The CLF thus embodied all the radical and violent traits the LAPD had attributed to the rest of the Chicano movement.[47]

The LAPD spent much time attempting to apprehend CLF members. Although these efforts proved nearly fruitless, toward the end of 1971, the bombings came to an end. Sporadic fire bombings continued into November, but after August no more dynamite bombs exploded in the city. Since no one has ever come forward to explain the bombings, we do not know why they ended. . . .[48]

While police inspired the urban terrorism of the CLF, police repression also helped politicize the larger Mexican-American community. Studies conducted in the early 1970s, soon after the conflict between Chicanos and the LAPD peaked, suggest that the movement and the hostile police response to movement activity heightened Los Angeles Mexican Americans' sense that they were an oppressed and exploited people, especially in their relations with the police. This increased sense of exploitation, in turn, led to a greater feeling of ethnic solidarity within the Mexican-American community and a greater inclination to engage in collective ethnic politics. . . .[49]

. . . Political scientists Biliana C. S. Ambrecht and Harry P. Pachón in a study that compared Mexican-American attitudes in 1965 and 1972 . . . [and] found that most Mexican Americans in Los Angeles "consistently reported negative views of police treatment of Mexican Americans," and that a higher percentage believed they were victims of discrimination in 1972 than in 1965. The authors surmised that . . . Mexican Americans had come to see themselves "as a subordinate exploited group in American society, thus sharing many of the problems faced by Black Americans." No doubt the LAPD's efforts to suppress legitimate Chicano dissent added to that sense of exploitation and subordination.[50]

Ambrecht and Pachón's research also showed that many Mexican Americans supported the goals and activities of the Chicano movement organizations. A large majority regarded the NCMC demonstrations and, by extension, the police-Chicano conflict that followed "as a 'general expression of frustration of the Mexican people' and as a strategy to 'obtain denied opportunities and equal rights.'" Despite the massive violence and great trauma that resulted from these

---

[47]Chicano Liberation Front, "Declaration from the Chicano Liberation Front," n.d., box 9884, Mayor Sam Yorty Papers (Los Angeles City Records Center).

[48]Los Angeles Police Department, Criminal Conspiracy Section, Weekly Activities Report, June 18, July 16, Sept. 24, 1971, box 43988, Chief of Police General Files.

[49]Armando Morales, "A Study of Mexican American Perceptions of Law Enforcement Policies and Practices in East Los Angeles" (Ph.D. diss., University of Southern California, 1972), 188–248.

[50]Biliana C. S. Ambrecht and Harry P. Pachon, "Ethnic Political Mobilization in a Mexican American Community: An Exploratory Study of East Los Angeles, 1965–1972," *Western Political Quarterly* 27 (Sept. 1974), 509, 509n50, 513–14, 514n63.

demonstrations, 44 percent judged the protests to have been for "the good of the community." The Mexican-American community sympathized with and supported Chicano activists in their conflict with police.[51]

The overall sense of exploitation and the sympathy and support of the Chicano movement stimulated what Ambrecht and Pachon call an "ethnic political mobilization." That is, Mexican Americans became more inclined to base their political choices primarily on their ethnicity and to engage in political activity in support of their ethnic interests. . . . The conflict between Chicanos and the LAPD thus helped Mexican Americans develop a new political consciousness—a consciousness that included a greater sense of ethnic solidarity, an acknowledgment of their subordinated status in American society, and a greater determination to act politically, and perhaps even violently, to end that subordination. While most people of Mexican descent still refused to call themselves Chicanos, many had come to adopt many of the principles intrinsic in the concept of *chicanismo*.[52]

Mexican Americans' new political consciousness had a slow but ultimately significant impact on electoral politics. During the seventies and eighties, voters elected a growing number of Los Angeles–area Mexican Americans to public office, including many who had been active in the movement. . . . This new consciousness had a[n] . . . immediate bearing on the 1973 Los Angeles mayoral election, which pitted, for the second time, the conservative incumbent Sam Yorty against the liberal black city councilman Thomas Bradley. . . .[53] The first mayoral contest between the two men took place in 1969, before much of the conflict between Chicanos and the LAPD. Yorty received 56 percent of the Mexican-American vote and won the election. By 1973, however, the politicized Mexican-American community had come to appreciate Bradley's criticism of the LAPD. Mexican Americans by a small majority (51 percent) joined African Americans . . . and a substantial minority of whites (46 percent) to make him the first African-American mayor of Los Angeles. The new mayor set out to regain control of the LAPD by appointing a strong Police Commission, which began to hear citizens' complaints of police misconduct. After Chief Davis retired in 1976, the commission established policies regarding the use of force and the discharge of weapons that earlier Police Commissions would never have accepted. . . . During the early 1980s it seemed that a modicum of civilian control had returned to the LAPD.[54]

---

[51]Ibid, 515–16.

[52]Ibid, 505, 507–8, 515–16.

[53]Guerra, "Ethnic Officeholders in Los Angeles County," 90–94; Charles G. Mayo, "The 1961 Mayoralty Election in Los Angeles: The Political Party in a Nonpartisan Election," *Western Political Quarterly* 17 (June 1964), 326; John C. Bollens and Grant B. Geyer, *Yorty: Politics of a Constant Candidate* (Pacific Palisades, 1973), 132, 169; *The Los Angeles Times*, Sept. 9, 1970; ibid., Sept. 16, 1970, sec. 1, p. 26; Bradley to the Police Commission, June 10, 1965, box 35328, Chief of Police General Files.

[54]Bollens and Geyer, *Yorty*, 163–73; Harlen Hahn, David Klingman, and Harry Pachón, "Cleavages, Coalitions, and the Black Candidate: The Los Angeles Mayoralty Elections of 1969 and 1973," *Western Political Quarterly* 29 (Dec. 1976), 514; Independent Commission on the Los Angeles Police Department, *Report of the Independent Commission on the Los Angeles Police Department* (Los Angeles, 1991); and Mike Davis, *City of Quartz: Excavating the Future in Los Angeles* (New York, 1992), 267–316.

Chicanos found the courts a more effective vehicle than the ballot for ending police abuse. In 1978 the Coalition Against Police Abuse and the American Civil Liberties Union filed a suit that sought to prohibit the LAPD from investigating peaceful political groups. . . . The court ordered the LAPD to cease all investigations of private groups or individuals "without reasonable and articulated suspicion" of wrongdoing and mandated the creation of an audit committee to monitor all LAPD intelligence-gathering activities. Finally, because pretrial discovery disclosed a wide variety of abuses by the LAPD's Public Disorder and Intelligence Division, the department agreed to dismantle that division.[55]

Chicanos also began developing their own organizations to protect their rights. Out of the protest of the sixties emerged the Mexican American Legal Defense and Education Fund (MALDEF), whose primary function is to defend Mexican Americans' civil rights in the courts. . . . Police officials across the nation . . . if they trample on the rights of Mexican-American political activists, . . . will have to contend with . . . a highly competent and committed legal organization.[56]

In a broader context, much of recent Mexican-American history seems to validate Ambrecht and Pachon's study: The political consciousness . . . significantly changed the way Mexican Americans viewed themselves and related to the larger society. Because they came to see themselves as an exploited minority group, Mexican Americans no longer opposed being categorized with African Americans for the purpose of protecting their rights. . . . Similarly, because they placed a greater value on their Mexican heritage, many Mexican Americans rejected assimilation and instead demanded educational programs at the elementary, secondary, and college levels that reinforced Mexican culture. . . .[57]

The story of the Chicano movement's struggle with the LAPD thus illuminates a critical period in American history and brings a new understanding of present-day social and political relations. The efforts and sacrifices of Chicano activists helped redefine our concept of what constitutes an exploited minority group and . . . helped give rise to the interest group politics that is so much a part of our political landscape today. For the Mexican-American community, the consequences of the struggle between Chicanos and the LAPD were even more profound. The LAPD may have succeeded in diminishing Chicano militant

---

[55]Acuña, *Occupied America*, 400–401; José Angel Gutiérrez, "Chicanos and Mexicans under Surveillance: 1940–1980," *Renato Rosaldo Lecture Series Monograph*, 2 (Spring 1986), 30–58; Donner, *Protectors of Privilege*, 271–89.

[56]NAACP Legal Defense and Education Fund, "A Mexican-American Legal Defense and Education Fund: A Proposal," Aug. 7, 1967, 8–11, box i4, Ernesto Galarza Papers (Special Collections, Stanford University Library); Mexican American Legal Defense and Education Fund, "The Year 1970: A Year of Expansion and Growth," Annual Report to the Board of Directors, ibid; Mexican American Legal Defense and Education Fund, "A Review of the Year's Pending Litigation," ibid; Mexican American Legal Defense and Education Fund, *Case Summaries*, 1978, box 39, Urban Policy Research Institute Papers; San Miguel, *"Let All of Them Take Heed,"* 169–75.

[57]San Miguel, "Let All of Them Take Heed," 177–81; Gutiérrez, "Sin Fronteras?" 5–37.

activity, but in gaining this victory, the department revealed to Mexican Americans their subordinated status in American society. More dramatic and convincing than the rhetoric of any sixties activist, the LAPD's repressive tactics . . . helped convince even conservative Mexican Americans that they, like African Americans, were an oppressed racial minority and that if they wanted a measure of equality, they must act collectively to attain their rights. Thus, while the LAPD may have curbed militant Chicano activism, the response to the department's tactics gave rise to a new consciousness that has the potential to empower the Chicano community.

Edward Escobar

I was once asked during a job interview how could I possibly have anything positive to say about American history given that I study such a grim topic as relations between Mexican Americans and the Los Angeles Police Department. After thinking about the question for a moment, I answered that I don't teach simply about brutality and victimization. Rather I teach about how ordinary people, even under the most difficult circumstances, assert their humanity to fight against the structures that limit their potential.

This perspective developed as much from my youthful experiences as from formal study. It was sparked by hearing my parents' stories about their involvement in the labor movement of the 1930s. By struggling alongside other working class groups, these otherwise ostracized but brave Mexican Americans gained dignity for themselves and a brighter future for their children. As a high school and college student, I witnessed the impact of the great social movements of the1960s. Through involvement in these movements, ordinary people managed to tear down the walls of segregation, help end the war in Vietnam, and bring a greater measure of equality to racial minority groups, women, and gays.

Formal study affirmed what I witnessed as a youth. During graduate school, the great historians of slavery influenced my thinking on the power of collective action. John Blassingame, Herbert Gutman, and Eugene Genovese wrote about how even slaves in the plantation South built communities, maintained families, and used the very ideological underpinnings of slavery to empower themselves.

QUESTIONS FOR CONSIDERATION

1. Characterize the context that led to the Chicano Moratorium of 1970 and its tragic end. Consider the assumptions and interests brought to the scene by both the protestors and the Los Angeles police department.
2. What assumptions on the part of the LAPD shaped their treatment of the Chicano rights movement? How did the United States Civil Rights Commission report *Mexican Americans and the Administration of Justice in the Southwest* contradict these assumptions? What conflict does this contradiction mark between the assumptions of local versus federal authorities?
3. Describe events before and after Rubén Salazar's death that led the Los Angeles Mexican-American community to assume that his death was intentional.
4. According to Escobar, how did the authorities' reaction to the Chicano Moratorium produce results counterproductive to the authorities' goals? In what ways did the Chicano movement draw inspiration from other protest movements during the 1960s?

CHAPTER FOURTEEN

✦◯

Security against Democracy: The Legacy of the Cold War at Home[1]

Elaine Tyler May

The first decade of the twenty-first century was marked by the events of September 11, 2001, and the war on terror that followed. We have seen a dramatic preoccupation with security spark a wide range of antidemocratic policies, from torture to people held without trial at Guantanamo to the Patriot Act. We have become accustomed to orange alerts, metal detectors, and taking off half our clothes at airports. But if we assume that all this started with 9/11 or that the trouble lies primarily with public policies, we miss the deeper roots of our national obsession with security, which began more than half a century ago, permeating not just public life but private life as well.

The preoccupation with security emerged during the same decades that American democracy expanded to become more inclusive and more tolerant. As a result of what some have called the rights revolution—the civil rights, feminist, gay liberation, and disability rights movements—the United States came much closer to reaching its full democratic promise. These two goals—to expand democracy and to achieve security—need not be in conflict. Democracy and security depend upon each other. In a thriving democracy, citizens engage with each other across differences, empowered to grapple with problems and address common concerns. Democracy fosters trust and a healthy public life. But when citizens retreat from public life, they are unable to achieve meaningful change on behalf of the common good. People are more likely to feel insecure and distrust each other, and democracy withers. Security also withers, shrinking to a negative concept that is little more than fear combined with force. Yet true security has more to do with trust and confidence than boundaries, bunkers, and weapons. In the United States since World War II, security and democracy have been on a collision course. Misguided ideas about security, along with an investment in private life at the expense of public life, have muted efforts to expand and strengthen democracy, resulting in a nation that is not as democratic, nor as secure, as it could be.

---

[1] Interested students are encouraged to read this essay in the original form. Elaine Tyler May, "Security against Democracy: The Legacy of the Cold War at Home," *Journal of American History* 97, no. 4 (March 2011), 939–57.

The reasons for this clash of national interests reach back far into American history. Citizens have long been willing to compromise their basic democratic rights to achieve national security, especially during wartime. Since World War II, however, that willingness to sacrifice rights for security has become chronic. The Cold War ushered in an uneasy era often described as "peacetime." But in fact the Cold War was more hot than cold, marked by more or less constant warfare. Despite all the talk of maintaining peace, war became a fixture of life. In the words of the historian Michael Sherry, Americans have been living in the "shadow of war" since the 1930s.[2]

Antidemocratic policies, from the early Cold War purges of suspected Communists and homosexuals to the erosion of individual rights in the war on terror, have received extensive attention from scholars. Less studied are the ways citizens, in their private lives, have adopted and internalized the preoccupation with security. I will argue that the undermining of democracy in the name of security has penetrated much deeper into American life than our public policies, right down to the level of daily life. In fact, the obsession with security at the personal level may be even more corrosive of democracy than the public policies promoted in the name of national security.

The Cold War laid the groundwork for this development. Cold War ideology wove together several strands of American political culture into a tough fabric constructed to withstand the harsh postwar climate and protect the American way of life. These strands included a belief in individual freedom, unfettered capitalism, the sanctity of the home, and a suspicion of outsiders. Capitalism, grounded in private life and consumerism, defined the United States against the Soviet Union. When then–vice president Richard M. Nixon traveled to Moscow in 1959 for the American exposition, in an event that came to be known as the Kitchen Debate, he articulated the American way of life in terms of domesticity and consumer goods.[3]

These historically rooted dimensions of Cold War ideology shaped how Americans responded to perceived dangers at home and abroad. For example, at the dawn of the atomic age, protection against external dangers took the form of a nuclear arsenal; protection against internal enemies took the form of a nuclear family. The two were profoundly connected. The United States vigorously opposed international control of nuclear weapons, insisting on accumulating weapons, which led to a spiraling nuclear arms race. This stance reflected a turning away from a concern for the common good in favor of self-protection secured by an arsenal of atomic weapons. Rather than diffusing international tensions to achieve a safer world through democratic practices in the global arena, American leaders chose preparedness in the face of danger.

A similar process unfolded at home. To avoid big government programs that might resemble socialism, policy makers rejected large-scale public civil defense

---

[2]Michael S. Sherry, *In the Shadow of War: The United States Since the 1930s* (New Haven, 1997).

[3]See, for example, Elaine Tyler May, *Homeward Bound: American Families in the Cold War Era* (New York, 2008), 19–22.

efforts, encouraging citizens instead to plan for a possible attack by fortifying their homes. The media did its part to keep citizens alert and insecure. For example, on July 26, 1950, the front page of *The Los Angeles Times* reported, "Experts Weighing A-Bomb Peril Here." . . . Civil defense officials and enterprising businesses offered homeowners tips on constructing basement shelters, backyard bunkers, or even the "all-concrete blast resistant house . . . for the atomic age."[4]

There were good reasons for people to be worried. Atomic war was a real possibility. The United States had already waged it, and Americans saw the results. Even those who opposed the proliferation of nuclear weapons fanned fears of an atomic catastrophe. Scientists calling for an end to the arms race pointed to the dire consequences of an atomic explosion to make their point, with the unintended consequence of heightening fears that could not be easily channeled into calls for peaceful coexistence. Americans became accustomed to the threat of nuclear annihilation, fueling a bunker mentality and a militarization of society.[5]

Very few homeowners actually constructed shelters. But the message was clear: the world was dangerous, and citizens were responsible for their own safety. Americans adopted a framework for security based on self-defense bolstered by private enterprise, rather than on cooperative democratic efforts to ease international and domestic tensions. Over time, a domestic arms race developed parallel to the nuclear arms race: citizens responded to perceived threats by fortifying their homes and arming themselves. Soon Americans could boast that they had more missiles, and more pistols, than anyone else. The United States' nuclear stockpile consistently outnumbered that of the Soviet Union from 1964 to 1982, and by the early 1990s the percentage of households in America with guns was far above that of other industrialized countries. It was not only the atomic age that made citizens fearful; there were also real domestic dangers. . . . There were . . . good reasons for citizens to distrust the government. In its investigative zeal, the government engaged in intrusive practices such as wiretapping and other types of surveillance. . . . By the time the Watergate scandal unfolded . . . , government officials had actually become . . . burglars. Americans' trust in government dropped from 75 percent in 1963 to 25 percent in 1979.[6]

---

[4]See Laura McEnaney, *Civil Defense Begins at Home: Militarization Meets Everyday Life in the Fifties* (Princeton, 2000). William S. Barton, "Experts Weighing A-bomb Peril Here," *Los Angeles Times,* July 26, 1950, p. 1A. Portland Cement Association, advertisement, *Better Homes and Gardens,* 33 (June 1955), 3.

[5]See Paul Boyer, *By the Bomb's Early Light: American Thought and Culture at the Dawn of the Atomic Age* (Chapel Hill, 1994).

[6]Gerald Segal, *The Simon and Schuster Guide to the World Today* (New York, 1987), 82. See also Edwin Bacon and Mark Sandle, eds., *Brezhnev Reconsidered* (New York, 2002). For comparative data on gun ownership see B. G. Krugg, K. E. Powell, and L. L. Dahlberg, "Firearm-Related Deaths in the United States and 35 Other High- and Upper-Middle-Income Countries," *International Journal of Epidemiology* 27 (April 1998), 216; and "International Homicide Comparisons," *GunCite,* http://www.guncite.com/gun_control_gcgvinco.html. The cartoon appeared in "A Response to Fear," *Time,* Aug. 3, 1970, p. 10. Kevin Diaz, "Cynicism Is Out, Trust in Government In," *Minneapolis Star Tribune,* Oct. 23, 2001, p. A11.

While dangers were real, citizens responded with exaggerated fear and distrust, much of it focused on crime. A 1974 study concluded that "The fear of crime in the United States is a fundamental social problem which has not yet received attention in proportion to its severity and which may well prove to be more difficult to treat than criminality itself." While it is difficult to quantify fear of crime, we do have poll data from particular years that indicate the level of fear. A poll taken in 1980 showed that while the chance of being murdered was a mere one in ten thousand and becoming a victim of violent crime was just six in one thousand, fully four in ten Americans polled reported that they were "highly fearful" of assault. More than half said that they dress plainly to avoid attracting the attention of attackers. A majority reported that they kept a gun for protection.[7]

So, how did this happen? I will offer some examples to suggest that the legacy of the Cold War fed this irrational response to crime, encouraged citizens to retreat from public life, and worked against the democratizing momentum of the rights revolution. Although the Cold War was not the sole cause of this fear, I argue that the ideological premises embedded in the Cold War shaped the response to it.

Long before crime filled the headlines and the airwaves, there was the alleged communist threat. Anticommunism was "in the air," according to the St. Paul native Patricia Hampl. She writes in her memoir of her terror as a child in the 1950s, unable to sleep for fear "of the *Communists* who lurked in the dark." . . . Noting the power of the new medium of television, she recalled watching TV shows, including the nightly news, which were filled with dire warnings about the Communists. Still, she wrote, "I could not concoct my Communists. . . . They remained, simply, dread."[8]

Such anxieties were not merely figments of an overly active imagination. Private enterprise did its part to whip up fear of Communists. Innocent children inside their homes appeared particularly vulnerable. In 1953, for example, a public service ad in Newsweek for the Norfolk and Western Railway pictured a frightened boy at home at night in a dark hallway, with the caption: "You needn't be ashamed of being afraid in the dark, son. . . . The darkness is a hiding place for confusion, greed, conspiracy, treachery, socialism . . . and its uglier brother, communism. . . . In the U.S.A. you are free to become vigilant to see what's going on . . . if you ignore this responsibility. . . . what you lose in the dark may be your freedom." Communists were not the only threat. The government was equally dangerous. A 1950 public service announcement in *U.S. News and World Report*

---

[7]James Brooks, "The Fear of Crime in the United States," *Crime and Delinquency*, 20 (July 1974), 241–44, esp. 241. "Crime: The Shape of Fear," *Economist*, Nov. 29, 1980, p. 36. For crime and population, see "Crime—State Level: Trends in One Variable," *U.S. Department of Justice: Bureau of Justice Statistics*, http://bjs.ojp.usdoj.gov/dataonline/Search/Crime/State/RunCrimeTrendsInOneVar.cfm; and Susan B. Carter et al., eds., "Table Aa6-8: Population; 1790–2000 (Annual Estimates)," *Historical Statistics of the United States: Millennial Edition Online*, http://hsus.cambridge.org/HSUSWeb/search/searchTable.do?id=Aa6-8.

[8]Patricia Hampl, *A Romantic Education* (Boston, 1981), 37–39.

from the Electric Light and Power Companies warned of increasing government control and assured readers that the company was "battling this move toward a socialistic government." The ad pictured a small boy in front of a table holding four symbols of freedom: a key, a bible, a pencil, and a ballot.[9]

These public service advertisements used familial images to raise fears among Americans that they and their children were vulnerable. They portrayed big government as akin to socialism and communism. Companies called on men to protect their families with do-it-yourself defense and to trust private enterprise, not the government, to keep them secure. This message was nowhere more explicit than in ads for the insurance industry, promising "self-made security" for the "do-it-yourself American" who is "creating his own security."[10]

As these ads suggest, the home gradually shifted from the place that *provides* protection to the place that *needs* protection. An example of that shift appeared in House Beautiful magazine. One of the most outspoken advocates of privatized single-family dwellings was Elizabeth Gordon, editor in chief of *House Beautiful* from 1941 to 1964. Gordon articulated the intertwined Cold War themes of individualism, free enterprise, the sanctity of the home, and suspicion of outsiders when, in a 1953 speech, she railed against the "International Style," the design of many postwar buildings, which she considered collectivist and un-American:

> We don't believe the International Style is simply a matter of taste; any more than we believe that Nazism or Communism are matters of taste, matters of opinion. . . . Either we choose the architecture that will encourage the development of individualism or we choose the architecture and design of collectivism and totalitarian control. . . . The International Style . . . masses families together in one giant building so that relatively few, strategically placed, block leaders could check on all movements and conduct classes of ideological indoctrination . . . [it is] a design for living that we associate with totalitarianism.

According to Gordon, families flourished in privacy, fenced in and walled off from public gaze. Joseph Howland, the magazine's garden editor, agreed with Gordon:

> Good living is NOT public living. We consider [privacy] one of the cherished American rights, one of the privileges we fought a war to preserve. Freedom to live our own lives, the way we want to live them without being spied on or snooped around, is as American as pancakes and molasses. . . . The very raison d'etre of the separate house is to get away from the living habits and cooking smells and inquisitive eyes of other people.[11]

[9]Norfolk and Western Railway, advertisement, *Newsweek*, Sept. 7, 1953, p. 13. Electric Light and Power Companies, advertisement, *U.S. News and World Report*, May 12, 1950, p. 25.

[10]These quotes appeared on a number of insurance industry posters that have been collected by Caley Horan for her Ph.D. dissertation in progress on the insurance industry. I am grateful to her for allowing me to use these materials.

[11]Elizabeth Gordon, "The Responsibility of an Editor," speech to the Press Club Luncheon of the American Furniture Mart, Chicago, June 22, 1953, quoted in Dianne Harris, "Making Your Private World: Modern Landscape Architecture and *House Beautiful*, 1945–1965," in *The Architecture of Landscape, 1940–1960*, ed. Marc Treib (Philadelphia, 2002), 181–82.

By the early 1960s, the broad Cold War consensus was beginning to fracture. The excesses of McCarthyism had discredited the most vehement expressions of anticommunism. But fears of internal as well as external danger continued to permeate the country. Along with communism, criminality seemed to threaten individual security. In 1964, *House Beautiful* commented on the shift with a full-page illustration of a fortified house, with cannons, boarded-up doors and windows, alarms, guard dogs, locks, loudspeakers, and a large sign announcing "Burglars Go Home." Companies that stood to profit from fear of crime did their best to whip up terror. In 1970, for example, General Telephone and Electronics took out a two-page ad in *Time* magazine promoting their new intercom system. One side of the ad was a full-page photo of a man wearing a trench coat, face obscured by a hat. The facing page said in large bold letters, "Who's downstairs ringing your bell? A friend? Or the Boston Strangler?" These rudimentary devices eventually gave way to elaborate security systems, alarms, and safe rooms. The total worth of the private security business in the United States increased from $3.3 billion in 1970 to $52 billion in 1991. By the early twenty-first century consumers could contemplate a custom-built "quantum sleeper," a bulletproof cocoon complete with CD and DVD player, microwave, and refrigerator.[12]

The locks, gadgets, barricades, and warnings against dangerous strangers revealed a growing siege mentality that began to solidify in the mid-1960s. It was not just about crime. Although crime was increasing, the rate of violent crime, even at its peak in the last half of the twentieth century, barely exceeded its highest point in the first half of the century. Throughout the twentieth century, the U.S. murder rate remained below 11 murders per 100,000 population. In the mid-1960s, the crime rate was relatively low, with violent crime affecting fewer than 2 people in 1,000. At its height, the rate of all violent crimes remained below 8 victims per 1,000 population. If we consider these numbers in terms of percentage of the population, these variations appear even slighter. The murder rate remained consistently below one one-hundredth of one percent of the population. The percentage of the population who were victims of all violent crimes remained consistently below one percent of the population. Regardless of the slim likelihood of becoming a crime victim, however, crime came to stand in for the many upheavals that were disrupting the Cold War order, including political protests, urban riots, and the many other challenges to the status quo and authority structures.[13]

---

[12]*House Beautiful*, 106 (July 1964), 100. General Telephone and Electronics, advertisement, *Time*, July 13, 1970, pp. 60–61. William C. Cunningham, John J. Strauchs, and Clifford W. Van Meter, *Private Security Trends, 1970–2000: The Hallcrest Report II* (Boston, 1990), 238. For population data, see Carter et al., eds., "Table Aa6-8." *Quantum Sleeper,* http://www.qsleeper.com.

[13]Federal Bureau of Investigation, *Uniform Crime Reports* (Washington, D.C., 1940–1960); "Crime—State Level"; Susan B. Carter, et al., eds., "Table Ec190-198: Reported Homicides and Homicide Rates, by Sex and Mode of Death, 1900–1997," *Historical Statistics of the United States,* http://hsus.cambridge.org/HSUSWeb/search/searchTable.do?id=Ec190-198. For population data, see "Population Estimates," *United States Census Bureau,* http://www.census.gov/popest/datasets.html; Carter et al., eds., "Table Aa6-8."

The civil rights movement challenged racial hierarchies, and women were challenging domesticity by entering careers and public life. The counterculture, the antiwar movement, and the sexual revolution added to the sense that the tight-knit fabric of Cold War social order was coming apart. Urban riots across the country, along with a new militancy that accompanied the shift from civil rights to black power, heightened racial anxieties among white Americans. A backlash began immediately as an attempt to restore a sense of security and social order. Cold War ideology, with its emphasis on privatization, self-defense, and suspicion of both government and outsiders, gave shape to the backlash. Although the McCarthy era was over, anticommunism was still alive and well, fueling the "domino theory" that propelled the war in Vietnam as well as the suspicion of subversives within the country. In this atmosphere it is not surprising that many individuals and government agencies, including the Federal Bureau of Investigation, believed that "outside agitators" with communist sympathies were responsible for political protests, civil rights activism, and social disorder.

Politicians were quick to respond with a call for law and order. This was a new campaign issue. In the early Cold War years, from 1948 until 1964, candidates warned of the communist menace and promised to be tough on organized crime. But there was no mention of street crime in any presidential candidate's acceptance speech or in any inaugural address. This changed dramatically in 1964. Law and order leaped into the center of political debates and stayed there for the rest of the century.[14]

Even as the issue of crime was taking hold, the Cold War still loomed large. Candidates in 1964 vied over which were the greatest dangers facing citizens and who offered the best protection. The Republican presidential candidate Barry Goldwater said that he would not rule out using tactical nuclear weapons in war. In response, the Democratic incumbent Lyndon B. Johnson aired a powerful television ad suggesting that his opponent would unleash nuclear war. In the ad, a little girl counts as she pulls daisy petals in a field of flowers. As a freeze-frame captures her innocent face, a man's voice-over begins an ominous countdown, followed by sounds of a blast and horrific scenes of a nuclear bomb exploding. Johnson speaks in an ominous voice-over: "These are the stakes: to make a world in which all of God's children can live, or to go into the dark. We must either love each other, or we must die." The ad was so controversial that it aired only once, but it received tremendous attention. News programs played the ad over and over in their coverage of the controversy. The "daisy girl" appeared on the cover of *Time* magazine, and two major television networks did stories on her. Many analysts claimed that this ad ushered in a new era of television attack-ad campaign advertising. Goldwater responded with his own fear mongering, not about

---

[14]The only mention of crime in any of those speeches referred to organized crime and political corruption. See Gregory Bush, ed., *Campaign Speeches of American Presidential Candidates, 1948–1984* (New York, 1985); and Davis Newton Lott, *The Presidents Speak: The Inaugural Addresses of the American Presidents from Washington to Clinton* (New York, 1994).

atomic war but about crime, political protest, and social chaos. Above scenes of crime, rioting youths, and jarring music are large bold words suggesting that Johnson was "soft" on the dangers facing the nation: "Graft! Swindle! Juvenile Delinquency! Crime! Riots! Hear what Barry Goldwater has to say about our lack of moral leadership."[15]

Although Johnson easily won the election, Goldwater's message on crime and social chaos set the tone for later campaigns. In 1968 both the Republican Richard Nixon and the candidate for the conservative American Independent party, George Wallace, focused on law and order. Nixon had a well-earned reputation as a fierce anticommunist; in 1968 he turned his attention to street violence and political protest. Nixon ran a television ad that turned the tables on "civil rights," using the term to address law and order. Amid scenes of urban chaos and violence, with a soundtrack of snare drum and dissonant piano chords, Nixon says, "It is time for an honest look at the problem of order in the United States. Dissent is a necessary ingredient of change, but in a system of government that provides for peaceful change, there is no cause that justifies resort to violence. Let us recognize that the first civil right of every American is to be free from domestic violence. So I pledge to you, we shall have order in the United States." Nixon drew no distinctions among crime, urban disturbances, and political demonstrations. In the ad, an eerie shot of an unclothed female mannequin torso tossed on the littered street underscored Nixon's pointed use of "domestic violence" to convey *public*, not *private* mayhem. His subtle use of language turned terms of the black freedom struggle and the feminist movement— "civil rights" and "domestic violence"—against them.[16]

The third-party candidate that year, George Wallace, had a well-earned reputation as a segregationist. In one ad he combined an antibusing message with a warning that city streets were dangerous, especially for women. As a school bus drives off, the narrator says, "Why are more and more millions of Americans turning to Governor Wallace? Follow, as your children are bussed across town." Wallace responds, "As President, I shall—within the law—turn back the absolute control of the public school systems to the people of the respective states." The ad then cuts to a darkened street with a woman walking, only her feet and the hem of her skirt visible. The narrator says, "Why are more and more millions of Americans turning to Governor Wallace? Take a walk in your street or park tonight." The sound of gunshots and breaking glass accompany the scene of a streetlight that is shot and then goes dark. Wallace says, "As President, I shall help make it possible for you and your families to walk the streets of our cities in safety."[17]

---

[15]Michael Carlson, "Obituary: Tony Schwartz; His Daisy Girl tv Ad Was a First, and Helped Put Lyndon Johnson in the White House," *Guardian* (London), June 28, 2008. *Time*, Sept. 25, 1964, front cover. For quotes from and descriptions of television ads, see "The Living Room Candidate: Presidential Campaign Commercials, 1952–2008," *Museum of the Moving Image*, http://www.livingroomcandidate.org.

[16]"Living Room Candidate."

[17]Ibid.

The Democratic candidate Hubert Humphrey was the only candidate to address crime as a social problem. In one ad he tells an assembled crowd, "You're not going to make this a better America just because you build more jails. What this country needs are more decent neighborhoods, more educated people, better homes. . . . I do not believe that repression alone builds a better society."[18]

Humphrey in 1968 was the only candidate to address the underlying causes of crime. Nixon and Wallace combined won 57 percent of the votes. Although Humphrey's loss was in large measure due to his association with Johnson and the Vietnam War, the election results taught the Democrats a lesson. Four years later, the Democratic candidate George McGovern embraced law and order and anticipated the war on drugs. In a campaign speech incorporated into a television ad, McGovern said, "You're never going to get on top of crime in the United States until you get on top of drugs, because half of all the crime in this country is caused by the drug addict. They'll kill, they'll steal, they'll do anything to get that money to sustain that drug habit." From that time on, the rhetoric of law and order became a political necessity, embraced by both parties.[19]

The framing of the crime issue reveals the escalating clash between security and democracy. The 1960s marked a shift in the black freedom struggle from civil rights to black power. While black people were not the only targets of racial profiling, media coverage of groups such as the Black Panthers and television images of urban riots fed a backlash that emphasized a black-white binary. The rise of the feminist movement also intensified the backlash against women entering public life. Just at the time when African Americans and women were asserting their rights as citizens, the news media fused the two issues by reviving the age-old trope that black men were dangerous and women—especially white women—were vulnerable.

The media contributed significantly to whipping up fear. By focusing disproportionately on rare but heinous crimes, television and newspapers contributed to exaggerated fears of random violence. The popular press saturated readers with the message that attacks on city streets were practically inevitable. As early as 1963 *U.S. News and World Report* exhorted women, "First Scream, Then Scram. . . . muggings, rapes and assaults have become common" (which, of course, they were not). *The Washington Post* warned women not to "walk around alone at night," to keep all doors and windows locked, and to install burglar alarms. In 1970, *Time* magazine asserted, "the universal fear of violent crime and vicious strangers . . . is a constant companion of the populace. It is the cold fear of dying at random in a brief spasm of senseless violence—for a few pennies, for nothing." Who were these vicious strangers? *Time* asserted that "the most crime-prone segment of the population—poor urban youths aged 15 to 24—will increase disproportionately at least until 1975. Sheer demography adds a racial factor: half the nation's blacks are under 21." *Time*'s warning was not subtle. Young blacks were "crime-prone," and their numbers were increasing. *Time* warned its white

---

[18]Ibid.
[19]Ibid.

readers that "it is chiefly young black males who commit the most common interracial crime: armed robbery."[20]

Time gave the impression that the city streets were swarming with young blacks eager to commit "interracial crime"—a term loaded with sexual associations. The police chief in Washington, D.C., trained his officers "to treat blacks decently mainly as a matter of self-protection. A mistreated kid, for example, may hurt a cop when he gets big and dangerous." In other words, police should treat blacks decently not because they deserve to be treated decently, but because black kids will get big and dangerous.[21]

The term "black militant" carried the most ominous weight, evoking power, violence, and danger. For example, *Time* quoted Julius Hobson, a critic of the city's leadership, and identified him simply as "a local black militant." Time failed to mention that Hobson was a longtime civil rights activist and World War II veteran who attended the Tuskegee Institute, Columbia and Howard Universities, held an M.A. in economics, was a member of the Washington, D.C., school board . . ., and taught at three universities.[22]

Like the reference to Hobson as a "black militant," these warnings twisted reality and exaggerated danger. The most likely victims of violent crime, then as now, were men of color. The least likely victims were white women. Moreover, women were much safer, statistically, on the city streets in the middle of the night than in their own homes, where most violence against women occurred. Nevertheless, the media focused on women who ventured out onto public streets as particularly vulnerable to attacks by strangers. Not surprisingly, public opinion polls showed that women were most likely to fear becoming a victim of crime, even though they were least likely to actually be victimized.[23]

Messages intended to scare women back into the home portrayed them not only as the most likely *victims* of crime but also as the *cause* of crime. As increasing numbers of women with children entered the work force, the media began to blame working mothers, not only for leaving their homes unprotected but also for leaving their children unsupervised and undisciplined. One article from

---

[20]Roberto Suro, "Driven by Fear; Crime and Its Amplified Echoes Are Rearranging People's Lives," *The New York Times,* Feb. 9, 1992, http://www.nytimes.com/1992/02/09/weekinreview/driven-by-fear-crime-and-its-amplified-echoes-are-rearranging-people-s-lives.html; Linda Heath, Jack Kavanagh, and Rae S. Thompson, "Perceived Vulnerability and Fear of Crime: Why Fear Stays High When Crime Rates Drop," *Journal of Offender Rehabilitation* 33 (no. 2, 2001), 1–14. "First Scream, Then Scram," *U.S. News and World Report,* April 1, 1963. *The Washington Post,* March 17, 1963. "Response to Fear." "What the Police Can—and Cannot—Do about Crime," *Time,* July 13, 1970, http://www.time.com/time/magazine/article/0,9171,909452,00.html.

[21]"What the Police Can—and Cannot—Do about Crime."

[22]Ibid.

[23]Susan J. Douglas, *Where the Girls Are: Growing Up Female with the Mass Media* (New York, 1995), 209–11. For data examined from online opinion polls, see "Self Defense, Personal Safety–Public Opinion Polls," Roper Center at the University of Connecticut Public Opinion Online, available at LexisNexis. For example, polls taken in 1981, 1990, 1995, and 1998 indicate that women are more fearful than men. On crime statistics, see Eric H. Monkkonen, *Murder in New York City* (Berkeley, 2001), 55–79, 134–50.

1981, noting an increase in crimes in the suburbs, explained, "As more and more husbands and wives hold down jobs, their unoccupied homes make tempting daytime targets for burglars. . . . The thieves are often the unattended sons of working couples who, say police, steal to keep up with the rising cost of marijuana."[24]

Meanwhile, as the backlash against feminism and civil rights intensified, so did the panic over crime. Calls for law and order led to harsher punishment for offenders. . . . Riding the wave of the backlash, Ronald Reagan became president in 1981 and breathed new life into the Cold War, calling for law and order, family values, and a "star wars" protective shield in outer space to keep the country safe from nuclear attack.

By this time, fear of crime had taken on a life of its own that continued to grow, independent of the crime rate. According to a 1981 report, "A pervasive fear of robbery and mayhem threatens the way America lives. . . . The fear of crime is slowly paralyzing American society." Houston police chief B. K. Johnson lamented, "We have allowed ourselves to degenerate to the point where we're living like animals. We live behind burglar bars and throw a collection of door locks at night and set an alarm and lay down with a loaded shotgun beside the bed and then try to get some rest. It's ridiculous." "Americans are arming themselves with guns," the report continued, "as though they still lived in frontier days." But Chief Johnson himself kept several loaded guns in his own bedroom. Countless citizens did the same, arming themselves with guns, guard dogs, chemical mace, burglar alarms, karate classes, and target-shooting practice. They emptied the streets, making the streets more dangerous. Officials warned that the worst was yet to come, basing their predictions on unfounded assumptions. The former director of the Bureau of Justice Statistics predicted that "within four or five years every household in the country will be hit by crime." In 1980, when the chance of becoming a murder victim was one in ten thousand, a Massachusetts Institute of Technology study made the absurd claim that one out of every sixty-one babies born in New York City in that year would be a murder victim. . . .[25]

. . . In December 1984 Bernhard Goetz, a white subway passenger, shot four black youths when they tried to rob him. . . . Goetz quickly became a folk hero. He was charged with attempted murder, assault, and several other crimes, but a Manhattan jury acquitted him of all crimes except one count of illegal possession of a firearm. According to a *Newsweek* poll taken three months later, 57 percent of respondents approved of Goetz shooting the youths. Half said they had little or no confidence in the police to protect them against violent crime. *U.S. News and World Report* was quick to comment with a telling political cartoon depicting the inside of a crowded subway car. All the passengers are armed to the teeth, including elderly women, as one passenger reads a newspaper with the headline,

---

[24]"The Curse of Violent Crime," *Time,* March 23, 1981, http://www.time.com/time/print-out/0,8816.952929,00.html.

[25]Ibid.

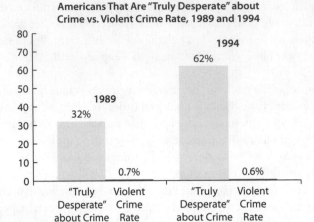

Figure 14.1
Sources: Rorie Sherman, "Crime's Toll on the U.S.: Fear, Despair, and
Guns," *National Law Journal*, April 18, 1994, pp. A1, A19–A20, reprinted
in John J. Sullivan and Joseph L. Victor, eds., *Criminal Justice 95/96*
(Guilford, 1995), 57–61; "Crime—State Level: Trends in One Variable,"
U.S. Department of Justice: Bureau of Justice Statistics, http://bjs.ojp.
usdoj.gov/dataonline/Search/Crime/State/RunCrimeTrendsInOneVar.
cfm; "Population Estimates," United States Census Bureau, http://www.
census.gov/popest/datasets.html; Susan B. Carter, et al., eds., "Table
Aa6-8: Population; 1790–2000 (Annual Estimates)," Historical Statistics
of the United States: Millennial Edition Online, http://hsus.cambridge.
org/HSUSWeb/search/searchTable.do?id=Aa6-8.

"Muggings down." The message was clear: the way to stop crime was for citizens
to carry weapons, become vigilantes, and protect themselves, like Goetz. . . .[26]

In the 1990s the clash between security and democracy reached a crescendo.
It was a decade of small government and big business. A Democratic president
presided over the end of the welfare program, a rapidly widening gap between
rich and poor, and mergers of giant corporations into even more gigantic con-
glomerates with vast power. Citizens expressed distrust toward the government
and each other. Although the crime rate declined in the 1990s, fear continued to
rise. Between 1989 and 1994 the percentage of those polled who said they were
"truly desperate" about crime nearly doubled, from 32 percent to 62 percent. At
the same time, the rate of violent crime declined, from seven hundredths of
1 percent to six hundredths of 1 percent.[27]

. . . Many people had little faith in government authorities and law enforcement. Because of a widespread belief that police could not be trusted to protect

---

[26]David M. Alpern, "A Newsweek Poll: 'Deadly Force,'" *Newsweek*, March 11, 1985, p. 53;
"Behind Tough Public Stance on Criminals," *U.S. News and World Report*, Jan. 21, 1985, p. 60.

[27]Rorie Sherman, "Crime's Toll on the U.S.: Fear, Despair, and Guns," *National Law Journal*,
April 18, 1994, pp. A1, A19–A20, reprinted in John J. Sullivan and Joseph L. Victor, eds., *Criminal
Justice 95/96* (Guilford, 1995), 57–61. For crime statistics, see "Crime—State Level." For population
data, see "Population Estimates"; and Carter et al., eds., "Table Aa6-8."

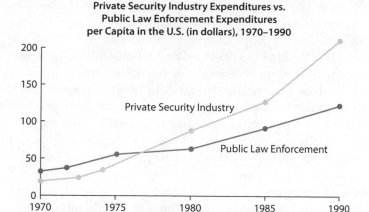

Figure 14.2

Sources: David M. Alpern, "A Newsweek Poll: 'Deadly Force,'" *Newsweek*, March 11, 1985, p. 53; Barry Meier, "Reality and Anxiety: Crime and the Fear of It," The New York Times, Feb. 18, 1993, p. A14; William C. Cunningham, John J. Strauchs, and Clifford W. Van Meter, *Private Security Trends*, 1970–2000: *The Hallcrest Report II* (Boston, 1990), 238.

citizens and may not be around when needed, private security companies began patrolling neighborhoods. From the 1970s onward, expenditures for private security exceeded expenditures for public law enforcement. A New Jersey security agency, for example, offered a "Family Protection Plan" that provided personal bodyguard service. Customers began hiring bodyguards to take them into New York City or to go shopping. During the 1980s the employment rate in the private security industry increased dramatically and far outstripped the rate in public law enforcement, which declined. By 1994 public perception of crime as the most important problem in America reached an all-time high.[28]

The Cold War was over, but the war on drugs took its place. Bringing atomic-age fears full circle, a 1996 TV ad for the Republican presidential candidate Bob Dole began with footage of the little girl with a daisy taken from the 1964 Johnson ad. The female narrator says, "Thirty years ago, the biggest threat to her was nuclear war. Today the threat is drugs. Teenage drug use has doubled in the last four years. What's been done?" The ad continues with images of pre-adolescent children using various forms of drugs in a public park. Dole's ad reflected the continuation of a trend that began in the 1950s panic over juvenile delinquency. Children, while often portrayed as vulnerable, also appeared as threatening. Although the crime rate was declining rapidly in the 1990s, especially crimes committed by youths, polls revealed a vastly exaggerated sense of the danger. In 1994 juveniles committed only about 13 percent of all violent crimes. But Americans polled at the

---

[28]Alpern, "Newsweek Poll." Barry Meier, "Reality and Anxiety: Crime and the Fear of It," *The New York Times*, Feb. 18, 1993, p. A14. Cunningham, Strauchs, and Van Meter, *Private Security Trends*, 238.

time believed that juveniles committed 43 percent of violent crimes—over three times the actual proportion. Not simply afraid *for* their children, Americans were becoming afraid *of* their children. Especially black children.[29]

In 1996 the Princeton University political scientist John DiIulio made a startling pre-diction. Looking at demographic trends, he asserted that by 2005 the number of fourteen- to seventeen-year-old males would increase by 23 percent and that the rate would rise faster among black children than among white children. Assuming that black boys would necessarily become violent teenage criminals, he coined the term "superpredator" and called the trend a "ticking time bomb" that would unleash "a storm of predatory criminality" on the nation. Critics who called DiIulio's warnings alarmist, racist, and inaccurate were correct. The crime wave he warned about never happened. Crime was declining dramatically in the 1990s, just when DiIulio made his prediction, and within a decade violent crime by juveniles dropped to its lowest point in twenty-five years. But DiIulio's claims about "superpredators" saturated the media. Michael Petit, the deputy director of the Child Welfare League of America, said that "superpredators" are "literally being manufactured, programmed, hardwired to behave in a certain way." A 1997 editorial in the *Omaha World Herald* described these children as "killing machines."[30]

False and frightening predictions such as DiIulio's had an impact. Black people were incarcerated far out of proportion to their crimes. In the 1990s white people comprised 70 percent of those arrested (in line with their percentage of the population), but only 30 percent of those who went to prison. The reverse was true for people of color, who comprised 30 percent of those arrested but 70 percent of prison inmates. By the end of the century, one out of every four young black men was in jail, on parole, or on probation. The overcrowding of prisons with nonviolent offenders guilty of such crimes as drug possession and immigration violations eventually brought private enterprise into the criminal justice system. For-profit prisons expanded across the country, with financial incentives to keep more people incarcerated for longer periods of time. Between 1980 and 2008, the prison population increased from just under 320,000 to over 1.5 million. The rate of increase for prison costs was six times greater than that for higher education spending.[31]

By the late twentieth century, it was not only criminals who lived behind bars and walls. Increasing numbers of nonincarcerated Americans locked themselves up in fortified homes. Nowhere is this bunker mentality more obvious

[29]"Living Room Candidate." On the panic over juvenile delinquency, see, for example, James Gilbert, *A Cycle of Outrage: America's Reaction to the Juvenile Delinquent in the 1950s* (New York, 1988). Sherman, "Crime's Toll on the U.S.," 57.

[30]John DiIulio, "Lock 'Em Up or Else: Huge Wave of Criminally Inclined Coming in Next 10 Years," *Lakeland (Fla.) Ledger,* March 23, 1996, p. A11; Joyce Purnick, "Youth Crime: Should Laws Be Tougher?," *The New York Times,* May 9, 1996, p. B1. Vincent Schiraldi, "Will the Real John DiIulio Please Stand Up," editorial, *The Washington Post,* Feb. 5, 2001, p. A19; "'Superpredators' Aren't Mere Kids," editorial, *Omaha World Herald,* May 16, 1997, p. 12.

[31]See, for example, Department of Justice, "Prison Statistics," Nov. 7, 2007, *U.S. Department of Justice: Bureau of Justice Statistics,* http://bjs.ojp.usdoj.gov/content/glance/tables/corr2tab.cfm; Ruth Wilson Gilmore, "Globalisation and U.S. Prison Growth: From Military Keynesianism to Post-Keynesian Militarism," *Race and Class* 40 (nos. 2–3, 1998–1999), 172–74.

than in the rapid proliferation of gated communities. . . . Residents of gated communities often own their own streets, pay for their own services and utilities, and provide their own security guards. Homeowners pay significant fees for their infrastructure and security, which are independent of public funding and oversight. . . . Not surprisingly, residents of these communities often resent paying taxes for the same services that are provided to the public. . . .[32]

In many gated communities, freedom and security remain elusive. Homeowner associations develop policies that restrict residents' freedom to construct and decorate their homes as they wish, and enforce rigid behavioral codes as well. Whether inhabited by the wealthy or those of modest means, gated communities sometimes actually heighten feelings of vulnerability. Residents often complain that security is lax and outsiders easily enter. . . .[33]

A 1995 study found that most residents chose gated communities for security, with the vast majority saying that security was "very important" in their decision. High-income residents of gated communities believed there was less crime in their neighborhood than in nongated communities, and they felt that crime was lower because of the gates. They believed they were safer, but in fact they were not: there was no significant difference in crime rates between gated and nongated communities with residents of similar income levels.[34] Unfriendly warnings and barriers did little to keep out crime, in part because some of the residents who lived inside the gates committed crimes against their neighbors.

Perhaps the perfect symbol of the trend toward privatized protection is the sport utility vehicle (SUV). Although sales of SUVs have declined in recent years due to rising gas prices and the economic crisis, these vehicles were the fastest growing segment of the auto industry during the last two decades of the twentieth century, outpacing minivans with similar size and features. Families often purchased SUVs because they appeared to offer safety. But SUVs are more prone to rollovers and braking failures than cars. The National Highway Traffic Safety Administration reported that SUV occupants are 11 percent more likely to die in a traffic accident than those in cars. . . .[35]

Most SUV owners were men, but by 1989 women owned one-third of SUVs. SUVs carried a different appeal than the family-oriented minivan. A market research study that compared 4,500 SUV and minivan purchasers showed little demographic difference: owners of both vehicles were typically affluent married couples in their forties with children. Yet consultants for the auto industry found

[32]Edward J. Blakely and Mary Gail Snyder, *Fortress America: Gated Communities in the United States* (Washington, D.C., 1997), 7. Georgeanna Wilson-Doenges, "An Exploration of Sense of Community and Fear of Crime in Gated Communities," *Environment and Behavior* 32 (Sept. 2000), 597–611.

[33]Sharon Waxman, "Paradise Bought in Los Angeles," *The New York Times,* July 2, 2006, style section, p. 1. On the impact of gated communities on residents and the ways children become fearful of outsiders, see Blakely and Snyder, *Fortress America.* See also Roger K. Lewis, "'Gated' Areas: Start of New Middle Ages,"*The Washington Post,* Sept. 9, 1995, available at LexisNexis.

[34]Blakely and Snyder, *Fortress America,* 126–27.

[35]Keith Bradsher, *High and Mighty: SUVs—The World's Most Dangerous Vehicles and How They Got That Way* (New York, 2002); Josh Lauer, "Driven to Extremes: Fear of Crime and the Rise of the Sport Utility Vehicle in the United States," *Crime, Media, Culture* 1 (no. 2, 2005), 149–68.

that the buyers were very different psychologically. SUV buyers were more restless, less social people with strong fears of crime. Minivan buyers were more self-confident and social, more involved with family and friends, more active in their communities. . . . These data suggest that minivan owners exhibited more democratic tendencies in terms of their sense of security and engagement with public life. SUV drivers, in contrast, exhibited more antidemocratic characteristics, insecurity, and a retreat from public life.[36]

One study concluded that the popularity of the SUV reflected American attitudes toward crime, random violence, and "the importance of defended personal space." Although advertised as rugged off-road vehicles, SUV owners almost never ventured off-road. But the large, intimidating vigilante vehicles offered the fantasy of escape, aggression, and conquest, even as their owners hunkered down. One researcher described SUVs as "weapons" and "armoured cars for the battlefield." The last incarnation of the SUV was, in fact, a military vehicle: the Hummer, a civilian version of the Humvee used by the armed forces in the first Gulf War. . . . Although at less than ten miles per gallon the Hummer did not survive the economic collapse, its presence on American streets at the turn of the twenty-first century was a symbol of the times.[37]

By the end of the twentieth century, Americans had altered the way they live because of fear of crime. One study shows that women often changed their lifestyles to avoid crime, by not going out alone or at night and by avoiding subways, downtown areas of major cities, and contact with people who look or seem dangerous to them. Although women are less likely to be victims of crime, research shows that they are more fearful. Fear of crime inhibits their participation in activities perceived as being too dangerous for women, and it maintains gender hierarchies that limit women's power, rights, and achievements.[38]

The personal response to fears of crime mirrored the national response to the dangers of the atomic age: a heightening of alarm, a proliferation of arms, and a bunker mentality, rather than investment in the common good. The number of guns in the United States has increased steadily, from 76 per 100 residents in 1994 to 90 per 100 residents in 2007. Per capita gun ownership in the United States is now far above that of other nations, including those often described as lawless, such as Iraq, Mexico, and Colombia.[39]

---

[36]Keith Bradsher, "Delving into Psyche of SUV v. Minivan Buyers; Automakers' Research: Minivan Owners Are Other-Oriented, SUV Owners Less Social," *Financial Post*, July 18, 2000, p. C3.

[37]Ibid. Elaine Cardenas and Ellen Gorman, *The Hummer: Myths and Consumer Culture* (Lanham, 2007), 101.

[38]Esther Madriz, *Nothing Bad Happens to Good Girls: Fear of Crime in Women's Lives* (Berkeley, 1997), 119–24.

[39]Graduate Institute of International Studies, *Small Arms Survey 2007: Guns and the City* (New York, 2007), 47; Graduate Institute of International Studies, *Small Arms Survey 2003: Development Denied* (New York, 2003), 4; Robert A. Hahn et al., "First Reports Evaluating the Effectiveness of Strategies for Preventing Violence: Firearms Laws. Findings from the Task Force on Community Preventive Services," Oct. 3, 2003, *Centers for Disease Control and Prevention*, http://www.cdc.gov/mmwr/preview/mmwrhtml/rr5214a2.htm; "Population Estimates"; Carter et al., eds., "Table Aa6-8."

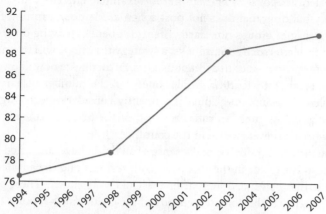

Number of Firearms in the United States per 100 Residents, 1994–2007

Figure 14.3

Sources: Graduate Institute of International Studies, *Small Arms Survey 2007: Guns and the City* (New York, 2007), 47; Graduate Institute of International Studies, *Small Arms Survey 2003: Development Denied* (New York, 2003), 4; Robert A. Hahn et al., "First Reports Evaluating the Effectiveness of Strategies for Preventing Violence: Firearms Laws. Findings from the Task Force on Community Preventive Services," Oct. 3, 2003, Centers for Disease Control and Prevention, http://www.cdc.gov/mmwr/preview/mmwrhtml/rr5214a2.htm; "Population Estimates"; Carter et al., eds., "Table Aa6-8."

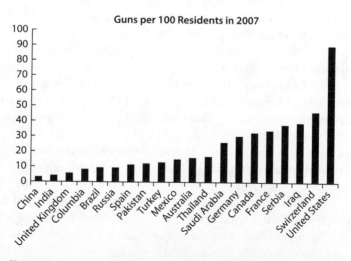

Guns per 100 Residents in 2007

Figure 14.4

Sources: Graduate Institute of International Studies, *Small Arms Survey 2007: Guns and the City* (New York, 2007), 47; Graduate Institute of International Studies, *Small Arms Survey 2003: Development Denied* (New York, 2003), 4; Robert A. Hahn et al., "First Reports Evaluating the Effectiveness of Strategies for Preventing Violence: Firearms Laws. Findings from the Task Force on Community Preventive Services," Oct. 3, 2003, Centers for Disease Control and Prevention, http://www.cdc.gov/mmwr/preview/mmwrhtml/rr5214a2.htm; "Population Estimates"; Carter et al., eds., "Table Aa6-8."

A vigilante mentality permeates society; forty states now allow citizens to carry concealed weapons. In Minnesota, for example, citizens can carry their guns into any building that does not post a sign at the door banning firearms. Members of pro-gun groups now carry firearms openly, showing off their guns on their hips in places such as Starbucks, a strategy they hope will intimidate the public into supporting concealed weapons laws. Firearms are now allowed in national parks. From 2008 to 2009, in just one year, the number of paramilitary militias tripled. The Supreme Court is currently considering striking down a Chicago law banning guns, an interpretation of the Second Amendment that would allow firearms everywhere in the country.[40]

So, as historians, how do we make sense of all this? I have suggested here that the Cold War was a factor in the obsession with security and the antidemocratic response to it that continued long after the Cold War ended. There are many outstanding studies of the domestic culture of the Cold War that point to several possible avenues for further exploration. We know that not all aspects of the Cold War were antidemocratic. After all, in an effort to eradicate inequalities and showcase to the world that the United States could live up to its ideals, national policies supported civil rights, women's rights, and the expansion of the welfare state in the Great Society programs. It is worth further study to examine why those liberal Cold War impulses were not powerful enough to prevent the antidemocratic tendencies that fostered the security obsession. It is also worth exploring the extent to which exaggerated concerns about security may have pushed the American political center to the right.

The principles of individualism, unfettered capitalism, the sanctity of the home, and a suspicion of outsiders that gained salience in the early Cold War era far outlived the Cold War itself. Those principles pushed back against the democratizing impulses of the rights revolution, fostered a bunker, vigilante mentality, and inhibited citizens from acting on behalf of the common good. Although Americans have largely accepted the gains made by the movements for civil rights and feminism, the security obsession has limited those achievements from reaching their full potential.

What, then, of security? Fear has made Americans feel less secure. As the twenty-first century unfolds, there is little evidence that Americans are safer or more empowered as a result of more weapons, more gated communities, and larger vehicles. But the security obsession has created an armed and defensive citizenry. There are more guns on the streets, locks on the doors, and walls around neighborhoods and along the nation's borders. Hostility to government and lack of concern for the common good may have made Americans considerably *less* safe. . . . Locks on the doors did not protect families against losing their homes through mortgage foreclosure. Guns in their pockets did not prevent citizens from losing their shirts to Wall Street. . . .

---

[40]Ian Urbina, "Locked, Loaded, and Ready to Caffeinate," *The New York Times*, March 8, 2010, p. A11; David G. Savage, "Justices May Rule for Gun Rights: A Pending Decision on Chicago's Ban Has National Implications," *The Los Angeles Times*, March 3, 2010, p. 1A.

And what about democracy? Democracy depends on citizens accepting their differences and trusting one another, at least to the extent that they understand themselves as belonging to a civic sphere as well as a private sphere. It requires investing in the common good and holding the government accountable as the institution that represents, and acts on behalf of, the citizenry. If, in the name of security, Americans distrust each other and the government, and value private protection at the expense of the public good, then the basic social and political practices that ensure a healthy democracy cannot survive.

Understanding the way that fear became a dominant force in American culture alongside the great achievements on behalf of democratic inclusiveness provides a historical perspective. . . . [Drawing on] Franklin D. Roosevelt: if we believe in the democratic project, "the only thing we have to fear is fear itself."[41]

---

[41] I am grateful to Daniel May for this insight.

Elaine Tyler May

I have always been interested in the connections between what we think of as private life and public life. We don't really live in two separate worlds. My scholarship seeks to understand how the personal and the public shape both individual lives and the broader world in which we live. Issues such as marriage, family, sexuality, and domesticity often seem to be removed from public life. Yet these issues are profoundly connected to public policies, political debates, and cultural shifts, as well as the experiences we have in our individual lives. My books have looked at the public and private dimensions of marriage and divorce, suburban family life during the Cold War, childlessness and birth control, and changing gender roles. The article in this collection is drawn from my current book in progress, a study of how efforts to achieve national and personal security affect the way we live as citizens, and how our democracy functions.

QUESTIONS FOR CONSIDERATION

1. May claims that the security measures after the 9/11 attacks have their origins in US policy and society during the twentieth century. Describe three examples of what Americans increasingly feared during the twentieth century and the way policymakers reacted to these fears.
2. According to May, how did politicians capitalize on the growing sense of insecurity among the American people during the twentieth century? How did business? How did the media?
3. According to May, how did Americans sense of insecurity between the 1960s and 1980s undermine the civil rights movements of this era?
4. In the aftermath of the Cold War, what other "wars" contributed to Americans' ongoing sense of insecurity?
5. In what ways were the security measures after the 9/11 attacks a continuation of US policies? In what ways were they a change?
6. According to May, how did twentieth-century fears contribute to the eroding of democracy in the United States? Compare these fears to American concerns about immigration as discussed in Ngai's article in this volume. What are some similarities and differences in Americans' reaction to these "threats?"

CHAPTER FIFTEEN

✦

Why Mass Incarceration Matters: Rethinking Crisis, Decline, and Transformation in Postwar American History[1]

Heather Ann Thompson

As the twentieth century came to a close and the twenty-first began, something occurred in the United States that was without international parallel or historical precedent. Between 1970 and 2010 more people were incarcerated in the United States than were imprisoned in any other country, and at no other point in its past had the nation's economic, social, and political institutions become so bound up with the practice of punishment. By 2006 more than 7.3 million Americans had become entangled in the criminal justice system. The American prison population had by that year increased more rapidly than had the resident population as a whole, and one in every thirty-one U.S. residents was under some form of correctional supervision, such as in prison or jail, or on probation or parole. As importantly, the incarcerated and supervised population of the United States was, overwhelmingly, a population of color. African American men experienced the highest imprisonment rate of all racial groups, male or female. It was 6.5 times the rate of white males and 2.5 times that of Hispanic males. By the middle of 2006 one in fifteen black men over the age of eighteen were behind bars as were one in nine black men aged twenty to thirty-four. The imprisonment rate of African American women looked little better. It was almost double that of Hispanic women and three times the rate of white women.[2]

---

[1] Interested students are encouraged to read this essay in the original form. Heather Ann Thompson, "Why Mass Incarceration Matters: Rethinking Crisis, Decline, and Transformation in Postwar American History," *Journal of American History* 97, no. 3 (Dec. 2010), 703–34.

[2] "Table 6.1.2006: Adults on Probation, in Jail or Prison, and on Parole," *Sourcebook of Criminal Justice Statistics Online,* http://www.albany.edu/sourcebook/pdf/t612006.pdf. "1 in 31: The Long Reach of American Corrections," March 2009, *Pew Center on the States,* http://www.pewcenteronthestates.org/uploadedFiles/PSPP_1in31_report_ FINAL_WEB_3-26-09.pdf; Heather West and William J. Sabol, "Prisoners in 2007," *Bureau of Justice Statistics Bulletin* (Dec. 2008), http://bjs.ojp. usdoj.gov/content/pub/pdf/p07.pdf; "One in Every 31 U.S. Adults Were in Prison or Jail or on Probation or Parole in 2007," press release, Dec. 11, 2008, *U.S. Department of Justice: Bureau of Justice*

Just as the American justice system changed dramatically in the wake of major historical revolutions such as the abolition of slavery, so too did it metamorphize much later in the twentieth century as the nation was further contested and transformed. This was particularly the case following the 1960s. ... In the thirty-five years leading up to and including the tumultuous 1960s, the number of Americans incarcerated in federal and state prisons had increased by 52,249 people. In the subsequent thirty-five years that group increased by 1,266,2435. There is little question that such numbers both reflected and shaped the history of postwar America. ... [3]

This essay will suggest ... that to understand why so many prosperous American cities became centers of poverty and pessimism during the postwar period—to fully locate the origins of urban crisis—we must reckon with the extent to which postwar urban spaces were compromised by the mass incarceration of the later twentieth century. Likewise, to make sense of why the American labor movement declined so dramatically after the 1970s, we must explore the significant changes to the law and the economy that accompanied mass incarceration—changes that directly and indirectly eroded the bargaining power and economic security of America's free-world work force. And finally, if we hope to sort out why the politics of postwar liberalism waned over this period, we must realize that the nation's rightward shift had more to do with mass incarceration than we have yet appreciated and less to do with rising crime rates and the political savvy of the Republican party than we have long assumed.

MASS INCARCERATION AND THE ORIGINS OF URBAN CRISIS

Historicizing mass incarceration can provide new perspectives on many of the questions that historians ask about the postwar period. One of the most central of these concerns why America's inner cities came to suffer such crisis toward the end of the twentieth century. ... As the postwar period unfolded not only did numerous urban centers across the country suffer deep racial and political conflicts but these same cities also experienced tremendous distress from substantial economic disinvestment. By the twenty-first century too many urban enclaves had become synonymous with unrelenting and seemingly inescapable poverty. ... [4] Historians have ... done a great deal of important work on the origins of its demise. Thomas Sugrue's pivotal study of Detroit, for example, highlights the role that deindustrialization and white racial conservatism played in creating

Statistics, http://bjs.ojp.usdoj.gov/content/pub/press/p07ppuspr.cfm. Michelle Alexander, *The New Jim Crow: Mass Incarceration in the Age of Colorblindness* (New York, 2010), 195. "One in a Hundred: Behind Bars in America, 2008," Feb. 2008, *Pew Center on the States*, http://www.pewcenteronthestates.org/uploadedFiles/One%20 in%20100.pdf.

[3]Manning Marable, *Race, Reform, and Rebellion: The Second Reconstruction in Black America* (1991; Jackson, 2003), 3. "Table 6.13.2008."

[4]Alison Isenburg, *Downtown America: A History of the Place and the People Who Made It* (Chicago, 2005); Fred Siegel, *The Future Once Happened Here: New York, D.C., L.A., and the Fate of America's Big Cities* (New York, 2000).

a crisis from which the city simply could not escape. Others, such as Matthew Lassiter, have pointed to the ways that mass suburbanization in the middle and later decades of the twentieth century also undermined urban America.[5] All of these phenomena clearly mattered, but so did the postwar expansion of the carceral state and its eventual byproduct, mass incarceration.

The dramatic postwar rise of the carceral state depended directly on what might well be called the "criminalization of urban space," a process by which increasing numbers of urban dwellers—overwhelmingly men and women of color—became subject to a growing number of laws that . . . subjected violators to unprecedented time behind bars. In the same way that rural African American spaces were criminalized at the end of the Civil War, resulting in the record imprisonment of black men that undermined African American communities in the Reconstruction and Jim Crow–era South, the criminalization of urban spaces of color, in both the South and North, during and after the 1960s civil rights era fundamentally altered the social and economic landscape of the late twentieth- and early twenty-first-century United States.[6]

As Khalil Muhammad and Donna Murch have both pointed out, the focus of law enforcement on urban African Americans, which became a hallmark of the last third of the twentieth century, was rooted in much earlier decades. As Muhammad shows, northern social scientists throughout the Progressive Era were using census data to try to "prove" that blacks were inherently prone to criminality and thus needed greater police scrutiny. He notes as well that such associations between blackness and crime only deepened as the twentieth century unfolded. . . . In stark contrast to white working-class Americans, who increasingly claimed the mantle of crime victim over the course of the twentieth century, poor blacks were increasingly blamed for any crime problem America had. As Murch also shows clearly, by the first decades of the postwar period, much of white America had come to see the presence of African Americans, and their concentration in inner cities in particular, as inherently threatening and it advocated policing them accordingly.[7]

---

[5]Thomas J. Sugrue, *The Origins of the Urban Crisis: Race and Inequality in Postwar Detroit* (Princeton, 1996); Matthew Lassiter, *The Silent Majority: Suburban Politics in the Sunbelt South* (Princeton, 2005); Arnold Hirsch, *Making the Second Ghetto: Race and Housing in Chicago, 1940–1960* (Chicago, 1998); Wendell Pritchett, *Brownsville, Brooklyn: Blacks, Jews, and the Changing Face of the Ghetto* (Chicago, 2002); Amanda Seligman, *Block by Block: Neighborhoods and Public Policy on Chicago's West Side* (Chicago, 2005); Robert O. Self, *American Babylon: Race and the Struggle for Postwar Oakland* (Princeton, 2004); Kenneth Jackson, *Crabgrass Frontier: The Suburbanization of the United States* (New York, 1987); Jane Jacobs, *The Death and Life of Great American Cities* (1961; New York, 1992); Kevin M. Kruse and Thomas J. Sugrue, eds., *The New Suburban History* (Chicago, 2006); Kevin M. Kruse, *White Flight: Atlanta and the Making of Modern Conservatism* (Princeton, 2005); David M. P. Freund, *Colored Property: State Policy and White Racial Politics in Suburban America* (Chicago, 2008).

[6]Clear, *Imprisoning Communities*. Loïc Wacquant, "Racial Stigma in the Making of the Punitive State," in *Race, Incarceration, and American Values*, ed. Loury, 57–70.

[7]Muhammad, *Condemnation of Blackness*, 12–13, 270, 272, 275; Khalil Gibran Muhammad, "Where Did All of the White Criminals Go? The Remapping of Racial Criminalities on the Road to Mass Incarceration," paper delivered at the "Historians and the Carceral State: Writing Policing and Punishment into Modern U.S. History" symposium, Rutgers University, March 5, 2009 (in Heather Ann Thompson's possession), 3. Murch, *Living for the City*.

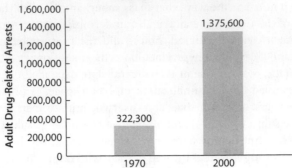

By the late 1960s, however, with African Americans across the country actively laying claim to equal citizenship, the urban spaces in which they lived were criminalized to an unprecedented extent. One of the most important mechanisms by which urban spaces were newly criminalized after the civil rights sixties was a revolution in drug legislation. The state of New York started this revolution by passing a series of new drug laws in 1973. . . . [8] As a result . . . the state's prison population soared. By the 1990s, 32.2 percent of inmates in New York's prisons were locked up for drug offenses, and significantly, the majority of them hailed from the state's most urban enclaves. In fact, New York's urban spaces were so impacted by drug legislation in the last decades of the twentieth century that by the new millennium 66 percent of the prisoners who filled the state's vast prison system had been arrested in, and were from, New York City.[9]

By the close of the twentieth century, New York–style drug laws had been implemented across the nation, and the incarceration rate of inner-city dwellers everywhere escalated dramatically. While in 1970 there had been only 322,300 drug-related arrests in the United States, in 2000 that figure was 1,375,600, and again, the majority of those taken into custody came from inner cities. There were eventually more Detroiters under correctional supervision than there were holding union jobs in the city's auto plants.[10]

---

[8]Rhonda Y. Williams, "The Dope Wars: Street-Level Hustling and the Culture of Drugs in Post-1940s America," unpublished manuscript (in Rhonda Y. Williams's possession); Julilly Kohler-Hausmann, "'The Attila the Hun Law': New York's Rockefeller Drug Laws and the Making of the Punitive State," *Journal of Social History* 44 (Fall 2010), 76; Vanessa Barker, *The Politics of Imprisonment: How the Democratic Process Shapes the Way America Punishes Offenders* (New York, 2009), 149; David F. Weiman and Christopher Weiss, "The Origins of Mass Incarceration in New York State: The Rockefeller Drug Laws and the Local War on Drugs," in *Do Prisons Make Us Safer? The Benefits and Costs of the Prison Boom*, ed. Steven Raphael and Michael A. Stoll (New York, 2009), 89.

[9]Aaron D. Wilson, "Rockefeller Drug Laws Information Sheet," *PRDI: Partnership for Responsible Drug Information*, http://www.prdi.org/rocklawfact.html. "Before the New York State Legislative Task Force on Demographic Research and Reapportionment: Testimony of Peter Wagner, March 14, 2002," *Prison Policy Initiative*, http://www.prisonpolicy.org/articles/ny_legis031402.pdf.

[10]Tina L. Dorsey and Priscilla Middleton, "Drug and Crime Facts," 2007, *U.S. Department of Justice: Bureau of Justice Statistics*, http://bjs.ojp.usdoj.gov/content/pub/pdf/dcf.pdf; Linda Ewing, United Auto Workers Union, telephone conversation with Heather Ann Thompson, July 19, 2010, notes (in Thompson's possession); "1 in 31," 9.

Law enforcement not only disproportionately targeted cities in its new war on drugs but it also particularly policed the communities of color within them; this, despite extensive and readily available data that these areas were not where most drug trafficking and usage took place. As studies done by the National Institute on Drug Abuse and the National Household Survey on Drug Abuse noted in 2000, not only did "white students use cocaine at seven times the rate of black students, use crack cocaine at eight times the rate of black students, and use heroin at seven times the rate of black students," but whites between the ages of twelve and seventeen were also "more than a third more likely to have sold illegal drugs than African American youth."[11] In the 1980s alone, however, African Americans' "share" of drug crimes jumped from 26.9 percent to 46.0 percent, and arrested black juveniles "were 37 percent more likely to be transferred to adult courts, where they faced tougher sanctions." If convicted, African Americans of every age "were more likely than whites to be committed to prison instead of jail, and they were more likely to receive longer sentences."[12]

As much as criminalizing drugs impacted urban America in general, and poor neighborhoods of color in particular, both spaces were also disproportionately affected after 1970 by an overhaul of state and federal sentencing guidelines related to drug convictions.... Over the next twenty-five years prison terms across the country lengthened substantially. Between the 1980s and the 1990s "the chances of receiving a prison sentence following arrest increased by more than 50 percent" and "the average length of sentences served increas[ed] by nearly 40 percent."[13]

Not only did possession of various illegal drugs eventually guarantee decades behind bars, but so did mere association with people who possessed such contraband. In 1978, for example, Michigan passed a "650 lifer law," which mandated a life sentence for anyone found guilty of the intent to deliver 650 grams or more of cocaine. By 1999 this law had resulted in two hundred people receiving a life sentence with no chance of parole—some of whom had not had drugs in their possession but were simply in proximity to someone who did. Indicative of how widespread punitive sentencing practices had become during the later twentieth century, by the new millennium "thirty-three states had abolished limited parole (up from seventeen in 1980), twenty-four states had introduced three strikes laws (up from zero), and forty states had introduced truth-in-sentencing laws

---

[11]Alexander, *New Jim Crow*, 97; Weiman and Weiss, "Origins of Mass Incarceration in New York State," 81.

[12]Weiman and Weiss, "Origins of Mass Incarceration in New York State," 81, 84.

[13]William J. Sabol et al., "The Influences of Truth-in-Sentencing Reforms on Changes in States' Sentencing Practices and Prison Populations," April 1, 2002, *Urban Institute*, http://www.urban.org/publications/410470.html. Jonathan Erlen and Joseph F. Spillane, eds., *Federal Drug Control: The Evolution of Policy and Practice* (Binghamton, 2004). See Edward M. Kennedy's introduction, along with Senators John McClellan of Arkansas and Hiram Fong of Hawaii, of Senate Bill 2698, in "Question of Mandatory Prison Sentence to Reduce Crime—Pro and Con," *Congressional Digest* 55 (Aug.–Sept. 1976), 204. Devah Pager, *Marked: Race, Crime, and Finding Work in an Era of Mass Incarceration* (Chicago, 2007), 17.

(up from three)." . . . In 2009 there were nevertheless more adult Americans serving life sentences (140,610) than at any other time in the country's history, and nineteen states had recently passed laws that also allowed minors to be sentenced to life without the possibility of parole.[14]

. . . By the close of the twentieth century, actions that had earlier not garnered the attention of the nation's criminal justice apparatus were netting serious sanctions. This played out most clearly in the nation's urban school districts beginning in the late 1960s. Youth challenges to racial inequality had escalated throughout that decade, targeting numerous civic institutions, including secondary schools. In response, school district officials across the country not only embraced more punitive policies but also began employing security staffs to enforce them.[15]

Throughout the 1960s Baltimore City Schools had experienced a great deal of civil rights activism, and in 1967 district officers decided to bring in a law enforcement presence of twenty-one officers. During the 1970s, and in no small part through resources made available to the city district from the federal Juvenile Justice and Delinquency Prevention Act of 1974, Baltimore City Schools, and other districts like it, dramatically increased the policing of their schools. By 1984 Baltimore had concluded that "security" was an insufficient descriptor for the level of policing it had come to expect of its school officers, so it created the Baltimore School Police Force, which was given additional, unprecedented power in 1991. The Maryland General Assembly determined that year that school police officers would be given the same training and be as heavily armed as all other law enforcement personnel in the state.[16]

The process of criminalizing urban space via urban schools continued into the twenty-first century. The school district of New York City eventually had "the tenth largest police force in the country—larger than the police forces of Washington, D.C., Detroit, Boston, or Las Vegas." It employed 4,625 school safety

---

[14]"The Huge Cost of Harsh Sentences," editorial, *St. Petersburg Times*, Dec. 22, 2002. "Fight for Justice, One State Group Works Miracles for Many Families," *Detroit Free Press*, Jan. 4, 1999. "Rethinking the Lifer Law," *60 Minutes*, http://www.cbsnews.com/stories/1999/06/04/60II/main49670.shtml; Glenn C. Loury, "Race, Incarceration, and American Values," in *Race, Incarceration, and American Values*, ed. Loury, 9; Solomon Moore, "Number of Life Terms Hits Record," *The New York Times*, July 22, 2009, http://www.nytimes.com/2009/07/23/us/23sentence.html. Stephanie Chen, "Teens Locked Up for Life without a Second Chance," April 8, 2009, *CNN*, http://www.cnn.com/2009/CRIME/04/08/teens.life.sentence/index.html.

[15]Sean Nicholson-Crotty, Zachary Birchmeier, and David Valentine, "Exploring the Impact of School Discipline on Racial Disproportion in the Juvenile Justice Systems," *Social Science Quarterly* 90 (Dec. 2009), 1003–18; Murch, *Living for the City.*

[16]Dollie Walker, Arthur L. Stinchcombe, and Mary S. McDill, "School Desegregation in Baltimore," Aug. 1967, report BR-6-1610, *ERIC: Education Resources Information Center*, http://www.eric.ed.gov/PDFS/ED013168 .pdf. Juvenile Justice and Delinquency Prevention Act, 42 U.S.C. 5601 sec. 101 (1974). For the text of this act, especially the "Congressional Statement of Findings," see *U.S. Department of Justice: Office of Juvenile Justice and Delinquency Prevention*, http://ojjdp.ncjrs.org/about/ojjjact.txt. "School Police History," *Baltimore City Public Schools: School Police*, http://www.baltimorecityschools.org/21671031716529880/blank/browse.asp?A=383&BMDRN=2000&BCOB=0&C=56274.

agents and stationed two hundred armed police officers in school buildings. As the law-and-order presence grew in city schools across the nation, students were increasingly subject to police scrutiny for infractions ranging from fighting to having food in class, carrying cell phones, skipping classes, and throwing temper tantrums. The subsequent dramatic rise of "arrests for minor noncriminal violations of school rules" in inner-city America not only disrupted urban learning environments but also ensured that the incarcerated population of America's big cities would become increasingly younger.[17]

Law enforcement more aggressively targeted adult urbanites who committed petty crimes. . . . Acts that had before resulted in misdemeanor citations at worst . . . could be considered serious criminal matters by the close of the twentieth century. . . . By the close of the twentieth century the list of illegal activities included urinating in public, sleeping outside, begging for food, and consuming food on the train. . . . In 2006 alone the New York Police Department "stopped and frisked" over half a million men and women.[18]

It is significant that law enforcement bodies of the later postwar period focused their attention overwhelmingly on urban spaces. . . . As a Columbia University study of incarceration in the boroughs of New York City found, "Like poverty, incarceration is spatially concentrated; much more than is crime," indicating clearly that the greater the incarceration rate a given city experienced, the less possibility there was that it could remain socially stable and economically vibrant. . . .[19]

---

[17]New York Civil Liberties Union, "Criminalizing the Classroom: The Over-Policing of New York City Schools," March 2007, http://www.nyclu.org/pdfs/criminalizing_the_classroom_report. pdf; Bob Herbert, "6-Year-Olds Under Arrest," *The New York Times*, April 9, 2007, http://select. nytimes.com/2007/04/09/opinion/09herbert.html?_r=1; Richard E. Redding, "Juvenile Transfer Laws: An Effective Deterrent to Delinquency?," *Juvenile Justice Bulletin* (Aug. 2008).

[18]Timothy Stewart-Winter, "Raids, Riots, and Rainbow Coalitions: Sexuality and Race in Chicago Politics, 1950–2000" (Ph.D. diss., University of Chicago, 2009). Mark Levin, "Not Just for Criminals: Overcriminalization in the Lone Star State," April 2005, *Texas Policy Foundation*, http:// www.texaspolicy.com/pdf/2005-04-pp-overcrim.pdf; "Homes Not Handcuffs: The Criminalization of Homelessness in U.S. Cities," July 2009, *National Coalition for the Homeless*; D.C. Code sec. 35-251(b) (2001). See also *Tracey V. Hedgepeth, as the Next Friend to Ansche Hedgepeth v. Washington Metropolitan Area Transit Authority*, No. 03-7149 (D.C. Cir. decided Oct. 26, 2004), http://www.ll. georgetown.edu/federal/judicial/dc/opinions/03opinions/03-7149a.pdf. *Terry v. Ohio*, 392 U.S. 1 (1968); Mary Frances Berry, ed., *Police Practices and Civil Rights in New York City: A Report of the United States Commission on Civil Rights* (Washington, D.C., 2000); and Harry G. Levine and Deborah Peterson Small, "Marijuana Arrest Crusade: Racial Bias and Police Policy in New York City, 1997–2007," April 2008, *New York Civil Liberties Union*, http://www.nyclu.org/files/MARIJUANA-ARREST-CRUSADE_Final.pdf, p. 25. Ray Rivera, Al Baker, and Janet Roberts, "A Few Blocks, 4 Years, 52,000 Police Stops," *The New York Times*, July 12, 2010, http://query.nytimes.com/gst/fullpage. html?res=9E04E5DF173AF931A25754C0A9669D8B63. Andrew Golub, Bruce D. Johnson, and Eloise Dunlap, "The Race/Ethnicity Disparity in Misdemeanor Marijuana Arrests in New York City," *Criminal Public Policy* 6 (no. 1, 2007), 131–64; Levine and Small, "Marijuana Arrest Crusade," 6.

[19]"Architecture and Justice," Sept. 2006, *Columbia University Graduate School of Architecture, Planning, and Preservation: Spatial Information Design Lab*, http://www.spatialinformationdesign-lab.org/MEDIA/PDF_04.pdf, p. 9; Clear, *Imprisoning Communities*, 165; Jeffery Fagan, Vivian West, and Jan Holland, "Reciprocal Effects of Crime and Incarceration in New York City Neighborhoods," *Fordham Urban Law Journal* 30 (2003), 1551–602.

The criminalization of urban space and the imposition of lengthy prison terms not only rendered an increasing percentage of urbanites unable to contribute to the cities where they grew up but it also made it difficult for them to provide for the dependents they left behind. According to the Bureau of Justice Statistics, at the close of the twentieth century, "state and federal prisoners were parents to 1,498,800 children under age 18." By 2002 one in every forty-five minor children had at least one parent in a state or federal prison, and by 2008 "52% of state inmates and 63% of federal inmates reported having an estimated 1,706,600 minor children"—the majority of whom were under the age of ten. That women eventually became the fastest growing population in the nation's jails and prisons only exacerbated the crisis faced by America's cities because so many of them were mothers no longer able to care for their young children still at home. . . . The increasing imprisonment of "women who are nonbiological caretakers of dependent children [and] women who are arrested while raising their younger siblings, nieces, and nephews, or children in their extended social network" also adversely impacted inner-city kids.[20]

Even when inner-city residents got out of prison . . . their status as formerly incarcerated still negatively impacted their children as well as the inner cities in which they lived. When men and women returned to cities such as Detroit or Brooklyn, the first thing they needed was a job to support themselves and their dependents. As a study of several of America's largest cities revealed in 1996, however, a majority of employers "would not knowingly hire an ex-offender." Several studies indicate that the formerly incarcerated could have their employment options reduced by as much as 59 percent and, if hired, their annual income reduced by as much as 28 percent, and their hourly wages reduced by as much as 19 percent. The nation's welfare system failed to mitigate much of this post-incarceration poverty because, after passage of the Personal Responsibility and Work Opportunity Reconciliation Act of 1996, offenders with drug-related felonies were saddled with "a lifetime ban on eligibility for TANF [Temporary Assistance for Needy Families] . . . and food stamps." . . . Almost a decade before the Clinton administration chose to "end welfare as we know it" in the mid-1990s, expenditures on incarceration had already "surpassed AFDC [Aid

---

[20]Christopher J. Mumola, "Incarcerated Parents and Their Children," Aug. 2000, *U.S. Department of Justice: Office of Justice Programs,* http://bjs.ojp.usdoj.gov/content/pub/pdf/iptc.pdf. "An Estimated 809,800 Inmates in the Nation's Prisons Were Parents to 1,706,600 Minor Children at Midyear 2007," press release, Aug. 26, 2008, *U.S. Department of Justice: Bureau of Justice Statistics,* http://www.ojp.usdoj.gov/newsroom/pressreleases/2008/bjs08101.htm. "Women in the Criminal Justice System: Briefing Sheets, 2007," May 2007, *Sentencing Project,* http://www.sentencingproject.org/doc/publications/womenincj_total.pdf; Christina Rathbone, *A World Apart: Women, Prison, and Life behind Bars* (New York, 2006). "Nell Bernstein Asks Us to 'See' the Children of Incarcerated Americans," Jan. 11, 2006, *BuzzFlash,* http://www.buzzflash.com/interviews/06/01/int06001.html. Nell Bernstein, *All Alone in the World: Children of the Incarcerated* (New York, 2005). Beth E. Richie, "The Social Impact of Mass Incarceration on Women," in *Invisible Punishment: The Collateral Consequences of Mass Imprisonment,* ed. Marc Mauer and Meda Chesney-Lind (New York, 2002), 139.

to Families with Dependent Children] by 130 percent and food stamps by 70 percent."[21]

... According to research scientists, by the close of the twentieth century human immunodeficiency virus/acquired immune deficiency syndrome (HIV/ AIDS) was "up to five times more prevalent in American prisons than in the general population," and given that the majority of inmates were eventually released to urban centers, numerous city residents were eventually at a higher risk for contracting the virus. With prison overcrowding leading to major outbreaks of tuberculosis in penal facilities across the country, inner-city dwellers were also at an increased risk of exposure to a disease that only decades earlier had been virtually eliminated. According to one scholar, "Several of the worst outbreaks of tuberculosis documented in the United States" (such as a 1989 "epidemic of drug-resistant tuberculosis in New York City" that took "more than a billion dollars" to bring to an end) had "their roots in overcrowded prisons and jails." ... [22]

As the postwar period wore on, America's urban centers were increasingly trapped in a vicious cycle of imprisonment and want, one that both undergirded and ensured civic distress: mass incarceration increased poverty, increased urban poverty led to even more urban incarceration, and so on. According to analysts, as many as 70 percent of the children whose parents were imprisoned at the close of the twentieth century would end up behind bars themselves, and African American children were more than eight times more likely to have a parent in prison than were white children in major cities such as Chicago. Therefore, to understand the origins of urban crisis in the postwar United States (in its myriad manifestations ranging from population loss to escalating poverty to a compromised educational system to poor public health to the ever-widening racial divide) historians must look much more closely at how the American justice

---

[21]Jennifer Fahey, Cheryl Roberts, and Len Engel, "Employment of Ex-offenders: Employer Perspectives," Oct. 31, 2006, *Crime and Justice Institute*, http://www.cjinstitute.org/files/ex_ offenders_employers_12-15-06.pdf; Bruce Western, "The Penal System and the Labor Market," in *Barriers to Reentry? The Labor Market for Released Prisoners in Post-industrial America*, ed. Shawn Bushway, Michael A. Stoll, and David F. Weiman (New York, 2007), 342, table 11.1; and Bruce Western and Katherine Beckett, "How Unregulated Is the U.S. Labor Market? The Penal System as a Labor Market Institution," *American Journal of Sociology* 104 (Jan. 1999), 1031; Gwen Rubenstein and Debbie Mukamal, "Welfare and Housing—Denial of Benefits to Drug Offenders," in *Invisible Punishment*, ed. Mauer and Chesney-Lind, 41; Wacquant, *Prisons of Poverty*, 140, table 9.

[22]Wil S. Hylton, "Sick on the Inside: Correctional HMOS and the Coming Prison Plague," in *Prison Profiteers: Who Makes Money from Mass Incarceration*, ed. Tara Herivel and Paul Wright (New York, 2008), 179–203. "Study Highlights HIV/AIDS Challenge in American Prison System," *Science Daily*, Sept. 30, 2009, http://www.sciencedaily.com/releases/2009/09/090929133246.htm; Ronald Braithwaite, Theodore M. Hammett, Robert M. Mayberry, eds., *Prisons and Aids: A Public Health Challenge* (San Francisco, 1996); Rucker C. Johnson and Steven Raphael, "The Effects of Male Incarceration Dynamics on Acquired Immune Deficiency Syndrome Infection Rates among African American Women and Men," *Journal of Law and Economics*, 52 (May 2009), 251–93; *Plata v. Schwarzenegger*, No. 3:01-cv-01351-THE (N.D. Cal. filed April 5, 2001); *Coleman v. Schwarzenegger*, No. 2:90-cv-00520-LKK-JFM (E.D. Cal. filed April 23, 1990); Sarah Valway, Robert Greifinger, and Mark Papania, "Multidrug-Resistant Tuberculosis in the New York Prison System, 1990–1991," *Journal of Infectious Diseases* 170 (July 1994); and Robert Greifinger, *Public Health behind Bars: From Prisons to Communities* (New York, 2009); Paul Farmer, "The House of the Dead: Tuberculosis and Incarceration," in *Invisible Punishment*, ed. Mauer and Chesney-Lind, 239.

system evolved after the 1960s, in general, and at the implications of mass incarceration for urbanites, in particular. Mass incarceration was not simply, as the sociologist Loïc Wacquant suggests, "a political response to the collapse of the ghetto."[23] It was a historical phenomenon that—like deindustrialization and white flight—*itself* caused crisis and collapse in America's inner cities.

MASS INCARCERATION AND THE DECLINE
OF THE AMERICAN LABOR MOVEMENT

Just as historians have overlooked key connections between the dramatic post-1960s rise in the American prison population and the crisis that subsequently befell U.S. inner cities, so too have we been slow to recognize how this turn to mass incarceration adversely impacted the American labor movement. . . . Just as the South's economy was transformed . . . when the leaders of that region embraced a more punitive labor system and locked up unprecedented numbers of African Americans right after the Civil War, so too did the national economy, and the American working class as a whole, feel the reverberations of the post–civil rights sixties turn to mass incarceration. In both periods there were important links between the criminalization of space—specifically spaces of color—and calls by the government and private business for unfettered access to a prison labor force. In both eras, when private and public employers managed to secure, and then began regularly to exploit, an unfree labor force, the American labor movement was undermined, the economic security of the free-world working class was compromised, and income as well as racial inequality was actively exacerbated.

The American labor movement's rise to a position of power and prominence remains a central event of the twentieth century. From the earliest days of industrialization, working people struggled to improve the conditions under which they labored as well as to increase their share of the profits extracted from their toil. Although workers made slow progress in this effort during the first couple of decades of the twentieth century, by the 1930s they had forged a powerful labor movement. By the early postwar period that movement had dramatically improved the standard of living and the nature of work across the United States. Toward the end of the century, however, such labor gains were in serious jeopardy. Whereas union density was at an all-time high soon after World War II, with 35 percent of the nation's work force in a labor union in 1954, by the early 1980s only 20.1 percent were unionized, by 2001 that figure was only 13.5 percent, and by 2008, it was only 8 percent.[24]

---

[23]Fagan, West, and Holland, "Reciprocal Effects of Crime and Incarceration in New York City Neighborhoods." Mumola, "Incarcerated Parents and Their Children." For Loïc Waquant's remarks, see Loury, ed., *Race, Incarceration, and American Values*, 63.

[24]U.S. Census Bureau, "Historical Statistics of the United States, Colonial Times to 1970," *U.S. Census Bureau: Statistical Abstracts,* http://www.census.gov/prod/www/abs/statab.html; Bureau of Labor Statistics, *Handbook of Labor Statistics, Bulletin 2070* (Washington, D.C., 1980). See various January issues for the years 1983–2002 of Bureau of Labor Statistics, *Employment and Earnings.* See also "Change to Win's Agenda for Restoring the American Dream," *Change to Win,* http://www.changetowin.org/issues.html.

As scholars of convict leasing in the nineteenth-century South have made clear, prisons have long been some of the most exploitative workplaces in America, and thus, the fate of American workers and the history of the American justice system are inexorably linked. . . . Until the mid-twentieth century, free-world employers had ready access to convict labor, and that cheap labor was so important to the American economy that politicians from both the South and North went to extraordinary lengths to ensure that penal institutions met the needs of private companies.[25]

. . . To an important extent the New Deal actually formalized and legiti-mated the practice of prison labor with the creation of the Federal Prison Indus-tries (FPI) in 1934. Thanks to the FPI, state and federal prisons forever after were in the business of manufacturing clothing, furniture, and other items, albeit only for sale to fellow state and federal government agencies. While New Deal regula-tions had largely barred private employers from using inmate labor and had blocked the sale of prison-made goods to private interests and across state lines, the federal government and the states in the postwar period were still able to force inmates to work for little or no pay, often under terrible conditions. . . .[26]

Just as the federal government and numerous state legislatures were inter-ested in overhauling criminal laws . . . , so too were they interested in ridding the books of laws that regulated prison labor to strengthen the economic position of both government and business. . . . At the federal level this meant passing a series of laws in 1979 that dramatically weakened New Deal–era restrictions on the sale of prison-made goods and the use of prison labor.[27]

This legislative shift had been realized thanks to a mobilization of conserva-tives desiring greater "privatization of government services" in the early 1970s. . . . Groups of businessmen had also begun agitating at the state level to gain access to penal work forces. . . . Thanks to . . . employer activism, in the last five years of the twentieth century thirty-six states granted private companies complete access to prison labor.[28]

---

[25]"Table 1: Convicts in Prison, and at Work—By States," in *Statistics of Convict Labor. Advanced Chapters from the Fourth Biennial Report of the Bureau of Labor Statistics of the State of Illinois* (Spring-field, Ill., 1886), 44. McLennan, *Crisis of Imprisonment*, 84. Thompson, "Blinded by a 'Barbaric' South."

[26]Douglas A. Blackmon, *Slavery by Another Name: The Re-enslavement of Black Americans from the Civil War to World War II* (New York, 2008); Records of Federal Prison Industries, Inc., 1930–43, Records of the Bureau of Prisons, rg 129.4 (National Archives, College Park, Md.); and "Factories with Fences: 75 Years of Changing Lives," 2009, *UNICOR*, http://www.unicor.gov/information/publications/pdfs/corporate/CATMC1101_C.pdf.

[27]Justice System Improvement Act of 1979, Pub.L. No. 96-157, 18 U.S.C. 1761(c) and 41 U.S.C. 35. Gwen Smith Ingley, "Inmate Labor: Yesterday, Today, and Tomorrow," *Corrections Today* 58 (Feb. 1996), 28, 30, 77; Robert D. Atkinson, "Prison Labor: It's More Than Just Breaking Rocks," May 2002, *Progressive Policy Institute*, http:// www.ppionline.org/documents/prison_labor_502.pdf.

[28]Judith A. Greene, "Entrepreneurial Corrections: Incarceration as a Business Opportunity," in *Invisible Punishment*, ed. Mauer and Chesney-Lind, 96; National Institute of Justice report, George E. Sexton, "Work in American Prisons: Joint Ventures with the Private Sector," July 26, 2004, *National Criminal Justice Reference Service*, http://www.ncjrs.gov/pdffiles/workampr.pdf, p. 5; Gordon Lafer, "Captive Labor: America's Prisoners as Corporate Workforce," *American Pros-pect*, Sept. 1, 1999, http://www.prospect.org/cs/articles?article=captive_labor. David Leonhardt, "As Prison Labor Grows, So Does the Debate," *The New York Times*, March 19, 2000, http://www.nytimes.com/2000/03/19/business/as-prison-labor-grows-so-does-the-debate.html.

As long-standing regulations on prison labor were substantially amended or eliminated in the latter third of the twentieth century, the American economy was also transformed.... The work already being done by prisoners in state facilities increased dramatically, both because the government began asking them to produce an ever greater number of products for sale to the private sector and because there had been an explosion of new contracts between private companies and state prisons that allowed for the leasing out of these convicts to perform jobs previously done by free-world workers. By the close of the twentieth century Supreme Court justice Warren Burger's 1985 wish to transform prisons into "factories with fences" had been fulfilled, with over 80,000 inmates holding "traditional jobs, working for government or private companies and earning 25 cents to $7 an hour." . . .[29]

There was clear evidence that free-world wages had been cut and jobs had been eliminated as a result of prison labor in the later postwar period as well. Free-world workers who made circuit boards at Lockhart Technologies in Austin, Texas, for example, found themselves unemployed in the mid-1990s because their company figured out that it was more cost-effective to reopen in a private prison thirty miles away. The prison had designed a facility to the company's specifications and charged it rent of only $1.00 per year. In that same decade a major hospital in Eugene, Oregon, "canceled its contract with a unionized linen service to redirect the work to a prison laundry," while a recycling plant in Georgia laid off its free-world employees so that it could replace "them with prison laborers from a nearby women's prison." Konica Corporation was also drawn to prison labor and eventually gave its copier repair jobs to workers behind bars, because it could pay them between 35 and 47 cents an hour. As the Ohio Civil Service Employees Association, which represented laid-off workers whose jobs had gone to prisoners in that state, put it, "'These aren't phantom jobs—these are real jobs, real people.'"[30]

Prison labor was attractive to American employers for more reasons than lower wages; they also did not have to deal with sick days, unemployment insurance, or workman's compensation claims, and they had few liability worries

---

[29]Kentucky Correctional Industries—"Kentucky's best kept secret" and New Jersey Department of Corrections— "And you thought we only made license plates." Pamela LiCalzi O'Connell, "New Economy: For Consumer Goods Producers, It Is Not So Bad to Be Behind Bars," *The New York Times*, May 14, 2001, http://www.nytimes.com/2001/05/14/business/new-economy-for-consumer-goods-producers-it-is-not-so-bad-to-be-behind-bars.html; Sexton, "Work in American Prisons"; Lafer, "Captive Labor." Warren Burger, "Prison Industries: Turning Warehouses into Factories with Fences," *Public Administration Review* 45 (Nov. 1985), 754–57; Leonhardt, "As Prison Labor Grows, So Does the Debate."

[30]Charles C. Cox and Roger E. Meiners, "Private Employment of Prison Labor," *Journal of Private Enterprise* 17 (Fall 2001), 18–63; "Prison Labor, Prison Blues,"*AFL-CIO Label Letter*, Dec. 16, 1995; Pens, "Microsoft 'Outcells' Competition," in *The Celling of America: An Inside Look at the U.S. Prison Industry*, ed. Daniel Burton Rose, Dan Pens, and Paul Wright (Monroe, 1998), 118; Lafer, "Captive Labor"; Danny Cahill, "The Global Economy behind Ohio Prison Walls," in *Celling of America*, ed. Rose, Pens, and Wright, 110; "Ohio: Ire over Inmate Labor Plan," *The New York Times*, April 17, 2009.

when it came to toxins or accidents in prison workplaces. . . . That employers could dodge safety regulations in prison shops undermined the free-world working class as significantly as did wage competition. In short, because prisoners were unable to demand decent working conditions, and employers saved a substantial amount of money on health and safety protections when they hired them, workers in the free world also found it increasingly difficult to insist upon a safe workplace for fear of losing their jobs."[31]

Crime clearly paid, at least for some actors in the American economy. Regaining access to prison labor in the later decades of the twentieth century was not the only way that business interests profited from the expansion of the carceral state. They also struck gold when it came to building and managing prisons. Indicative of how lucrative the expansion of the carceral state could be, by 2007 Colorado was paying out "almost 95 million dollars a year in taxpayer money to corporate jailers," and one of the nation's eighteen private-sector, for-profit, prison-building and management companies, Corrections Corporation of America, posted "revenues of over $1.4 billion" that year. Crime, and more precisely mass incarceration, also meant major profits for companies that could provide prison goods and services—items ranging from telephones to tampons and tasers. During the later postwar period, annual meetings of the American Correctional Association became little more than trade shows where for-profit firms hawked their goods and services. . . . As Irving Lingo, the chief financial officer for Corrections Corporation of America put it in 2006, "Our core business touches so many things—security, medicine, education, food service, maintenance, technology—that it presents a unique opportunity for any number of vendors to do business with us."

The benefits of mass incarceration were also obvious to employers who saw prison expansion as an antidote to the shrinking migrant labor pool of the later postwar period. From Maryland's crab industry to farms in states such as Colorado, employers flocked to prisoner-workers when their access to cheap immigrant labor began to dry up. Indeed, prisons and the labor they could provide were touted as more lucrative than moving operations to *maquiladoras* or sweatshops. As one study for the National Institute of Justice put it, "inmates represent

---

[31]Pat Beall and Chad Terhune, "Job Program at Prison Draws Fire," *The Wall Street Journal*, Jan. 15, 1997. Anne-Marie Cusac, "Toxic Prison Labor," *Progressive* 73 (March 2009), 26–31; Elizabeth Grossman, "Toxic Recycling," *Nation*, Nov. 21, 2005, pp. 20, 22, 24. S. Randall Humm, investigative counsel, U.S. Department of Justice Inspector General, to Bruce Bernard, chief medical officer, Centers for Disease Control and Prevention/National Institute for Occupational Safety and Health, Nov. 27, 2007, *ABC News*, http://abcnews.go.com/images/Blotter/OIGLetter.pdf; National Institute for Occupational Safety and Health preliminary report on work conditions at Federal Correctional Institution Elkton, July 16, 2008, Public Employees for Environmental Responsibility, http://www.peer.org /docs/doj/08_28_7_elkton_prison_niosh_report.pdf; Elena H. Page and David Sylvain, "Exposure to Hazardous Metals during Electronics Recycling at Four UNICOR Facilities," Dec. 2009, Centers for Disease Control and Prevention: National Institute for Occupational Safety and Health, http://www.cdc.gov/niosh/hhe/reports/pdfs/2008-0055-3098.pdf. "Federal Prisons, Inc., Annual Report, 2009," *UNICOR*, http://www.unicor.gov/information/publications/pdfs/corporate/catar2009_C.pdf.

a readily available and dependable source of entry-level labor that is a cost-effective alternative to work forces found in Mexico, the Caribbean Basin, Southeast Asia, and the Pacific Rim countries." Such marketing did not escape the notice of the American Federation of State, County, and Municipal Employees, which grimly summed up the situation in 1992: "Convict labor is thus used to directly compete with organized labor and drive down wages." . . .[32]

While mass incarceration undercut the postwar gains of the American labor movement by dampening the wages of all free-world workers, it particularly eroded the economic standing of African Americans. Even though many thought that "the wage gap between black and white young men" had narrowed substantially over the postwar period, the disproportionate incarceration of African Americans not only hid black unemployment and thus masked real income inequality but it also ensured that such inequality would deepen over time since blacks faced a more severe "wage penalty" than whites when they were finally freed.[33] Not only did black men find less work than white men when they tried to reenter the free-world labor force, but when they did secure employment their hourly wages were at least "10 percent lower after prison than before."[34]

Mass incarceration also widened the income gap between white and black Americans because the infrastructure of the carceral state was located disproportionately in all-white rural communities. The Adirondack district of upstate New York only had two prisons in the early 1970s, but by the late 1990s it had eighteen correctional facilities and another under construction. . . . The small Midwestern town of Ionia, Michigan, eventually housed six state prisons, and the state of California, which had built only twelve prisons between 1852 and 1964, built twenty-three more after 1984.[35]

Whenever a prison came to a rural white community it certainly created jobs, and given that a corrections officer's salary could be 50 percent higher than

[32]Hilary Dick, "Making Mexicans Illegal in Small Town USA," *Journal of Linguistic Anthropology* (Winter 2011); Stephanie Desmon, "Shortage of Pickers Has Crab Houses Pondering Hiring State Prisoners," *The Baltimore Sun,* April 16, 2009, http://articles.baltimoresun.com/2009-04-16/news/0904150157_1_crab-foreign-workers-prisoners; "Prison Labor," *State Legislatures* 33 (June 2007), 14. Sexton, "Work in American Prisons," 3; Jennifer Grzeskowiak, "Inmate Labor Pays Off for Business, Counties," *American City and County,* June 1, 2005, http://americancityandcounty.com/mag/government_inmate_labor_pays/, pp. 12–14. Weiss, "'Repatriating' Low-Wage Work," 275. "AFSCME Resolution No. 10: Prison Labor Programs," June 1992, *American Federation of State, County, and Municipal Employees,* http://www.afscme.org/resolutions/1992/r30-010.htm.

[33]Bruce Western, Becky Pettit, and Josh Guetzkow, "Black Economic Progress in the Era of Mass Imprisonment," in *Invisible Punishment,* ed. Mauer and Chesney-Lind, 175, 178; David F. Weiman, Michael A. Stoll, and Shawn Bushway, "The Regime of Mass Incarceration: A Labor-Market Perspective," in *Barriers to Reentry?,* ed. Bushway, Stoll, and Weiman, 42.

[34]Becky Pettit and Christopher J. Lyons, "Status and the Stigma of Incarceration: The Labor-Market Effects of Incarceration, by Race, Class, and Criminal Involvement," in *Barriers to Reentry?,* ed. Bushway, Stoll, and Weiman, 221. Loury, "Race, Incarceration, and American Values," 20.

[35]Eric Schlosser, "The Prison-Industrial Complex," *Atlantic Monthly* 282 (Dec. 1998), http://www.theatlantic.com/magazine/archive/1998/12/the-prison-industrial-complex/4669/. Tracy Huling, "Building a Prison Economy in Rural America," in *Invisible Punishment,* ed. Mauer and Chesney-Lind, 207; Gilmore, *Golden Gulag,* 7.

that paid to most other unskilled workers, this expansion of the carceral state had the potential to benefit key segments of America's white working class. By 2006 the department of corrections had become California's "largest state agency," employing 54,000 people; across the nation as a whole, state, federal, and private penal facilities were employing more people than any Fortune 500 company. Not only did whites enjoy new employment options with the boom in prison growth but areas that received new penal facilities also reaped other less obvious benefits simply because prisoners inflated the region's population. In 1990, when the presence of a large prison artificially boosted the census population of Coxsackie, New York, by 27.5 percent, its recorded median income dropped substantially from what it had been in the previous census year. As a result, the overwhelmingly white resident population became "eligible to receive more funding from the federal Department of Housing and Urban Development," such as that which came from Community Development Block Grants.[36]

While there is no question that whites benefited disproportionately from the rise in income that the expansion of the carceral state had produced, these gains did not offset the broad and deep economic losses that their communities had in fact experienced as a result of mass incarceration. Although corrections-commissioned studies sold the idea that rural outposts and small towns had much to gain from expanding the carceral state, those locales benefitted far less than they had hoped. In Corcoran, California, for example, corrections officials had promised local residents that their town would prosper and "gain more than 950 people in 353 households" if they built a prison. Ultimately, however, "fewer than 10 percent of the jobs at the prison were filled by Corcoran residents," and the city's housing vacancy rate, which, at the height of a major economic depression in 1977, had been 3.31 percent, rose to 7.5 percent by 1989.[37]

Not only were there fewer jobs for "low-wage workers in struggling rural areas" than had been promised, but the meager gains in employment they did secure were often undercut by the fact that the other local employers with jobs that did need filling were, ironically, turning to prison labor rather than to the resident white labor pool. In short, when cities such as Coxsackie wanted community centers painted, blacktop sealed, or other projects done "for local government, churches, hospitals, [and] libraries," the many white residents who needed those jobs simply could not compete with area inmates who could be paid "an industrial rate which amounts to 42 cents an hour." As one study of rural prison towns by the policy analyst Tracy Huling concludes, "local governments and other organizations save money on work they would otherwise have had to contract out to workers at a prevailing wage, prison labor may result in displacement of workers in these communities and can deepen local poverty."[38]

---

[36]Gilmore, *Golden Gulag*, 10; Leonhardt, "As Prison Labor Grows, So Does the Debate." Huling, "Building a Prison Economy in Rural America," 211.

[37]Gilmore, *Golden Gulag*, 152, 159.

[38]Huling, "Building a Prison Economy in Rural America," 203, 204, 211.

Ultimately, then, although white workers were able to benefit from the expansion of the carceral state in ways that black workers could not, prison employment never came close to replacing the living wages and decent benefits that U.S. workers had enjoyed before the turn to mass incarceration. . . .

. . . Why did unions such as the United Auto Workers lose so many members in the latter decades of the twentieth century? Why did so many service-sector workers become unemployed in this same period? These questions simply cannot be answered without reckoning with the fact that federal prisons were, by the 1990s, "making $150 million in automobile parts" and were also newly allowed to sell services "to the private commercial sector."[39] To be sure, organized labor found it almost impossible to withstand the deleterious effects of deindustrialization and globalization in the postwar period, but mass incarceration also mattered to the fate of the American labor movement in this era.[40]

MASS INCARCERATION AND THE RISE OF THE RIGHT IN POSTWAR AMERICA

. . . From a more careful examination of postwar justice, policy historians can not only learn more about why cities and workers lost significant power during the later twentieth century but we also can gain needed new perspective on why political power shifted the way that it did in that same period. More specifically, we are given an opportunity to think in completely new ways about why the politics of postwar liberalism—the political ethos that had dominated the nation since the 1930s—became so overshadowed by the politics of conservatism as the twentieth century came to a close.

Although there is widespread agreement among historians of the period that postwar liberals and the Democratic party lost significant ideological and policy ground to the Right during the latter part of the twentieth century, there is little consensus regarding why this happened. One influential argument, however, is that Americans moved rightward in response to rising crime rates and an increasing feeling among the nation's working-class and middle-class taxpayers that the Democratic party simply did not take this threat seriously. . . .[41]

---

[39]Federal Prison Industries, Inc., "Hoover's Company Records—In-depth Records," April 2, 2010, available at LexisNexus.

[40]AFL-CIO Executive Council, "The Exploitation of Prison Labor," May 7, 1997, *Southern Automotive Wholesalers,* http://www.southernautomotive.com/fpi/aflciofpi.htm.

[41]Steve Frasier and Gary Gerstle, eds.,*The Rise and Fall of the New Deal Order, 1930–1980* (Princeton, 1990); Jonathan Rieder, *Canarsie: The Jews and Italians of Brooklyn against Liberalism* (Cambridge, Mass., 2005); Allen J. Matusow, *The Unraveling of America: A History of Liberalism in the 1960s* (New York, 1987); Thomas Byrne Edsall and Mary D. Edsall, *Chain Reaction: The Impact of Race, Rights, and Taxes on American Politics* (New York, 1992); Tamar Jacoby, *Someone Else's House: America's Unfinished Struggle for Integration* (New York, 2001); Michael W. Flamm, *Law and Order: Street Crime, Civil Unrest, and the Crisis of Liberalism in the 1960s* (New York, 2007); Rick Perlstein, *Nixonland: The Rise of a President and the Fracturing of America* (New York, 2008); Jonathan M. Schoenwald, *A Time for Choosing: The Rise of Modern American Conservatism* (New York,

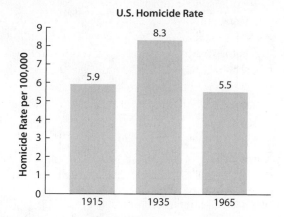

There are elements of this argument that are valuable. This scholarship has, for example, deftly captured the deep-seated fears of many Americans in this period, and without question, perception was important to the evolution of postwar political ideology and party practice. But perception was not necessarily reality, and historians must more carefully examine how the politics of crime and punishment played out in the postwar period to determine that reality.[42] A closer look at the politics of crime and punishment in the latter third of the twentieth century reveals that, somewhat ironically, historians have failed to historicize "crime" sufficiently and, as a result, they have missed the extent to which mass incarceration, rather than crime, undergirded the Right's rise to power in the later postwar period.

From one perspective Americans might have had good reason to fear for their safety as the 1960s unfolded. Whereas the national homicide rate was 5.5 per 100,000 in 1965, by 1968 it had risen to 7.3 per 100,000. What is more, this increase followed decades of remarkably stable crime rates overall. The nation's citizenry was not, however, experiencing a crime wave, and even this sort of jump in the murder rate cannot explain Americans' turn away from the Democratic party and their embrace of law and order. Certainly, the 1968 murder rate of 7.3 per 100,000 was significant, but in 1921 it had been 8.1 per 100,000 and in 1933 it had been 9.7 per 100,000. Furthermore, in major cities such as Detroit, substantially fewer murders were committed in 1965 than a decade earlier. In fact, if one looks at the entire twentieth century, it is clear that Americans of the mid-1960s— the years when the crime issue first took center stage in national political discourse—were experiencing the lowest homicide rate since 1910.[43]

2001); and Maurice Isserman and Michael Kazin, *America Divided: The Civil War of the 1960s* (New York, 2007). Edsall and Edsall, *Chain Reaction,* 48. Flamm, *Law and Order,* 168.

[42]Weaver, "Frontlash," 230–65; Dennis D. Loo and Ruth-Ellen M. Grimes, "Polls, Politics, and Crime: The 'Law and Order' Issue of the 1960s," *Western Criminology Review* 5 (no. 1, 2004), 50–67.

[43]"Key Facts at a Glance: Homicide Rate Trends," *U.S. Department of Justice: Bureau of Justice Statistics,* http:// bjs.ojp.usdoj.gov/content/glance/tables/hmrttab.cfm. "Major Crimes by Precinct," in *Annual Report for 1955,* by Detroit Police Department (1955) (Detroit Police Department Museums and Archives Unit, Detroit, Mich.); "Total Crime and Prosecution Arrests—Twenty-five Year Comparison," ibid.

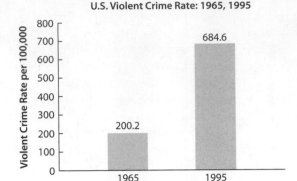

U.S. Violent Crime Rate: 1965, 1995

Still, crime rates did begin a steady rise in the latter years of the 1960s. It is important, however, to take a much closer look at the crime statistics of America's largest cities for those years because the way that cities counted crime changed dramatically in the second half of the 1960s. After 1965, thanks to a new federal commitment to fighting crime, local law enforcement could net substantial infusions of money and equipment by demonstrating that crime was on the rise in their area. Significantly, when crime rates began to inch up in Detroit in the later 1960s, even the city's mayor admitted that "new methods of counting crime" had played an important role in "distorting the size of the increase."[44]

Not only were Americans less likely to be murdered in the 1960s than they had been in earlier decades but they were also more likely to be murdered *after* the nation began funding a more punitive law-and-order state. By creating urban crises and by undercutting gains made by the American working class, mass incarceration had created a greater crime problem in America. Prisons not only impoverished people, leading them to commit more crimes of necessity, but they also made people more violent and antisocial. Not surprisingly then, the homicide rate jumped from 6.8 per 100,000 in 1967, when Lyndon B. Johnson was heading into his last year in office, to 10.5 per 100,000 in 1991, after more than a decade of solidly conservative rule, a thorough retreat from the liberal welfare state, and the unprecedented buildup of the carceral state. Moreover, while the violent crime rate in 1965 was 200.2 per 100,000, it grew to 556.6 in 1985 and to 684.6 in 1995.[45]

---

[44]"Detroit's Mayor Assails Critics," *The New York Times,* May 18, 1967, p. 33; Heather Ann Thompson, "Rethinking the Politics of White Flight in the Postwar City: Detroit, 1945–1980," *Journal of Urban History* 25 (Jan. 1999), 163–98; and Gebhard Long et al., "Detroit Police Department— A Research Report on Previous Studies; Criminal Statistics; and Police Technology, Productivity, and Competence," May 1970, box 37, Kenneth Cockrel/Sheila Murphy Cockrell Collection (Walter Reuther Library of Labor and Urban Affairs, Detroit).

[45]Amy E. Lerman, "The People Prisons Make: Effects of Incarceration on Criminal Psychology," in *Do Prisons Make Us Safer?*,ed. Raphael and Stoll, 168; Key Facts at a Glance"; "Crime—State Level: Trends in One Variable," *U.S. Department of Justice: Bureau of Justice Statistics,* http://bjsdata. ojp.usdoj.gov/dataonline/Search/Crime/State/TrendsInOneVar.cfm; "Crimes Known to the Police by Type and Area: 1965," in *Statistical Abstract of the United States: 1967,* by U.S. Department of Commerce, Bureau of the Census (Washington, D.C., 1967), 149, table 209; "Crimes and Crime Rates

... Despite the fact that the crime rate was rather unremarkable compared with that of previous decades, Democratic politicians at the local and national levels focused substantial attention on the issue; they not only took great pains to speak to constituent fears about safety but they also fueled them.

President Johnson tackled the issue of crime head on when he spoke to Congress and the nation in March 1965, insisting that "streets must be safe" and that "homes and places of business must be secure." As important, he assured the public that he saw "the preservation of law and order" as "one of the most legitimate functions of government." A year later he again faced the nation, passionately acknowledging that "the fear of crime marks the life of every American" and that such fear made law-abiding citizens "afraid to walk city streets by night or public parks by day". . . .[46] President Johnson did not merely speak of the need for a safer society and for tougher measures to achieve it; he also made it clear that he would earmark substantial resources for beating back the lawlessness that inflicted so much "death, injury, suffering and anguish" in the United States. Crime, he indicated in actions as well as words, was something that "a truly free people cannot tolerate." In fact, the Johnson administration created the largest crime-fighting bureaucracy the nation had ever seen. Soon after taking office, Johnson oversaw passage of the Law Enforcement Assistant Act (LEAA) and created a national crime commission staffed by a blue-ribbon panel that was committed to probing "fully and deeply into the problems of crime in our nation." In 1967 he endorsed the sweeping District of Columbia Crime Bill and issued a voluminous report on crime, "The Challenge of Crime in a Free Society," which recommended, among other things, that the federal government provide more financial assistance to state and local governments for law enforcement. In 1968 the Johnson administration passed the Omnibus Crime Control and Safe Streets Act of 1968. Even though Johnson had grown increasingly ambivalent about this piece of legislation as its more rehabilitative components were watered down in committee, when the time came to sign it he did so most willingly. In his words, "I signed the bill because it responds to one of the most urgent problems in America today—the problem of fighting crime in the local neighborhood and on the city street." Only four senators and seventeen representatives in a Congress that was overwhelmingly Democratic voted against this sweeping legislation.[47]

---

by Type of Offenses: 1985–1995," in *Statistical Abstract of the United States: 1997,* by U.S. Department of Commerce, Bureau of the Census (Washington, D.C., 1997), 201, table 313; and "United States Crime Rates, 1960–2009," *Disaster Center,* http:// www.disastercenter.com/crime/uscrime.htm.

[46]Lyndon Baines Johnson, "Special Message to the Congress on Law Enforcement and the Administration of Justice," March 8, 1965, Papers of Lyndon Baines Johnson, Presidential Documents Archive, *American Presidency Project,* http://www.presidency.ucsb.edu/ws/index.php?pid=26800. Lyndon Baines Johnson, "Special Message to the Congress on Crime and Law Enforcement," March 9, 1966, ibid., http://www.presidency.ucsb.edu/ws/index .php?pid=27478.

[47]Johnson, "Special Message to the Congress on Crime and Law Enforcement." Johnson, "Special Message to the Congress on Law Enforcement and the Administration of Justice." Law Enforcement Assistant Act, of 1965, Pub. L. No. 89-197, 79 Stat. 2135 (1965); President's Commission on Law Enforcement and Administration of Justice, *The Challenge of Crime in a Free Society* (Washington, D.C., 1967); District of Columbia Omnibus Crime Bill, Pub. L. No. 90-226, 81 Stat. 734 (1967);

This was not simply, as some have argued, "the Democratic leap upon the law and order bandwagon." There is little question that "law and order" became the platform on which many conservative politicians sought elected office from the mid-1960s onward, but postwar liberals were some of the first to flesh out that platform and give it substance on the ground.[48] The Democratic party of the 1960s had its own clearly articulated anxieties about social disorder and its own discomfort with African Americans' new determination to achieve meaningful social and economic equality by any means necessary—concerns that hardening laws and strengthening law enforcement directly addressed. By 1968 twenty-one states had received sophisticated new equipment to quiet civil disturbances, as well as new funding to train more police officers in riot control and more "correctional officers in prison, probation, and probation work" because the Johnson administration itself believed that the country needed more law and order. Indeed, thanks to the Democratic party's creation of the LEAA the federal government was able to spend approximately $7.5 billion to beef up the nation's law-and-order apparatus in little more than a decade.[49] Ultimately, postwar liberals had been high-ranking generals in the nation's new war on crime, not its unhappy conscripts.[50]

In ways deeply ironic, however, the very law-and-order era that the Democratic party of the 1960s had actively, and even proactively, ushered in when it had created entities such as the LEAA, would be the party's undoing. Democratic politicians had failed to predict the extent to which fueling fears of crime would eventually undermine the politics of postwar liberalism. . . . In short, mass incarceration, the ultimate and most devastating legacy of the nation's new war on crime, eventually weakened the liberal (and particularly the black liberal) vote in America, while simultaneously strengthening the conservative (and particularly white conservative) vote, to an extent that historians have yet to appreciate.

The most direct and obvious mechanism by which the phenomenon of mass incarceration undermined African American voting power was legislation that barred those with criminal records from the ballot. . . . Laws disfranchising convicts proliferated . . . in the wake of the civil rights movement. The most significant disfranchisement decision of the post–World War II era was handed down by the U.S. Supreme Court in 1974 in *Richardson v. Ramirez.* . . . Following *Richardson v.*

President's Commission Report, *The Challenge of Crime in a Free Society* (Honolulu, 2005); Omnibus Crime Control and Safe Streets Act, Pub. L. No. 90-351, 82 Stat. 197 (1968). Simon, *Governing through Crime,* 54.

[48]Katherine Beckett, *Making Crime Pay: Law and Order in Contemporary American Politics* (New York, 1997), 38; Flamm, *Law and Order,* 36; and Gary Donaldson, *Liberalism's Last Hurrah: The Presidential Campaign of 1964* (Armonk, 2003), 252; Elaine Tyler May, "Gimme Shelter: Do-It-Yourself Defense and the Politics of Fear," in *The Cultural Turn in U.S. History: Past, Present, and Future,* ed. James W. Cook, Lawrence B. Glickman, and Michael O'Malley (Chicago, 2008), 226.

[49]"Annual Report to the President and the Congress on Activities under the Law Enforcement Assistance Act of 1965 (3rd)."

[50]"Question of Mandatory Prison Sentence to Reduce Crime," 204. Abstract of "Annual Report to the President and the Congress on Activities under the Law Enforcement Assistance Act of 1965," April 1968, available to order at *U.S. Department of Justice: National Criminal Justice Reference Service,* http://www.ncjrs.gov/App/Publications/abstract.aspx?ID=368.

Ramirez, states across the country began passing laws that disproportionately disfranchised African Americans. By the year 2000, 1.8 million African Americans had been barred from the polls because of felon disfranchisement laws and, as one legal scholar pointed out, "the potential black electorate" had been "decimated."[51]

The proliferation of such laws was not the only reason African American votes were diluted in the age of mass incarceration. The way that the U.S. Census Bureau calculates population came to undermine black political power as well. The census has always counted prisoners as residents of the counties where they are incarcerated, even though these prisoners could not vote. . . . Just as inner city vitality was sapped when increasing percentages of urbanites were sent to prisons in rural counties—in turn giving those all-white areas claims on government aid that had formerly been theirs—so too did urban spaces of color lose political power when they, in effect, were forced to give the votes of the incarcerated to those who confined them.[52]

By the year 2000 African American voting power had been purloined by numerous all-white counties in the United States—dozens of which eventually owed more than 21 percent of their population to prisoners. Thirty-five percent of the population of Crowley County, Colorado, were in fact disfranchised prisoners, while in Concho County, Texas, the figure was 33 percent, and in Union County, Florida, it was 30 percent. Whereas overwhelmingly white areas of the United States such as Lassen County, California (where prisoners made up 25.49 percent of the census population in 2000), came to enjoy greater political clout, people of color in Oakland and Los Angeles (whose neighborhoods had lost census population in the wake of mass incarceration) saw their power weaken. In ways quantifiable, the mass incarceration of the later twentieth century had given whites an amount of political power that had not been so disproportionate since before the Civil War, when they had been able to count each African American body as three-fifths of a white person for the purposes of political representation.[53] Ultimately, the rise of the carceral state had undercut one of the most

---

[51]Pippa Holloway, "Disfranchised for Crime: Voting Rights and Criminal Convictions in the South, 1865–1920" (unpublished manuscript) (in Pippa Holloway's possession); *Richardson v. Ramirez,* 418 U.S. 24 (1974); Elizabeth A. Hull, *The Disenfranchisement of Ex-felons* (Philadelphia, 2006), 99; U.S. Const. amend. XIV, sec. 2. Pamela S. Karlan, remarks in forum, in Loury, *Race, Incarceration, and American Values,* 48.

[52]Gary Hunter and Peter Wagner, "Prisons, Politics, and the Census," in *Prison Profiteers,* ed. Herivel and Wright, 80–89; Todd Clear, "The Problem with 'Addition by Subtraction': The Prison-Crime Relationship in Low Income Communities," in *Invisible Punishment,* ed. Mauer and Chesney-Lind, 181–93; Jonathan Tilove, "Minority Prison Inmates Skew Local Populations as States Redistrict," March 12, 2002, *Prison Policy Initiative,* http://www.prisonpolicy.org/news/newhousenews031202.html; Eric Lotke and Peter Wagner, "Prisoners of the Census: Electoral and Financial Consequences of Counting Prisoners Where They Go, Not Where They Come From," *Pace Law Review* 24 (Spring 2004), 587–607.

[53]Peter Wagner, "Twenty-one Counties Have Twenty-one Percent of Their Population in Prisons and Jails," April 19, 2004, Prisoners of the Census, http://www.prisonersofthecensus.org/news/2004/04/19/twenty-one/.Andrew Marantz, "The Five-Fifths Clause: How We Count, and Use, Our Prisoners," *Slate,* Nov. 6, 2006, http://www.slate.com/id/2152994/. Ryan S. King and Marc Mauer, "The Vanishing Black Electorate: Felony Disenfranchisement in Atlanta, Georgia," Sept. 2004, Sentencing Project, http://www.sentencingproject.org/doc/publications/fd_vanishingblack-electorate.pdf.

important victories of the American civil rights movement, the Voting Rights Act of 1965.[54]

The fact that 98 percent of some states' prison cells were by 2003 located not just in all-white counties but specifically in Republican state senate districts also had real implications for the Democratic party. Indeed, one could argue that distorted population counts, had, over time, empowered the Republican party to a degree that no single redistricting effort could have . . . One New York state senator, Republican Dale Volker, admitted publicly that he was glad "that the almost 9,000 people confined in his district cannot vote because 'they would never vote for me.'"[55]

Felon disfranchisement laws and the rules governing census population eventually undermined the Democratic party well beyond the state level. According to research by Christopher Uggen and Jeff Manza, disfranchisement policies "affected the outcome of seven U.S. Senate races from 1970 to 1998 . . . [and] in each case the Democratic candidate would have won rather than the Republican victor." The distorted outcomes of these elections, in turn, "prevented Democratic control of the Senate from 1986 to 2000." Disfranchisement legislation also benefitted Republicans over Democrats in major contests such as the presidential elections of 2000 and 2004 because a full ten states "had African American disenfranchisement rates above 15%" by those years. Excluding Americans with criminal records from the democratic process seems to have provided "a small but clear advantage to Republican candidates in every presidential and senatorial election from 1972 to 2000."[56]

By 2006 forty-eight states had passed laws that took away prisoners' voting rights, and with more than 47 million Americans (one-fourth of the adult population) having a criminal record by that year, there is little doubt that the nation's political process had been fundamentally altered.[57] Historians, therefore, need to reckon with the myriad consequences of mass incarceration, including its less obvious political fallout. There is little question that the rise of the carceral state over the last forty years eroded the political power of the Democratic party and fueled the rise of the Right, in ways structural, and thus, changes in American justice policy did not just reflect the nation's move rightward after 1968; they

[54]Lauren Handelsman, "Giving the Barking Dog a Bite: Challenging Felon Disenfranchisement under the Voting Rights Act of 1965," *Fordham Law Review* 73 (March 2005), 1875–1940.

[55]Peter Wagner, "Temporary Populations Change the Political Face of New York," Aug. 30, 2004, *Prisoners of the Census*, http://www.prisonersofthecensus.org/news/2004/08/30/temporary-populations/. Peter Wagner, "Locked Up, but Still Counted: How Prison Populations Distort Democracy," Sept. 5, 2008, ibid., http://www.prisonersofthecensus.org/news/2008/09/05/stillcounted/.

[56]On the statistics for 2006, see Hull, *Disenfranchisement of Ex-felons*, 1.

[57]Marc Mauer, "Mass Imprisonment and the Disappearing Voters," in *Invisible Punishment*, ed. Mauer and Chesney-Lind, 53; Hull, *Disenfranchisement of Ex-felons*, 1, 11; Mauer, "Mass Imprisonment and the Disappearing Voters," 50–58; and "Felon Disenfranchisement by State," March 11, 2008, *FairPlan 2020: Precision Mapping for Community-Based Redistricting and GOTV*, http://www.fairvote2020.org/2008/03/felon-disenfranchisement-by-state.html. "Criminal Disenfranchisement Laws across the United States," *Brennan Center for Justice*, http://www .brennancenter.org/page/-/d/download_file_48642.pdf. Manza and Uggen, *Locked Out*, 191.

actually fueled it to an extent that liberal leaders at the time never predicted and scholars today have yet to appreciate.

MASS INCARCERATION AND THE REWRITING OF POSTWAR AMERICAN HISTORY

Focusing new historical attention on how the American criminal justice system evolved after World War II, and specifically on the advent of mass incarceration after the 1960s, helps us understand some of the most dramatic political, economic, and social transformations of the postwar period. By the close of the twentieth century almost 5.6 million U.S. adults had served time in a state or federal prison, and the lives of all Americans had been shaped in fundamental ways by mass incarceration.[58]

There were, of course, many forces undermining the vitality of America's inner cities in the latter part of the twentieth century; the American labor movement also had numerous forces eroding its power, and the new political order that came to dominate by the 1980s was multidimensional and was rooted in everything from the sexual revolution to stagflation to battles over religion to the way gender politics played out in the postwar period. It is important, therefore, not to place too much causative weight on any single event, process, or phenomenon. No one historical episode— no matter how epic it may have been—would have, on its own, caused changes as drastic and sweeping as those that took place in this period. Clearly, though, mass incarceration mattered a great deal to the way that the postwar United States evolved; it must then also matter when we write the history of that period.

---

[58]Thomas P. Bonczar, "Prevalence of Imprisonment in the U.S Population: 1974–2001," Aug. 2003, *U.S. Department of Justice: Bureau of Justice Statistics,* http://bjs.ojp.usdoj.gov/content/pub/pdf/piusp01.pdf.

Heather Ann Thompson

I am very interested in how cities and workplaces have changed over the last fifty years. As important, I want to know how various civil rights struggles to make both of these places more equal and just actually unfolded after World War II. Growing up in Detroit, Michigan, made me wonder so much about why my city was so racially polarized and economically depressed, and my history teachers encouraged me to research the past to find out! I then knew that I loved history because I got to be a bit of a detective. Eventually my researching led to my first book about the history of Detroit, *Whose Detroit? Politics, Labor, and Race in a Modern American City*, which cast a new light on the many civil rights protests that took place in the 1960s and 1970s. It tried to make sense of why so many whites later abandoned the city rather than agree to live there under black leadership. Today I write about the protests that have taken place in America's prisons throughout the twentieth century in order to make them more humane as well. I actually just finished a history of one such very famous civil rights rebellion that took place in the Attica State Correctional Facility back in 1971. While researching that book I also began wondering why it is that this country has more people in prison today that any other on the globe. I also wondered what impact that high level of imprisonment had on our cities, our workplaces, and on our very democracy. This too led to me to history—I needed to know a lot more about the past to make sense of this present—and this history article is what you are reading here.

QUESTION FOR CONSIDERATION

1. What trend in incarceration during the late twentieth century does Thompson cite?
2. What does Thompson mean by the "criminalization of urban space?" How did the "War on Drugs" contribute to this criminalization? How did mandatory sentencing? Describe how, according to Thompson, schools likewise became criminalized space.
3. Thompson compares the criminalization of urban space to the repression of African Americans in the South during and after Reconstruction. Review Eric Foner's article "Rights and the Constitution in Black Life During the Civil War and Reconstruction" at the beginning of this volume and find examples of this "criminalization" of rural spaces in the South in the late nineteenth century.
4. According to Thompson, mass incarceration also undermined the American working class in the late twentieth century. What evidence does she provide to support this argument? What did business owners find attractive about the prospect of using prisoners as laborers?
5. Thompson argues that the "carceral" (prison-centered) state arose when Americans elected politicians who were "tough on crime." She also argues that racism shaped the politics of crime. To what extent is her argument similar to Thomas Sugrue's in "Crabgrass-Roots Politics: Race, Rights, and the Reaction Against Liberalism in the Urban North, 1940–1964," also found in this book?
6. What were the political, economic, and social effects of mass incarceration for African Americans in the late twentieth century?